D0966254

THE
AMERICAN POLITICAL
DICTIONARY

THE
AMERICAN POLITICAL
DICTIONARY

JACK C. PLANO
MILTON GREENBERG
Western Michigan University

HOLT, RINEHART and WINSTON
New York — Chicago — San Francisco

⌐1962⌐

To
Ellen
and
Sonia

Preface

THE WORLD OF POLITICS is as close to the citizen as his daily newspaper, weekly news magazine, radio, or television set. Confronted with problems ranging from parking places to survival, the American people have turned to government— national, state, and local—for solutions. As a consequence, countless numbers of agencies, laws, officials, programs, and politicians surround, and often confuse, the citizen trying to play his political role. While American government has become complex and detailed it is not beyond the understanding of the interested citizen. Indeed, for the citizen in a democratic republic, understanding is essential if he is wisely to choose his leaders and give direction to their actions.

Politics, like other fields of knowledge, has a technical language. Unlike such other fields of knowledge as medicine, however, the language of politics is not limited to professional journals or to the practitioner. It is broadly and freely used in public and private conversations and by mass media of communication. While this is basically a healthy situation, lack of precision in the use of political terminology serves only to obscure the issues of today. This dictionary is intended to help the citizen who seeks a deeper and more precise understanding of the historical, social, economic, and institutional forces which make up the lifeblood of the most exciting political system in the world.

This book consists of more than 1100 terms, agencies, court cases, and statutes which are the most relevant for a basic comprehension of American government institutions, practices, and problems. Each item is defined or described, followed by a statement of its significance to American government and to the citizen. Terms are discussed within subject matter chapters to place them in their proper frame of reference.

This book can be used in two ways. First, it is a dictionary in which terms are listed alphabetically by subject matter; the reader can find a term by consulting a particular chapter or, when in doubt as to the usage of a term, by consulting the Index. Second, a complete reading of a chapter will provide a useful, basic understanding of an entire subject area. State and local government issues and procedures are integrated with national government practice in most instances since similar terms are used at all levels of government. A separate chapter on state and local government is included, however, which focuses on terms that have specific application to state and local government problems and practices. With the exception of the case of *Eakin v. Raub*, discussed on page 219, all cases discussed were decided by the United States Supreme Court.

It has become commonplace to speak of the need for an informed citizenry in order to maintain a free society. Ignorance and lethargy about our government pose as great a danger to American democracy as do external threats. The authors hope that this book will help to meet this challenge.

Kalamazoo, Michigan   JCP
August 1962   MG

Contents

THE
AMERICAN POLITICAL
DICTIONARY

1

Political Ideas

Absolutism.   The theory and practice by which full and unbridled powers are exercised over the people by government. Absolutism is the opposite of constitutionalism which provides for limited government under a constitution. • *Significance:* Prior to the American Revolution, absolutism commonly took the form of absolute monarchy based on the theory of the divine right of kings. In modern times, it has emerged in the form of dictatorship of the right (fascism) or dictatorship of the left (communism). The Founding Fathers feared absolutism and created a system of separation of powers with checks and balances to safeguard against it. Today, the rival ideologies of absolutism and democratic constitutionalism are arrayed against each other in a world-wide ideological struggle.

Accountability.   The concept underlying democratic representative government that elected officials must be held responsible to the people for their actions while serving in office. Accountability under law is one of the features distinguishing governments based on the principle of absolutism from those embracing the concepts of liberal democracy. • *Significance:* Accountability implies that the citizens in a democracy know their elective officials and the decisions they make, and have an opportunity to pass judgment on them. This, in turn, requires relatively short ballots, roll call votes, frequent elections, and an effective opposition voice. In the national government, the voters can hold the President accountable for all decisions and actions undertaken in the executive branch because he alone is accorded the authority and the responsibility under the Constitution. In the Congress, accountability is based on individual performance; frequent roll call votes on important bills enable voters to judge their congressman every two years and their senators every six years. When bills are killed through minority blocking tactics or parliamentary maneuvers are used to conceal political motives or to confuse voters, accountability is reduced.

Anarchism.   The doctrine that government is an unnecessary evil and should be replaced by free and voluntary cooperation among individuals and groups.

1

Anarchists regard the state as an instrument used by the propertied classes to dominate and exploit the people. There have been many strains of anarchist thinking running the gamut from individualism to collectivism, from pacifism to advocates of violent revolution. All, however, hold the state's coercive system to be responsible for the warping of man's personality and look to the day when all governments will be abolished.

• *Significance:* In Europe, anarchism has been represented primarily by syndicalist parties; similarly, in the United States, anarchists have worked through the Industrial Workers of the World. Anarchism has never been a successful political ideology, but its advocates have had considerable influence on other political theorists and movements. Marxian communism, for example, views government as an evil instrument of class exploitation and provides for a "final stage" in which government "withers away" and people in a "stateless, classless society" spontaneously cooperate with each other.

Aristocracy.   A system of government in which political power is exercised by a small ruling clique of a state's "best" citizens. The selection of the aristocrats may be made on the basis of birth, wealth, or ability.

• *Significance:* Aristocracies are characterized by limited suffrage and great emphasis on property rights. Post-Revolutionary America had many of the characteristics of aristocracy until the democratic reforms ushered in during the age of Jackson provided a leveling influence.

Authoritarianism.   A dictatorial form of government in which political authority is concentrated in one man or a small group. Authoritarian regimes emphasize obedience by the people to their rulers, and the unlimited power of rulers over their subjects. The term is used generally to describe modern forms of absolutism.

• *Significance:* The political history of the world has been characterized by a continuing struggle between the rival doctrines of authoritarianism and democracy. Although authoritarianism was set back by the defeat of the Axis powers in World War II, today it is on the rise again, owing to the numerous Communist countries and to developments in the newly emerged states of Asia and Africa. In many cases, modern authoritarian regimes operate behind a façade of democratic and constitutional institutions.

Capitalism.   An economic system based on the private ownership of the means of production and a supply-demand market economy. Capitalism is based on the laissez-faire theory which emphasizes the absence of governmental restraints on ownership, production, and trade.

• *Significance:* Capitalism as a working economic system developed in Europe and the United States in the late eighteenth and early nineteenth centuries replacing the state-fostered mercantilist system. Capitalism has never been practiced for long in its pure state in any country since each major economic group soon looks to government for an improvement of its economic position. In time, this results in a substantial promotional and regulatory role being played by government. Today, all capitalist states have mixed economies in which private ownership and market economies are matched with extensive governmental intervention. Free trade, a hallmark of capitalism, has been replaced by national and regional international trade restrictions. For some years, the fundamental concepts of economic freedom which characterize capitalism have been challenged by socialism and communism.

Collectivism. A generic term which describes various theories and social movements calling for the ownership and control of all land and means of production by the state or groups rather than by individuals. Collectivism is often used synonymously with socialism and communism, and it rejects the economic freedoms of capitalism.

• *Significance:* The major ideological conflicts of modern times have involved clashes between the supporters of collectivist doctrines and the defenders of the concepts of individualism. The former have emphasized the advantages of cooperation and group effort, the latter the advantages of competition and individual enterprise. Collectivism has also been frequently used in American election campaigns as a "scare" word to describe the opposition candidate's position or his party's philosophy.

Communism. A political, economic, and social theory based on a collectivistic society in which all land and capital are socially owned and political power is exercised by the masses. Modern communism is based on the theories and practices of Karl Marx, V. I. Lenin, Josef Stalin, and Nikita Khrushchev, with some new variations provided by Mao Tse-tung and the Chinese Communists. Communism in theory espouses the doctrines of historical inevitability, economic determinism, labor value, the "inner contradictions" of capitalism, class conflict, capitalist colonialism and imperialism, world wars resulting from competition for markets, the destruction of the bourgeoisie, the dictatorship of the proletariat, the socialist revolution, and the final "withering away" of the state. Plato and other political theorists as well as various church and social groups have also advocated, and some of the latter have practiced, communism in the form of communal living.

• *Significance:* Since World War II, communism as an ideology has been used by the Communist states, especially the Soviet Union, in a massive, world-wide offensive against capitalism and democracy. Communism in theory is largely a destructive philosophy, basing its main attack on the evils and basic weaknesses of nineteenth century capitalism. In practice, communism has been highly pragmatic: Soviet leaders often use capitalist practices to provide incentives and to secure some degree of political stability and economic viability. The "dictatorship of the proletariat" during the period of transition from socialism to communism has proved to be a quite permanent dictatorship by one man or a ruthless oligarchy. Communists have been unsuccessful in winning mass support and political elections, but they have been highly successful in infiltrating and capturing control of mass independence movements in Asia and Africa.

Concurrent Majority. The political doctrine expounded by John C. Calhoun of South Carolina prior to the Civil War which held that democratic decisions should be made only with the concurrence of all major segments of society.

Without such concurrence, Calhoun argued, a decision should not be binding on those groups whose interests it violated.

• *Significance:* This doctrine was central to a careful and systematic effort by Calhoun to justify the secession of southern states from the Union, for he held that the decisions made by Congress concerning tariffs and slavery were inimical to the interests of the South. Each southern state, therefore, had to decide whether it would accept these decisions or would reject them and withdraw from the Union. The idea of the concurrent majority has more recently been evoked in protecting substantial minority interests from majority rule.

Conservatism.   Defense of the status quo against major changes in the political, economic, or social institutions of a society. The philosophy of conservatism has been expounded most effectively by the English writer and statesman, Edmund Burke. He held that political stability could be maintained only if the forces of change could be moderated by a slow and careful integration of new elements into time-tested institutions.

• *Significance:* Both major American political parties have their conservative wings which frequently unite in opposing liberal legislation. Today in American politics the term has no precise meaning and is often used as a term of opprobrium against a rival party or candidate. The general conservative position on issues, however, has been fairly consistently opposed to governmental regulation of the economy and to civil rights legislation, and has favored state action over federal, emphasized fiscal responsibility, and supported decreased government spending and lower taxes.

Constitutionalism.   The political principle of limited government under a written or unwritten constitution. Constitutionalism assumes that the sovereign people draw up a contract (constitution) by the terms of which government is created and given its powers. In the American system, the Supreme Court acts as the guardian of the constitutional contract through its power to void government actions which exceed these limitations (judicial review). The Founding Fathers also incorporated various limitations into the system which restrain the individuals who exercise power. The most significant of these include the separation of powers, checks and balances, federalism, subordination of military to civilian control, and a Bill of Rights.

• *Significance:* The American system of constitutional government has been fairly effective in maintaining limitations upon government throughout most of American history. In recent years, however, public sentiment has favored bigger government with expanded powers. Fear of the consequences of the Industrial Revolution, depressions, wars, alien ideologies, and other domestic and foreign threats has overridden the fear of stronger government. Expanding democratic government is viewed by many as a means of achieving better protection for their personal rights, values, and welfare, rather than as a threat. The problem remains essentially one of maintaining an equilibrium between the needs for liberty and for order, of enabling government to meet new and challenging responsibilities, while still maintaining the restraints of constitutionalism.

Contract Theory. A class of theories which seeks to explain the origin of society and government and to set out the respective authority and responsibility of government and individuals under their contractual obligations. Contract theorists regard man as having lived in a state of nature prior to the organization of civil society. Once a "body politic" has been created through a contract or compact among the people, government is then created and empowered through a second contract or constitution concluded between the people and the government. The nature of the relationship established by the governmental contract varies, in these theories, from the individualism of John Locke's popular sovereignty and limited government democratic system to the authoritarianism of Thomas Hobbes's *Leviathan.*

• *Significance:* The contract theory was developed by various political philosophers during the Middle Ages as an intellectual challenge to the existing absolutism based on the theory of the divine right of kings. Progressively the new doctrine gained adherents and the absolute power of some monarchs was mildly curtailed, but its full flowering and broad democratic implications emerged during the Age of Enlightenment. The advocacy of the doctrine by John Locke, Jean Jacques Rousseau, and James Harrington helped to gain the support of the intellectual classes and laid the foundations for the English, American, and French Revolutions. The American Declaration of Independence, described by Thomas Jefferson as "pure Locke," based its justification of revolution on the violation of the contract by the English government. Although the theories of the social contract are somewhat out of vogue today, the great ideas they fostered remain part of the concept of democracy based on limited government and individual rights.

Democracy. The term is derived from the Greek words "demos" (the people) and "kratos" (authority). Democracy may be direct, as practiced in ancient Athens and in New England town meetings, or indirect and representative. The Democratic Creed includes the following concepts: (1) individualism, which holds that the primary task of government is to enable each individual to achieve the highest potential of development; (2) liberty, which allows each individual the greatest amount of freedom consistent with order; (3) equality, which states that all men are created equal and have equal rights and opportunities; and (4) fraternity, which postulates that individuals will not misuse their freedom but will cooperate in creating a wholesome society. As a political system, democracy starts with the assumption of popular sovereignty, vesting the ultimate political power in the people. It presupposes that man can control his destiny, that he can make moral judgments and practical decisions in his daily life. It implies a continuing search for truth in the sense of man's pursuit of improved ways of building social institutions and ordering human relations. Democracy requires a decision-making system based on majority rule with minority rights protected. Effective guarantees of freedom of speech, press, religion, assembly, petition, and equality before the law are indispensable to a democratic system of government. Politics, parties, and politicians are the catalytic agents which make democracy workable.

• *Significance:* Democracy, for many centuries regarded as a dangerous but unworkable doctrine, swept the western world during the nineteenth and twentieth centuries with the forces unleashed by the American and French Revolutions. In the twentieth century, democracy has clashed head-on with new authoritarian ideologies, and the struggle continues today on a world-wide basis, particularly in the emerging nations of Asia and Africa. Democracy is under attack not only from the ideologies of the extreme right and left, but from within as well, by those who oppose it as mob rule which vulgarizes society and makes a virtue out of incompetence and mediocrity. Others charge that democracy is a sham, impossible in practice because of an "iron law of oligarchy." Supporters of democracy reject such attacks, pointing to the evidence of superiority of democracy as practiced in the United States, Britain, France, and Scandinavia. Yet, façade democracy exists in many nonwestern countries where, despite forms and appearances, a small oligarchic group manipulates all power. Workable democracy seems to require a special environment, including an educated and responsible people, some degree of economic stability, and some social cohesion and consensus. Above all, it demands an acceptance of the democratic "rules of the game," viz., that there will be frequent elections, that the losers will accept the verdict of the voters and allow the majority to govern, that the majority will respect the right of the minority to furnish opposition, and that if the minority wins a future election it will then be permitted to take over the reins of government. Although democracy in practice will never achieve the perfection of the Democratic Creed, yet so long as such goals are held worthy and efforts are made to move in their direction, the system may be called democratic. American democracy, like its British counterpart, is an evolutionary and organic system which has overcome obstacles and crises pragmatically.

Democratic Socialism.   An economic system established by a democratic nation in which the people, through their government, take over ownership and direction of basic industry, banking, communication, transportation, and other segments of the economy. The extent of the government's role in the economy is determined by free elections rather than by ideological dogma. Although a private sector of the economy may continue to exist, much effort is expended by government in planning, directing, and regulating it, and in providing welfare services for the needy.
• *Significance:* Democratic socialism has been partially instituted in several countries, particularly Britain and the Scandinavian countries. Some observers regard it as the best answer to the economic challenge of communism. Communists are especially hostile toward democratic socialism because they fear it will correct the evils and "inner contradictions" of capitalism upon which they place their hope for economic collapse. American conservatives also oppose it as a dangerous leftward step toward communism.

Direct Democracy.   A system of government in which the political decisions are made by the people directly rather than by their elected representatives. Under direct democracy, the citizens assemble periodically and act as a legislative body.
• *Significance:* Direct democracy has been used in ancient Greece and Rome,

in some Swiss cantons, in New England town meetings, and in some midwestern township meetings. A modern adaptation of direct democracy is found in fewer than one half of the American states—those which provide for initiative, referendum, and recall action by the people. Many local units of government also use binding and advisory referendums in reaching decisions on important issues. Direct democracy, however, is not provided for nor recognized by the national government. Ordinarily, direct democracy is practicable only in small communities and in resolving simple issues.

Divine Right.   A political system based on the divinity of a person or his office, or on a right to rule inherited from ancestors who were divinely appointed. A natural corollary of the divine right theory is that the monarch has been given absolute powers to rule by a Supreme Being.
• *Significance:* The divine right of kings was the accepted political philosophy in theory and practice throughout most of the western world from the fifteenth through the eighteenth century. The system was perpetuated through family inheritance of the ruling power, and the intermarriage of ruling families. Any challenge to or revolt against a king was regarded not only as a treasonable act but as a sin. In time, the divine right of kings was first weakened and then overcome by the new contract theory, which held that a ruler's power was granted to him not by God but by the sovereign people.

Economic Determinism.   The theory that economic factors, the methods of production and exchange of goods, control the form of political and social organization and shape the intellectual and moral development of the people. Economic determinists view history in terms of epochs in which the prevailing economic system pits the servile class against the dominant class resulting eventually in a new alignment.
• *Significance:* Vague beliefs in some aspects of economic determinism are widespread and held by people of many persuasions. The most celebrated systematic theory was set forth by Marx and Engels, who used it to explain the movement of history in response to changing economic relationships. It is at the core of such concepts as class struggle and the predicted collapse of capitalism.

Fascism.   The political system of the extreme right which incorporates the principles of the Leader (dictator), a one-party state, totalitarian regimentation of economic and social activity, and the arbitrary exercise of absolute power by the regime. Benito Mussolini fashioned the fascist prototype in Italy after 1922, emulated by Adolph Hitler in Germany, Francisco Franco in Spain, Juan Peron in Argentina, and others in Europe and Latin America. Fascism, unlike communism, retains the private ownership of land and capital, but most economic activity is controlled and regimented by the state through a system of national socialism.
• *Significance:* Fascism is contemptuous of democratic parliamentarianism and personal liberty, but is actively hostile toward communism. Fascists generally have come to power during a crisis in which the landed or industrial leaders of a state have feared the rise of communism. Although fascism was dealt a

destructive blow by the defeat of the Axis powers in World War II, neo-fascism is again on the rise throughout much of the world. As the Communist world-wide offensive intensifies, fascism may gain new adherents.

Government.   The political and administrative hierarchy of an organized state. Governments exercise legislative, executive, and judicial functions; the nature of the governmental system is determined by the distribution of these powers. Government may take many forms, but it must be sufficiently powerful and stable to command obedience and maintain order. A government's position also depends on its acceptance by the community of nations through its diplomatic recognition by other states.
• *Significance:* Questions concerning the form of government and who will exercise political power within a state have always been matters of bitter contention. Government has helped to bring peace and order to many states, but it has also been the cause of civil wars, revolutions, ideological struggles, and conflicts between states. As populations grow and technology develops, people become increasingly interdependent and turn to government for help in solving their problems. Government cannot help but become a more significant force, either for good or evil, in the future.

Ideology.   The "way of life" of a people reflected in terms of their political system, economic order, social goals, and moral values. Ideology is particularly concerned with the form and role of government and the nature of a state's economic system. Ideology may also describe the ideas and views held by a party, class, or group. *See* IDEOLOGICAL WARFARE, page 310.
• *Significance:* The world today is caught up in a massive conflict between two rival ideologies—communism and democracy. Other ideologies exist, but are overshadowed by the size and intense rivalry of the main struggle. Ideology provides the basic propaganda ammunition for psychological warfare. Each side in the Cold War seeks to sell its ideology to the world's peoples by emphasizing its own good points and highlighting its opponent's weaknesses.

Individualism.   The political, economic, and social concept which places primary emphasis upon the worth, freedom, and well-being of the individual rather than that of the group, society, or nation.
• *Significance:* Individualism is the central idea in the political doctrine of constitutional democracy and in the economic theory of laissez faire. The broad guarantees afforded to individuals and their property rights by the Constitution exemplify the American focus on the worth of the individual.

Jacksonian Democracy.   A political and social equalitarian movement in the United States which rejected political aristocracy and emphasized the "common man." The chief apostle of the new equality and democracy was Andrew Jackson, who brought to the presidency the leveling influences of the frontier.
• *Significance:* The election of Jackson in 1828 ushered in an era of democratic changes on the national, state, and local governmental levels. Jacksonian democracy emphasized and largely achieved universal manhood suffrage, popular election of officials, short terms of office, and the spoils system.

Laissez Faire.   The economic theory propounded by the French physiocrats and popularized by Adam Smith (*The Wealth of Nations,* 1776), which calls for a "hands off" policy by government toward the economy. Laissez faire rejects state control and regulation and emphasizes economic individualism, a market economy, and natural economic laws to guide the production and consumption of goods. Tariffs and other trade restrictions are rejected in favor of a world-wide system of free trade. The economic system becomes self-regulatory in nature, and each individual's pursuit of his own self-interest contributes to the well-being of all.

• *Significance:* The wide acceptance in practice of the theory of laissez faire in the western world during the eighteenth and nineteenth centuries ushered in the new economic era of capitalism. Laissez faire was largely a reaction to the severe production and trade restrictions imposed by governments under the preceding mercantilist system. The American Revolution was a product of these economic forces of change as well as of new political ideas, both of which sprang out of individualism. Today laissez faire has been modified by the expanding role of government in economic affairs, resulting in a "mixed economy" combining capitalism with governmental promotion and regulation.

Leftist.   An individual or political group advocating liberal or radical political or economic programs, an expanded role by democratic government, or the empowering of the masses. Leftists include such categories as "welfare-statists," democratic socialists, Marxian socialists, Communists, and anarchists. The use of the term stems from the practice in European parliaments of seating radical parties to the left of the presiding officer.

• *Significance:* The moderate leftist has played a significant role in advocating government action to correct injustices and shortcomings in existing societies. Leftists have been particularly active in calling for changes and modifications in capitalism and political democracy. Leftist views on social, economic, and political matters have often been in advance of popularly held beliefs. Extremes of the political left, like those of the right, tend to culminate in dictatorship.

Liberalism.   A political view which seeks to change the political, economic, or social status quo to foster the development and well-being of the individual. Liberals regard man as a rational creature who can use his intelligence to overcome human and natural obstacles to a good life for all, without resorting to violence against the established order. Liberalism is more concerned with process, with the method of solving problems, than with a specific program.

• *Significance:* Liberalism evolved in the eighteenth and nineteenth centuries as a doctrine which emphasized the full development of the individual free from the restraints of government. The twentieth century liberal, conversely, looks to government to step in and correct the abuses and shortcomings of society through a positive program of action. In the civil rights area, for example, the liberal of today views government as a positive force to correct abuses and to expand the freedom of the individual rather than in the traditional sense, as constituting the major threat to an individual's freedom. Liberals have fought totalitarianism of the left and right by pursuing policies

which seek to reduce economic and social inequalities and to produce political
stability.

Majority Rule.   A basic principle of democracy which asserts that the
greater number of citizens in any political unit should select officials and determine policies. Majority rule has been justified on the grounds that it rests
on superior force, that it is commonly accepted in practice, and that, pragmatically, no reasonable alternative exists.
• *Significance:* Political philosophers have long debated whether it is any more
justifiable for the majority to impose its will on the minority than for the
minority to rule. Some theorists reject majority rule in favor of government by
consensus or by a concurrent majority. In the United States, majority rule is
not rigidly adhered to, as in many cases only a plurality is needed to win an
election. Other practices which depart from majority rule include the equal
representation of the states in the Senate, gerrymandering, failure to redistrict
on a population basis, and the election of the President by the Electoral College.

Monarchy.   Any form of government in which the supreme powers of the
state are exercised by, or ceremoniously held by, a king, queen, emperor, or
other regal potentate. Monarchs may acquire their position through inheritance
or election, although the latter is unusual. Absolute monarchs exercise full
ruling powers, whereas constitutional monarchs either share governmental
powers with elected parliaments or are mere figureheads.
• *Significance:* Absolute monarchs once ruled nearly all of the states of
Europe. Today in the few states that retain their monarchs—Britain, Sweden,
Norway, The Netherlands, for example—the king or queen is assigned a ceremonial role as chief of state. However, in several semifeudal states of Asia,
Africa, and the Middle East, monarchs continue to wield absolute powers.

Nation.   Any sizable group of people who are united by common bonds of
geography, religion, language, race, custom and tradition, and through shared
experiences and common aspirations. The term is often used interchangeably
with *state,* but not all national groups have achieved statehood, although they
all aspire to it. Modern nations began to emerge from feudalism in the ninth
century. The community of nation-states was given political and legal recognition by the Peace of Westphalia in 1648.
• *Significance:* In the modern era, the nation has provided the unifying force
with which the individual can identify himself. The results have not always
been good, for many national groups have built their unity on a shared hatred
of other groups or on a desire to bring others under their dominion. These
conflicting national interests, which characterize the world's state system, have
contributed to the instability of international relations and the outbreak of wars.

Nationalism.   A sociopsychological force which springs from unique cultural and historical factors which provide unity and inspiration to a given
people through a sense of belonging together and shared values. Nationalism
binds together people who possess common cultural, linguistic, racial, historical,

or geographical characteristics or experiences and who give their loyalty to the same political group.

• *Significance:* The spirit of nationalism subjects people to the intangible forces of group psychology and collective behavior, especially when a crisis confronts them with a real or imaginary enemy. Nationalism tends to emphasize the separateness and differences between groups, as for example, Germans versus French and Arabs versus Jews. Most modern wars have been products of extreme nationalism in which mass emotional enthusiasm has been marshaled for one nation against another. Nationalism is currently playing a significant role in the march to independence of numerous peoples in Asia and Africa. Nationalism is also a powerful internal force which helps produce unity, loyalty, and durable political, economic, and social institutions.

Natural Law.   The concept that human relations are governed by an immutable set of laws, similar to the physical laws of the universe, which are recognizable through human reason. The theory originated with the Stoics and was developed and expanded by the eighteenth century natural rights philosophers.

• *Significance:* The concept of natural law has been influential in the development of legal and political theories and institutions, morals and ethics, and religion. Today it is particularly associated with conceptions of justice and standards of individual conduct. It constitutes the basis for the natural rights philosophy which has fundamentally affected the development of democratic systems of government.

Oligarchy.   Any system of government in which a small group holds the ruling power. Oligarchical systems are usually based on wealth, military power, or social position.

• *Significance:* Oligarchies traditionally rule with absolute power unencumbered by democratic restraints. However, even in democratic systems oligarchic groups may temporarily hold a decisive influence over the government because of their economic position or social status. Two European philosophers, Robert Michels and Vilfredo Pareto, have developed a theory of the "iron law of oligarchy" which propounds the impossibility of democracy in practice because of the tendency of small groups to dominate and control the majority.

Parliamentary System.   A system of government, often based on the British prototype, in which ultimate governmental authority is vested in the legislative body (parliament), and a cabinet headed by a prime minister or premier. The cabinet exercises political leadership and directs the administration. Cabinet ministers are entirely or largely selected from the membership of parliament and the cabinet continues in power so long as it commands the support of a majority of the parliament. Substantial disagreement between the parliament and the cabinet results either in appointment of a new ministry or election of a new legislature.

• *Significance:* The major advantage of the parliamentary system is that it avoids continuing controversy or deadlocks between the legislative and executive branches and provides for clear accountability to the people. These advantages, however, result in the loss of checks and balances and the American people have never seriously considered its adoption. Most of the world's democracies are patterned after the British or continental European parliamentary systems, rather than after the American presidential system with its separation of powers.

Pluralism.   The concept of modern society as made up of heterogeneous institutions and organizations which have diversified religious, economic, ethnic, and cultural interests.
• *Significance:* The greater the variety in a population, the greater the degree of pluralism likely to exist. Some react with fear in the presence of differences; others derive satisfaction. While diversity is a potential threat to unity, uniformity is a threat to freedom. In countries like the United States, pluralism has given rise to a tremendous proliferation of organized groups, many with some impact on public policy, representing all manner of interests. It has also resulted in a greater variety of solutions to problems than will be found in homogeneous societies.

Political Science.   One of the divisions of the social sciences which deals with the theory and practice of politics, government, and administration. Political science as an academic discipline includes the fields of political theory, governmental institutions, public law, politics and public policy, public administration, and international relations and foreign policy.
• *Significance:* Political science in its broadest sense dates back to Plato and Aristotle and even earlier. For many centuries, the study of politics was mainly concerned with deducing the characteristics of the ideal or utopian state. In the modern era, students of government embraced the scientific method to create an intellectual discipline based on the postulating of hypotheses followed by empirical verification and the ascertainment of probable trends, and on generalizations concerning state and individual political actions.

Popular Sovereignty.   The natural rights concept that ultimate political authority reposes in the people and can be exercised in creating, altering, or abolishing government.
• *Significance:* Popular sovereignty was enunciated by all of the natural rights philosophers in their general attack upon governmental absolutism based on the theory of divine right. The concept that the people possess supreme political power pervades the Declaration of Independence and is implicit in the United States Constitution. The Civil War involved the question of whether the people of the entire nation or the people within each state are sovereign. Popular sovereignty is most directly practiced by the American people when engaged in the writing, amending, and revising of constitutions.

Presidential Government.   A system which features a separation of powers between the legislative and executive branches, and an independently elected executive serving a fixed term.
• *Significance:* The main advantages claimed for the presidential system are the choosing of the executive by the voters rather than by the legislature, the effective use of checks and balances, and the encouragement of strong executive

leadership. Critics, however, claim that it creates a gulf between the legislature and the executive, encourages disagreement and deadlock, and disperses responsibility. Many American political scientists and statesmen have urged the modification of presidential government by the adoption of some features of the parliamentary system which make for a closer working relationship between the executive and legislature.

Radical.   An advocate of substantial political, social, and economic changes. Although no precise use of the term exists, a radical is generally regarded as a leftist who is extreme in his demands for change.

• *Significance:* The American guarantees of freedom of speech, press, and association have permitted the holding and the expression of radical views. Some radical parties have played a significant role in gaining popular support for some of their proposals which were then incorporated into the platforms of the major parties. Extreme radical parties are often Marxist-oriented. The term is freely used in political campaigns in attempts to discredit opponents or their proposals.

Reactionary.   A person who advocates substantial political, social, or economic changes favoring a return to an earlier, more conservative system. A reactionary believes that most social problems result from democratic excesses favoring the propertyless masses, and usually prefers government by oligarchy. Although the use of the term is not precise, reactionaries are political rightists who are more extreme in their views than conservatives.

• *Significance:* Some of the new nations of Asia and Africa have come under the control of reactionary regimes after the early failures of democracy following independence. In American politics, reactionaries have generally favored laissez faire and have opposed social welfare legislation. The term is freely used in political campaigns in an attempt to discredit opponents or their proposals.

Representative Government.   Any democratic system of government in which the people elect representatives to act as their agents in making and enforcing laws and decisions. Authoritarian regimes often have a façade of representative institutions, but they lack the vital element of accountability of democratic governments.

• *Significance:* Any large and populous political unit must resort to some form of representative government, although small units may provide for decision making by the people directly. Representatives may act for a special class or group, as in medieval assemblies; an occupational or social group, as in a system of functional representation; or, a geographical community, as in most contemporary legislatures. One theory holds that the representative should exercise his own intelligent discretion in reaching decisions; another views the role of the representative as an agent of the people who is expected to vote according to their wishes and interests.

Republic.   A form of government in which sovereign power resides in the electorate and is exercised by elected representatives who are responsible to the people. Republican government stands in contradistinction to monarchial or oligarchic government in which the rulers have a vested right to office. It is also to be distinguished from pure democracy in which the people govern directly.

• *Significance:* Republican government emerged in many states to replace monarchial systems in the century following the American Revolution. The Founding Fathers significantly wrote into the Constitution a guarantee by the national government of a republican form of government in every state. In American politics, the distinction between a republic and a democracy is one frequently drawn by conservatives to emphasize the representative character of the American system.

Rightist. An individual or political group advocating conservative or reactionary political or economic programs, a restriction upon the power of the masses, and oligarchical rule. Rightists tend to favor laissez faire and strong executive power; the extreme right wing supports fascist dictatorships. The term stems from the common practice in European parliaments of seating conservative parties to the right of the presiding officer.

• *Significance:* Rightist parties exercise considerable influence in most democratic states. In the United States, both major parties have conservative members who hold many positions of influence in the Congress. Extreme right-wing or left-wing forces have never found much support in American politics.

Rule of Law. An Anglo-American concept which emphasizes the supremacy of the law and restricts the discretionary power of public officials. The rule of law particularly stresses the protection of individual rights from the arbitrary interference of officials.

• *Significance:* The rule of law provides the foundation for democratic constitutionalism. In the United States, for example, each individual accused of crime is treated equally under the law, receives a fair trial with established procedures, and must be accorded due process in all official actions undertaken against him. Guarantees provided by the rule of law are more fully appreciated today when contrasted with the operations of a police state. A vital maxim of democratic government is "government of law and not of men."

Socialism. A doctrine that advocates economic collectivism, seeking collective or governmental ownership of the means of production and distribution of goods. Its basic aims are to replace competition for profit by cooperation and social responsibility and to secure a more equitable distribution of income and opportunity. Though these aims are common to all socialists, a wide variety of schools of thought have arisen, distinguished mainly by their approaches to the problem of how best to achieve socialism. These many distinct schools of thought vary from the peaceful and democratic ideas of utopian and Christian socialists to the aggressive, and ofttimes violent, approaches of anarchists and Communists.

• *Significance:* Socialism has been a significant force, particularly in Europe, since the middle of the nineteenth century. In the United States, socialist parties have had little success at the ballot box, but their ideas have gained some measure of acceptance through liberal economic and social welfare programs. The democratic Socialist party of Eugene Debs and Norman Thomas has had great influence on American politics but has waned in recent years. The more radical Socialist Labor party still runs a presidential candidate, but has few adherents.

Sovereignty.   The supreme power of a state, exercised within its boundaries and free from external interference. The idea behind sovereignty is an ancient one, but it was first developed into an elaborate doctrine by philosophers of the fifteenth and sixteenth centuries who sought to justify the absolutism of the kings of the new state system.
• *Significance:* The early absolutist implications of sovereignty developed by Jean Bodin and Thomas Hobbes gave way in time to the new concept of popular sovereignty developed by Jean Jacques Rousseau and John Locke. Today the idea of sovereignty remains a significant factor in international relations. The concept of absolute sovereignty, however, has been modified by state consent as demonstrated in treaties, international law, and world organizations.

State.   A political community occupying a definite territory, having an organized government, and possessing internal and external sovereignty. Recognition of a state's claims to independence by a sufficient number of other states to enable it to enter into international engagements is important to the establishment of its sovereignty. The term is also used to describe territorial divisions within a federal system, such as in the United States.
• *Significance:* Today over 100 states comprise the community of nations. The state as the basic political unit of the world since the sixteenth century is slowly giving way to evolutionary internationalism in the form of world and regional organizations. The basic challenge to the world of today is whether a stable system of international cooperation can be created before the state system commits suicide in the holocaust of a third world war.

Theocracy.   Any political system in which political power is exercised directly or indirectly by a clergy, and in which church law is superior to or replaces civil law. The implication is that decisions are made by a Supreme Being and are transmitted to man through agents who rule in a theocracy.
• *Significance:* Theocracies typically are nondemocratic systems in which political power is exercised by an oligarchic council of priests, ministers, monks, or other church officials, or by a single church leader. Examples of theocracies include Geneva under John Calvin and Tibet prior to the Communist conquest.

Totalitarianism.   A modern form of authoritarianism in which the state controls nearly every aspect of the individual's life. Totalitarian governments do not tolerate activities by individuals or groups, such as labor unions and youth organizations, which are not directed toward the state's goals. They maintain themselves in power through a secret police, by the use of propaganda disseminated through all media of communication, by the elimination of free discussion and criticism, and through widespread use of terror tactics. Internal scapegoats and foreign military threats are created and used to foster unity through fear.

• *Significance:* Totalitarianism has developed in the twentieth century through new techniques which mobilize entire populations in support of an authoritarian government and a political ideology. The main totalitarian governments have included Nazi Germany, Fascist Italy, and the Soviet Union.

Utopia.   An imaginary human paradise created in the mind and writings of Sir Thomas More. More's ideal commonwealth was located on an island untouched by worldly vices and provided a nearly perfect society. The word "utopia" means literally "no place" and is taken from the title of More's book published in 1516.

• *Significance:* More's *Utopia* is part of the stream of speculative political theory which has fostered the imaginative creation of ideal states and social systems, such as found in Plato's *Republic* and Tommaso Campanella's *City of the Sun*. The adjective "utopian" is also used to describe the idealistic nineteenth century socialistic programs offered by Robert Owen, Claude Saint Simon, and François Fourier. American democracy has been influenced by utopianism and has established ideals of perfect freedom, equality, and brotherhood in the Democratic Creed.

Welfare State.   A modern role of the state seeking to improve the daily life and to provide security for the individual through government economic programs.

• *Significance:* The welfare state has been occasioned mainly by the Industrial Revolution, urbanization, and the social and economic consequences of depressions and wars. Opponents of government's welfare role charge that "cradle to the grave" security destroys the individual's initiative and enterprise and promotes fiscal irresponsibility. Supporters point out that programs involving social security, health, subsidized housing, and the like provide necessary minimum standards of life for all, and that no civilized society can avoid this responsibility. Nearly all western governments have engaged in some such practices.

●
●
●
●
●
●
●
● **2**
●
●
●

The United States Constitution:
Background, Principles, Development

Amendment.   Changes in, or additions to, a constitution. In the United States Constitution, Article V spells out the methods. Amendments may be proposed by a two-thirds vote of both houses of the Congress or by a convention called by the Congress at the request of the legislatures of two thirds of the states. Only the first method has been used. Such proposals must be ratified by either the legislatures of three fourths of the states or by conventions called for that purpose in three fourths of the states, as determined by the Congress. Only the 21st Amendment (repealing prohibition) was submitted to conventions. The President may not veto an amendment proposal. Congress may stipulate a time limit, usually seven years, within which a proposal must be ratified. A state which has rejected an amendment may change its mind, but once a proposal is ratified by a state legislature, it stands. Ratification by a state may not be accomplished by a referendum of the people, but only by the legislature or convention. Though thousands of proposals have been made in the Congress to amend the Constitution, only 28 have received endorsement from both houses; of these 23 have been adopted. Amendments are appended to the Constitution and not placed within the article or section which may have been changed, as is done in some state constitutions. *See* CONSTITUTIONAL AMENDMENTS, STATE, page 343.
• *Significance:* A constitution, no matter how well designed, requires adjustment from time to time. A reasonable amendment procedure makes adjustment possible, without resort to force, in basic governmental arrangements. While most amendments adopted to date have not involved fundamental changes in American government, a few, such as the 14th, have had a profound effect. The present methods of amendment have been criticized largely on the ground that minorities may block the majority will because of the two-thirds and three-fourths vote requirements. However, the methods have proved workable. More important, other less formal methods of change, such as judicial interpretation and custom and usage, have made frequent resort to the amendment process unnecessary. (For specific amendments, *see* Index.)

Annapolis Convention.   A conference called by the Virginia legislature in 1786, inviting the states to send delegates to Annapolis, Maryland, to discuss trade regulations. Though nine states appointed delegates, only five states were represented. Under the leadership of Alexander Hamilton and James Madison, the group urged the Congress and the states to call another convention in Philadelphia in 1787 to consider revision of the Articles of Confederation.

• *Significance:* The Annapolis Convention was an important prelude to the framing of the Constitution of the United States, accomplished in Philadelphia the following year. Dissatisfaction with the Articles of Confederation, particularly in the areas of trade and commerce, led to this movement for reform.

Antifederalists.   Persons who opposed adoption of the Constitution framed in Philadelphia in 1787. They opposed the centralist tendencies of the Constitution and attacked the failure of the framers to include a bill of rights. The group included many who had signed the Declaration of Independence or had strongly supported the Revolution.

• *Significance:* It is often forgotten that a substantial number of people opposed the ratification of the Constitution. Strong opposition to the Constitution rapidly dwindled after its adoption. The Antifederalist group, however, became the supporters of Thomas Jefferson whose views on the nature of the Union, as distinguished from those of Alexander Hamilton and other Federalists, continues to mark many of the divisions in American politics today.

Articles of Confederation.   The name of the compact made among the original 13 states. Though prepared in 1776, it was not officially adopted by all states until 1781, and lasted until 1789 when it was replaced by the United States Constitution. The Confederation was a league of sovereign states. Each state had one vote in a one-house legislature. No provision was made in the Articles for a separate national executive or judiciary. The Congress was assigned a limited number of powers but the approval of nine states was necessary for effective action. Significant powers which the central government lacked included the power to tax, to regulate commerce or the currency, or to make its laws directly applicable to the people without further state action. In short, the Congress could not force states or individuals to comply with its decisions, resembling, in many respects, an international organization. Any amendments to the Articles required the unanimous approval of the 13 states.

• *Significance:* The Articles, and the lessons learned under their operation, formed the backdrop against which the states could move toward "a more perfect union." The government brought the Revolutionary War to a conclusion, accomplished much toward the development of the American continent through the Northwest Ordinance, and established the principle of interstate cooperation through such things as interstate rendition and full faith and credit. Many of the defects of the Articles were rectified in the United States Constitution.

Charter Colony.   One of the three types of colonial governments—charter, proprietary, royal—found in colonial America. Charter colonies, namely Rhode Island and Connecticut, operated under charters agreed to by the colony and the king. The legislature was elected and was allowed a good deal of autonomy by England. The governor was chosen by the legislature.

• *Significance:* Charter colonies enjoyed the greatest degree of independence from the Crown. The charters of Connecticut and Rhode Island proved so satisfactory for local self-government that they served as state constitutions until 1818 and 1842 respectively.

Checks and Balances.   A major principle of the American governmental system whereby each department of the government exercises a check upon the actions of the others. The principle operates not only among the legislative, executive, and judicial branches but between the two houses of the legislature and between the states and the national government. Each has some authority to control the actions of the other by participation in the functions of the other. Examples include the President's veto power and congressional power to override the veto, judicial review of legislative and executive actions, presidential appointment of judges with senatorial approval, and the congressional power to impeach.

• *Significance:* Through the various devices of check and balance, the framers of the Constitution sought to prevent the accumulation of all power in one branch or in one or several persons by giving each branch the authority to prevent the encroachment of the others. The check and balance system stresses the interdependence (rather than the complete separation) of the various units of government. It stresses the need for compromise and prevents the usurpation of power. One major defect of the system is its tendency to create deadlocks and to prevent swift action during crises.

Commerce and Slave Trade Compromise.   An agreement reached at the Constitutional Convention of 1787 which gave the national government power to regulate foreign commerce, required the consent of two thirds of the Senate to treaties, and prohibited the national government to tax exports or to interfere with the slave trade until the year 1808.

• *Significance:* One of the major purposes for which the Convention was called was to strengthen national control over commerce. Southern delegates, however, feared that northern majorities might cut off the slave trade and discriminate against the profitable cotton trade. They agreed to grant the national government control over foreign commerce provided that the South was given a check over treaties and that the Congress would not tax exports. It was believed that sufficient numbers of slaves would be available by 1808. The treaty and foreign commerce provisions continue to influence the making of American foreign policy.

Connecticut Compromise.   The agreement reached in the Constitutional Convention of 1787 which resolved the question of representation in the national Congress. Each state is represented in the House of Representatives according to population and in the Senate each state is represented equally. The Compromise, also called the "Great Compromise," satisfied the small states in particular and made it possible for them to agree to the establishment of a strong central government.

• *Significance:* While the Connecticut Compromise was the "price of union" in 1787, it has been of lasting significance. The equal representation of states in the Senate has resulted in a disproportionate influence of sparsely settled states and regions. Though the states are represented by population in the House, bills must pass both houses to become law. Thus the Compromise of 1787 is felt in the daily workings of the Congress. It is generally agreed that the Compromise was the crucial step in the formulation of the Constitution.

Constitution.   The fundamental or organic law which establishes the framework of government, assigns the powers and duties of governmental agencies, and establishes the relationship of the people to the government. Constitutions may be written or unwritten. The English operate under an unwritten constitution, i.e., one which consists largely of legislative acts, legal decisions, and customs which have never been comprehensively gathered in one document. American constitutions are written, but much fundamental law is unwritten, in the forms of custom and usage. The United States Constitution went into effect on March 4, 1789, and has been amended 23 times. It is the supreme law of the land. Its basic principles include limited government, popular sovereignty, separation of powers, checks and balances, and federalism. *See* CONSTITUTIONS, STATE, page 345.
• *Significance:* The United States Constitution, the oldest and most successful written constitution in history, has served the nation with remarkably little formal alteration during periods of rapid social changes. This is due to the wisdom of the framers who wrote a brief and flexible instrument, and to the policy of liberal construction which has characterized Supreme Court decisions. The Constitution has not only served as an effective instrument of government and a guardian of human rights but has come to be a revered symbol of how free men with diverse interests, and spread over a large area, can live together in freedom.

Constitutional Construction.   The method of interpreting the Constitution. People or groups are generally divided into those who favor a "loose" or "liberal" construction of constitutional phrases and those who favor a "strict" interpretation. The difference is largely expressed in terms of one's attitude toward broad grants of power to the national government as opposed to retaining more power in the states.
• *Significance:* The issue of loose versus strict construction arose early in American history and contributed to the emergence of political parties. The famous case of *McCulloch v. Maryland,* 4 Wheaton 316 (1819), involved the issue of whether the national government was limited to those powers *expressly* delegated to it or whether it had *implied* powers. Chief Justice Marshall resolved the issue in favor of the implied powers doctrine and established the principle of, if not the necessity for, loose construction of the Constitution. From time to time, the strict constructionists have had their way, depending largely on the party in power and the attitude of the Supreme Court. Loose construction, however, remains the basis for constitutional interpretation and has facilitated adaptation of the Constitution to the needs of the time.

Constitutional Convention of 1787. The convention held in Philadelphia from May 25 to September 18 which framed the Constitution of the United States. Called by the Confederation Congress to revise the Articles of Confederation, the delegates proceeded to draft an entirely new document. Rhode Island sent no delegates and only 55 of the 74 men originally appointed as delegates attended. George Washington presided. The deliberations were conducted in secret but have been made known through notes kept by James Madison. The delegates compromised various differences between large and small states, North and South, agrarian and commercial interests, and advocates of a strong and weak central government. They not only ignored their instructions merely to revise the Articles of Confederation, but also ignored the provision of the Articles requiring unanimous consent of the states for revision by providing that the new constitution would go into effect when nine states ratified it in state conventions.
• *Significance:* The Convention was a conservative reaction to the excesses of the Revolutionary period and the commercial disorder under the Articles of Confederation. The Constitution produced by the delegates is considered to be the greatest written constitution in history. The Convention's membership was exceedingly young and well-informed on government and politics, and was representative of propertied and commercial interests. The Convention has been the only national constitutional convention in American history, but one can be called upon the request of two thirds of the states.

Continental Congress. The body of delegates representing the colonies which first met to protest the British treatment of the colonies and eventually became the government of the United States. The First Continental Congress met in 1774 and drafted a Declaration of Rights. The Second Congress, meeting the following year, adopted the Declaration of Independence, conducted the War of Independence, and served as the national government until the Articles of Confederation went into effect in 1781.
• *Significance:* The First Congress met in an atmosphere in which the colonists still considered themselves as Englishmen who were being abused. The Second Congress convened after open conflict with England began. Though the Second Congress rested on no legal base, it served as a *de facto* government. Delegates were selected by the state legislatures. While the states did not feel bound by decisions of the Continental Congress, it succeeded in bringing the war to a successful conclusion. It also developed an American consciousness which led to the adoption of the Articles of Confederation and, eventually, the Constitution of the United States.

Declaration of Independence. The document adopted by the Second Continental Congress on July 4, 1776, declaring the independence of the American colonies from Great Britain and justifying the rebellion. It was drafted by a committee composed of Thomas Jefferson, John Adams, Benjamin Franklin, Roger Sherman, and Robert Livingston. The draft was largely the work of Jefferson who drew heavily from the natural rights doctrine of the English philosopher, John Locke. The Declaration enumerated the grievances against the Crown and contained an eloquent defense of the rights of man and the right of self-government.

• *Significance:* The Declaration of Independence does not have any legal effect today. Nevertheless, it is recognized the world over as a basic statement of the American creed. Its famed opening passage declares the equality of man, the natural rights of man endowed by God, the principle of limited government, government by consent, and the right of people to rebel against tyrannical government.

Distribution of Powers.   An underlying principle of the American constitutional system designed to prevent tyranny through assignment of powers to different governments and agencies, and by placing checks upon the exercise of power. The distribution takes the following forms: (1) dividing power between the national and state governments under a federal system; (2) separating power among the three major branches of the government—legislative, executive, and judicial—giving each branch a check upon the operations of the others; (3) selecting the personnel of the three branches by different procedures and electorates, making them responsible to different pressures; (4) limiting all governments by specific constitutional restrictions.

• *Significance:* The framers sought to prevent all governmental power from falling into the hands of any individual or group. They feared majority tyranny as much as minority or individual tyranny. Hence they provided for a wide distribution of authority, limited in scope, and designed to effect a balancing of interests. The distribution of powers has been modified by the expanding role of the national government, the increasing influence of the President over legislation and foreign affairs, and the development of independent regulatory agencies which exercise some legislative and judicial power in their supervision of the economy.

Economic Interpretation of the Constitution.   A theory which holds that the framers of the Constitution represented the well-to-do classes and that the Constitution was designed to protect their interests. The theory was developed by the distinguished historian, Charles A. Beard, in his book, *An Economic Interpretation of the Constitution of the United States* (1913).

• *Significance:* Beard did not attribute any malice to the framers but tried to show that they had a good deal to gain from the creation of a strong and stable national government. He pointed out that the delegates were professional or propertied men with extensive holdings in public securities, land, manufacturing, shipping, and slaves. Although the framers were a conservative-minded group who were affected by their own backgrounds and interests, Beard and other historians have emphasized that economic interest was only one of the factors which motivated them.

Federalist Papers.   A series of 85 essays written by Alexander Hamilton, James Madison, and John Jay (all using the name *Publius*), which were published in New York newspapers in 1787 to convince New Yorkers to adopt the newly proposed Constitution drafted in Philadelphia. These essays have been collected and published under the title *The Federalist.*

• *Significance: The Federalist,* though written in haste and for the specific purpose of winning support for the Constitution, is widely regarded as the best single commentary on the Constitution. Moreover, it is considered to be the outstanding American contribution to political theory.

Madison's Journal.   Notes kept by James Madison of the proceedings of the Constitutional Convention of 1787. Though an official journal of the Convention was kept, this contained only formal motions and votes by states. Madison kept a record of the debates as well. These notes were not published until 1840, four years after Madison's death.
• *Significance:* The proceedings of the Convention were conducted in secrecy and Madison's notes are the only reliable source of information. For more than 50 years, the Constitution was interpreted without the benefit of these materials which cast important light upon the intentions of the framers.

New Jersey Plan.   A plan submitted by William Patterson of New Jersey to the Constitutional Convention of 1787 representing the views of the small states and states' rights advocates. It was expressly designed as a counterproposal to the strongly nationalistic Virginia Plan. The essence of the New Jersey Plan was a single-house Congress with each state having an equal vote. Moreover, the Plan looked toward a moderate modification of the Articles of Confederation rather than the drafting of a new document.
• *Significance:* The New Jersey Plan, along with the Virginia Plan, drew the major battle lines of the Convention. Though the basic idea of the New Jersey Plan to retain the Articles of Confederation was defeated by the Convention, the demand for equal representation resulted in the Connecticut Compromise. The assurance that the states would receive equal representation in one house of the Congress made it possible for the Convention to complete its deliberations.

Preamble.   The statement affixed at the beginning of the Constitution, stating the source of its authority and the purposes which it is to serve. The Preamble to the United States Constitution is of no legal effect but may serve as a guide to the intent of the framers.
• *Significance:* Particular importance is attached to the fact that the Preamble begins with the words "We the people" rather than "The states of New York . . . ," etc. This establishes the supremacy of the national Constitution as emanating from all the people rather than as a contract among sovereign states. This was of particular significance in the great debate over the nature of the Union prior to the Civil War. The Preamble is also noted as a concise statement of the enduring principles of a free people.

Proprietary Colony.   One of the three types of colonial governments—charter, proprietary, royal—found in colonial America. Proprietary colonies were governed by charters issued by the "proprietor," an individual to whom the king had made a land grant. Pennsylvania was established under such a charter bestowed by William Penn. Other proprietary colonies were Delaware and Maryland. Though the lower house of the legislature was elected, the upper house and the governor were chosen by the proprietor, subject to approval of the Crown.

• *Significance:* The proprietor was, in effect, a miniature king representing the Crown, and the colonies were largely ruled from England. Nevertheless, important lessons in self-government were learned. Increasing efforts by the Crown to control these colonies was a contributing factor to the Revolution. The "frame of government" drawn up by William Penn for Pennsylvania, was a relatively democratic document.

Royal Colony.   One of the three types of colonial governments—charter, proprietary, royal—found in colonial America. Eight colonies were royal colonies. The lower house of the legislature was elected but the upper house and the governor were appointed by the king. Royal governors exercised almost complete authority over the colony through instructions received from England.

• *Significance:* It was in the royal colonies that much of the resentment against the king grew, resulting in the Revolution. The royal governor, in particular, was the object of resentment and fear, and the first state constitutions reflected this by giving little authority to the governor. This tradition has lasted until recent times, but the current tendency is to strengthen executive power in the states.

Separation of Powers.   A major principle of American government whereby power is distributed among three branches of government—the legislative, the executive, and the judicial. The officials of each branch are selected by different procedures and are independent of each other. The separation is not complete in that each branch participates in the functions of the other through a system of checks and balances. However, the separation serves to ensure that the same person or group will not make the law, enforce the law, and interpret and apply the law.

• *Significance:* The separation of lawmaking, law enforcement, and law interpretation is designed to prevent tyranny. It also serves to make the three branches responsive to different pressures. At the same time, the system frequently results in lack of unity between the legislative and executive branches, particularly when they are controlled by different parties. This fragmentation of power is a major factor in the operation of the American governmental system. The judiciary plays the critical role in maintaining the branches within their assigned powers.

Shays' Rebellion.   An armed revolt by farmers in western Massachusetts in 1786–87, seeking relief from debts and possible foreclosures of mortgages. Led by Daniel Shays, a Revolutionary War officer, the group prevented judges from hearing mortgage foreclosure cases and attempted to capture an arsenal. They were repelled by the state militia.

• *Significance:* Shays' Rebellion, while its seriousness may be questioned, is credited with being a major factor in the demand for a revision of the Articles of Confederation. The event highlighted the economic difficulties facing the states at that time and caused alarm among the creditor and commercial interests.

State Sovereignty.   Independence of a state from external control. The concept of state sovereignty was an integral part of government under the Articles of Confederation and part of the great debate on the Union, prior to the Civil War. In effect, state sovereignty is a rejection of the principle of national supremacy under the United States Constitution.
• *Significance:* The states of the Union were sovereign under the Articles of Confederation. Prior to the Civil War, it was claimed by southern states that the Constitution was a compact among states rather than the people and that the states were free to secede. This doctrine is now rejected, although the issue has arisen again in connection with the problem of racial integration.

Three-Fifths Compromise.   An agreement reached at the Constitutional Convention of 1787 to count only three fifths of the slave population in determining representation in the House of Representatives and in apportioning direct taxes.
• *Significance:* This provision of the Constitution (Art. I, sec. 2) is no longer pertinent. Nevertheless, at the Constitutional Convention, the issue of whether to count slaves for representation and tax purposes sharply divided the northern and southern delegates. The resultant compromise was one of many made at the Convention.

Usage.   A term used to describe a custom which, because well-established, is regarded as a part of the American constitutional system. Though not precisely provided for in the words of the Constitution, such practice forms an important element of the actual operations of government. Among these are such vital components as the role of political parties, the operations of the Electoral College, the presidential cabinet, and the inner organization of Congress.
• *Significance:* Little can be learned about how American government works solely by a reading of the Constitution. Usage is one of the major methods by which the Constitution has been developed to meet practical problems. A full understanding of the American constitutional system requires not only knowledge of the written document itself, but also of the various usages. A well-established usage becomes part of the "unwritten constitution" and may have the same effect as, or greater than, an actual constitutional amendment.

Virginia Plan.   A plan, submitted by Edmund Randolph of Virginia to the Constitutional Convention of 1787, which called for scrapping the Articles of Confederation and establishing a new and strong national government. It provided for a two-house legislature based on state population or wealth, a national executive, and a judiciary. The Congress would have had power to disallow state legislation and was to be invested with broad power over matters of national concern.
• *Significance:* The Virginia Plan served as the major basis for discussion in the Convention. Once the compromise over representation was reached to the satisfaction of the small states (equal representation in one house) the dele-

gates proceeded to draft a constitution as envisaged by the Virginia Plan. A strong central government was established with power to operate directly upon individuals rather than through the states.

IMPORTANT CASES

Coleman v. Miller, 307 U.S. 433 (1939): A case establishing the principle that the process of amending the Constitution is essentially political in nature and not subject to judicial interference. Specifically, the Court held that a state legislature may ratify the child labor amendment proposal after once rejecting it, and that whether the pending proposal was still valid after many years is a political question for the Congress to determine.

• *Significance:* No case involving the amending clause of the Constitution has come before the Supreme Court since *Coleman v. Miller. Coleman v. Miller* has the effect of removing the Court from control of the amending process, leaving Article V to the political branches of the government.

IMPORTANT STATUTES

Northwest Ordinance. An enactment of the Congress under the Articles of Confederation for the government of the territory north of the Ohio River and west of New York to the Mississippi River. The Ordinance provided for the eventual statehood of areas of the territory when they acquired 60,000 inhabitants. Liberal provision was made for local self-government, civil and political rights, and education. Slavery was forbidden in the territory. A previous ordinance of 1785, establishing the township system of dividing land and providing for local schools, was reaffirmed in the Ordinance of 1787.

• *Significance:* The Northwest Ordinance is the most significant measure passed by the Confederation Congress. It was readopted by the Congress under the Constitution and served as the basis for later territorial acts. It established the important policy that territories were not to be kept in subjection but were to be developed for admission to statehood on an equal footing with other states.

3

The Federal Union and the Territories

Admission of New States.   The Constitution empowers the Congress to admit new states to the Union (Art. IV, sec. 3). Limitations on this power are, that no state may be created within an existing state, nor may any state be formed by the union of two or more states or parts of states without the consent of the states concerned and of the Congress. The usual procedure for admission is (1) the people of the territory through their territorial assembly petition the Congress; (2) the Congress passes an "enabling act" which, when signed by the President, authorizes the territory to frame a constitution; (3) the Congress passes an act of admission approved by the President. Though the Congress and the President may insist upon certain conditions for admission to the Union, a state, once admitted, stands on an equal footing with all other states. No state may constitutionally withdraw from the Union.

• *Significance:* The Founding Fathers recognized the desirability of expanding the federal Union by giving the Congress power to admit new states. Political considerations, such as which political party the people of the area are likely to support, may influence the majority party in the Congress. With the exception of the 13 original states, 30 were elevated from territorial status, five (Vermont, Kentucky, Tennessee, Maine, and West Virginia) were formed by separation from other states, and two, Texas and California, were formed from an independent republic and by acquisition from Mexico, respectively.

Centralization.   The tendency for political power and authority to gravitate from state governments to the national government. Though the functions performed by all governments in the United States have increased, the nationwide impact of economic, social, and defense problems has led to an increased assumption of responsibility by the national government.

• *Significance:* The proper division of powers between national and state governments has been a cause for controversy throughout American history. It is argued that centralization permits more efficient handling of problems which are nationwide in scope. Opponents contend that decentralized activity prevents tyranny, permits experimentation, and encourages local solutions to

27

problems. Various groups tend to support the handling of a function by that level of government which is most responsive to their needs.

Commerce Power.   The authority granted to the Congress by the Constitution to regulate commerce with foreign nations and among the states. The term "commerce" has been interpreted to include the production and buying and selling of goods as well as the transportation of commodities. Any of these functions are subject to national regulation and control if they affect more than one state. *See* COMMERCE, page 246.

• *Significance:* The commerce power is one of the major constitutional provisions used by the Congress to expand national power. A broad interpretation of what constitutes interstate commerce has enabled the Congress to regulate such matters as manufacturing, child labor, farm production, wages and hours, labor unions, and even criminal conduct which involves the crossing of state lines, such as car theft or kidnaping. Any activity which in any way "affects" interstate commerce is subject to national rather than state control. So many functions are now interstate in character that the role of the states in the federal system has been considerably altered.

Concurrent Power.   Authority possessed by both the national and state governments. Examples include the power to tax, to maintain courts, and to charter banks. The states may exercise concurrently with the national government any power that is not exclusively conferred on the national government by the Constitution and that does not conflict with national law.

• *Significance:* Under the American federal system, it is essential that both national and state governments possess those powers necessary to enable them to function. The power to tax is a noteworthy example: the fact that this power is delegated to the national government does not mean that the states may not also tax. States frequently legislate in areas in which the national government has not sought to legislate, although the power to do so by the national government exists. Should the national government determine to occupy a particular field of activity delegated to it under the Constitution, then the principle of national supremacy prevails. In the regulation of interstate commerce, the national government has frequently allowed state control over some elements of such commerce. The Supreme Court has disallowed state action when it has determined that national uniformity is desirable.

Confederation.   An alliance of independent states. A central government or administrative organ handles those matters of common concern delegated to it by the member states. The central unit may not make laws directly applicable to individuals without further action by the member units. The governments under the Articles of Confederation and the Confederate States of America are two examples from American history. The United Nations is often referred to as a confederation.

• *Significance:* A confederation is generally distinguished from a federation in which, as in the United States today, the central unit is invested with supreme authority and may act directly upon individuals. American experience under the Articles of Confederation is credited with being an essential step toward the formation of the "more perfect union." The confederated structure of the United Nations, for example, enables sovereign states to cooperate in seeking solutions to mutual problems without giving up their autonomy.

Contract Clause.   Article I, section 10 prohibits any state from passing laws impairing the obligation of contracts. This applies to contracts between individuals and to contracts made by the states. The state may neither weaken the effect of a contract nor make it more difficult to enforce. However, all contracts are subject to the limitation that they may not endanger the health, safety, and welfare of the people—the areas of the states' "police powers."
• *Significance:* At one time, the contract clause was a major constitutional defense against state regulation of private property. The framers of the Constitution sought to guard against state practices of relieving private persons (e.g., debtors) of their contractual obligations. The clause was also used to favor corporations receiving charters from the states by making it impossible to change the charters at a later date. State constitutions or statutes now make specific provision permitting revocation or alteration of corporation charters and other state contracts, subject to the limitations of due process of law. This development, along with police power limitations, has modified the restrictive nature of the contract clause.

Cooperative Federalism.   A concept which views the state and the national government as cooperating partners in the performance of governmental functions rather than as antagonistic competitors for power. The grant-in-aid programs typify this relationship between the national and state governments.
• *Significance:* Many current problems cut across traditional divisions of authority between the national and state governments. Cooperation between these units to meet common problems has enabled American federalism to adjust to new problems and to find some middle ground between extreme centralization of power and unworkable decentralization. For example, a vast interstate highway system would be unlikely without national and state cooperation.

Delegated Powers.   Those powers granted to the national government under the Constitution. Generally, the delegated powers are those found enumerated in the first three articles of the Constitution relative to the legislative, executive, and judicial branches of the national government. Article I, section 8 contains the main compilation of these powers. The terms "delegated," "enumerated," "granted," and "specific" may be used interchangeably.
• *Significance:* Under American federalism, the national government is one of delegated powers. With the exception of foreign affairs, the national government must find justification for its actions in a specifically authorized power, or one which can be reasonably implied from those specifically authorized. The national government does not possess unlimited or general governmental power but only such power as is given to it in the Constitution.

Enabling Act.   An act of the Congress authorizing the people of a territory to take the necessary steps to prepare for statehood. This would include calling a convention to frame a constitution.

• *Significance:* The enabling act constitutes an official indication that the Congress and the President look with favor upon a territory's petition for statehood. The Congress and the President are vested with considerable authority over what areas and under what conditions statehood will be granted. They must still approve the territory's constitution before officially granting statehood. On occasion, such as in the case of Alaska, a state has bypassed the petition and enabling act steps and has gone directly to Congress with its proposed constitution.

Exclusive Powers.   Those powers of either the national or the state governments which, under the Constitution, may be exercised only by that government. An example of an exclusive national power is that over foreign affairs; an exclusive state power is control over local government.

• *Significance:* The concept of exclusive power emphasizes the federal nature of the United States—two governments, existing side by side, each supreme within its own sphere of authority. Many problem areas, once considered within the exclusive realm of state power, have, however, under changing social conditions, fallen under national control. The regulation of child labor illustrates how the national government has, through judicial interpretation, moved into a field previously under exclusive state control.

Federalism.   A system of government in which power is divided between a central government and regional or subdivisional governments. The division of authority is delineated by a constitution. Both governments operate directly upon the people through their officials and laws. Both are supreme within their proper sphere of authority. By contrast, a "unitary" system of government is one in which the central government is supreme and the regional governments derive their authority from the central government. Federal systems are found in the United States, Canada, Switzerland, Mexico, Australia, India, West Germany, and others. Great Britain is a unitary state. The term "federal" is also commonly used in the United States to describe the national government.

• *Significance:* Federalism is a compromise between an extreme concentration of power and a loose confederation of independent states for governing a variety of people usually in a large expanse of territory. It has the virtue of retaining local pride, traditions, and power, while making possible the existence of a strong central government to handle common problems. In the United States, federalism has facilitated the growth of the country through the admittance of new states to the Union. In 1787, at the Constitutional Convention, it was a compromise essential to convincing the independent states to join together. The basic principle of American federalism is fixed in the 10th Amendment to the Constitution which provides that the national government is to have those powers delegated in the Constitution, all other powers to be reserved to the states. In some countries using the federal system, as in Canada, the pattern is reversed, the regional governments possessing only delegated authority. Federalism is one of the major principles underlying the American Constitution and has a significant impact upon American life and politics.

Full Faith and Credit.   One of the obligations of each state in its relations with other states. Article IV, section 1, of the Constitution provides that "Full faith and credit shall be given in each state to the public acts, records and judicial proceedings of every other state." The clause applies to civil proceedings. It ensures that rights established under wills, contracts, deeds, and other property rights will be honored in all states. A judicial decision in one state will be honored and enforced in all states. One area of difficulty has arisen with regard to divorce decrees. Some states have refused to recognize uncontested divorces granted by sister states because of questions over domicile.

• *Significance:* This clause was originally put into the Articles of Confederation to promote "mutual friendship and intercourse among the people of the different states in this Union." It was carried over to the Constitution and has since contributed to the unity of the American people. It protects the legal rights of citizens as they move about the various states and prevents evasion of legal responsibilities. The increasing mobility of the American people and the expanse of business operations have increased the importance of the clause.

Grant-in-Aid.   Funds made available by the Congress to the states and local governments for expenditure in accordance with prescribed standards and conditions. State legislatures also make such grants to local governments. Some measure of supervision over the expenditure of the funds accompanies the grants. In addition, the receiving government is required to match the contribution dollar for dollar or on some other ratio. Highways, airports, agricultural education, welfare, and health are among the major functions financed through the grant-in-aid device.

• *Significance:* Extensive use is being made of grants-in-aid to make available the superior tax resources of the national government for financing activities administered by the state and local governments. It has enabled the national government to enter into fields formerly considered to be within the reserved powers of the states. The states have accepted some national control because they need the funds. Often, because state governments have been unwilling or unable to deal with pressing problems, their people have turned to Washington for help. In recent years this has also been true in local areas. It has enabled all sections of the country to benefit from governmental services which otherwise might be available only in wealthier states. In addition, states have been stimulated to undertake needed activities and to improve their administrative and technical standards. The major disadvantage of the grant-in-aid system is that it transfers policy-making authority to the national government in areas formerly handled by state and local governments. However, the system represents an alternative to extreme centralization of the administration of services.

Guam.   A territory of the United States acquired from Spain after the Spanish-American War in 1898. Guam, largest of the Marianas Islands in the Pacific Ocean, is under the supervision of the Department of the Interior. Since 1950, the Congress has granted it a large measure of self-government and has conferred United States citizenship upon its inhabitants. Guam is governed by a one-house legislature of 21 members chosen at large by the people of Guam and by a governor appointed for a four-year term by the President of the United States with the Senate's approval.

• *Significance:* Guam has long served as an American naval station. During World War II, the island was occupied by Japan from 1942–1944 and was retaken after severe fighting. The conferral of American citizenship upon the inhabitants was in recognition both of their loyalty and of the importance of Guam to American interests in the Pacific.

Horizontal Federalism.   The relationships among the states of the Union which are imposed by the Constitution or undertaken voluntarily. This term is used to distinguish state-state relations from "vertical" federalism which denotes national-state relations. Requirements imposed by the Constitution are that each state afford full faith and credit to the public acts, records, and judicial proceedings of other states, grant the citizens of each state the privileges and immunities of citizens of their own state, and return fugitives from justice. Voluntary arrangements include interstate compacts, uniform laws, reciprocal agreements, and cooperation through consultation.

• *Significance:* Under federalism, the relationships between the states may be of equal importance to the relationship between the national and state governments. Since each state retains a good deal of authority, certain requirements have been laid down to assure cooperation. The requirement of full faith and credit, for example, helps to guarantee legal rights of citizens throughout the country. The states have sought to forestall national intervention into problem areas which cross state lines by entering into voluntary agreements. However, states have not shown sufficient initiative in meeting mutual problems, resulting in increasing dependence by the people upon the national government.

Implied Powers.   Authority possessed by the national government by inference from those powers delegated to it in the Constitution. For example, the power to draft men into the armed forces may be deduced from the power delegated to raise armies and navies. The implied power concept derives from the "necessary and proper" clause in Article I, section 8, which empowers the national government to do all those things necessary and proper to carry out its delegated powers. This principle was officially enunciated by the Supreme Court in *McCulloch v. Maryland,* 4 Wheaton 316 (1819).

• *Significance:* In the early days of the Union, conflicting opinions arose over whether the national government was limited to exercising only those powers expressly delegated to it in the Constitution. It is unlikely that the national government could have emerged as a powerful force had the more limited view prevailed. Through the use of implied powers, the national government has been able to strengthen and broaden the scope of its authority to meet many problems not foreseen by the framers.

Incorporated Territory.   A term coined by the Supreme Court in the *Insular Cases,* 182 U.S. 1 (1901), to describe those territories of the United States destined for statehood. The people of incorporated territories must be accorded all rights and privileges of the Constitution. In "unincorporated" territories, the Court ruled, only "fundamental" rights need be guaranteed. Since the admission of Alaska and Hawaii to statehood, there are no remaining incorporated territories.

• *Significance:* The Court, by drawing a distinction between incorporated and unincorporated territories, enabled the Congress to pass laws appropriate to the situation existing in each territory. Areas with relatively backward people could be denied rights which might prove unworkable or dangerous, such as the right to bear arms. People being prepared for statehood could receive proper tutelage for self-government.

Inherent Powers.   Authority vested in the national government, particularly in the area of foreign affairs, which does not depend upon any specific grant of power in the Constitution. Inherent powers grow out of the fact that the United States is a sovereign power among the nations. The Supreme Court has pointed out that even if the Constitution made no mention of it, the national government could still, for example, make international agreements or acquire territory. Whether or not the President has inherent powers to meet emergencies in internal affairs by virtue of his position as chief executive, is a matter of dispute. *See* INHERENT POWERS, page 310.

• *Significance:* Since the national government is one of delegated powers, justification for its actions must be found either directly or by implication from a specific grant of power. In the field of international affairs, however, the United States must be presumed to have the same power as any other nation in the world. With regard to presidential power, many presidents have taken unauthorized action to meet emergency situations, notably Abraham Lincoln during the Civil War. However, in 1952, the Supreme Court ruled that the President could not seize private property (steel mills) without authorization from the Congress (*Youngstown Sheet and Tube Co. v. Sawyer,* 343 U.S. 579).

Intergovernmental Tax Immunity.   The exemption of state and national governmental agencies and property from taxation by each other. The doctrine of intergovernmental tax immunity had its origin in the case of *McCulloch v. Maryland,* 4 Wheaton 316 (1819), in which the Supreme Court declared that the states may not burden the national government by the taxation of its agents or functions. This doctrine was later extended to national taxation of state agents and functions. For a time, even the salaries of governmental employees and contractors were exempt from taxing; this is no longer the case. National government functions and properties are exempt from state taxation but where hardship may result, because of extensive federal holdings in a state, payments in lieu of taxes may be authorized by the Congress. State or local activities may be taxed by the national government if the function is non-governmental in character. An example of this is national taxation of state-owned liquor stores.

• *Significance:* Intergovernmental tax immunity prevents undue interference by one government with the proper exercise of power by another government. This rule is essential to the effective operation of a federal system of government. Without such a rule, one level of government might use its tax power to weaken or to destroy operations of the other. National taxation of state nongovernmental functions remains a matter of controversy since it is questionable whether any state or local activity can be classified as nongovernmental in character. The courts have been reluctant to interfere with congressional judgment on this matter.

Interposition.   A concept which holds that a state may place itself between its citizens and the national government so as to prevent the enforcement of national law upon its citizens. According to this doctrine, each state may be the judge of the legality or constitutionality of national action, and may "interpose" its sovereignty to nullify invalid federal action. This theory was propounded by Thomas Jefferson and James Madison in the Kentucky and Virginia Resolutions of 1799 protesting the Alien and Sedition Acts, and by the South prior to the Civil War. Recently, southern leaders have reactivated the theory in opposition to the school desegregation ruling of the Supreme Court. However, the federal courts have rejected the doctrine as contrary to the national supremacy clause of Article VI.

• *Significance:* Interposition represents a challenge to national supremacy in an extreme form. Obviously, 50 different interpretations of the Constitution would dissolve the Union. From time to time, the right to interpose state sovereignty has been claimed by states in all sections of the country. Generally, this claim of state sovereignty has been made to cover up underlying social and economic interests of particular groups which feel themselves threatened by national policy. Certainly, when interposition is claimed, it is a sign that the federal principle is under strain.

Interstate Compact.   An agreement between two or more states. The Constitution (Art. I, sec. 10) requires such agreements or compacts to have the consent of the Congress. However, many agreements on minor matters are made without such consent. Generally, the rule appears to be that any compact which tends to increase the power of the contracting states relative to other states or to the national government requires consent. One of the earliest and best-known compacts was concluded between New York and New Jersey, in 1921, to establish the Port of New York Authority for purposes of regulating the New York harbor and other facilities. A great variety of other compacts are in existence covering a wide range of subjects from flood control to petroleum conservation. Congress has, at times, granted advance blanket approval to certain kinds of compacts, as in civil defense matters and water pollution.

• *Significance:* One intent of the requirement that congressional consent be acquired was to prevent the states from threatening the Union through alliances among themselves. Today, interstate compacts serve as a means for the states to solve regional problems without resort to national aid. In this way the states may avoid the centralizing tendencies of recent years.

Interstate Rendition.   The return of fugitives from justice by a state upon the demand of the executive authority of the state in which the crime was committed. This is one of the obligations imposed upon the states by Article IV, section 2. Though the language of the Constitution is positive on this obligation, the federal courts will not order a governor of one state to deliver up a fugitive wanted in another state. Compliance by a governor is viewed as a moral duty. Rendition is routinely followed in the overwhelming number of cases but, on occasion, a governor has refused to comply. Refusal may be based on such grounds as the good behavior of the fugitive since his escape, the suspicion that a fair trial will not be granted, or for political or other reasons known only to the governor. The Congress has supplemented the requirement by making it a federal crime to flee across state lines to avoid prosecution for certain felonies. When apprehended by federal agents, the fugitive is usually turned over to the state from which he fled. The term "extradition" is used to describe this practice among nations under international law.

• *Significance:* The practice of rendition is designed to prevent "beating the rap" by leaving a state. Although the governor may refuse to return the fugitive, he may invite retaliation of the other state by such action. Considerable doubt exists as to whether or not the Congress could compel a governor to return a fugitive, despite a Supreme Court decision suggesting that this could not be done (*Kentucky v. Dennison,* 24 Howard 66 [1861]).

National Supremacy.   A basic constitutional principle of American government which provides for the superiority of national law. This principle is rooted in Article VI which provides that the Constitution, laws passed by the national government under its constitutional powers, and all treaties, are the supreme law of the land. The Article requires that all national and state officers and judges be bound by oath to support the Constitution regardless of any state constitutional or legislative provisions. Thus, any legitimate exercise of national power supersedes any state action which is in conflict. Determination of whether such a conflict exists rests in the hands of the judiciary, the final decisions being made by the Supreme Court.

• *Significance:* National supremacy is crucial to the successful operation of the federal system. The national government is the government of all the people; a state speaks for only part of the people. The application of the principle of national supremacy has been a source of constant conflict, with such extreme results as the Civil War. Broad construction of national authority in recent years has tended to weaken the position of the states. A contemporary example of the application of national supremacy is in the controversy over ending racial segregation in public facilities.

Necessary and Proper Clause.   The final paragraph of Article I, section 8, which delegates legislative powers to the Congress. It authorizes all laws "necessary and proper" to carry out the enumerated powers. This clause, sometimes called the "elastic" clause, was used by the Supreme Court in *McCulloch v. Maryland,* 4 Wheaton 316 (1819), to develop the concept of "implied powers."

• *Significance:* Congressional authority is limited to its delegated powers. However, the necessary and proper clause allows Congress to choose the *means* by which it will execute its authority. Broad construction of this phrase has enabled the national government to adapt its powers to the needs of the times. It has given elasticity to our constitutional system and has reduced the need for frequent constitutional amendment.

Nullification.   A declaration by a state that a national law is null and void and not binding upon its citizens. This was done by South Carolina in 1832, in opposition to the Tariff Acts of 1828 and 1832. The theory of nullification, a logical extension of the theory of interposition, was formulated by John C. Calhoun. Essentially, the theory holds that the Union is a compact among sovereign states and that the national government is not the final judge of its own powers; a state may nullify any national law and even secede from the Union.

• *Significance:* Though nullification is a discredited theory, the racial segregation problem of recent years has given rise to nullification talk by some southern leaders. The Supreme Court has rejected the theory as contrary to the principle of national supremacy. Nevertheless, some southern states have continued to thwart the Supreme Court's desegregation decision.

Panama Canal Zone.   A territory of the United States leased in perpetuity from the Republic of Panama in 1903. The Zone comprises territory five miles wide on each side of the Canal. It is administered by a governor appointed by the President for a four-year term, under general supervision of the Secretary of the Army. Laws governing the territory emanate from the Congress, or the President through executive orders. The Bill of Rights has been made applicable in the Zone.

• *Significance:* Panamanian resentment against United States control over the Zone erupted into violent demonstrations in 1959. The United States has recognized the Republic of Panama's titular sovereignty over the Zone and has made certain economic concessions to it relative to wage rates and purchasing of supplies. Continued control over the Canal is of strategic importance to the United States in view of Communist infiltration into Central and South America.

Police Power.   Authority to promote and safeguard the health, morals, safety, and welfare of the people. In the context of the American federal system, the police power is reserved to the states. The national government, exercising only delegated powers, does not possess a general police power. However, many national laws enacted under the commerce and postal powers, for example, have the effect of police power regulations. Laws designed to prevent shipment of impure drugs in interstate commerce or mailing of obscene literature are examples of what may be termed "federal police power." State laws enacted under the police power may invade national jurisdiction if such laws are pertinent to the health, safety, or welfare of the people of the state. An example of this is a state law regulating grade crossings for interstate trains.

• *Significance:* Police power regulations frequently come into conflict with the constitutional requirement of due process of law. The need for legislation must be clear and any limitation imposed upon individual rights must be justified. The judiciary plays a large role in determining the proper scope for the exercise of the police power. The police power has greatly enlarged the area of state and local control over the individual as well as over business, labor, and property.

Privileges and Immunities.   The Constitution contains two clauses which use the term "privileges and immunities." Article IV, section 2, provides that, "The citizens of each state shall be entitled to all privileges and immunities of citizens in the several states." The 14th Amendment provides that, "No state shall make or enforce any law which shall abridge the privileges or immunities of citizens of the United States." The first provision is considered to be an instrument of federalism, one of the obligations of states in their relations with each other. Basically, it means that a citizen of one state is not to be treated as an alien when in another state; he may not be discriminated against by denial of legal protection, access to courts, travel rights, or property rights. However, out-of-state residents may be denied certain political rights such as voting, or other privileges reserved to that state's residents such as lower tuition at state institutions. The full and precise meaning of the term has never been established by the courts. The 14th Amendment's privileges and immunities clause has, similarly, not received complete definition. It is basically an instrument of civil liberties, placing certain restrictions upon each state in its dealings with United States citizens. The clause has been interpreted to apply only to those privileges which one enjoys by virtue of national citizenship. These include the right to travel, to have access to national officials, and to engage in interstate and foreign commerce. As interpreted, the clause confers no new rights upon citizens nor does it affect the citizen in those privileges which he enjoys by virtue of state citizenship.
• *Significance:* Neither of these clauses has proved to be of great importance in American history. The narrow interpretation given by the courts to the 14th Amendment has disappointed those who saw in it a boon to Negro rights after the Civil War. Article IV has served, in part, to strengthen economic and social ties among the people of the various states, but the vagueness of its language, and uncertain judicial interpretation, has made it of only limited use.

Puerto Rico.   A territory of the United States acquired from Spain in 1898. Congress conferred citizenship upon the inhabitants in 1917. In 1952, the Congress approved a constitution framed by the inhabitants and officially designated Puerto Rico as a free, self-governing commonwealth, closely associated with the United States. Though subject to many national laws, such as the draft, the people of the island are now self-governing in most respects, with their own elected governor, bicameral legislature, and court system. The defense of the island and the conduct of foreign affairs are the responsibility of the United States, and appeals may be made from Puerto Rico courts to the regular federal courts. In addition, the people elect a "resident commissioner" who represents Puerto Rico in the Congress; he may speak but not vote.
• *Significance:* The precise status of Puerto Rico is far from clear. Though the Congress has left the door open to eventual statehood, there is agitation for complete independence. Statehood is opposed by many Puerto Ricans because they are exempt from the income tax. The island suffers from overpopulation and serious economic problems and many Puerto Ricans have migrated to

the United States. Attempts are being made to raise the standard of living and to make Puerto Rico a model of American territorial relations.

Regionalism.   A method of decentralizing power on a geographical basis. In the United States, regionalism is often proposed as an alternative or supplement to the states. For example, the country could be divided into nine or ten regional subdivisions instead of 50 states. The term is also applied to regional administration of federal projects, such as the Tennessee Valley Authority, and to regional interstate compacts.

• *Significance:* Advocates of regionalism argue that the states do not reflect realistic economic and social patterns. The country could be divided into regions having genuine unity, such as the Missouri Valley area, New England, etc. People of the United States tend to take a regional or sectional rather than state outlook on many problems. The strong tradition and constitutional power of the individual states make their elimination unlikely, but states are increasingly acting together to meet common problems.

Republican Form of Government.   A republican government operates through elected representatives of the people and is generally distinguished from a pure democracy in which the people govern directly. Article IV, section 4 provides that the national government shall guarantee to each state a republican form of government.

• *Significance:* The precise meaning of the guarantee of a republican form of government has never been determined; the Supreme Court has held this to be a "political question" to be answered by the Congress or the President. A state government is considered to be republican in form if the houses of Congress accept the elected representatives of the state. In addition, the President could conceivably use the armed forces to dispossess a state government considered by him to be other than republican in form. This guarantee is classified by political scientists as one of the obligations of the national government toward the states in maintaining the federal system. State citizens are thereby protected against arbitrary seizure of power of state government and abuse of state electoral systems.

Resident Commissioner.   A delegate elected by the people of a territory to represent them in the House of Representatives. He may speak in the House, serve on committees, but may not vote. His salary is the same as for all congressmen. At present, only Puerto Rico has a resident commissioner.

• *Significance:* By permitting a territory to elect a delegate to the Congress, we demonstrate our willingness to prepare the territory for self-governance and possible statehood or independence. Since the people of Puerto Rico are subject to many federal laws, they are entitled to representation of their interests.

Reserved Powers.   Powers of state governments under the American federal system. The states retain all powers not delegated to the national government in the Constitution or prohibited to them by it. These powers are frequently referred to as "residuary" powers. It is not possible to make a definitive list of state powers since, in the very nature of the federal system, the states may exercise any power which is not delegated to the national government. Generally, this includes authority over internal affairs of the state and general police power over the health, safety, and welfare of the people. State constitutions may place specific restrictions upon state powers.

• *Significance:* A basic principle of American federalism is the division of authority between national and state governments. The concept that certain powers are "reserved" to the states is stated in the 10th Amendment. Exactly what constitutes a reserved power is often a matter of dispute. With problems continuously changing in scope, a power formerly exercised by a state may fall under national control. This is particularly true in matters of commerce as subjects of commerce increasingly become interstate in character. The judiciary is frequently called upon to determine the proper division of authority between the nation and the states.

Resulting Powers.   Powers of the national government derived from a combination of delegated or implied powers; hence, powers which "result" from a given set of powers, rather than by implication (implied) from one of the delegated powers. For example, the United States Criminal Code provides for punishment for violation of any national law. The Constitution does not explicitly delegate such power nor is it implied by any single grant of power. Rather, it "results" from the aggregate of power delegated to the national government.

• *Significance:* In a sense, resulting powers are an extension of the implied powers doctrine. It makes possible an exercise of national power which may logically follow from a series of powers. Thus, it is not necessary for the Congress to point to some single grant of authority to substantiate an exercise of power.

Samoa (American Samoa).   A protectorate of the United States consisting of the Island of Tutuila and four lesser islands in the Pacific Ocean, about 4200 miles west of California. The islands were acquired under an agreement with Great Britain and Germany in 1899 and were formally accepted by Congress in 1929. Samoa is under complete control of the Department of the Interior. Its inhabitants are not citizens of the United States. In 1960, Samoa drafted its first constitution, although the Secretary of the Interior appoints the governor and may veto legislative and judicial actions.

• *Significance:* Samoa is important largely for strategic reasons. It also serves as a way station on trans-Pacific air routes. The United States has given the islands an increasing amount of autonomous power, thereby demonstrating our interest in developing the people in American territories for self-government.

States' Rights.   A term used to connote opposition to increasing national government power at the expense of the states. States' rights adherents call for an interpretation of the Constitution which would place limits on the federal assumption of implied powers and give expanded interpretation of the reserved powers of the states.

• *Significance:* Strong support for states' rights usually comes from those groups who feel that their particular interest will be better served by state action than by national action. Though the term is common in American political life, it has rarely been used with consistency by particular groups. For example, certain industries which sought to be free of state regulation by claiming that their operations were interstate in nature, changed their position when the national government sought to regulate them. The proper balance between national and state power is a continuing American problem under the federal system. The balance is usually determined by the strength of political forces rather than by the language of the Constitution.

Tenth Amendment.   The final item of the Bill of Rights in the Constitution which defines the principle of American federalism: "The powers not delegated to the United States by the Constitution, nor prohibited by it to the states, are reserved to the states respectively, or to the people."
• *Significance:* The 10th Amendment was added to the Constitution to make clear the position of the states in the Union. Though it was generally understood that the framers intended that the states would retain all powers not prohibited by the Constitution or delegated to the national government, the people insisted upon an express provision to that effect. Exactly what is meant by the phrase "or to the people" has never been determined.

Territory.   An area belonging to the United States which is not included within any state of the Union. Though the Constitution does not expressly grant the power to acquire territory, Article IV, section 3 authorizes the Congress to make rules respecting the territory of the United States. Power to acquire territory also results from the national government's power to make treaties, to admit new states, and to make war which might result in conquest. The District of Columbia, though not a part of any state, is not considered a territory. Major territorial possessions of the United States now include Guam, Puerto Rico, the Panama Canal Zone, Samoa, the Virgin Islands, and the Territory of the Pacific Islands.
• *Significance:* Most of the territory acquired by the United States through purchase, conquest, or treaty has eventually become part of the United States, enabling us to grow from 13 to 50 states. Current possessions are important mainly for strategic reasons. The United States has rarely used its territories as "colonies" to be exploited. Rather, inhabitants have been trained for self-government and, as in the case of the Philippine Islands, given independence, or, as in the case of Hawaii, given statehood.

Territory of the Pacific Islands.   A number of island chains acquired by conquest from Japan in World War II and administered by the United States under a United Nations Trusteeship. Chief among these are the Marshall, Caroline, Mariana, and Gilbert Islands, which though small in size, cover a vast expanse of area. The Territory is governed by a High Commissioner under the Secretary of the Interior.
• *Significance:* Though the United States could have taken outright possession of the islands, it volunteered to govern them under the United Nations Trusteeship. Under terms of the trust, the islands may be used for strategic defense

purposes. Many are fortified as naval and air bases, and nuclear weapons have been tested in the area.

Twenty-First Amendment. An amendment to the Constitution permitting the sale of intoxicating beverages in the United States. The Amendment protects states which retain prohibition by barring the importation or transportation of liquor into such states. It repealed the 18th Amendment which had imposed prohibition upon the entire country.

• *Significance:* The 21st Amendment is the only one which repeals a prior amendment. It is also the only one to have been ratified by conventions in the states rather than by state legislatures; ratification was accomplished in just one year. National support for state law is also a feature of the Amendment in that it prohibits the transportation of intoxicants into states preferring to remain "dry."

Unitary State. A system of government which vests control in a central authority. Local or subdivisional governments exercise only those powers given to them by the central government. It is distinguished from a federal system wherein power is constitutionally divided between a central and sub-divisional government. England and France are examples of the unitary form. In the United States, local governments, such as cities and counties, stand in a unitary relationship to the state governments which assign specific rights and duties to them. An exception to this is found in those states where cities are given "home rule" by constitutional provision.

• *Significance:* A unitary system provides a unified and consistent administration of policy while, at the same time, permitting variations to be made by the central authority. It allows more efficient handling of nationwide problems and is more sensitive to national majorities. Opponents of unitary government claim that federalism is superior in that it permits more experimentation in local government and greater freedom in meeting local needs.

Virgin Islands. Territory purchased by the United States from Denmark in 1917. It consists of three small islands east of Puerto Rico—St. Croix, St. John, and St. Thomas. American citizenship was granted to the inhabitants in 1927. The islands have been given an increasing measure of home rule over the years. At present it is governed by a popularly elected legislature but the governor is appointed by the President. Laws are subject to disallowance by the governor, the President, and the Congress.

• *Significance:* The islands were originally purchased in 1917 in order to forestall annexation by Germany. They serve a strategic purpose in protecting American interests in the Caribbean.

Washington, D.C. The capital of the United States of America, the District of Columbia. It consists of some 70 square miles of land carved out of the state of Maryland. Land originally ceded by Virginia for this purpose was returned in 1846. Article I, section 8, clause 17 grants the Congress exclusive control over the capital. The District is governed by a three-man Board of Commissioners appointed by the President and the Senate, one of whom is an Army engineer. Congress is the legislative body for the District and spends two days each month acting as the city council. Funds for the District are secured largely through local taxation. The District is a highly urbanized area of about one million inhabitants. The people of the District do not choose local officers, but, under the 23rd Amendment adopted in 1961, they may vote in presidential elections.

• *Significance:* In recent years, attention has turned toward securing a measure of self-government for the people of the District. Major obstacles appear to be the inability of the Congress to agree on a scheme of government, and southern opposition based on the fact that a large portion of the residents are Negroes. Criticism has also been made of the great amount of time devoted by Congress to affairs of the District, which would be unnecessary if home rule were granted.

IMPORTANT AGENCIES

Office of Territories.   A part of the Department of the Interior which supervises the territorial possessions of the United States except for the Panama Canal Zone, which is under the Department of the Army.

• *Significance:* The Office of Territories replaced the former system whereby several agencies were concerned with territorial matters. The Hoover Commission recommended in 1949 that an independent Administration of Overseas Affairs be established to report directly to the President. Although this has not been done, the Office of Territories does concentrate authority over most territories in a single agency.

Port of New York Authority.   An agency created by an interstate compact between New York and New Jersey to manage important public works, such as the New York harbor, metropolitan area airports, bridges, and tunnels. It is administered by a nonsalaried board appointed by the governors of both states.

• *Significance:* This agency was the first major compact between states for the common administration of mutual needs. Its success is credited with encouraging a variety of compacts among the states.

Social Security Administration.   A unit of the Department of Health, Education, and Welfare (HEW) which supervises the administration of national grants-in-aid to the states for welfare purposes under the Social Security Act of 1935. Its functions include supervision of grants for old-age assistance, aid to the blind, to dependent children, and to the totally and permanently disabled. This agency also is responsible for Old-Age and Survivors' Insurance, a service administered directly by the federal government.

• *Significance:* Welfare programs have accounted for a major share of federal grants-in-aid in recent years. In many cases, controversy exists over the proper share of the costs to be borne by state and national governments and over the degree of supervision which the national government should exercise. The Social Security Administration has become a major agency in the development of national-state cooperative federalism.

IMPORTANT CASES

Coyle v. Smith, 221 U.S. 599 (1911): Established the principle that all states are admitted to the Union on an equal footing. Congress may not enforce conditions which would undermine the equality of the states. In this case, the Court upheld the right of Oklahoma to change its capital city contrary to a requirement in the congressional enabling act which preceded statehood.
• *Significance:* Congress may stipulate any conditions it chooses for the admission of a state. Once admitted to the Union, a state may not be compelled to abide by any condition which would interfere with its right to manage its internal affairs or which would create different classes of states.

Graves v. New York ex rel. O'Keefe, 306 U.S. 466 (1939): Held that a state may tax the income of a federal employee and that such a tax does not impose an unconstitutional burden upon the national government.
• *Significance:* This was one of the last in a long line of cases which arose out of the decision in *McCulloch v. Maryland* that a state may not tax an instrumentality of the federal government since the power to tax is the power to destroy. This doctrine was carried to the point that neither the state nor the national government could tax each other in any way including the salaries of their respective employees. In the *Graves* case, the Court reversed its position and sustained congressional authorization of state taxation of federal employees' incomes. Federal taxation of state employees had been upheld the previous year in *Helvering v. Gerhardt,* 304 U.S. 405 (1938).

Kentucky v. Dennison, 24 Howard 66 (1861): Decided that the constitutional duty of a governor to return a fugitive to the state from which he fled is only a moral obligation rather than a mandatory one. The Court found that a national statute of 1793 dealing with the return of fugitives provided no means by which a governor could be compelled to perform his duty and, in any case, that the national government lacked authority to coerce a state officer.
• *Significance:* This opinion enabled the Court to shun the difficult practical question of how a state governor could actually be compelled to perform his duty. Though the supremacy of the national government is clear in most national-state controversies, this decision has been respected by the national government and all states, thereby keeping interstate rendition a discretionary act for the governors.

Luther v. Borden, 7 Howard 1 (1848): Held that the question of whether a state has a republican form of government is a political and not a judicial question. The Supreme Court refused to define a republican form of government, holding that the Congress and the President must decide. The case arose out of Dorr's Rebellion in Rhode Island in 1841 when rival groups claimed to be the true government of the state.
• *Significance:* The constitutional requirement that the national government guarantee each state a republican form of government will not be enforced by the courts. Congressional power to accept the state's representatives, and

the President's power to use force to quell a rebellion are the means by which the guarantee is honored.

McCulloch v. Maryland, 4 Wheaton 316 (1819): Upheld, in a landmark decision of the Supreme Court, the power of the national government to establish a bank, and denied the state of Maryland the power to tax a branch of the bank. In the opinion by Chief Justice John Marshall, the Court held that it was not necessary for the Constitution expressly to authorize the Congress to create a bank. Rather, the power to do so was implied from the Congress' power over financial matters and from the "necessary and proper" clause of the Constitution. Maryland could not tax a legitimate instrumentality of the national government, said the Court, since this would be an invasion of national supremacy. "The power to tax is the power to destroy . . . ." From this was derived the principle of intergovernmental tax immunity.

• *Significance:* Two important principles of American government were firmly established by this decision. First was the doctrine of "implied powers" which has given the national government a vast source of power. Second was the principle of "national supremacy" which denies to the states any right to interfere in the constitutional operations of the national government. Had the decision favored Maryland, the national government would not have been able to meet the problems of an expanding nation and the Constitution would not have become a "living" document.

Virginia v. Tennessee, 148 U.S. 503 (1893): Denied a suit brought by Virginia to have the boundary line voided between it and Tennessee on the ground that the line had been established by agreement between the states without consent of the Congress. The Court held that the agreement did not constitute a compact between the states which required positive approval of the Congress. The only compacts or agreements requiring approval are those which tend to increase state power at the expense of the national government. In other instances, the Congress may give its approval by implication.

• *Significance:* Although the Constitution prohibits states from entering into agreements or compacts without consent of the Congress, this decision made it clear that the restriction did not apply to each and every agreement between states. This has made it possible for states to solve mutual problems without the necessity of involving the Congress. Yet, the Congress is always free to step in if it feels that the agreement threatens the national government in any way.

Williams v. North Carolina, 325 U.S. 226 (1945): Decided that North Carolina could legally refuse to accord full faith and credit to a "quickie" Nevada divorce decree, since the parties to the suit had not relinquished their North Carolina residence and had gone to Nevada merely to get a divorce.

• *Significance:* The decision concerned one of the few trouble spots in the constitutional requirement that states give full faith and credit to the legal proceedings of other states. In later cases, the Court tended to narrow the scope of the *Williams* case, but many people believe that a constitutional amendment may be needed to resolve the divorce problem. However, most states honor the full faith and credit clause with regard to out-of-state divorces.

IMPORTANT STATUTES

Federal Aid Highway Act.   A major example of federal grants-in-aid to the states, which began in 1916 for the building of highways. Grants have been given for trunk roads, secondary roads, urban extensions of highways, and, since 1956, for an extensive interstate highway system. The states must meet national requirements as to matching funds, maintenance of roads, location, and engineering details. The 1956 Act provides for a 13-year program for the building of 41,000 miles of multilane highways connecting all major cities. The national government is financing 90 percent of the cost.

• *Significance:* This is a leading example of a successfully operated program of grants-in-aid. Through it, the national government has shaped state and local road policy, although it does not actually build the highways. Highway expenditures of state and local governments are exceeded only by expenditures for education. The grant-in-aid program has provided states with substantial revenue. But, it has limited the discretion of the state and local authorities over a major function.

4

Immigration and Citizenship

Alien. An individual living in a state of which he is not a citizen or national. Aliens generally owe allegiance to a foreign power but may acquire citizenship by following prescribed procedures.

• *Significance:* In the United States, aliens enjoy many of the civil rights which the Constitution accords to "persons" as distinguished from citizens. These include most provisions of the Bill of Rights and freedom from arbitrary discrimination. Aliens are subject to the laws of the United States, must pay taxes, and may be drafted. Military service and other duties and rights of aliens are generally in accord with treaties between the United States and other nations. At present, an alien who objects to the draft forfeits his right ever to become a citizen. Under the laws of most American states, an alien may not engage in certain professions, own firearms, hold government employment, or, in some states, own real estate. In no case may he enjoy such political rights as voting or holding public office. The most serious disability imposed upon an alien is the ever-present possibility of deportation. Since an alien has no *right* to live in the United States, he may be deported for moral turpitude or for past or present affiliation with the Communist party. In time of war, aliens who are subjects of enemy states may be severely restricted. Under present law, all aliens must register with the Attorney General every year.

Citizen. An individual who is a native or naturalized member of a state, owes allegiance to that state, and is entitled to the protection and privileges of its laws. Citizenship in the United States is defined in the 14th Amendment to the Constitution as follows: "All persons born or naturalized in the United States, and subject to the jurisdiction thereof, are citizens of the United States and of the state wherein they reside." Citizenship is based mainly on one's place of birth (*jus soli*) but may be acquired through naturalization and, under circumstances defined by the Congress, through blood relation (*jus sanguinis*).

• *Significance:* Two basic problems were raised prior to the Civil War: (1) Should Negroes born in the United States be considered citizens? (2) Is state citizenship secondary and incidental to national citizenship? The 14th Amendment provides affirmative answers to both. Recent developments include the extension of citizenship by birth to American Indians and to the people of Guam, Puerto Rico, and the Virgin Islands. Prior to 1922, a married woman took the citizenship of her husband, but now women are treated the same as men with the exception that an alien woman marrying an American citizen may be naturalized after a shorter residence requirement. Children born here of foreign diplomatic agents are not citizens since they are not "subject to the jurisdiction" of the United States.

Denaturalization.   Revocation of citizenship which has been acquired by naturalization. This may be done only by court order in accordance with due process of law.

• *Significance:* The most common ground for denaturalization is fraud or willful misrepresentation when being naturalized. Lengthy residence abroad by a naturalized citizen may also result in termination of citizenship. Recent legislation permits denaturalization of those who affiliate with subversive organizations within five years after naturalization or who are convicted of contempt of Congress for refusal to testify in an investigation into subversive activities within ten years. Many observers charge that such provisions make "second-class" citizens of naturalized persons since native born citizens are not affected by such laws. A commonly held assumption, that one loses his citizenship when convicted of a serious crime, is not true. One may lose certain privileges of citizenship, such as the right to vote or hold certain jobs, but citizenship is retained.

Deportation.   Compulsory expulsion of an alien from a state to his country of origin. Deportation is a civil rather than a criminal proceeding under American law, and, hence, various constitutional safeguards do not apply. With the exception of naturalized citizens who lose their citizenship, a citizen may not be deported.

• *Significance:* Aliens remain in the United States at the sufferance of the Congress, which has virtually unlimited power to establish grounds for deportation. Illegal entry is the most common cause of deportation, but, in recent years, the Congress has considerably increased the number of grounds for deportation, particularly for Communists and other political undesirables and for aliens convicted of serious crimes. Constitutional safeguards with regard to bail and ex post facto laws, for example, do not apply to deportation proceedings, and great discretion is vested in the Attorney General. Many public officials and citizens have questioned the fairness of procedures used in deportation cases. The courts have been reluctant to interfere since the issue involves the plenary powers of the national government in international affairs.

Dual Citizenship.   Holding citizenship in two or more countries. This may occur since most countries recognize as citizens those who are born within their boundaries as well as children of their subjects born abroad. Thus a person born abroad of American parents, for example, is considered to be an American citizen and may also be considered to be a citizen by the country in which he was born.

• *Significance:* With increasing mobility, dual citizenship may affect numerous people. It may cause hardship when, for example, conflicting claims are made over the right to require military service. Under American law, a person who, after reaching the age of 22, lives for three years in another country which also claims him as a citizen, forfeits his American citizenship unless he takes an oath of allegiance to the United States before a diplomatic official.

Expatriation.   Voluntary withdrawal of allegiance or residence from the country in which citizenship is held. Since 1865, the Congress has expressly recognized the right of expatriation, setting forth specific grounds. Actions which constitute expatriation include: naturalization in a foreign state, taking an oath of allegiance to another state, serving in a foreign army without consent, taking a job open only to citizens of another state, voting in a foreign election, leaving the United States to avoid military service, and conviction of treason or attempt to overthrow the government by force. A citizen living abroad may voluntarily renounce his citizenship before a diplomatic officer but renunciation is permitted within the United States only during wartime with consent of the Attorney General.
• *Significance:* Congress recognized the right of expatriation as "a natural and inherent right of all people," essential for the rights to life, liberty, and the pursuit of happiness. The major purpose of this declaration was to justify before the world the great number of people from foreign lands who were emigrating to the United States. The expatriation laws assume that the person committing certain acts, whether intended as acts of expatriation or not, acted voluntarily and with full knowledge of the consequences. A recent Supreme Court decision declared unconstitutional a statutory provision that a person who was convicted of wartime desertion expatriated himself, on the ground that this was cruel and unusual punishment (*Trop v. Dulles,* 356 U.S. 86 [1958]), but the Court upheld loss of citizenship for voting in a foreign election (*Perez v. Brownell,* 356 U.S. 44 [1958]).

Immigration.   Admittance of a person to a country of which he is not a native for the purpose of establishing permanent residence. Early attempts by seaboard states to regulate immigration into the United States were invalidated by the Supreme Court, which declared immigration to be an exclusive function of the national government, incidental to its power over foreign affairs. Immigration into the United States was unlimited until 1882, when the Congress began to impose restrictions on the admission of criminals, the mentally ill, paupers, diseased persons, illiterates, the Chinese, anarchists, and advocates of violent governmental change. In 1924, the Congress barred Asiatics and established the "national origins quota" system which assigns a quota to each country based on the numerical contribution it has made to our national stock as of 1920, and fixed the total number of immigrants from Europe at 154,000 per year. Recent legislation has erased racial exclusions but has retained the quota system and the numerical limitation (now 156,387). Restrictions against the admission of Communists or other suspected subversives have been increased. Canadians and Latin Americans have almost unrestricted permission to enter. Immigration laws are administered by the Department of State and the Department of Justice, and each has been given extensive discretion to determine who may enter the United States.

• *Significance:* More than 40 million people have come to the United States from all over the world. The figure would be higher had not the Congress imposed a variety of restrictions. From time to time, the Congress has relaxed the quota restrictions by admitting large numbers of refugees and displaced persons from war-torn and iron curtain countries. Pressures for limiting immigration have come largely from labor organizations, from those who fear the introduction of alien ideologies, and from those who, though immigrants or descendants of immigrants themselves, look down upon new groups seeking admission. Criticisms of the quota system as discriminatory have come from official and unofficial sources, and many have protested the red tape required for admission to the country, and the vast discretion vested in immigration officials to deny entrance to aliens. On the whole, however, the United States has a proud record of achievement in absorbing millions of immigrants and, in turn, the nation has benefited immeasurably from the contributions of so many people of varied backgrounds and talents.

Jus Sanguinis.   "Law of the blood"—a principle by which citizenship is determined by parentage rather than by place of birth (*jus soli*).

• *Significance:* The 14th Amendment recognizes only birth and naturalization as bases for citizenship, but the Congress has adopted the rule of *jus sanguinis* to apply in special circumstances. Thus, one may be a citizen of the United States if born abroad, provided that either or both of one's parents are citizens. If only one parent is a citizen, that parent must have lived in the United States or one of its possessions for ten years, five of them after the age of 14, and the child, in order to remain a citizen, must come to the United States prior to his twenty-third birthday and live here for five years between the ages of 14 and 23. Because large numbers of Americans are working and traveling abroad, *jus sanguinis* has taken on increasing significance.

Jus Soli.   "Law of the soil"—the basic rule under which American citizenship is determined by place of birth rather than by parentage (*jus sanguinis*).

• *Significance:* The 14th Amendment's provision that all persons born in the United States are citizens (with the minor exception, for example, of children born to foreign diplomats who are not under American jurisdiction) is far-reaching. Anyone born here is a citizen whether his parents are resident aliens or merely visitors. For purposes of citizenship, the Congress has declared the soil of the United States to include Puerto Rico, Guam, and the Virgin Islands.

National.   A person who owes allegiance to a country, though not a citizen thereof. The term is used at times, however, in the same sense as the term citizen. Under American law, a national is an inhabitant of an outlying possession of the United States to whom Congress has not granted citizenship. Residents of the Philippine Islands were considered nationals until independence was granted, whereas the people of Puerto Rico were granted citizenship in 1917 after a period as nationals.

• *Significance:* The term national is basically a concept of international law.

American nationals are accorded most of the protections which citizens have, and the actual distinction is hazy. By granting the status of nationals to a people, the Congress identifies them as belonging to and entitled to the protection of the United States, particularly for purposes of international relations.

National Origins Quota System.   The allotment assigned to a foreign country for purposes of admitting immigrants to the United States. The quota assigned to each country is based, in the main, on the number of people of a given national background living in the United States in 1920. At present, 156,387 immigrants may be admitted each year. The quota assigns nearly 150,000 places to Europeans (over 126,000 from northern and western Europe) and the remainder to Asia and Africa (limited to 100 to each country, except Japan, assigned 185). The quota does not apply to natives of the western hemisphere.

• *Significance:* The national origins quota system has made immigration a minor factor in American population growth. The allotments are extremely small for people from southern and eastern Europe, Asia, and Africa, many of whom are anxious to immigrate, whereas the quotas assigned to northern and western Europe are seldom filled. The system has been attacked from many quarters as racist in philosophy and detrimental to our international relations. Both Presidents Truman and Eisenhower unsuccessfully sought an increase in the quotas or the assignment of unfilled quotas to other countries. When admitting large numbers of displaced persons or political refugees, the Congress has often charged the number admitted against future quotas with the result that some countries have "mortgaged" their quotas to the year 2000 and beyond. By private acts, the Congress has exempted numerous people from quota restrictions.

Natural-Born Citizen.   A native of the United States. The term is used in Article II, section 1, which stipulates that "No person except a natural born citizen" may be President of the United States.

• *Significance:* The language of Article II is the only place in the Constitution where a distinction is drawn between a natural-born and a naturalized citizen. Whether or not a person born abroad of American parents, and, therefore, a citizen under the rule of *jus sanguinis,* is eligible for the presidency has never been resolved. Although the Constitution makes no other distinctions between natural-born and naturalized citizens, the former cannot be denaturalized or deported.

Naturalization.   The legal procedure by which an alien is admitted to citizenship. Congress is authorized by Article I, section 8 to establish uniform rules for naturalization. Naturalization may be individual or collective. Collective naturalization confers citizenship upon entire populations by statute or treaty as was done in the cases of Alaska, Hawaii, Texas, Puerto Rico, Guam, and the Virgin Islands. An individual over 18 years of age may be naturalized after meeting certain qualifications. These include (1) residence in the United States for five years, (2) ability to read, write, and speak English, (3) proof of good moral character, (4) knowledge of the history and attachment to the principles of American government, (5) nonadvocacy of Communist or other subversive doctrine nor membership (unless involuntary) in any subversive or totalitarian organization, and (6) taking of an oath of allegiance to the United States and renouncing allegiance to his former country. Detailed administration of naturalization is handled by the Immigration and Naturalization Service of the Department of Justice with final examination and administration of the oath by a judge of a federal court or a state court of record. The residence requirement is lowered for spouses of citizens and for aliens who serve in the armed forces. Minor children become citizens when their parents are naturalized.

• *Significance:* Millions of people have met the requirements established by the Congress and have become American citizens. Serious criticism has been directed against efforts to measure moral standards and political views, particularly during times of crises, since officials may abuse their discretion. Others, though not critical of the naturalization procedure itself, point out that a naturalized citizen is a "second-class" citizen since he may lose his citizenship under conditions which would not affect the citizenship status of the native born. On the whole, however, the procedure is designed to foster the "Americanization" of the alien and many become more knowledgeable and appreciative citizens than many of the native born. Through collective naturalization, the United States has demonstrated to the world its desire to give equal rights to all people under its control and, in some cases, prepare them for eventual statehood.

Nonimmigrant. One who comes to the United States on a temporary basis. This includes visitors, seasonal workers, tradesmen, crewmen, students, members of the press, and accredited representatives of foreign nations. No quota restrictions are applied but nonimmigrants must meet many of the qualifications imposed upon regular immigrants.

• *Significance:* For a time a good deal of controversy raged over the stringent red tape which visitors, many of whom were distinguished persons, had to face to enter the United States. This included many searching questions, delays in securing visas, and even fingerprinting. Some of these requirements have been relaxed but rather close inspection continues.

Nonquota Immigrant. An alien admitted to the United States who is not covered by the national origins quota system. Nonquota immigrants include people from Canada, Latin America and other parts of the western hemisphere, spouses and minor children of American citizens, clergymen, and aliens who reside in the United States but leave for a visit to their native lands. They must meet the standards established for quota immigrants.

• *Significance:* The policy of admitting nonquota immigrants is clearly designed to show friendliness to our neighbors of the western hemisphere, to avoid family hardships, and to encourage religion.

Passport. A certificate issued by an official government agency which identifies a person as a citizen of a country and authorizes him to travel abroad. Passports are granted to Americans by the Passport Office of the State Department, by territorial governors, and by diplomatic officials abroad.

• *Significance:* No American citizen may leave the country without a passport (except for trips to Canada, Mexico, and certain other nearby areas), and few countries will admit a traveler without a valid passport. A passport entitles a person to the privileges accorded travelers by international custom and various treaties. In 1958, the Supreme Court ruled that the Secretary of State could not deny a passport to a citizen because of his political beliefs or associations without explicit authorization from the Congress (*Kent v. Dulles,* 357 U.S. 116). The Internal Security Act of 1950 forbids issuance of passports to members of Communist organizations, and the Immigration and Nationality Act of 1952 vests some discretion in the Secretary of State, but the validity of these laws is yet to be tested. The State Department has refused to issue passports for travel to Communist China. Some limits on the right to travel may be valid if the person's trip is likely to prove detrimental to the foreign policy interests of the United States.

Visa.   A permit to enter a country. Persons seeking admission to the United States must get a visa from a United States consul located abroad. Most countries now require visas as well as passports. Visas are usually stamps of approval affixed to the passport by the official of the country to be visited or entered permanently.
• *Significance:* The visa procedure enables a country to screen applicants prior to their departure for that country. In the United States, before 1924, screening was done at ports of entry, causing great hardship to those rejected. Consular officers stationed abroad have unlimited discretion to grant or refuse visas, resulting in occasional charges of abuse of power.

IMPORTANT AGENCIES

Board of Immigration Appeals.   A board appointed by the Attorney General to hear appeals from decisions of the Immigration and Naturalization Service relative to the exclusion or deportation of aliens.
• *Significance:* Only on rare occasions will the courts hear appeals on immigration or deportation matters, since the Congress has broad authority in these areas. Hence, for most aliens, the Board is the "court of last resort" on matters of entry or deportation.

Bureau of Security and Consular Affairs.   A part of the State Department which supervises the issuance of passports and visas. The Bureau was established by the Immigration and Nationality Act of 1952 and, under its supervision, consular agents abroad determine whether foreigners will be permitted to enter the United States.
• *Significance:* Fear of Communist and other subversive elements has led to the extensive screening of applicants for visas to enter the United States. The decisions of consular officers are final.

Immigration and Naturalization Service.   A part of the Department of Justice which administers the laws regarding the admission, naturalization, and deportation of aliens. The Service investigates the credentials of immigrants at ports of entry. Immigration and Naturalization Service officers also patrol the Canadian and Mexican borders to prevent illegal entry of aliens. Aliens seeking to become citizens are investigated by agents of the Service who recommend to the courts whether or not the alien should be naturalized.

• *Significance:* Agents of the Immigration and Naturalization Service exercise considerable discretion in determining whether persons may enter the United States, become citizens, or be subject to deportation. Some critics have charged that the Service does not always follow fair procedures in reaching its decisions, particularly with regard to determining the character and political beliefs of aliens. Decisions of the Service may be appealed to the Board of Immigration Appeals in the Department of Justice.

IMPORTANT CASES

Fong Yue Ting v. United States, 149 U.S. 698 (1893): Supported the authority of the national government to deport aliens under its sovereign power in the field of international affairs. The Court upheld a federal law which authorized deportation of Chinese laborers who had failed to get certificates of residence. Furthermore, the Court held that deportation is not criminal punishment and, therefore, does not require a judicial trial.

• *Significance:* The major points of the case, that the Congress has full power to deport aliens and that such action is not considered to be punishment, remain basic to American law. While the Court has, in subsequent cases, demanded that basic elements of fairness or due process be observed in deportation proceedings, it has not insisted that a judicial trial is required.

Girouard v. United States, 328 U.S. 61 (1946): Established that an alien may be admitted to citizenship even if he refuses, on religious grounds, to swear that he will bear arms in defense of the United States. In this case, the Supreme Court reversed its earlier stand on this question and upheld Girouard's right to become a citizen since he was otherwise eligible and was willing to perform noncombatant duties.

• *Significance:* In the Immigration and Nationality Act of 1952, the Congress voiced its approval of the *Girouard* decision. The Act provides that conscientious objectors may be admitted to citizenship if they are willing to perform noncombatant service. It specifies that the exception applies only to persons who object to bear arms on religious and not on general philosophical grounds.

Perez v. Brownell, 356 U.S. 44 (1958): Upheld a law which provides that native-born citizens forfeit their citizenship by voting in a foreign election. The Court reasoned that this problem fell within the realm of foreign affairs and that voting abroad by American citizens could prove embarrassing to the conduct of foreign relations.

• *Significance:* The Court rarely, if ever, interferes with the conduct of foreign affairs and here extended this principle to expatriation. Under current law, two other acts by a citizen in relation to a foreign state may result in loss of citizenship—serving in its armed forces or assuming public office therein.

The Passenger Cases, 7 Howard 283 (1849): Declared that immigration is the exclusive concern of the national government and not subject to state control. The seaboard states had sought to regulate the heavy flow of immigrants to their shores by levying a tax on ships carrying immigrants.

• *Significance:* This decision helped to promote a uniform immigration policy prior to the great influx of immigrants in the late nineteenth and early twentieth centuries. However, it was not until 1882 that the national government assumed the full responsibility of regulating immigration.

Trop v. Dulles, 356 U. S. 86 (1958): Decided that the deprivation of citizenship for wartime desertion is a cruel and unusual punishment. The Supreme Court held that native-born citizenship is a basic right and cannot be taken away without voluntary expatriation. The Court noted that desertion does not always indicate disloyalty to one's country.

• *Significance:* This case raises citizenship to the level of a constitutional right and declared unconstitutional the law which provided that a citizen expatriates himself if he is convicted by court-martial for wartime desertion. Ordinarily, when a person expatriates himself, he becomes a citizen of another country, but this law would leave a person completely stateless.

Truax v. Raich, 239 U.S. 33 (1915): Declared unconstitutional an Arizona law requiring that at least 80 percent of the employees of any private business must be citizens, as a denial of equal protection of the law. The Court held that a state may not deny a person the right to earn a living, regardless of his race or nationality.

• *Significance:* This case and others which have followed it underscore the fact that an alien is entitled to most of the rights of a citizen since the Constitution speaks of "persons" rather than citizens with regard to most rights. While an alien may be denied access to specific jobs, such as government employment, he may not be deprived of any right to work in ordinary occupations.

United States v. Wong Kim Ark, 169 U.S. 649 (1898): Established that all persons born in the United States are citizens of the United States even if the parents are aliens ineligible for citizenship. The only major exceptions are children born to foreign diplomats stationed here. The Court held that a Chinese person born in California who went to China for a visit could not be denied readmission to the United States.

• *Significance:* This was a major interpretation of the meaning of the 14th Amendment which confers citizenship upon "all persons" born in the United States and subject to its jurisdiction. The Court made it clear that citizenship by birth, regardless of parentage, is the basic rule of American citizenship.

IMPORTANT STATUTES

Alien Registration Act of 1940.   An act requiring the annual registration of all aliens over the age of 14. Aliens are required to be fingerprinted, to inform the government of their address, occupation, and other data, and to carry registration cards at all times.

• *Significance:* The Alien Registration Act is part of a major sedition law, known as the Smith Act, which makes it criminal to teach, advocate, or join an organization advocating violent overthrow of government. The alien registration requirement is designed to make it easier for the government to know the whereabouts of aliens who might prove dangerous in time of war.

Cable Act.   A law passed in 1922 and amended in 1930, 1931, and 1934, which equalized the citizenship status of women with that of men. Prior to that, a woman's citizenship had been determined by that of her husband. Hence, an American woman who married a foreigner lost her citizenship while an alien woman who married an American citizen gained American citizenship.
• *Significance:* A woman's citizenship is no longer affected by the citizenship status of her husband. However, the law provides for a shorter residence requirement for naturalization of alien women who marry American citizens.

Immigration and Nationality Act of 1952 (McCarran-Walter Act).   A major revision and restatement of the immigration and citizenship policies of the United States. The Act, passed over the veto of President Truman, maintains the quota system for immigration and places restrictions upon the immigration and naturalization of Communists and other totalitarians. All racial barriers to immigration were eliminated by the Act, but Asians, Africans, and southern and eastern Europeans are assigned small quotas. Communists or other persons advocating violent overthrow of government are denied admission to the United States. Further, such persons residing in this country may not be naturalized, and citizenship may be taken from naturalized persons who join the Communist party or refuse to testify before a congressional committee investigating subversive activities.
• *Significance:* The Immigration and Nationality Act of 1952 is a comprehensive collection of the immigration and citizenship laws of the United States. Most opponents of the Act protest its retention of a discriminatory immigration policy and its continuation of the policy of making naturalized citizens subject to loss of citizenship on grounds not applicable to native-born citizens. Many political leaders have advocated changes in the law, but the Congress has not been sympathetic.

Civil Liberties

Arraignment.   A stage in criminal proceedings in which the accused is brought before the court to hear the formal charges against him as prepared by a grand jury or prosecutor. The accused is then asked to plead guilty or not guilty. The Supreme Court has ruled that there must be no unnecessary delay between arrest and arraignment. A confession or other evidence obtained as a result of such delay will be barred as evidence (*Mallory v. United States,* 354 U.S. 449 [1957]).

• *Significance:* A major factor in fair criminal procedure is that the accused be informed of the charges against him so that he can prepare his defense. Speedy arraignment acts as an additional safeguard against arbitrary arrest, prolonged detention, and unsavory police tactics.

Arrest Warrant.   An order issued in writing by a court or magistrate authorizing the detainment of a person. The Fourth Amendment specifies that such warrants are to be issued only upon "probable cause" supported by oath, describing the person to be seized. All state constitutions have similar provisions.

• *Significance:* This guarantee has the effect of protecting persons against overzealous officers. Arrests may be made without a warrant if the law officers have "probable cause" for making the arrest. For example, an officer who witnesses a crime need not secure a warrant. Whether an arrest has been properly made is a matter for judicial determination. An arbitrary arrest may void any subsequent conviction.

Attorney General's List.   A list of organizations, deemed to be subversive, compiled by the Attorney General of the United States. The Attorney General's list was drawn up as part of the loyalty program established by President Truman in 1947. Membership in any listed organization has been taken into account in determining the loyalty of government employees. In *Joint Anti-Fascist Refugee Committee v. McGrath,* 341 U.S. 123 (1951), the Supreme Court declared that an organization could not be listed without being given notice and an opportunity to be heard.

• *Significance:* The Attorney General's list of subversive organizations does not carry any legal weight. The legal determination of what constitutes a subversive organization is now in the hands of the Subversive Activities Control Board, established under the Internal Security Act of 1950. However, the Attorney General's list may be used informally in determining the loyalty of particular persons. Some critics of the list point out that it does not distinguish between organizations in terms of the time of their inception or the degree of their subversive connections, and that its very existence imputes guilt by association to the members of these groups. Some state and local governments have accepted the list at face value in determining the loyalty of employees. The list does put innocent individuals on notice of the possible subversive character of their organizations.

Bad Tendency Rule.　　A test used by the Supreme Court to determine the permissible bounds of free speech. The bad tendency rule holds that speech or other First Amendment freedoms may be curtailed if they may lead to some evil. It is to be distinguished from the "clear and present danger" doctrine which holds that one's liberty may not be curtailed unless it presents some imminent danger of illegal action.
• *Significance:* The bad tendency test, like the clear and present danger test, proceeds from the search for some formula to solve the problem of balancing individual freedom against the rights of society. Both tests have been used by the Supreme Court over the years, with results determined by the nature of the times and the ideas of the justices. In recent years, in cases involving communism and loyalty, the Court has used the bad tendency rule frequently.

Bail.　　Funds provided as assurance that a person will appear in court at the proper time. Bail is permitted after arrest and before trial, as well as after conviction pending appeal or sentencing. Bail is usually denied in capital cases. The Eighth Amendment forbids excessive bail; wide discretion is left the courts to determine the amount in relation to the severity of the offense, the record and resources of the defendant, and the likelihood of his reappearing in court.
• *Significance:* This is part of the theory that one is innocent until proved guilty and should not have punishment inflicted by unnecessary internment until guilt is established.

Bill of Attainder.　　A legislative act which declares the guilt of an individual and metes out punishment without a judicial trial. The state legislatures and the Congress are forbidden to pass such acts by Article I, sections 9 and 10.
• *Significance:* A legislative body may not exercise the judicial function of ascertaining guilt and pronouncing sentence. Rather, the legislature is limited to passing general laws, specific applications being left to the courts. This is an important ingredient of the separation of powers and of freedom itself.

Bill of Rights.　　A popular term used to describe the first ten amendments to the United States Constitution. Bills of rights, sometimes called declarations of rights, are found in all state constitutions as well. They contain a listing of the rights which a person enjoys against infringement by government. Many important rights are stated in other parts of the United States Constitution, such as trial by jury and the guarantee of habeas corpus. All bills of rights contain provisions designed to protect the freedom of expression, the rights of property, and the rights of persons accused of crime.

• *Significance:* Bills of rights are restrictions on government rather than on individuals or private groups. History teaches that unchecked governmental powers lead to the decay of freedom. A bill of rights provides the legal mechanism through which the individual can challenge the oppressive acts of government officials in courts of law. It contains the essential elements of government by the people. Without guarantees for individual freedom, democracy would become meaningless and unworkable. The federal Bill of Rights was added to the Constitution as a condition for its ratification, upon the insistence of people who feared a strong central government. Some state bills of rights antedate the federal Bill of Rights.

Censorship.   The curbing of ideas either in speech or writing *before* they are expressed rather than punishment for illegal expression. The latter would include libel and slander, obscenity, incitement to crime, contempt of court, or seditious utterance. Except in time of war or other national emergency, any prior restraint upon freedom of speech or press is forbidden.

• *Significance:* The right of freedom of speech or press would be meaningless if prior censorship could be exercised. While a person must bear the consequences of any illegal expression, no government official may determine in advance what may be said or written. The Supreme Court has made an exception in the case of motion pictures, holding that a city may require submission of films to a censor (*Times Film Corporation v. Chicago,* 365 U.S. 43 [1961]).

Civil Liberties.   Those liberties usually spelled out in a bill of rights or a constitution which guarantee the protection of persons, opinions, and property from the arbitrary interference of governmental officials. Restraints may be placed upon the exercise of these liberties only when they are abused by individuals or groups and when the public welfare requires it.

• *Significance:* Civil liberties lie at the base of a free society as contrasted with the absence of such guarantees in a totalitarian society. They are a restraint upon the government rather than upon individuals. Civil liberties may be distinguished from "civil rights" in that the latter is generally understood to refer to positive policies of government to protect individuals from arbitrary treatment both by government and by other individuals. However, the terms are often used interchangeably.

Civil Rights.   Positive acts of government designed to protect persons against arbitrary or discriminatory treatment by government or individuals. Civil rights are sometimes written into constitutions but frequently take the form of statutes. Though the term is often used interchangeably with "civil liberties," the latter generally refers to negative restraints upon government as found in bills of rights. It is also to be distinguished from political rights which generally refer to the rights to participate in the management of government through such practices as voting. Civil rights have taken on special importance since the

Civil War as the Congress and state and local legislatures have endeavored to secure equal treatment for Negroes.

• *Significance:* The decades of the 1940's and 1950's witnessed extensive attempts by government at all levels to secure civil rights for Negroes and other minorities in such areas as employment, housing, and public facilities. Traditional constitutional civil liberty provisions have not proved workable to meet the challenge of discrimination against minority groups. The precise role and extent of governmental action to secure civil rights remains a controversial question in the 1960's. Examples of recent civil rights legislation include the Civil Rights Acts of 1957 and 1960 and the fair employment practice laws enacted in many states.

Clear and Present Danger Rule.   A test adopted by the Supreme Court to measure the permissible bounds of free speech. The test was formulated by Justice Oliver Wendell Holmes in *Schenck v. United States,* 249 U.S. 47 (1919): "The question in every case is whether the words are used in circumstances and are of such a nature as to create a clear and present danger that they will bring about substantive evils that Congress has a right to prevent. It is a question of proximity and degree." The application of this test has varied a good deal since 1919. Some judges have preferred to determine whether certain speech has a "bad tendency" while others have raised the right of free speech to a "preferred position" among constitutional rights.

• *Significance:* Freedom of speech is not absolute, particularly when its exercise has a close relationship to some unlawful act, such as the violent overthrow of the government. Yet, a legal distinction exists between mere speech or the advocacy of a doctrine and the performance of an act, although not always easy to determine. As Justice Holmes put it, one could not falsely shout "Fire!" in a crowded theatre and claim one's right to do so as an element of free speech. The clear and present danger rule is one attempt to establish a criterion for the protection of the individual's right to speak in the light of society's right to protection.

Confession.   An admission of guilt by one accused of a crime.
• *Significance:* A confession must be voluntary and not induced by force, "third degree" methods, prolonged interrogation, threats, psychological coercion, or promise of leniency. A confession exacted by any illegal means is not admissible in a trial and may result in the release of the accused. A confession must be corroborated with evidence that a crime has actually been committed. This prevents the conviction of deranged persons who confess to crimes they have not committed. The courts have been quite strict in demanding proof that a confession was voluntarily made.

Conscientious Objector.   A person who refuses to render military service because of religious scruples or other grounds of conscience. While the right to religious freedom does not extend to refusal to serve in the military service, the Congress has, as an act of grace, authorized noncombatant service or, for those opposed to any form of military duty, service in public conservation projects.

• *Significance:* A person does not have the right to refuse military duty. A high regard for the beliefs of those who cannot participate in a war effort has led the Congress to this policy of leniency. In effect, such people are given preferred treatment when excused from actual combat, rather than penalized by being required to do other service. Whether or not a person is a true conscientious objector and not a "draft dodger" is a question to be determined by draft boards and, at times, the courts.

Conspiracy.   Any agreement between two or more persons to commit an unlawful act. Conspiracy is a crime under numerous criminal statutes; in the realm of business and labor activities the law forbids conspiracies in restraint of trade. The most prominent conspiracy provision in the field of civil liberties is that found in the Smith Act of 1940 which makes it a crime to conspire to teach, advocate, or organize groups which advocate the overthrow of government by force.
• *Significance:* Conspiracy laws are designed to apprehend persons in the planning stage of a criminal act. In the area of speech, press, and association, conspiracy laws pose the danger that persons may be punished for foolish conjecture rather than actual plans to do evil.

Counsel.   Under the Sixth Amendment, an accused is entitled to the assistance of counsel (an attorney) in a federal criminal case. In the states, the assignment of counsel to those unable to afford their own varies from state to state and with the nature of the offense. The Supreme Court has ruled that a state must provide counsel in capital cases where death or life imprisonment may result or where the defendant is clearly unable to defend himself because of youth or mental infirmity. An accused may waive his right to counsel, but the waiver must be an intelligent one in which the defendant recognizes the consequences of his action.
• *Significance:* Right to counsel is based on the fact that the average person is unable to understand the intricacies of the law or to know the full extent of his rights. The problem arises largely in connection with indigent defendants who cannot afford an attorney. Since counsel is always furnished in federal trials, many observers argue that the same treatment should be expected in state trials. However, the Supreme Court is reluctant to impose this requirement upon the states unless gross injustice is likely to result from the lack of competent legal assistance.

Cruel and Unusual Punishment.   Such punishment is forbidden by the Eighth Amendment. The scope of the ban is determined by the courts both in terms of the method of punishment and the severity of a sentence. Generally, any lingering torture, mutilation, or degrading treatment is condemned as well as any sentence which is too severe for the offense committed.
• *Significance:* The idea of humane treatment for criminals is a relatively modern concept. The dignity of the individual is to be preserved even for the undesirable elements of the community. Whether a particular punishment is cruel depends upon community standards as determined by the courts.

Double Jeopardy.   The Fifth Amendment guarantees that one may not be twice put in jeopardy of life or limb for the same offense. One who has been tried for a crime may not be tried again for the same offense. However, the guarantee does not apply to trials by both the national government and a state, or by two different states for offenses growing out of a single criminal act. Trial following a mistrial is not double jeopardy unless the prosecution deliberately forces a mistrial in order to get better evidence or a more favorable jury.

• *Significance:* Although considerable confusion exists as to what constitutes double jeopardy in specific instances, this guarantee does afford protection against continual harassment of accused persons. Also, the courts and the accused are spared endless costs and time-consuming litigation.

Due Process of Law.   Protection against arbitrary deprivation of life, liberty, or property. The Fifth and Fourteenth Amendments forbid the national and state governments, respectively, to deny any person his life, liberty, or property without due process of law. While no precise definition of this term has ever been made, it establishes the principle of limited government. Two types of due process have emerged in the course of litigation—procedural and substantive. Though used sparingly in recent years, substantive due process has been used by the judiciary to strike down legislative and executive acts which are arbitrary or lacking in reasonableness or which cover subject matter beyond the reach of government. Procedural due process was defined by Daniel Webster as procedure "which hears before it condemns, which proceeds upon inquiry, and renders judgment only after trial." The Supreme Court, in a long series of cases, has marked out the general meaning of the phrase so as to forbid any procedure which is shocking to the conscience or which makes impossible a fair and enlightened system of justice for a civilized people.

• *Significance:* Protection against arbitrary treatment lies at the base of the American system of government. Due process functions both as a limitation on public officials and as a power in the hands of the judiciary which has wide latitude in applying it. Judges can determine whether a law bears a reasonable relationship to a proper governmental function and whether the procedure used, particularly in criminal cases, is fair and reasonable.

Eminent Domain.   The power inherent in all governments to take private property provided that it is taken for a public purpose and that just compensation is awarded. Disputes as to purpose or price are generally settled in courts.

• *Significance:* The right to own and use private property is high in the American scheme of values. The right of the public to take that property is recognized provided just compensation is made. Without this power, slum clearance or highway projects, for example, would be impossible.

Equal Protection of the Law.   A requirement of the 14th Amendment that state laws may not arbitrarily discriminate against persons. Identical treatment is not required. Classification of persons is permitted provided that the classification is reasonable and bears some relationship to the end sought. Hence, taxation in accordance with ability to pay has been held to be a reasonable classification, whereas classification according to color or religion has been held to bear no reasonable relationship to the functions of government. Current interest in the application of equal protection centers on the segregation of races in public facilities. Though the Constitution does not contain a similar restriction on the national government, the courts have read this into the meaning of the due process clause of the Fifth Amendment.

• *Significance:* Equal protection of the law emanates from the democratic concepts of the equality of men under the law and their right to equality of opportunity. Arbitrary or irrelevant barriers to full enjoyment of rights are forbidden. Although the prohibition does not extend to private discrimination, both the national and many state governments have acted to forbid private discrimination against persons based on color, creed, or national origin.

Ex Post Facto Law.   A criminal law which is retroactive and has an adverse effect upon one accused of a crime. Thus, an ex post facto law is one which makes an act a crime which was not a crime when committed, which increases the penalty for a crime after its commission, or which changes the rules of evidence so as to make conviction easier. Neither the state nor the national governments may enact such laws under provisions of Article I, sections 9 and 10. The prohibition does not extend to civil laws or to laws favorable to an accused person.

• *Significance:* A basic principle of American law is that each individual is free to do those things not specifically forbidden without fear of future punishment. This is pertinent to the concept that ours is a government of laws and not of men.

Fair Employment Practices Laws.   Some 22 states have laws which forbid private and/or public employers, labor unions, or employment agencies to discriminate against persons in hiring or in other personnel policies, on the grounds of race, color, creed, or national origin. The Congress has never enacted such legislation although a nondiscriminatory policy exists in federal employment by executive order.

• *Significance:* Such laws represent recent tendencies toward positive governmental action in the field of private rights as contrasted with the traditional concept of civil liberties as a restraint against government. Whether the governments of the states and nation should use their power to secure private rights against discrimination remains a controversial question.

Fifth Amendment.   A part of the Bill of Rights which imposes a number of restrictions on the national government in respect to the rights of persons accused of crime. It provides for indictment by grand jury and protection against double jeopardy and self-incrimination, and it forbids denial of life, liberty, or property without due process of law. In addition, the Fifth Amendment prohibits the taking of property without just compensation. *See* GRAND JURY, page 64; DOUBLE JEOPARDY, page 60; SELF-INCRIMINATION, page 73; DUE PROCESS, page 61; EMINENT DOMAIN, page 61.

• *Significance:* Together with the Fourth, Sixth, and Eighth Amendments, as well as provisions in the Constitution relative to habeas corpus, ex post facto laws, and bills of attainder, the Fifth Amendment serves as a significant source of liberty. The Amendment has come into contemporary prominence because of the self-incrimination clause. Persons refusing to testify before congressional committees have frequently "taken the Fifth," a shorthand phrase for claiming the privilege against self-incrimination.

Fourteenth Amendment.   A post–Civil War Amendment (1868) which defines citizenship, restricts the powers of the states in their relations with their inhabitants, requires reduction of a state's representation in the Congress for denials of suffrage, disqualifies former officeholders who participated in the rebellion, and invalidates any war debts of rebellious states. The most important provisions are those which forbid a state to abridge the privileges and immunities of citizens, to deprive any person of life, liberty, or property without due process of law, or deny to any person the equal protection of the law. The provision on reduction of representation in the Congress is a potential source of power but the Congress has never exercised it.
• *Significance:* The due process clause and the equal protection clause have held the center of the constitutional stage for many years. Both have made possible federal intervention against alleged state encroachment on the rights of the people. For a time, the due process clause was used mainly to limit the states in the exercise of their taxing and police powers in business regulation. Since 1925, the due process clause has been interpreted by the courts to forbid state denials of First Amendment freedoms as well as of essential procedural rights. The equal protection clause has been invoked to restrain racial segregation practices by state governments.

Freedom of Assembly.   The right of the people to congregate for the discussion of public questions and to organize into political parties or pressure groups for the purpose of influencing public policy. The right of assembly does not authorize meetings designed to accomplish an illegal purpose or which lead to a breach of the peace or resistance to lawful authority. This right is guaranteed by the First Amendment and by state constitutions. In addition, the Supreme Court has ruled that the due process clause of the 14th Amendment protects the individual's freedom of assembly against infringement by state governments.
• *Significance:* In a democratic society, the people must have the right to meet freely in peaceable assemblage to consider public questions. This right is closely related to those of freedom of speech and of petition. All act as a restraint upon the legislature and other public officials.

Freedom of Association.   The right to organize into organizations or groups for political, religious, or other social purposes. The Constitution makes no mention of freedom of association, but it is implicit in guarantees of freedom of speech, assembly, and religion.
• *Significance:* The American people are noted for being organization-minded; most Americans belong to several organizations. In recent years, the right to associate has received much attention, particularly with regard to Communist or other subversive organizations, since numerous laws have been passed to curtail their activities. Such laws have been attacked in some quarters as imputing guilt by association since members of a group may not necessarily subscribe to all the beliefs or actions of a group. However, persons do not have

a right to organize to accomplish illegal aims. Another recent problem in connection with freedom of association has arisen out of attempts by some southern states to impede the activities of the National Association for the Advancement of Colored People. However, the courts have frowned upon any limitations placed upon lawful groups. On the whole, the right to associate is recognized as essential in a democratic society since, generally, an individual can accomplish more with a group than by acting alone.

Freedom of Religion.   Freedom of worship and religious practice, and the separation of church and state. The national government through the First Amendment, and the states through their constitutions and the 14th Amendment, may not abridge this right of worship, nor support nor discriminate against any religious group or church. Any religious practice which is contrary to public peace or morality may be outlawed, such as snake-handling or polygamy. No public funds may be expended on behalf of any church nor may the government favor one church over another. Public schools may not be used for sectarian religious observances although released time programs for religious study off school property are permitted. Public bus transportation for parochial schools is permissible, but other forms of aid to parochial schools and other religious practices in the public schools remain controversial questions and have not yet been resolved by the courts.

• *Significance:* In a nation with such diversity of religious groups, the free exercise of religion and the separation of church and state are essential. This was foremost in the minds of the Founding Fathers who provided that there be no religious test for public office. Religious freedom is the first item in the Bill of Rights, reflecting the need for freedom of conscience in a free society. Any interference of state with church or church with state constitutes a danger to both.

Freedom of Speech and Press.   The right to speak and publish without prior restraint, subject to penalties for abuse of the right. Abuses include libel and slander, obscenity, incitement to crime, contempt of court, or sedition. By virtue of the First and Fourteenth Amendments and state bills of rights, neither the national government nor the states may abridge freedom of speech and press.

• *Significance:* Freedom is hardly possible without the right to disseminate ideas. Generally, the courts have treated the guarantee liberally. In recent years, problems have arisen with regard to the advocacy of Communist doctrine. The courts have distinguished between the mere advocacy of abstract doctrine and conspiratorial advocacy. In placing limitations on freedom of speech or press, the courts have attempted to apply such concepts as "clear and present danger" to determine whether a given situation justified restriction.

Grand Jury.   A body of from 12 to 23 members who hear evidence presented by the prosecuting attorney against persons accused of a serious crime. The Fifth Amendment requires that this be done for any capital or infamous crime, generally those for which death or imprisonment may result. The grand jury, meeting secretly, votes whether or not to present a "true bill" which "indicts" the accused. If indicted, the accused will be bound over for trial; if not, he goes free. The grand jury may also conduct investigations on its own when a prosecutor is lax or when official misconduct is suspected. In such cases, any resulting accusation is called a "presentment." The grand jury exercises vast powers under the common law, being empowered to subpoena witnesses and records and to compel testimony under oath. More than half of the states have abolished or limited grand jury indictments to capital cases, replacing it with the "information" which permits the prosecutor alone to bring charges.

• *Significance:* It is charged that the grand jury is too time-consuming and expensive and that it tends to follow the dictates of the prosecutor. It has been abolished in England, the place of its origin, as well as in many states. However, the grand jury does serve as a protection against overzealous prosecutors and serves as a watchdog against official wrongdoing. It had its origins in the idea that before an individual could be subjected to the costs and humiliation of a public trial, sufficient evidence to justify such action must be shown and be acceptable to a majority of the grand jury.

Guilt by Association.   Attribution of criminal or other wrongful acts to a person because of the people or groups with whom he associates. The term has come into prominence as a result of the loyalty investigations of recent years.

• *Significance:* Guilt by association is viewed as a denial of the concept underlying American justice that guilt is personal and that one should not suffer any disabilities because of conduct or ideas attributed to one's associates. The issue has been raised in connection with those who have lost their jobs or suffered other penalties as a result of membership in the Communist party or alleged subversive groups. It is argued that mere membership or association does not prove agreement with all the tenets of the group. Nevertheless, the Supreme Court has sustained the power of national, state, and local governments to impose disabilities upon members of particular groups or exponents of certain ideas. The Court has noted that people are often judged by the company they keep and this factor may properly be considered in determining loyalty (*Adler v. Board of Education,* 342 U.S. 485 [1952]). Guilt by association should not be confused with conviction for conspiracy to commit a crime which involves actual and deliberate participation in the planning of the wrongful act.

Habeas Corpus.   An order directing an official who has a person in custody to bring the prisoner to court and to show cause for his detention. Congress is authorized to suspend the writ in cases of rebellion or invasion (Art. I, sec. 9). Though President Lincoln suspended the writ on his own volition, the Congress subsequently affirmed his action. A number of states absolutely forbid its suspension.

• *Significance:* This is generally considered to be the most important guarantee of liberty in that it prevents arbitrary arrest and imprisonment—the fearful knock at the door and disappearance of the seized person. A prisoner must be released unless sufficient cause to detain him can be shown.

Immunity.   A privilege granted to a person which exempts him from prosecution for any self-incriminating testimony given by him before a court, grand jury, or investigating committee. No evidence revealed by a witness who has been granted immunity may be used against him in a criminal prosecution, or in order to subject him to any penalty. Many states and the national government make provisions for the granting of immunity to witnesses under specified circumstances. One who has been granted immunity may not refuse to testify under penalty of contempt.

• *Significance:* A grant of immunity is designed to compel testimony from persons who refuse to answer questions on the ground that their answers would tend to incriminate them and subject them to prosecution. Immunity will not be granted unless the information likely to be secured is of great public importance. Care must be taken not to make immunity a loophole for notorious criminals to escape punishment.

Indictment.   The formal accusation, drawn up by the prosecutor and brought by a grand jury, charging a person with the commission of a crime.

• *Significance:* One of the essential elements of due process is that the accused be informed of the precise charges against him so that he can prepare his defense. A faulty or vague indictment justifies dismissal of the case.

Information.   An accusation made under oath by a prosecuting attorney before a court, charging a person with a crime. Though regularly used for minor offenses, more than half the states have substituted the information for indictment by grand jury in serious cases as well.

• *Significance:* The trend has definitely been in the direction of increased use of the information instead of the grand jury. Thus, the prosecuting attorney bypasses the grand jury and final determination of whether the evidence justifies a trial is placed in the hands of the judge. Increasing use of the information instead of the grand jury results from considerations of both efficiency and economy.

Involuntary Servitude.   The 13th Amendment provides that neither slavery nor involuntary servitude, except in punishment for crime, may exist anywhere in the United States. Forcing a person to work in order to fulfill a contract or to work out a debt constitutes peonage or involuntary servitude. Certain types of employment are not covered by the prohibition when it might jeopardize the public safety. These include police, fire, seamen, and train crews.

• *Significance:* Though aimed primarily at putting an end to slavery, the 13th Amendment serves as a guarantee of free and voluntary labor which may be threatened by situations less drastic than outright slavery. Congress has supplemented this Amendment by passage of the Antipeonage Act of 1867.

Jim Crow Law.   A term applied to laws requiring the segregation of white and colored races in the use of public facilities.

• *Significance:* Although many Jim Crow laws are still on the statute books of many southern states, the Supreme Court has invalidated them in such areas as education, public recreational facilities, and interstate transportation. No blanket rule outlawing any form of Jim Crow law has yet come from the Court.

Custom prevails in many states, both north and south, which has the effect of preserving Jim Crow.

Jury. An impartial body which sits in judgment on charges brought in either criminal or civil cases. A trial jury is known as a petit jury to distinguish it from a grand jury. In federal courts, the trial jury must consist of 12 persons and their decision must be unanimous. Many states authorize trial by less than 12 in certain cases and a decision by less than a unanimous vote. Jury trials may be waived by the accused. Generally, the jury is the judge of the facts, though some states permit the jury to determine the law as well as the facts. The jury must be impartial and no specific class of persons may be deliberately and systematically excluded from jury service. Trial by jury is required by Article III, section 2, and by the Sixth and Seventh Amendments of the United States Constitution.
• *Significance:* The right to be judged by a jury of one's peers is a long-standing tradition of the common law. The competence of the average jury and the motivations which may lead it to a particular verdict are frequently questioned. Yet, the jury system brings the common sense of the community to bear upon the laws of the state or nation. It permits the citizen to participate in the administration of justice and gives the people more confidence in the application of the law.

Libel and Slander. Libel is a written, and slander an oral, defamation of character. They include statements which expose a person to hatred, contempt, or ridicule, or injure his reputation by imputing to him a criminal act, or harm him in his trade or profession. Libel is generally considered more serious than slander because the written word is more durable than a passing remark. But the reputation of those involved, the nature of the audience, and the conditions under which the words were written or spoken may prove pertinent in a suit for damages. Truth of a statement is generally an absolute defense.
• *Significance:* Libel and slander are limitations on the freedom of speech and press, and many state constitutions expressly make this distinction. Libel and slander rarely apply to "fair and reasonable" comment made about public officials or newsworthy people, since such comments are considered to be in the public interest. Major recent problems concern (1) the harm done to private reputations by legislative or executive officials who enjoy immunity from suit for remarks made in the line of duty; (2) whether remarks made on radio and television are libel or slander (e.g., do oral remarks made on these mediums have the impact of the printed word?); and (3) the legality of "group libel" laws which make it illegal to impugn the reputation of an entire minority group.

Loyalty Oath. An oath which requires one to disavow or abjure certain beliefs and associations. Such oaths were exacted during the Revolutionary War, the Civil War, and during the "red scare" of the 1920's. Recent loyalty oaths, inspired by the Cold War, generally require one to swear that one does not advocate the violent overthrow of government, nor belong to any organization so advocating. Both the national and state governments require loyalty oaths of public employees, teachers, attorneys, defense workers, recipients of government benefits, and, in one state, boxers and wrestlers. The courts have generally upheld impositions of loyalty oaths unless the oath did not excuse those whose associations were innocent of wrongful intent, or if the oath was required of persons totally unrelated to any governmental purpose.

• *Significance:* Few people object to taking an ordinary oath of allegiance wherein one declares one's loyalty to the United States and swears to uphold the Constitution. However, loyalty or "test" oaths have met numerous objections based largely on the reversal of the presumption of innocence, since one may be considered disloyal unless one swears that one is not. It is also charged that such oaths abridge freedom of speech and assembly by the discretion vested in the imposer of the oath to determine suitable beliefs and associations. Moreover, many doubt the utility of oaths as a weapon against Communists since a real Communist would probably swear falsely to the oath. Its major utility lies in bringing the oath taker to a serious consideration of his activities and in the possibility of charging real Communists with perjury.

Loyalty-Security Programs.   Programs carried on by national and state governments to rid the public service of disloyal persons or persons suspected of being security risks. The national government loyalty program had its inception in 1947 when President Truman ordered that government employees be removed if grounds existed to doubt their loyalty. President Eisenhower extended the program to include all "security risks" including disloyal as well as generally untrustworthy people. The programs have also been applied to the armed forces, defense plants, maritime workers, and other government-connected facilities. Both the Truman and Eisenhower programs provided for appeal procedures for discharged persons but did not permit confrontation of secret informers. The courts, in a series of cases, have held that the loyalty programs apply only to sensitive security posts and that, under certain circumstances, a person has a right to face his accusers. However, one has no right to a government job and the programs have resulted in numerous dismissals. In the states, similar programs have been undertaken, although most states have limited their loyalty requirements to the taking of a loyalty oath.

• *Significance:* Few people insist that disloyal persons should work for the government. However, many people have protested the procedures used in the loyalty-security programs, preferring normal police work to uncover dangerous persons. The use of unidentified informers raised much criticism. Many persons are concerned with the effects on the morale of government employees who are subject to investigation of all their activities and beliefs. Loyalty-security programs will undoubtedly be part of the American scene as long as the international situation continues to be dangerous.

Magna Carta.   The Great Charter of freedom granted by King John of England upon demand of the barons in 1215.

• *Significance:* The source for many of the basic freedoms found in American law are traceable to the Great Charter. Among these are trial by a jury of one's peers and the guarantee that no person shall lose his life, liberty, or property except by due process of law.

National Association for the Advancement of Colored People (NAACP). A major national interest group which seeks to improve and promote the economic and political status of the Negro.
• *Significance:* The NAACP has been one of the most vigorous and successful pressure groups in the United States. It has been particularly successful in bringing and winning lawsuits designed to secure equal protection of the law for Negroes. The NAACP is a major example of a group which has used the resources of the courts to achieve what could not be achieved through legislative lobbying. Attempts by some southern states to curtail NAACP activities have been declared unconstitutional by the Supreme Court (*NAACP v. Alabama,* 357 U.S. 449 [1958]).

Natural Rights. An underlying assumption of the American political creed which holds that men are endowed by their Creator with certain rights that may not be abridged by government.
• *Significance:* The Judaeo-Christian doctrine, as embodied in the American creed, assumes the inviolability of man's basic rights. The history of civilization is largely a struggle between the natural rights philosophy and the forces of totalitarianism which assume that man has only such rights as the government decides to give him. The doctrine of natural rights assumes that man had his rights in a "state of nature" and creates government to protect those rights.

Ninth Amendment. A part of the Bill of Rights which reads, "The enumeration in the Constitution, of certain rights, shall not be construed to deny or disparage others retained by the people." This provision was a catchall, in the tradition of the natural rights philosophy, supported by those who feared that a listing of rights in the Bill of Rights might be interpreted to mean that no other rights were held by the people.
• *Significance:* The "other" rights which the people retain have never been defined. The Amendment has not been prominently used in litigation and no law has been declared unconstitutional because of conflict with the Ninth Amendment. In the case of *Mitchell v. United States,* 313 U.S. 80 (1941), the Supreme Court noted that the Amendment protected the right to political activity by the people.

Petition. A request to a public official seeking to correct a wrong or to influence public policy. The First Amendment guarantees to the people the right to "petition the government for a redress of grievances." This provision, like all provisions of the First Amendment, is applicable to the states through the 14th Amendment, although most state constitutions contain a similar provision. The right of petition, closely related to freedom of speech, press, and assembly, is generally exercised through letter writing to public officials and through pressure group activity.
• *Significance:* It is vital in a free society that persons be able to call the attention of their representatives to their grievances. In this way, government can remain continually responsive to the people and can be made aware of their opinions at times other than at elections.

Police Power. The power inherent in state governments to protect the health, safety, and welfare of the people. In the area of civil rights and liberties, a lawful exercise of the police power may justify abridgment of personal or property rights. For example, through use of the police power, a state may destroy property which endangers public health or may limit freedom of speech or assembly when the public safety is jeopardized. *See* POLICE POWER, page 36.

• *Significance:* The police power rests on the assumption that rights are not absolute. The extent of the power is generally determined by the courts when faced with concrete situations in which the police power comes into conflict with personal liberties. In a typical civil liberty–police power case, the courts must strike a balance between the needs of society and the rights of the individual.

Political Right.   The right to participate in the management of government and to influence public policy. Typical political rights include the right to vote, to form a political party, and to participate in pressure group activity.

• *Significance:* Political rights are essential for the operations of a free government. Each citizen must be given opportunity not only to speak out on public issues but to take positive action to influence or control the government. So long as these rights remain inviolate, regardless of the party in power, dictatorship cannot take hold. Any group denied these rights is left with the sole recourse of violent revolution to accomplish its goals. In recent years, emphasis has been placed on securing political rights for Negroes and other minority groups who may be denied access to the polls. Limitations, however, have been placed upon the political activities of Communists who seek to eliminate such rights.

Privilege.   An advantage or opportunity granted to an individual or group to which they have no right. The courts have held, for example, that government employment is a privilege and not a right. Nor does one have a right to a professional license or to public housing. The government may establish reasonable qualifications or demands before it grants a privilege, such as a loyalty oath or other demonstration of fitness or reliability.

• *Significance:* One may lose a privilege under procedures and circumstances which would not be permissible if a right were abridged. Hence, a person could be discharged from public service on suspicion of disloyalty without a trial, but he could not be punished for disloyalty by fine or imprisonment without the constitutional safeguards accorded accused persons. This distinction has drawn some criticism because an individual may suffer a great deal when discharged for disloyalty.

Procedural Rights.   The manner in which rights are protected. Under American constitutional law, no person may be deprived of his life, liberty, or property or any other right guaranteed him except under well-defined procedures, including a fair hearing before a judicial tribunal. American procedural rights are generally considered to be those listed in the Bill of Rights, particularly in the Fourth through the Eighth Amendments. *Procedural* rights are to be distinguished from *substantive* rights. The latter include those elements which are considered to be of the very essence of freedom, such as freedom of speech, whereas the former are concerned with the methods by which rights are protected.

• *Significance:* A crucial difference between a free society and a totalitarian society lies in the procedures afforded citizens to protect them against arbitrary treatment. Under American law, one may not be tried and condemned except in conformity with due process of law, and any errors in procedure may render a conviction void.

Quartering of Soldiers.   The Third Amendment prohibits the government from housing soldiers in private homes during time of peace without consent of the owner. In wartime, it may be done under conditions prescribed by law.

• *Significance:* The Third Amendment resulted from the practice of the British, during the colonial era, of housing soldiers in private homes. This has never been done in the United States, and no cases have arisen concerning this provision. It stands as a symbol of civilian control over the military.

Religious Test.   A requirement that one profess belief in a particular religious faith or in a Supreme Being as a condition to holding public office. Article VI prohibits such tests. Several state constitutions contain a requirement that public officials profess a belief in God, but in 1961 the Supreme Court held such a Maryland provision unconstitutional (*Torcaso v. Watkins,* 367 U.S. 488).

• *Significance:* The prohibition against religious tests for office is a necessary component of the separation of church and state. Until the election of John F. Kennedy, a Catholic, to the presidency in 1960, there appeared to be an "unofficial" religious test for the office of President, since it was widely believed that a Catholic could not be elected. Kennedy's victory and the Supreme Court decision in the Maryland case have contributed to the effectiveness of the religious test prohibition.

Restrictive Covenant.   An agreement entered into by property owners in which they agree not to sell their property to Negroes or other minority groups.

• *Significance:* Individuals do not violate any constitutional provisions by entering into restrictive covenant agreements. However, the Supreme Court held (*Shelley v. Kramer,* 334 U.S. 1 [1948]) that such agreements cannot be enforced in the courts since such action would constitute government support of discrimination contrary to the equal protection clause of the 14th Amendment.

Right to Bear Arms.   The Second Amendment guarantees the right to bear arms, recognizing that "A well regulated militia [is] necessary to the security of a free state." Similar provisions are found in many state constitutions. However, the possession of weapons is extensively regulated. Possession of certain types of weapons is prohibited, such as machine guns or sawed-off shot guns, and registration of certain types of other weapons is required.

• *Significance:* In practice, this Amendment has been of little importance. It is, however, an implicit recognition of the right of revolution, stemming from the idea that a tyrant could not be overthrown if the people were denied the means. In addition, it was included in the Bill of Rights to assure the states that the national government would not disarm the state militias.

Search and Seizure.   The Fourth Amendment prohibits "unreasonable" searches and seizures. Under ordinary or "reasonable" circumstances, a search warrant must be secured from a judge, commissioner, or magistrate. This is a written order issued under oath; it describes the place to be searched and the person or things to be seized. A warrant is not essential if it can be shown that time or circumstances did not reasonably permit securing it. Evidence gathered through illegal or unreasonable means is not admissible in federal trials nor, under the 14th Amendment, in state trials (*Weeks v. United States,* 232 U.S. 383 [1914]; *Mapp v. Ohio,* 367 U.S. 643 [1961]).

• *Significance:* The Fourth Amendment has proved to be one of the more troublesome provisions of the Bill of Rights. What constitutes an "unreasonable" search and seizure? No precise definition can be made and the courts have treated the issue on a case-to-case basis, considering all the circumstances involved. The most serious contemporary problem is the reasonableness of search through wiretapping and other electronic devices. Evidence which is obtained through an unreasonable search and seizure is inadmissible on the ground that it constitutes self-incrimination—forcing the accused to reveal what he has a right to conceal. See WIRETAPPING, page 75.

Sedition.   Actions which incite rebellion or discontent against duly established government. Espionage, sabotage, or attempts to overthrow the government constitute sedition, as does advocacy by publication or speech to accomplish these goals. The Sedition Acts of 1798 and 1918 put severe limitations on mere criticism of the government. Recent sedition legislation has been aimed at outlawing Communist conspiracies and advocacy of doctrines aimed at overthrow of government by force. See ALIEN AND SEDITION LAWS, page 86; SMITH ACT, page 88; INTERNAL SECURITY ACT, page 87; COMMUNIST CONTROL ACT, page 87.

• *Significance:* Though closely akin to treason, sedition does not require the precise standard of proof which the Constitution requires for treason convictions. Few people question the legality or wisdom of outlawing and punishing seditious *actions.* However, punishment for seditious *speech* resulted in severe restrictions on nonconformists in post-Revolutionary America and during World War I. The Supreme Court has sustained recent convictions of Communists but has drawn a distinction between mere advocacy of abstract doctrine and conspiracy to advocate concrete action (*Yates v. United States,* 354 U.S. 298 [1957]). A law which makes mere criticism of government a crime makes free government impossible since one may criticize and be loyal at the same time.

Segregation.   The separation of the white and colored races in public and private facilities. Laws requiring the segregation of the races (Jim Crow laws) are on the statute books of several states. In 1896, the Supreme Court upheld such laws under the doctrine of "separate but equal" whereby the Negro could be segregated if he were provided with equal facilities (*Plessy v. Ferguson,* 163 U.S. 537). Under this doctrine, a wide pattern of segregation developed in schools, transportation, recreation, and housing. Beginning in the 1940's, the Supreme Court began to weaken the separate but equal doctrine by insisting that the facilities provided for Negroes, particularly in education, be equal, indeed. Finally, in 1954, the Supreme Court struck down the separate but equal formula, holding that segregation based on color denied the equal protection of the law (*Brown v. Board of Education of Topeka,* 347 U.S. 483). Later, the Court declared unconstitutional segregation in transportation and recreational facilities.

• *Significance:* Segregation has been part of the pattern of life in 17 southern states and the District of Columbia. The Supreme Court's 1954 decision has simultaneously strained and improved the status of the American Negro. Since 1954, integration has proceeded at various speeds and, in some states, no progress has been made at all. In some areas, integration has precipitated violence. However, since 1954, with the law no longer compelling separate treatment, the Negro has sought to make the ruling a reality by such actions as "sit-ins" in restaurants, "kneel-ins" at churches, and "wade-ins" at public beaches, all of which were closed to him previously. Moreover, the Congress has passed civil rights measures to increase Negro political and civil rights. Southern states have sought to resist integration by various evasive schemes but few have found favor in the courts. Informal patterns of segregation still exist on a wide scale in both the North and the South and are likely to continue for many years.

Self-Incrimination.   Testimony by a person which reveals facts which may result in a criminal prosecution against him. The Fifth Amendment provides that no person "shall be compelled in any criminal case to be a witness against himself." Though originally applied to persons on trial, the concept has been extended to cover testimony before legislative committees or executive agencies. A person may not refuse to testify in order to protect another person, nor because his answers might bring disgrace upon himself. The guarantee extends only to testimony which might involve the person himself in a criminal prosecution. A person who has been given immunity or a pardon, or who has already been convicted of the particular offense, may not refuse to testify. In a federal trial, no unfavorable inferences may be drawn from a refusal to testify. This is true in most states, too, but about six states permit such inferences to be drawn. The Supreme Court has given its approval to this practice, holding that it does not violate the due process clause of the 14th Amendment (*Adamson v. California,* 332 U.S. 46 [1947]).

• *Significance:* In a criminal prosecution, the burden of proof is on the prosecution. The right against self-incrimination is designed to prevent the shifting of the burden to the defendant by forcing him to reveal incriminating facts. It also prevents the use of torture or inquisitorial procedures to coerce confessions, as well as the use of evidence illegally obtained. A major problem involves the question of whether the witness has waived his right by answering questions directly or indirectly related to a matter which might incriminate him. Once the witness begins to answer a line of questions he may have unknowingly waived the right; for this reason, many witnesses have refused to answer any questions. This has been particularly true in congressional investigations into subversion and racketeering. However, a person may be found in contempt if he uses the right as a mere dodge and refuses to answer proper questions. While one may not suffer any legal penalty for invoking the Fifth Amendment, loss of reputation or employment may result. The protection against self-incrimination is one of the hallmarks of a free society, but, like many rights, it is often abused.

Seventh Amendment.   A part of the Bill of Rights which guarantees the preservation of the right to a jury trial in a suit at common law where the value in controversy exceeds $20. It also provides that facts tried by the jury may not be re-examined in any court except in accordance with common law rules.
• *Significance:* The Seventh Amendment is a rarely litigated item which applies only to cases in which the Congress permits common law rules to be used. It does not apply to cases arising out of statutory law nor in equity proceedings. The Seventh Amendment is frequently pointed to as a concrete example of a portion of the Bill of Rights which is not made applicable to the states by the 14th Amendment, since it involves no right which is basic to fairness or is so important as to be ranked fundamental.

Sixth Amendment.   A part of the Bill of Rights which stipulates the basic requirements of fairness in federal criminal court procedures. These include a speedy and public trial, an impartial jury, trial in the area where the crime was committed, notice of the charges, the right to confront witnesses and to obtain favorable witnesses, and the right to counsel. *See* TRIAL, page 215; JURY, page 67; VENUE, page 216; WITNESS, page 75; COUNSEL, page 60.
• *Significance:* The brief but highly important Sixth Amendment sums up the essential procedures of a fair and impartial trial. An improper denial of any of these ingredients may be sufficient to void a conviction.

Substantive Rights.   Rights essential for personal liberty. These generally include those rights listed in the First, Thirteenth, and Fourteenth Amendments—freedoms of speech, press, religion, assembly, and petition, freedom from involuntary servitude, and the right to equal protection of the law. *Substantive* rights are to be distinguished from *procedural* rights which are concerned with the manner in which the substantive rights are protected, as by due process and fair trial.
• *Significance:* No precise listing of substantive rights is possible, but certain ingredients, such as those listed above, are generally considered to be of the very essence of freedom. One can hardly be considered to be free if he is a slave, has no liberty to express himself in speech, press, or prayer, and is arbitrarily discriminated against. It is important, too, that procedures be established whereby necessary limitations may be placed on substantive rights. Thus, one may be confined to jail or have his speech limited but only in accordance with due process of law.

Treason.   A disloyal act which, as defined by Article III, section 3, "shall consist only in levying war against [the United States], or in adhering to their enemies, giving them aid and comfort." The Constitution further provides that one may not be convicted of treason "unless on the testimony of two witnesses to the same overt act, or on confession in open court."

• *Significance:* Treason is the only crime precisely defined in the Constitution as a safeguard against irresponsible charges for this most serious of crimes. Levying war or adhering to enemies of the United States are the only grounds for bringing a prosecution and unless the suspect confesses, two witnesses must testify that they saw him commit the act. Acts of disloyalty which do not fall within the constitutional definition may be prosecuted under sedition laws. Communist subversive activities are not considered as treason since the Soviet Union is not, technically, an enemy. Many state constitutions contain treason provisions, but it is questionable whether one could commit treason against a state and not against the United States. John Brown, hanged in 1859 for his raid on Harper's Ferry, Virginia, is believed to be the only person executed for treason against a state. Treason trials have not been numerous and no one has been executed for treason by the national government.

Wiretapping.   The use of listening devices to intercept telephone messages. The term is generally applied to the use of any electronic device to intercept private conversations. Congress, in 1934, forbade the interception of telephone messages without the consent of the sender. Evidence so secured is excluded from federal trials but not all state trials, and the rule with regard to the use of other listening devices is not clear.

• *Significance:* The availability of electronic devices has vastly complicated traditional rules of search and seizure. Though intercepted telephone messages may not be used as evidence in federal trials, the Supreme Court has refused to enjoin a state from doing so. Most states, however, follow the federal rule. It appears that other electronic devices may be used provided no invasion of property takes place, as when conversations are overheard by sensitive listening devices placed outside a home. In spite of the federal law on telephone taps, it is widely recognized that wiretapping is done by law enforcement agencies at all levels, with an apparent distinction being drawn between listening and using the information as evidence. Legislation has been introduced in the Congress and in several states to permit wiretapping in such cases as subversion or kidnaping but no useful formula has been discovered whereby the innocent may be protected. New York State has a constitutional provision permitting wiretapping with court approval.

Witness.   A person who presents information or evidence in a trial or investigation. Under the Sixth Amendment and most state constitutions, a person accused of a crime is entitled to confront the witnesses against him and to compel the attendance of witnesses in his favor.

• *Significance:* In a criminal case, the government must permit cross-examination of any witness it uses. If it wishes to conceal the identity of an informant then that person may not be put on the stand, nor may his testimony be introduced. In addition, the defendant is entitled to see any reports made to the police by a witness, unless the judge rules otherwise. The right to compel the attendance of favorable witnesses is an important corollary to the right of confrontation and the defendant has the right to government aid to subpoena any reluctant witness. Though these rights are fairly well established in criminal trials, attention in recent years has been directed to the lack of these rights in congressional investigations. In hearings on subversion in particular, criticism has been made of the fact that while persons accused of subversion are usually permitted to testify, they are not permitted to confront and cross-examine accusers nor to compel the attendance of favorable witnesses.

IMPORTANT AGENCIES

Civil Rights Commission.   Established by the federal Civil Rights Act of 1957 as a bipartisan commission of six members to investigate the broad area of civil rights. The Commission has conducted investigations and studies in such matters as voting rights, education, housing, employment, and the administration of justice. Originally created for a two-year period, the life of the Commission was extended for two more years in 1959 and again in 1961. Its first two reports, filed in 1959 and 1961, contained numerous recommendations on voting, education, housing, employment, and justice.
• *Significance:* The Commission has uncovered evidence of abuses of civil rights in all areas of its investigations. Its findings and recommendations played a vital role in the enactment of the Civil Rights Act of 1960.

Department of Justice.   Three divisions of the Department of Justice are particularly concerned with civil liberty matters. The Federal Bureau of Investigation (FBI), established in 1908, has charge of investigations of violations of federal laws except for those assigned to another agency. The Internal Security Division of the Department of Justice was formed in 1954 to handle all criminal laws relating to subversive activities. These include prosecutions for treason or sedition, and prosecutions under the Atomic Energy Act, the Smith Act, and the Internal Security Act. It also conducts cases before the Subversive Activities Control Board and handles matters relating to security requirements for government employees. The third is the Civil Rights Division established under the Civil Rights Act of 1957. It is responsible for enforcement of all statutes affecting civil rights including the Civil Rights Acts of 1957 and 1960, antipeonage laws, election frauds, and obstructions of justice. It also investigates complaints brought by persons claiming deprivations of their civil rights.
• *Significance:* The Department of Justice is playing an increasingly large role in the field of civil liberties. The Internal Security and the Civil Rights Divisions underscore national government concern in these two areas in recent years and the expansion of activity against communism on the one hand and in defense of Negro rights on the other. The role of the FBI has been enlarged, too, as the scope of federal law enforcement grows.

Subversive Activities Control Board.   An independent agency established in 1950 under the Internal Security Act. The Board is composed of five members appointed by the President, with the consent of the Senate, for five-year terms. Its major function is to conduct hearings, upon the request of the Attorney General, to determine whether an organization is a Communist action or front group subject to the registration requirements of the Internal Security Act. It also considers petitions from organizations ordered to register to have their names removed from the list of Communist organizations if the group has undergone a change of character.

• *Significance:* The Subversive Activities Control Board formalizes the procedures formally used to put allegedly subversive organizations on the Attorney General's List. The Board has ordered a few organizations to register, including the Communist party, and the Supreme Court has upheld the order with regard to the party (*Communist Party v. Subversive Activities Control Board,* 367 U.S. 1 [1961]).

IMPORTANT CASES

Adamson v. California, 332 U.S. 46 (1947): Decided that a state may, without violating the due process clause of the 14th Amendment, permit unfavorable inferences to be drawn from the refusal of a defendant in a criminal trial to testify. Though this is not permitted in federal trials, a state is not bound to follow the procedures used in federal courts under the Bill of Rights unless state procedures are shockingly unjust.

• *Significance:* In this case, the Supreme Court refused to reverse its ruling in *Twining v. New Jersey,* 211 U.S. 78 (1908) that the guarantee against self-incrimination does not apply to the states. The *Adamson* ruling underscored the refusal of the Court to bring the entire Bill of Rights under the scope of the 14th Amendment and make it applicable to the states.

Adler v. Board of Education, 342 U.S. 485 (1952): Established that a state has the right to remove a public employee from his job if the employee belongs to an organization advocating violent overthrow of government.

• *Significance:* Many persons viewed the *Adler* decision as endorsing guilt by association, but the Court indicated that persons are often known by the company they keep. The Court felt that inquiries into such associations were valid to determine one's fitness for public service. In related cases, the Court has upheld discharges of public employees for refusing to answer questions asked by their employers about political affiliations since such questions may be relevant to an employee's fitness (e.g., *Lerner v. Casey,* 357 U.S. 468 [1958]). However, a public employee may not be discharged solely for invoking his right against self-incrimination before an investigating committee since he would then be penalized for exercising a constitutional right (*Slochower v. Board of Higher Education,* 350 U.S. 551 [1956]). The Court has taken the view that no one has a *right* to public employment and that the schools, in particular, should be kept free from subversive influences. However, one may not arbitrarily be discharged.

Ashcraft v. Tennessee, 322 U.S. 143 (1944): Ruled that a confession obtained from a suspect after prolonged interrogation under hot lights by a relay of officers is not admissible in a state trial. Such coercive methods to obtain confessions violate the 14th Amendment.

• *Significance:* Earlier, in *Brown v. Mississippi,* 297 U.S. 278 (1936), the Court announced for the first time that a confession extracted through brutality and torture violated the 14th Amendment. In the *Ashcraft* case, the Court extended this rule to confessions which were derived through psychological rather than physical maltreatment. Since that time, the Court has heard a number of cases involving charges that confessions were coerced, and in each instance, the Court has had to determine the nature and extent of the coercion.

Barron v. Baltimore, 7 Peters 243 (1833): Held that the Bill of Rights limits only the national government and not the state governments.

• *Significance:* This decision is still operative today although its impact has been greatly modified in practice through interpretations of the 14th Amendment which make state and local government infringement of civil liberties subject to Supreme Court review.

Bartkus v. Illinois, 355 U.S. 281 (1958): Denied a claim of double jeopardy in a conviction in a state court for bank robbery in spite of the fact that the person had been acquitted by a federal court for the same bank robbery.

• *Significance:* This case underscores the rule that double jeopardy refers only to repeated trials on the same charge by the same jurisdiction. One may be tried by both the national and state courts for a single offense.

Bolling v. Sharpe, 347 U.S. 497 (1954): Declared, in one of the school segregation cases, that segregation in the public schools of the District of Columbia violated the due process clause of the Fifth Amendment.

• *Significance:* The Constitution contains no requirement that the national government afford "equal protection of the law." The "equal protection" clause is found in the 14th Amendment and is a limitation on the states. Nevertheless, the Court held that segregation of the races by the national government is an arbitrary denial of liberty without due process of law.

Brown v. Board of Education of Topeka, 347 U.S. 483 (1954); 349 U.S. 294 (1955): Established in a major decision that segregation of the races in public schools violates the equal protection clause of the 14th Amendment. The Supreme Court overruled the "separate but equal" doctrine which had been in effect since 1896, noting that "Separate educational facilities are inherently unequal." In the 1955 case, the Court ordered desegregation to proceed "with all deliberate speed," leaving it to the federal district courts to determine implementations of the ruling in specific cases brought before them.

• *Significance:* This decision ranks among the most important of American constitutional history. School desegregation has taken place in many southern communities, sometimes with violent results. Other segregation practices have also been declared unconstitutional in the wake of this decision. The *Brown* case has created a crisis in national-state relations with many southern states seeking means of evading the decision. The case has undoubtedly given impetus to much of the federal government's activity in the field of civil rights, such as the Civil Rights Acts of 1957 and 1960.

Communist Party v. Subversive Activities Control Board, 367 U.S. 1 (1961): Upheld provisions of the Internal Security Act of 1950 which require the registration of officers and members of Communist action organizations after a finding by the Subversive Activities Control Board that the organization is controlled by a foreign power. The Court rejected claims that the law was a bill of attainder or required self-incrimination and justified any restriction on freedom of speech or association on the ground that the nation had a right to self-preservation. Further, the Court found no conflict between the Internal Security Act and the Smith Act since registration does not subject one to prosecution under the Smith Act unless illegal activities are undertaken.
• *Significance:* This case was the first test of the Internal Security Act before the Supreme Court after years of hearings before the Subversive Activities Control Board and the lower courts. The Communist party has refused to register as required by the decision. Several other controversial provisions of the Internal Security Act remain to be tested in the courts.

Dennis v. United States, 341 U.S. 494 (1951): Sustained, in a major decision, the conviction of 11 top Communist party leaders for conspiring to teach and to advocate the violent overthrow of the government. The decision upheld the Smith Act of 1940.
• *Significance:* The *Dennis* case attracted wide notice because of the sharp conflict between freedom of speech guaranteed by the First Amendment and the indictment against the Communist leaders for advocating their doctrine. The Supreme Court narrowed the interpretation of the clear and present danger rule by holding that in the interest of self-preservation it was not essential for the government to wait until the conspiracy ripened into action. This decision led to numerous prosecutions of other Communist leaders. However, in 1957, in *Yates v. United States,* 354 U.S. 298, the Supreme Court modified its ruling in the *Dennis* case by holding that a distinction must be drawn between urging people to *believe* in something and urging people to *do* something. In the *Yates* case, the Court found that the defendants were merely preaching Communist doctrine in the abstract and were not teaching or advocating unlawful conduct. The *Yates* case has restored the clear and present danger rule to some extent and has made it more difficult for the government to prosecute Communists without proving some measure of concrete action to overthrow the government by force.

Everson v. Board of Education of Ewing Township, 330 U.S. 1 (1947): Decided that it is not a violation of the First Amendment's establishment of religion clause for a state to pay for the transportation of children to parochial schools. The Court found this to be of benefit to the children rather than an aid to the church.
• *Significance:* This case was the first major test of the establishment of religion clause which has become largely a problem of the separation of church and state in public schools. In its decision, the Court emphasized that the First Amendment was designed to "erect a wall of separation between church and state." Nevertheless, it found that in this instance the wall had not been breached.

Garner v. Board of Public Works, 341 U.S. 716 (1951): Sustained a municipal law requiring a noncommunist affidavit and loyalty oath from public employees. The Court took the view that loyalty was a reasonable requirement for public employment in spite of any limitations which the law placed upon freedom of speech and of association.

• *Significance:* The Court has upheld numerous state and local laws requiring loyalty oaths of public employees and school teachers. However, the Court has insisted that the oaths be interpreted to mean that the person knew that any organizations to which he belonged had illegal aims (*Wieman v. Updegraff,* 344 U.S. 183 [1952]). Further, the Court has held that a state may not require a loyalty oath of individuals in order to get general public benefits, such as tax exemptions (*Speiser v. Randall,* 357 U.S. 513 [1958]).

Gitlow v. New York, 268 U.S. 652 (1925): Established, in a landmark case, that freedom of speech and press are protected against state impairment by the due process clause of the 14th Amendment. Nevertheless, in this case the Court upheld a conviction for publishing and circulating materials advocating the overthrow of government by force.

• *Significance:* Prior to this decision, the Court had consistently held that the 14th Amendment did not incorporate any part of the Bill of Rights. Since the *Gitlow* decision, the Court has applied the entire First Amendment to the states under the due process clause of the 14th Amendment, as well as some other portions of the Bill of Rights. The net effect has been an increasing involvement of the national government in the protection of the people against abuse of their liberties by the states.

Hague v. CIO, 307 U.S. 496 (1939): Declared unconstitutional under the 14th Amendment an ordinance of Jersey City, N.J., which required permission to hold a meeting in or upon public streets, parks, or buildings. Under the ordinance, the officials of Jersey City had molested union organizers of the CIO and had denied them permission to hold meetings or to circulate handbills.

• *Significance:* This is an important freedom of assembly decision. The right to assemble applies not merely to meetings of private groups but to public meetings in public places. The Court has, in other cases, frowned upon any prior restraints upon public meetings unless some reasonable standards are established for the granting of permission. These standards must in some way be related to the health, safety, and welfare of the people. For example, one might legally be required to secure a permit in order to hold a parade (*Cox v. New Hampshire,* 312 U.S. 569 [1941]).

Hurtado v. California, 110 U.S. 516 (1884): Established that a state is not required by the due process clause of the 14th Amendment to provide for indictment by grand jury in felony cases. Indictment by information is consistent with fair procedure.

• *Significance:* This was the first major test of the meaning of the due process clause of the 14th Amendment. In this case, the Court made it clear that the 14th Amendment did not make the Bill of Rights applicable to the states and that merely because indictment by grand jury is required by the Fifth Amendment did not mean that the states were bound thereby. To this day, the states are given considerable discretion to vary their procedures in criminal matters provided they do not violate fundamental fairness.

Jehovah's Witnesses Cases: Involved, in a series of cases, the religious sect known as Jehovah's Witnesses, testing the scope of religious freedom under the First and Fourteenth Amendments. Among the various decisions were those which held unconstitutional laws requiring prior official approval to solicit funds for religious purposes (*Cantwell v. Connecticut*, 310 U.S. 296 [1940]); laws levying license taxes on peddlers of religious tracts (*Murdock v. Pennsylvania*, 319 U.S. 105 [1943]); laws prohibiting door to door distribution of religious handbills (*Martin v. Struthers*, 319 U.S. 141 [1943]); and laws requiring official approval to hold public worship meetings in public parks (*Niemotko v. Maryland*, 340 U.S. 268 [1951]). In a famous decision, the Court held that children of Jehovah's Witnesses could not be compelled to salute the flag contrary to their religious beliefs (*West Virginia State Board of Education v. Barnette*, 319 U.S. 624 [1943]). On the other hand, the Court has held that the sect may not hold a parade without permission (*Cox v. New Hampshire*, 312 U.S. 569 [1941]); or have a young child sell magazines on a street corner late at night contrary to state child welfare laws (*Prince v. Massachusetts*, 321 U.S. 158 [1944]; or create a breach of peace in the course of a public meeting (*Chaplinsky v. New Hampshire*, 315 U.S. 568 [1942]).
• *Significance:* Through these and other cases, Jehovah's Witnesses have forced the courts to consider the proper scope of, and limitations on, the practice of religion. For the most part, the Supreme Court has been sympathetic with the proselytizing activities of the sect except when their actions were in conflict with reasonable measures designed to protect the public welfare.

McNabb v. United States, 318 U.S. 332 (1943): Held that the federal courts may not convict a person of a crime on the basis of a confession secured while the prisoner was unlawfully detained. The Court ruled that the prisoner must be taken before a judicial officer for arraignment without delay.
• *Significance:* The rule here is designed to prohibit police officials from unduly detaining a suspect in order to secure a confession. The Court reaffirmed this in *Mallory v. United States*, 354 U.S. 449 (1957), which involved the release of a confessed criminal because of a delay in arraignment. This led to demands from some members of the Congress that the rule be changed to permit use of legally secured evidence regardless of such delay, but no law has been enacted. Neither the *McNabb* nor *Mallory* rule applies in state courts.

Mapp v. Ohio, 367 U.S. 643 (1961): Ruled that a state may not use illegally seized evidence in criminal trials.
• *Significance:* This decision is of far-reaching importance since it overruled the decision in *Wolf v. Colorado*, 338 U.S. 25 (1949), which held that a state may use evidence secured through an illegal search and seizure. About half the states have admitted such evidence in criminal trials, although in federal criminal trials illegally secured evidence is not admissible. In *Mapp v. Ohio*, the Court declared that the *Wolf* rule made the constitutional protection against

unlawful search and seizure meaningless. The *Mapp* decision is a major example of continuing national supervision of state activities in the field of civil liberties through the 14th Amendment.

Moore v. Dempsey, 261 U.S. 86 (1923): Declared that a trial conducted under the influence of a mob, in which public passion dominates the judge, jury, witnesses, and defense counsel, is a denial of due process of law. In this case, the trial of five Negroes was conducted under the duress of a mob, making the outcome a certainty.

• *Significance:* It is not enough that the mere forms of a trial be observed. The proceedings must be fair and provide the defendant with the full measure of his rights. While the Court is usually concerned with specific aspects of a case, it will, as it did here, insist that the entire proceedings be conducted in an atmosphere which will assure a fair trial.

National Association for the Advancement of Colored People v. Alabama, 357 U.S. 449 (1958): Established that a state may not compel the disclosure of the membership lists of an organization which is pursuing lawful ends if members are likely to suffer physical, economic, and other hostile reprisals.

• *Significance:* One result of the integration movement in the South has been an effort on the part of some states to harass and impede the activities of the NAACP which has been particularly active in behalf of Negro rights. In this case, the Court stressed the importance of the freedom to associate, noting that any interference is subject to close scrutiny.

Near v. Minnesota, 283 U.S. 697 (1931): Defined freedom of the press to mean that the press is to be free from prior restraint or censorship. A state may not, under the due process clause of the 14th Amendment, permanently enjoin a newspaper from being published. If a newspaper abuses its privilege, it may be punished subsequently. The Court held unconstitutional a Minnesota statute which authorized officials to forbid publication of "malicious, scandalous and defamatory" newspapers.

• *Significance:* The *Near* case was the first important decision of the Supreme Court on censorship. The Court admitted that under exceptional circumstances, such as war, a paper might be prevented from publishing but stressed that freedom of the press means freedom from governmental censorship or ban. Otherwise, government officials would be in a position to suppress news which, as in the *Near* case, was critical of them.

Norris v. Alabama, 294 U.S. 587 (1935): Held, in what is popularly known as the Second Scottsboro case, that Negroes could not be systematically excluded from jury service.

• *Significance:* A Negro defendant does not have a right to have Negroes serve on the jury in his trial. However, Negroes may not deliberately be excluded. In this case, the Court found that no Negroes had ever served on juries in the counties involved and showed that it would look behind the nondiscriminatory wording of the state law to see what the actual practice was with regard to jury selection.

Palko v. Connecticut, 302 U.S. 319 (1937): Ruled that the double jeopardy provision of the Fifth Amendment does not apply to the states through the 14th Amendment. A state may appeal a conviction of a defendant and ask for a more severe sentence.

• *Significance:* The *Palko* case is particularly noteworthy because of the Court's opinion written by Justice Benjamin N. Cardozo in which he set down the criteria by which the Court will determine whether a state has violated the rights protected by the due process clause of the 14th Amendment. These include those rights which are "implicit in the concept of ordered liberty," which are "so rooted in the traditions and conscience of our people as to be ranked as fundamental" or "essential to a fair and enlightened system of justice," or, if the denial of given rights would be "shocking to the sense of justice of the civilized world." Within this framework, Justice Cardozo indicated that freedom of speech, press, religion, and assembly were essential for liberty and hence covered by the 14th Amendment, but that variations in criminal procedures were permissible so long as they violated no fundamental principles of justice. On a case-to-case basis, the Court has marked out the limits of the due process clause, permitting the states to abolish the grand jury, to hold trial in certain cases without a jury, or to permit trial without counsel. On the other hand, the Court has forbidden states to conduct unreasonable searches and seizures or to permit cruel and unusual punishment. The *Palko* decision emphasizes that the Court has wide latitude in determining the meaning of the 14th Amendment.

Plessy v. Ferguson, 163 U.S. 537 (1896): Upheld, in a famous decision, a state law requiring segregation of the races in public transportation. The Court held that under the equal protection clause of the 14th Amendment, a state could provide "separate but equal" facilities to Negroes. This case was overruled in *Brown v. Board of Education of Topeka,* 347 U.S. 483 (1954).

• *Significance:* The *Plessy* case served as justification for the segregation policies of many states until 1954. Although it is no longer effective, the decision demonstrates the great power of the Supreme Court in giving direction to the law. Until the case was overturned, the Court limited itself to considering whether facilities provided to Negroes were indeed equal though separate.

Pollock v. Williams, 322 U.S. 4 (1944): Decided that a state lends support to slavery or peonage, contrary to the 13th Amendment, when it requires that a person must work to discharge a debt or go to jail. The Court held unconstitutional a law which made it a crime to take money in advance and then refuse to perform the required labor. A state may punish fraud but it cannot make failure to work a crime.

• *Significance:* A surprisingly large number of persons appear to be involved in forced labor due to their ignorance of their rights. The Justice Department gets numerous complaints of involuntary servitude involving persons who are forced to work through indebtedness to their employer. The Court's decision has made it clear it will outlaw practices which are just short of outright slavery.

Powell v. Alabama, 287 U.S. 45 (1932): Held, in what is popularly known as the First Scottsboro case, that the due process clause of the 14th Amendment requires that counsel be provided to defendants in a capital case.

• *Significance:* The Supreme Court has never held that a state must furnish counsel to a defendant in all cases, although this is the practice in federal courts. In several cases involving noncapital offenses, the Court has taken the position that counsel need be furnished by a state only when circumstances require it in order to assure a fair trial. These circumstances include such factors as the age, mental competence, and experience of the defendant.

Reynolds v. United States, 98 U.S. 145 (1879): Established that religious freedom does not protect one who commits a crime or an act contrary to accepted public morals. In this case, the Court upheld the enforcement of antipolygamy laws against Mormons who, prior to 1890, practiced polygamy as a religious doctrine.

• *Significance:* This case established one of the clearest legal principles involving the free exercise of religion. A person is free to believe and worship as he pleases so long as his conduct violates no laws which validly protect the health, safety, or morals of the community.

Roth v. United States, 354 U.S. 476 (1957): Excluded obscenity from the area of constitutionally protected speech and press. The Court held that the proper standard to determine obscenity is "whether to the average person, applying contemporary community standards, the dominant theme of the material taken as a whole appeals to prurient interest."

• *Significance:* Publication of obscene materials has long puzzled American courts. In denying constitutional protection to such publications, the Court expressed the view that obscenity was without the "redeeming social importance" which the First Amendment is designed to protect. In a companion case, *Alberts v. California,* 354 U.S. 476 (1957), the Court applied the same rule to state obscenity laws. Whether or not a particular publication is obscene is determined on a case-to-case basis.

Scales v. United States, 367 U.S. 203 (1961): Sustained that portion of the Smith Act of 1940 which makes it a crime to be a member of an organization that advocates overthrow of government by force, knowing that to be the purpose of the organization. The Court drew a distinction between active membership and mere membership, noting that active membership in a party that has illegal aims is not constitutionally protected.

• *Significance:* The *Scales* decision strengthened the government's hand in its fight against the Communist party. However, the Court sought to avoid imputing guilt by mere association by insisting that the government must prove that an individual was an active participant in illegal activities.

Schenck v. United States, 249 U.S. 47 (1919): Upheld a conviction against Schenck who had circulated materials urging men to resist the call to military service during World War I. The Court held that this was a justified infringement upon freedom of speech and press in view of the wartime emergency.

• *Significance:* This case is particularly noteworthy because of the opinion of Justice Oliver Wendell Holmes which established the clear and present danger doctrine. Justice Holmes wrote that "the question in every case is whether the words used are in such circumstances and are of such a nature as to create a clear and present danger that they will bring about the substantive evils that Congress has a right to prevent." In these words, Justice Holmes provided the formula which has been used in many free speech cases since that time. The *Schenck* case is also noted for the distinction drawn between speech that may be permissible in peacetime but not when the nation is at war.

Times Film Corporation v. Chicago, 365 U.S. 43 (1961): Ruled that a city may require the submission of motion pictures to a censor prior to exhibition of the film to the public.
• *Significance:* From time to time, the Supreme Court has invalidated censorship of specific films on the ground that the films were not obscene or otherwise offensive. However, in this case, the nature of the film was not in question. Rather the film company had refused to submit the film for approval. The Court, which usually frowns upon prior restraint of any kind, held that this practice was permissible with regard to motion pictures. Officials of the entertainment industry were much upset by this ruling. Earlier, in *Burstyn v. Wilson,* 343 U.S. 495 (1952), the Court brought movies within the protection of the First and Fourteenth Amendments guaranteeing freedom of speech and press.

United States v. Lovett, 328 U.S. 303 (1946): Declared unconstitutional as a bill of attainder an act of Congress which named three individuals as ineligible for continued government employment, in that it punished the individuals without judicial trial.
• *Significance:* Few cases have arisen in American constitutional history involving bills of attainder. After the Civil War, the Supreme Court found certain laws imposing disabilities upon all persons who participated in the rebellion to be bills of attainder (*Cummings v. Missouri,* 4 Wallace 277, *Ex parte Garland,* 4 Wallace 333 [1867]). Recent legislation designed to keep Communists out of public service has been upheld by the Court on the ground that it established general qualifications for employment rather than naming specific individuals (*Garner v. Board of Public Works,* 341 U.S. 716 [1951]).

Zorach v. Clauson, 343 U.S. 306 (1952): Supported New York's released time program in public schools under which students are released from classes to attend religious exercises in their respective churches. The Court found no conflict between this practice and the establishment of religion clause in the First Amendment.
• *Significance:* The teaching of religion in public schools is one of the most controversial questions in public education, going to the very heart of the issue of the separation of church and state. The *Zorach* decision attracted wide notice since it followed on the heels of the Court's decision in *McCollum v. Board of Education,* 333 U.S. 203 (1948). In the *McCollum* case, the Court declared unconstitutional a program of released time under which children attended religious classes on school grounds. The *Zorach* ruling rested largely on the fact that the religious classes were not held on school property.

IMPORTANT STATUTES

Alien and Sedition Laws.   Acts passed in 1798 authorizing the President to deport undesirable aliens and making it a crime to criticize the government or its officials. Through these Acts, the Federalist party sought to silence opposition. About 25 persons were jailed or fined for criticizing the President. These Acts are credited with being a major cause in the defeat of the Federalist party in the election of 1800. Thomas Jefferson, the winner of that election, pardoned those convicted under the Acts.

• *Significance:* With the exception of these laws, Congress did not find it necessary to pass antisedition legislation until World War I. It is generally agreed that the Alien and Sedition Laws were unconstitutional, but they were never tested in the courts. They serve as a reminder that civil rights are under constant threat unless zealously guarded by the people. Free government is not possible unless it is understood that one may be loyal to his nation and, at the same time, criticize those who make its policies.

Civil Rights Acts of 1866, 1870, 1871, and 1875.   Laws passed by the Congress after the Civil War to guarantee the rights of Negroes. Most of the provisions of these laws were declared unconstitutional by the Supreme Court as a federal invasion of the police power of the states, and many were repealed by the Congress. Today, a few major provisions remain from the Acts of 1866 and 1871. One makes it a federal crime for any person acting under the authority of state law to deprive another of any rights protected by the Constitution or laws of the United States. Another authorizes suits for civil damages against state or local officials by persons whose rights are abridged. Similar provisions apply to persons who conspire to deprive another of his rights.

• *Significance:* The failure of the post–Civil War Acts represented the general attitude of the time that the national government had a limited role to play in the enforcement of individual rights. The remaining provisions have served occasionally as a weapon in the hands of national officers to restrain state officials who violate the constitutional rights of persons in their charge. Today, as the national government expands its role in the protection of individual rights, particularly in the area of race relations, the laws have taken on new importance.

Civil Rights Act of 1957.   This is the first civil rights law passed by the Congress since Reconstruction and is designed to secure the right to vote for Negroes. Its major feature empowers the Department of Justice to seek court injunctions against any deprivation of voting rights and authorizes criminal prosecutions for violations of an injunction. In addition, the Act establishes a Civil Rights Division in the Department of Justice to be headed by an Assistant Attorney General, and creates a six man bipartisan Civil Rights Commission to investigate civil rights violations and to recommend legislation.

• *Significance:* This statute marks a major breakthrough in positive federal action in the field of civil rights. It is based on the theory that if the Negro is protected in his voting rights, he will be in a better position to seek reform in other areas of discrimination.

Civil Rights Act of 1960.   This second post-Reconstruction civil rights law is also basically designed to secure the right to vote for Negroes although it also includes provisions to meet certain contemporary problems arising from racial upheavals in the South. The major provision authorizes federal courts to appoint referees to help Negroes to register to vote. This may be done following a conviction under the 1957 Civil Rights Act and a court finding of a "pattern or practice" of discrimination against qualified voters. Other provisions (1) authorize punishment for persons who obstruct any federal court order by threats or force, such as a school desegregation order; (2) authorize criminal penalties for transportation of explosives for purposes of bombing a building; (3) require preservation of voting records for 22 months and authorize the Attorney General to inspect the records; (4) provide for schooling of children of armed forces personnel in the event that a school closes in an integration dispute.

• *Significance:* Continuing the pattern established in the 1957 Civil Rights Act, the Congress sought to strengthen the voting rights of citizens and reached out into other problem areas. The debate on the Act in the Senate was marked by a filibuster which was overcome through "round-the-clock" sessions.

Communist Control Act of 1954.   An act of Congress which deprives the Communist party of the rights and privileges of other legally organized bodies or political parties and declares it to be a clear and present threat to the security of the United States. The law does not make it a crime to be a Communist, but a member of the party is subject to the requirements of the Internal Security Act.

• *Significance:* The full meaning of the law is not clear. It was passed in the Congress with little discussion and has not been vigorously enforced. Many authorities question its constitutionality. The main effect has been to keep the Communist party off the ballot. This is the first time in American history that a party has been denied use of the ballot as a means of gaining adherents to its programs.

Immunity Act of 1954.   An act designed to compel testimony from witnesses who claim self-incrimination when questioned on matters of national security. Either house of the Congress, a congressional committee, or a federal district attorney may, after notifying the Attorney General, request a federal district court to grant immunity. Once granted, the witness must testify on those matters covered by the immunity order and may never be prosecuted for any crimes revealed by his testimony in any state or federal court.

• *Significance:* Congress was disturbed by the hundreds of persons who claimed self-incrimination when called to testify on security matters. The law has been used sparingly, since it can result in complete freedom for dangerous persons. The Supreme Court upheld this act in *Ullmann v. United States,* 350 U.S. 422 (1956).

Internal Security Act of 1950 (McCarran Act).   An act designed to place the Communist party and other totalitarian groups under rigid controls. The Act outlaws any conspiracy, peaceful or violent, which has as its purpose the establishment of a foreign-controlled dictatorship in the United States. A Subversive Activities Control Board has been established to designate Communist "action" groups, "fronts," or Communist "infiltrated" organizations. Once identified, action and front groups must register with the Attorney General, listing their officers and members, financial records, and any printing equipment under their control. Publications of these organizations must be labeled as Communist propaganda. Infiltrated trade unions lose all rights under national labor laws. Individual members of any of these groups may not hold office in a labor union, obtain a passport, or work in any public office, and members of action groups are barred from defense plants. The law also strengthens espionage and sedition laws and immigration requirements and provides for deportation of Communist aliens. Another provision establishes procedures for detention of suspected saboteurs in the event of an emergency.

• *Significance:* The Act was passed over the veto of President Truman. Many serious constitutional questions are raised by its provisions and, to date, the Supreme Court has upheld only the registration requirement (*Communist Party v. Subversive Activities Control Board,* 367 U.S. 1 [1961]). A good deal of litigation undoubtedly will take place before the full impact of the Act can be known.

Smith Act of 1940.   The first peacetime sedition law, officially known as the Alien Registration Act, since the Alien and Sedition Laws of 1798. The provision requiring the annual registration of aliens is merely one part of the law which, as a whole, is aimed at organizations and activities which advocate violent overthrow of government. Its major provisions make it unlawful to teach, advocate, or distribute information advocating the forcible overthrow of government or to knowingly organize or join an organization which so advocates. Other provisions outlaw activities designed to create disloyalty in the armed forces or to encourage participation in a violent revolution or the assassination of public officials.

• *Significance:* The Smith Act is the first law passed in peacetime since 1798 which outlaws particular forms of speech and writing. It is also the first act to make it a crime to be a member of an organization which, some critics claim, imputes guilt by association. The advocacy and membership provisions of this Act have been upheld by the Supreme Court (*Dennis v. United States,* 341 U.S. 494 [1951]; *Scales v. United States,* 367 U.S. 203 [1961]). Though the Act does not mention the Communist party by name, and was intended, in part, to apply to Nazi and fascist groups, it has been successfully applied against the Communist party leadership.

Parties, Politics, Pressure
Groups, and Elections

Absentee Voting.   Provisions of state laws or constitutions which enable qualified voters to cast their ballots in an election without going to the polls on election day. If a person expects to be unavoidably absent from his voting precinct on election day, he obtains a ballot within a specified period preceding the election, marks it, has it notarized, and returns it to the proper official.
• *Significance:* All states except New Mexico have provisions for absentee voting. Several states limit the practice to members of the armed forces. Congress has sought to encourage uniformity in state provisions for servicemen and for civilians employed abroad. Absentee voters can sometimes affect the outcome of an election, as occurred in 1960 when a late count of absentee ballots in California swung that state's electoral votes from John F. Kennedy to Richard M. Nixon.

Absolute Majority.   Any number over 50 percent of the total votes cast by *all* the voters participating in a given election. A *simple* majority, in contrast, is any number over 50 percent of the votes cast on any single issue in an election, even though many voters who go to the polls may not vote on the specific issue.
• *Significance:* No federal and only a few state and local elections are conducted with a requirement of an absolute majority. Some states require an absolute majority of all voters participating in any phase of the election to vote "yes" on a question of calling a constitutional convention or on ratifying an amendment to a state constitution. Hence, the failure to vote on the issue is the equivalent of a "no" vote.

At Large.   The election of members of a legislative body by the voters of an entire governmental unit rather than from subdivisions thereof. Congressmen at large are elected by the whole electorate of the state when a state legislature fails to redistrict after a decennial census. United States Senators and Electoral College Electors are elected at large in each state. On the local level, members of city commissions are, in some cases, elected at large by the voters of the entire city rather than from wards, especially under the commission and city manager forms.

• *Significance:* Election of representatives at large tends to foster a broader state-wide or city-wide approach to issues rather than the more restrictive "mirroring" of local interests by those chosen from districts or wards. The case against election at large is that representatives so chosen will not respond to the wishes or interests of the voters because of the size, population, and variety of views of the larger electorate. Proponents of election at large claim that it reduces parochialism in politics and makes fuller use of available political talent by allowing several good candidates living in the same area to run for election simultaneously, which would not be possible under the district system.

Australian Ballot.   A secret ballot prepared by government officials at public expense.

• *Significance:* For over a century many American voters were denied a secret ballot. Oral voting and differently colored ballots, prepared by the parties, were used. Extreme pressures could be exerted upon voters who were forced to cast their ballot publicly. Threats of retaliation frequently coerced voters into voting against their choice of candidates. Since 1888, all states have used the Australian ballot. Voting machines are mechanical adaptations of the Australian ballot.

Availability.   The qualifications of a potential candidate which are analyzed by his party in making its selection of a nominee. A candidate whom the party believes has the qualities and background to make him a winner is "available."

• *Significance:* The question of availability is especially important in the selection of presidential nominees. Millions of members of each party meet the constitutional and legal requirements for the presidency, but few have the qualifications needed to win. Availability depends on whether the potential nominee has ever alienated a large economic, ethnic, or religious voting group, whether he comes from a key state or strategic section, whether he has demonstrated real vote-getting ability, whether he is too closely identified with one wing or faction in the party, whether he is a good family man—in short, whether his background and his personal and political qualities all appear to add up to victory for the party in the presidential election.

Border States.   Those states—Delaware, Kentucky, Maryland, Missouri, and Virginia—which served as a dividing barrier in 1860 between the Deep South and the North. Although all were slave states, only Virginia seceded. The western part of the state remained loyal to the Union and broke away to become the new state of West Virginia. In recent years, the term has also included the states of West Virginia, Tennessee, and Oklahoma, while omitting Virginia.

• *Significance:* The Border States traditionally have voted Democratic but in recent congressional and presidential elections, the Republican party has made strong inroads into them. Dwight D. Eisenhower carried Delaware, Maryland, Tennessee, Oklahoma, and Missouri in 1952 and won all Border States except Missouri in 1956. In 1960, Richard Nixon carried Kentucky, Tennessee, and Oklahoma. In school desegregation, all of the Border States have integrated the races in some of their public schools. This stands in contrast to the states of the Deep South where there has been little or no compliance with the Supreme Court's desegregation decision.

Boss.   An autocratic political leader who dominates a highly disciplined state or local party organization which tends to monopolize power in its area. Political bosses retain power through patronage disposition, control over nominations, use of "honest" and dishonest graft, and through manipulation of voting and elections. Sometimes the term is used merely to try to discredit the successful leaders of an opposing party.
• *Significance:* American politics has proved to be a fertile ground for the growth of political machines and party bosses. This stems largely from the decentralization of power in the party system and the apathy of large numbers of voters. Some of the leading party bosses in recent years have been Edward J. Flynn of New York's Bronx County, Edward "Boss" Crump of Memphis, Ed Kelly of Chicago, Frank Hague of Jersey City, and Carmine DeSapio of the Tammany Hall machine in New York City. Political bosses have been equally successful in the countryside and in the big cities. The day of the political boss has been waning for some years and only a few who could be truly called bosses in the old tradition remain. Causes for the demise of "bossism" include the direct primary, an educated electorate, and public welfare programs.

Canvassing Boards.   Official groups, usually bipartisan, which tabulate the election returns and certify the election of the winners. When the polls close on election day, the returns from each precinct are forwarded to city and county canvassing boards. These consolidate the returns and forward them to the state canvassing authority which, usually in a few days, certifies the election of the winners. The local group is the county board of supervisors or county board of election. The state canvassing board consists of several ex officio members of the state government, headed by the secretary of state. Each election winner receives a certificate of election from the county or state board.
• *Significance:* Because of the extensive coverage of election returns by newspapers, radio, and television, the results in most elections are known by the public before the canvassing boards certify them. However, in exceptionally close elections, the final outcome may turn on the official tabulation and certification. Disputed elections are commonly settled in the courts or through an official recount.

Caucus.   A closed meeting of party leaders to select party candidates. Party members in the Congress and in the state legislatures selected their respective party's candidates for national and state office during the early years of the Republic. Presidential candidates were chosen by party caucuses in the Congress. Locally, leading members of each party met behind closed doors

to select candidates for various local offices. Some local candidates are still
nominated by caucus.
• *Significance:* "King Caucus" flourished for several decades of early American
history. Because Andrew Jackson had been refused nomination for the presidency by the congressional Democratic caucus in 1824, he repudiated the
system when he won the office in 1828. By 1835, the legislative caucus as a
means of making nominations for public office had almost disappeared. On
both national and state levels the caucus lost ground to the convention method.
Reasons for the demise of the caucus included (1) its unrepresentative character; (2) violation of the separation of powers theory; (3) use of secret deals
and logrolling to manipulate the caucus; and (4) widespread use of the "snap
caucus," by which small cliques control the nominating process by not notifying all eligible participants of a caucus meeting.

Challenge.   An allegation by a poll watcher that a potential voter is un-
qualified or that a vote is invalid. Most states provide for a bipartisan group of
election judges in each precinct to help decide disputes. An inspector is usually
in charge of each precinct and makes the final decision. In some closed-primary
states, a voter's party affiliation may be challenged. If he cannot prove it to
the satisfaction of that party's poll watcher, he can be deprived of his vote in
the primary.
• *Significance:* Bipartisan selection of poll watchers and their right to challenge
voters and votes are designed to prevent fraud in elections. This builds confidence, not always warranted, in the incorruptibility of the ballot.

Closed Primary.   The selection of a party's candidates in an election limited
to avowed party members. Voters must declare their party affiliation either
when they register or at the primary election.
• *Significance:* The closed-primary system is designed to stop the "crossover"
of registered voters into the other party's primary for the purpose of trying to
nominate its weakest candidates. Such "raiding" is common in open-primary
states. Party organizations tend to favor the closed primary because it promotes
party regularity and responsibility. Many voters oppose it because it limits
their freedom of action to select anew at each primary election the party in
which they wish to choose nominees. Independent voters are altogether excluded from participating in the nominating process in closed-primary states.
Thirty-seven states use the closed primary.

Coalition.   This term is used to describe the fusion of various political
elements into a major American party. In multiparty countries the fusion involves a coalition of a number of individual parties into a working majority.
In the United States, both major parties combine factions of liberals, moderates,
and conservatives.
• *Significance:* Because of the coalition character of American major parties,
black and white extremes of position that might split the American people
into two hostile groups are avoided. Conversely, the American system has been
criticized on the ground that, because both parties are so similar in their
make-up, satisfactory alternatives are not presented to the voters.

Committee on Political Education (COPE).   The political action organization of the AFL-CIO, the national federation of trade unions. COPE combines the political tactics developed over the years by the CIO Political Action Committee (PAC) and the AFL League for Political Education. These were the political action organizations of the two labor federations prior to their merger into the new AFL-CIO in 1955. Funds for COPE's activities are raised through voluntary contributions of trade union members.
• *Significance:* The Taft-Hartley Act of 1947 forbids the use of union dues for partisan political activity. This has resulted in the establishment of political "education" committees financed through voluntary contributions. COPE has been active in state and national campaigns since 1956. It educates workers and the general public on candidates and on issues of interest to labor. Its activities have had a considerable effect on elections, especially in the industrial states. Opponents have criticized COPE on the grounds that, allegedly, members are pressured into making contributions and that its education consists, in reality, of partisan political propaganda.

Congressional Campaign Committees.   Two groups consisting, respectively, of Republican and Democratic members of the House of Representatives who have been selected by fellow party members in the House to organize and to help finance their campaigns. Senatorial campaign committees are selected by party members in the upper chamber. The Republican Congressional Campaign Committee consists of one congressman from each state having Republican representation in the House. Democrats use this formula also, but supplement it with private citizens, selected by the committee chairman, from those states not having Democratic representation in the House.
• *Significance:* In a presidential election year, each committee integrates its efforts with those of its respective national committee. In off-year contests, they operate more independently. Maintaining permanent staffs, the committees raise funds, furnish speakers, distribute literature, and generally take charge of congressional campaigns. Their efforts are usually integrated with those of state and local committees of their parties.

Conventions.   A meeting of party delegates at the national, state, or local levels to decide upon party policy and strategy and to nominate candidates for elective office. Each party holds a national convention every four years to nominate its presidential candidate and adopt a platform. In most states, both parties hold county and state conventions annually. Typically, delegates to the county conventions are selected by party voters in precinct elections, delegates to state conventions are selected by county conventions, and delegates to national conventions are selected by state conventions, or, in approximately one third of the states, by voters in presidential primaries.
• *Significance:* Although state and local conventions have lost most of their nominating power, they continue to serve as the basic policy makers of the American political parties. Decisions made at national, state, and local conventions give direction to party committees and chairmen in the periods between conventions. On the state and local scene, nominating for most elective offices has been taken from conventions and placed under direct primary

systems. This has been the result, partly, of increasing democratization of elections and, partly, of convention malpractices which allowed small cliques to dominate them through manipulation. An advantage of the convention system in making policy and deciding nominations is that it tends to force conflicting wings of the party to work out compromises which help hold tenuous intraparty coalitions together.

Corrupt Practices Acts.   State and federal laws which seek to limit and regulate the size and sources of contributions and expenditures in political campaigns. Concerning contributions, federal limitations specify (1) no individual can give more than $5,000 each year to any national committee; (2) corporations and labor unions cannot contribute to national committees; (3) labor union members and corporation officials can set up organizations for voluntary contributions by their members, stockholders, or customers; (4) national committees may not accept more than $3 million in any one year. Federal regulations of expenditures include (1) each national committee can spend up to $3 million annually; (2) in the Congress, campaign expenditures may not exceed in any instance $25,000 for senatorial candidates and $5,000 for House candidates. Contributions to and expenditures by state and local political groups are regulated by state laws, which vary considerably.

• *Significance:* Most corrupt practices legislation now in existence has proved to be ineffective in achieving its purposes. Various loopholes exist by which individual and group donors and party committees can circumvent restrictions. Means of avoiding regulations include the subdividing of contributions among family members, creation of additional "committees," establishment of business and labor political "education" groups, and a general decentralization of expenditures. The underlying purpose of corrupt practices legislation, to free public officials from being beholden to heavy contributors while serving in office, has not been satisfactorily achieved. State laws are largely concerned with publicizing contributors and amounts received and spent by candidates and committees. This type of legislation has been more successful than attempts to control, limit, and regulate.

Countervailing Theory of Pressure Politics.   The concept that in American politics competition among major business, labor, farm, racial, religious, and other interest groups tends to balance off each other's power and influence.

• *Significance:* The countervailing theory of pressure politics seeks to explain the failure of a single, dominant social group to control the direction of American politics and policies. From this competition of diverse interests, the public interest tends to emerge.

Credentials Committee.   An important committee used by both major parties in their national conventions to determine which delegates may participate. The credentials committee prepares a roll of all delegates entitled to be seated at the convention. Controversy over contested seats arises when rival groups within a state claim to be the official party organization. In such cases, the committee makes recommendations to the convention.

• *Significance:* Recommendations made by the credentials committee to the convention are usually approved informally without debate or roll call. However, the convention has on occasion rejected these recommendations in whole or in part. Decisions on seating of delegates from certain states, when two or more rival delegations appear at the convention, may be a decisive factor in the selection of the presidential nominee. As an example, in 1952 at the Republican Convention, rival delegations supporting General Dwight D. Eisenhower and Senator Robert A. Taft arrived from five southern states. The success of the Eisenhower supporters in getting their delegates seated was instrumental in securing the nomination for him.

Cross-Filing.   A direct primary election system in which a candidate may run on other party tickets as well as on his own. Under a system which permits cross-filing, for example, a candidate for the Congress might place his name on both Democratic and Republican primary ballots.
• *Significance:* In California, the only state which permits this, some candidates for state and national office have succeeded in winning nomination by both parties, thus assuring their election. A recent California law requires candidates to identify their party affiliation on the other party's ballot, which has reduced the possibility of a candidate winning both party nominations. Advocates of cross-filing defend it on the ground that it permits greater freedom of choice by voters in primary elections while still accomplishing the purpose of a primary. Opponents of the system decry its effects on party responsibility and point out that it tends to confuse the voters.

Cumulative Voting.   A method of voting in which the individual casts more than one vote in the simultaneous election of several officials, as a means of securing greater representation for minor parties. Each voter is allowed two or more votes, which he can cast for a single candidate or distribute among several. Candidates of minor parties can usually win seats because their supporters concentrate their additional votes for them whereas major party supporters tend to distribute their votes among several candidates. This system is used in electing members of the lower house of the Illinois legislature, with three representatives elected from each district.
• *Significance:* Cumulative voting is an attempt to provide some direct representation for minority groups. Proponents support it as more accurately representative (and, hence, more democratic) than the two-party system. Opponents point out that it has a tendency to foster a host of splinter parties with the result that, frequently, none is able to gain a majority.

Demagogue.   An unscrupulous politician who seeks to win and hold office through emotional appeals to mass prejudices and passions. Half-truths, outright lies, and various means of card-stacking may be used in either subtle or bold-faced attempts to dupe the voters. Typically, a demagogue may try to win support from one group by blaming another for its misfortunes. Another useful demagogic technique is to promise all things to all men.
• *Significance:* Demagogues may thrive in either a dictatorship or a democracy. In the latter, however, because of free speech and press guarantees and

frequent elections, the chances of unseating a demagogue are infinitely greater. Generally, the success of American demagogues has been rather short-lived.

Democratic Party.   One of the two major parties in the United States to-day. The Democratic party evolved out of the Democratic-Republican group which supported Thomas Jefferson. Andrew Jackson, regarded by Democrats as cofounder with Jefferson of their party, changed the name to Democratic party in keeping with his ultrademocratic philosophy. Further development of party principles occurred under the more recent leadership of Woodrow Wilson and Franklin D. Roosevelt. Today, the Democratic party finds its basic strength in a loose coalition of the agricultural South and the urban, industrial North. To achieve national victory, others need to be added to the coalition, such as the midwestern farming and western ranching and mining regions.
• *Significance:* Many studies show strong Democratic party preference by low-income groups, organized labor, and religious and racial minority groups. In recent years, the Democratic party has generally stood for freer trade, more extensive international commitments, a greater measure of governmental regulation of the economy, and for expanded civil rights guarantees. On the issue of states' rights, the party has reversed its early position and, in modern times, has consistently favored expanded national responsibilities. Polls indicate that approximately 60 percent of all registered voters in the United States are Democrats.

Democratic-Republican Party.   An early party led by Thomas Jefferson which evolved into the present-day Democratic party. The party was created in opposition to the Federalist party and its program, and was first referred to as the Anti-Federalist party, then the Jeffersonian Republican or Democratic-Republican party. Finally, under Andrew Jackson, it became the Democratic party.
• *Significance:* The Democratic-Republican party played an important role in developing the two-party system as we know it today, when it assumed the role of opposition to the Federalist party. It stood for strict interpretation of the Constitution, states' rights, free trade, and for protection of agrarian interests.

Direct Primary.   An intraparty election in which the voters select the candidates who will run on a party's ticket in the subsequent general election. Primaries are also used to choose convention delegates and party leaders. In a closed primary, the selection process is limited to avowed party adherents whereas, in an open primary, voters participate regardless of party affiliation or lack of it. Some state and local governments use nonpartisan primaries. Candidates get their names on a primary ballot, typically, through petitions signed by a required number of registered voters. Other means include caucus, pre-primary convention, and self-announcement.
• *Significance:* Since 1900, the direct primary has gradually superseded the convention as a nominating device. All states today use the direct primary system in one form or another. Advantages of the primary are that it permits a larger voice in party affairs to rank and file voters and enables the voters to get rid of an unpopular but strongly entrenched elected official or party leader.

Disadvantages include greater expense both for the candidate and for the taxpayer and, generally, a weakening of party organization and party responsibility.

Disfranchise. Taking away the privilege of voting. Persons may be disfranchised if they lose their citizenship, if they fail to reregister when required, or if convicted for certain crimes. Many people are disfranchised temporarily when they move, either within the state or from state to state, until they establish new residence. Voters may also be wholly or partially disfranchised indirectly as a result of dishonesty in ballot counts or through political manipulation, such as gerrymandering. In the South, fear and intimidation fostered by occasional acts of violence serve to keep eligible Negro voters from the polls. • *Significance:* Each election finds many Americans denied the privilege of voting despite their previous participation. Disfranchisement for loss of citizenship and conviction for crime are infrequent and probably justified. Other reasons are of doubtful validity. Suggestions for reducing voter disfranchisement would include (1) reduce residence requirements for most elections and eliminate them for presidential contests; (2) provide federal oversight of state redistricting to ensure substantial equality in voting power; (3) increase federal action to prevent disfranchisement because of color or race—the Civil Rights Acts of 1957 and 1960 are steps in this direction.

Electoral College. The presidential electors from each state who meet in their respective state capitals, following their popular election, and cast ballots for president and vice president. The process starts with the nomination of partisan slates of electors by party conventions, primaries, or committees in each state. The number of electors in each state is equal to its representation in both houses of the Congress. In the November presidential election, the slate of electors receiving a plurality of popular votes is elected. The electors have pledged themselves to vote for their party's candidates for president and vice president, although the Constitution still permits them to use discretion. After casting electoral ballots in their respective state capitals in December, the ballots are forwarded to Washington, D.C., counted, and certified before a joint session of the Congress early in January. The candidates who receive a majority of the electoral votes are certified as president-elect and vice president-elect. If none receives a majority of the electoral vote, the election of the president is thrown into the House of Representatives where each state has one vote, and that of the vice president into the Senate where each senator has one vote. Normally, the people of the United States know who has been elected following the popular election in November, and the rest of the process is largely a formality. The rise of political parties which nominate pledged electors has distorted the original intention of the Founding Fathers. They had intended that the electors should be chosen as each state would determine and that they would exercise complete discretion in the selection of the President. • *Significance:* The Electoral College system has come under severe criticism at times in American history. Several recurring grounds for criticism have been (1) sometimes candidates with a minority of the popular vote have won election; (2) the machinery has become an anachronism, since the electors no longer actually perform the selecting function envisioned by the Founding Fathers; (3) the unit system under which all of a state's electoral votes go to that party which polls a state-wide plurality is unfair to other candidates and their supporters; and (4) the complicated nature of the entire system tends to confuse voters and complicate the selection process. Proposals for reform include (1) discarding the Electoral College machinery and placing the election on a direct popular vote on the basis of a nationwide constituency; (2) eliminating the electors but retaining a state basis for voting, with a plurality needed in a majority of states to win; (3) eliminating the electors but retaining an electoral vote divided in each state at approximately the same ratio as the popular vote (Lodge-Gossett proposal).

Favorite Son.   A state political leader whose name is placed in nomination for the presidency at a national nominating convention by members of his state's delegation. Usually his nomination is merely a means of honoring him. • *Significance:* A "favorite son" nominee is seldom given serious consideration by the convention. Delegation members generally vote for their favorite son on the first ballot, especially if a real contest between leading candidates is shaping up. In this way, the delegation can remain noncommital until after the first ballot gives some indication of the relative strength of leading candidates. At this point, the favorite son will probably withdraw his own nomination and throw his delegation's votes to one of the front runners. If the recipient of these votes should go on to win the presidency, the favorite son will be in a good bargaining position to obtain a high-level, patronage appointment.

Federalist Party.   The first American political party which evolved during the later phases of George Washington's presidency. Its leaders, Alexander Hamilton and John Adams, gained the support of the financial, industrial, and commercial interests for the new party. Many of its members had strongly supported the adoption of the new Constitution and the creation of the federal Union. • *Significance:* The Federalist party developed national financial and economic programs. These included a protective tariff, an excise tax, the creation of a National Bank, and the assumption of state debts by the national government. To justify the expansion of national powers, the Federalists insisted on a loose interpretation of the Constitution. As a reaction to these policies, Thomas Jefferson and James Madison rallied the small farmers and artisans and the planters of the South into a coalition of Anti-Federalists. In this manner the two-party political system was given birth in the United States. After Jefferson's defeat of the Federalists in the election of 1800, the party began to decline in popularity. In 1816, it disappeared completely from the American scene. Its demise resulted from quarrels among its leaders, and discredit both from its attempt to silence the opposition through the Alien and Sedition Acts and its failure to support the War of 1812. In 1832, the Whig party evolved as a successor to the Federalists, and, in 1860, the Republican party superseded the Whigs.

Fifteenth Amendment.   An amendment to the Constitution, enacted after the Civil War, which forbids a state to deny a person the right to vote because of race, color, or previous condition of servitude.

• *Significance:* Although the 15th Amendment does not give anyone the right to vote, it does prohibit any discrimination because of race or color. Not until recent years has the Negro made significant advances in realizing the goals established by the Amendment. The Civil Rights Acts of 1957 and 1960 were passed by the Congress to aid the Negro in overcoming the various devices used by some southern states to frustrate the purposes of the Amendment.

Filing.   The legal act of declaring candidacy for a public elective office. Most states provide that aspirants first circulate candidacy petitions to be signed by a stipulated number of registered voters. The aspirant presents the petitions, and files for candidacy with the appropriate official (secretary of state, county clerk, or city clerk). The candidate may then run against other candidates of his party for the office in a direct primary election to determine which of them will become the party's standard-bearer in the general election. In some states, persons seeking candidacy for local office may file by simply declaring their intentions before an official. In other states, a candidate may file by depositing a sum of money in lieu of petitions, which may be refunded if the candidate polls enough votes.

• *Significance:* Filing is a means by which running for office can be limited to "serious" candidates. A balance must be struck: if the requirements are too difficult, competent, public-spirited citizens may be discouraged from seeking candidacy; if too lenient, a horde of candidates may confuse the voters. In Britain, this problem is met by requiring all candidates to deposit a modest filing fee which is forfeited if the candidate fails to secure a minimum number of votes.

General Election.   A state-wide election, usually held shortly after a primary election, to fill state and national offices in which the incumbents' terms are expiring. States hold national presidential elections every four years, in November, and national congressional elections in the even-numbered years. Typically, states hold state and county general elections every November in the even-numbered years, although some states elect some important state officials and judges in general elections held in odd-numbered years, frequently in the spring.

• *Significance:* Voters make their final choice in selecting their public officials in the general election. It is to be distinguished from a primary election which is a nominating process, and from a special election which is called at irregular intervals.

Grandfather Clause.   A device used in several southern states to restore the vote to whites who had been disfranchised by property and literacy qualifications aimed at barring Negroes from voting. The "grandfather clause," which was adopted as a constitutional amendment in as many as seven states, provided that a person disfranchised for certain reasons could become a permanently registered voter if either he or a lineal ancestor (father, grandfather) had been an eligible voter on January 1, 1867, two months before the Congress had passed legislation designed to enfranchise the Negro.

• *Significance:* The grandfather clause was not used to bar Negroes from voting—this had already been accomplished—but rather was intended to restore the ballot to poor, illiterate whites. In 1915, the Supreme Court declared the grandfather clause to be discriminatory, in violation of the 15th Amendment (*Guinn v. United States,* 238 U.S. 347). However, most such clauses had already expired and had served their purpose of getting the names of the disfranchised whites on the permanent registration lists.

Hare Plan. A system of proportional representation, occasionally used in the United States, which is based on a single, transferable vote. Candidates vie in open competition for a number of elective offices. A quota is established and all candidates obtaining sufficient votes to meet it are declared elected. Surplus votes of winning candidates and the votes of the eliminated candidates are then distributed according to the second choices expressed by the voters on their ballots. Votes are transferred in this manner until sufficient candidates have been declared elected to fill all elective seats.

• *Significance:* The Hare Plan seeks to record the voters' wishes more accurately than can be achieved through the common American elective system of single-member districts, in which all votes not cast for the winning candidate are discarded. Economic and social minority interest groups are more likely to gain representation under it, giving a broader consensus to the government. The obvious weakness of the Hare Plan, and a characteristic shortcoming of all proportional representation systems, is the difficulty of building a majority in the government which can make decisions. Diverse interest groups often have conflicting views on matters of public policy, and frequently these cannot be reconciled. Government by consensus tends to replace government by majority rule. Only a dozen or so municipalities have adopted the Hare Plan in the United States, many of these dropping it after a short trial period.

Independent. A voter who disregards party affiliation of candidates running for elective office and casts his ballot for the best qualified or on the basis of issues. Most independents are not party members, but a few retain membership in a party, enabling them to vote in primaries while exercising their own best judgment in general elections.

• *Significance:* Although independents are often criticized for not contributing actively through political parties to the democratic process, they are wooed by both major parties. Independent votes may be decisive in determining the outcome of many elections, including presidential contests. A large number of independent voters encourages political parties to focus on crucial issues in the campaigns and to act responsibly when elected. Some political analysts question whether there is such a thing as an independent, holding the view that all voters have a predisposition toward one party or the other.

Literacy Test. A suffrage qualification used in less than one third of the states to determine fitness for voting through literacy, educational, or "understanding" tests. Some southern states require an oral examination of prospective voters who must demonstrate ability to understand and interpret passages from the national or their state constitution.

• *Significance:* Literacy tests are used to bar Negroes from voting in six southern states and to exclude Orientals in several western states. They are an effective means of practicing discrimination because examining officials have great discretion, especially when the tests are administered orally. In some southern states, for example, Negro college graduates have been disqualified because they failed to interpret constitutional passages to the satisfaction of a white board of examiners. New York's system is generally regarded as the best in the nation. It consists of a reading and writing test administered through the state educational department to all persons who have not completed sixth-grade school work. Some observers regard a nondiscriminatory, fairly administered literacy test as a useful qualification for voting, in view of the complexity of issues involved in contemporary elections.

Lobbyist.   A person, usually acting as an agent for a pressure group, who seeks to bring about the passage or defeat of legislative bills or to influence their contents. Lobbyists, often called the "Third House" of the legislature, are experts who testify before committees and present important facts on legislative proposals to support their clients' interests. Several states and the national government require the registration of lobbyists and the disclosure of information concerning their employers, their salaries, and the amounts spent to influence legislation. Lobbyists are also active in trying to influence decisions made by executive officials and administrators.

• *Significance:* Lobbyists are useful in the legislative process because they furnish important factual data to legislators and because they provide effective representation for organized groups. They are criticized, on the other hand, because they use selected facts, often distorted, to bolster their cases and are more concerned with particular interests than with the general interest. Except for laws prohibiting bribery and similar criminal offenses, governmental action toward lobbyists has not sought to restrict their activities but to publicize them. Attempts by government to restrict lobbyists and lobbying unduly might be regarded by the courts as an infringement of the First Amendment freedom to petition the government.

Long Ballot.   The typical state and local ballot, ofttimes referred to as the "bedsheet ballot" or "jungle ballot," which has a large number of offices to be filled, candidates to be selected, and issues to be decided.

• *Significance:* The long ballot was created during the era of Jacksonian Democracy on the assumption that the way to expand democracy is to increase the number of elective officials and the role of the participating citizen. Today, political scientists refute this assumption by emphasizing that a smaller number of elective officials means that the voter can more likely become acquainted with the candidates, their qualifications, and the issues of the campaign. The long ballot has also frequently enabled political machines to retain power because of voter apathy and lack of knowledge sufficient to cope with the magnitude of the citizen's job under this system. The short ballot movement, begun around the turn of the century, has had some small success in reducing the length of the ballot in a few states, but the basic problem remains.

Mass Media.   The technical means by which communications can be maintained with millions of people, exemplified by television, radio, newspapers, motion pictures, magazines, and periodicals.
• *Significance:* The mass media of communications have become extremely important to government as a means of influencing and educating millions of citizens. Objectives include the winning of elections, the marshaling of support for or opposition to programs, and the education of the public on major issues. Political scientists, aware of the increasing significance of the mass media in decision making, and taking note of its abuse in totalitarian states, have expressed concern for its effect on the democratic process. The trend in the United States is toward concentration of ownership of mass media in fewer hands. The problem of seeking corrections for this situation is recognized as a difficult one, replete with serious issues including those concerning constitutional rights.

Minor Party.   A party movement, often based on a single idea or principle, which usually has little influence on elections because its support is either localized or widely scattered. Some observers distinguish it from a third party, a new party based on a protest movement which often does influence the outcome of elections.
• *Significance:* Minor parties have played a significant role in American political life in initiating and successfully publicizing political, economic, and social reforms over a period of years. When a minor party gains a substantial number of adherents to its principle, a major party often incorporates this principle into its own platform so as to gain voter support. The Prohibition party, for example, convinced large numbers of people of the wisdom of prohibition; the Republican party thereupon included a prohibition plank in its platform and, after winning at the polls, instituted prohibition. Minor parties found on the ballot in many states today include the Prohibition, Socialist Labor, and Socialist Workers. Several right-wing conservative and tax reform parties have also appeared on the political scene in recent years.

Multiple Party System.   A government based on an electoral system of proportional representation resulting in the need for a coalition of several parties to form a majority to run the government. Multiple party systems are typical of continental European democracies. The system can be distinguished from the Anglo-American two-party system, not by the existence of numerous parties, but rather in the sense that in a multiple party system many parties seriously compete for, and actually win, seats in the legislature.
• *Significance:* Multiple party systems tend to provide a broader, more diverse representation of the electorate. This strength is, at the same time, a major weakness. Coalition governments, by their very nature, are unstable governments which tend to disintegrate when the parties comprising the coalition have a falling out over a major issue. France, as an example, had 21 coalition governments during the period of the Fourth Republic, from 1946 to 1958.

The American people have shunned a multiple party approach to politics by refusing to give substantial support to any but the two major parties. Moreover, the single-member district system, as distinguished from proportional representation, tends to perpetuate the two-party system.

National Chairman. The chairman of a political party's national committee who is generally chosen by his party's presidential candidate.
• *Significance:* The major responsibility of a national chairman is the management of the national election campaign. Working through the national committee, the chairman may exercise a considerable influence over state and local party organizations, although no formal control mechanism exists. His specific responsibilities include establishing national party headquarters, directing party affairs during and between campaigns, and raising and distributing campaign funds. An adroit and skillful national chairman can be a great asset to a presidential nominee and his party.

National Committee. A standing committee of a national political party established to direct and co-ordinate party activities during the four-year periods between national party conventions. The Democratic National Committee includes two members, a man and a woman, from each state, from the District of Columbia, and from several territories; the Republican National Committee uses the same formula but adds state chairmen from all states which elected Republican governors or senators in the preceding election. National committeemen and committeewomen are chosen every four years by the various delegations to the national convention. Each committee ratifies the presidential nominee's selection of a national chairman who acts as spokesman for his party.
• *Significance:* Although the national committee appears to top the hierarchical permanent structure of each party, its power and influence are not great. The real locus of power in both party organizations remains at the local and state levels. Each national committee is concerned mainly with the presidential election and points most of its activities toward planning the next campaign. Other important functions include planning the national convention, securing financial contributions, and publicizing the party.

National Convention. A quadrennial meeting held by each major party to select presidential and vice presidential candidates, write a platform, choose a national committee, and conduct party business. Presidential candidates have been nominated by the convention method in every election since 1832. Delegates are apportioned on the basis of state representation with bonuses for states showing voting majorities for the party in preceding elections. Delegates are selected by party conventions or committees in approximately two thirds of the states and by presidential primaries in one third of the states. Both parties also accredit delegates from the District of Columbia, Puerto Rico, and the Virgin Islands. The nomination of, and voting on, candidates is conducted by a call of the states in alphabetical order. Democratic party conventions permit state delegations to use the unit rule. Both conventions nominate their candidates by an absolute majority vote.

• *Significance:* Although national party conventions are typified by excitement, both artificial and natural, their responsibilities are extremely important. Most convention efforts and oratory are pointed toward the imminent fall campaign. Despite extensive television coverage in recent years, the national convention remains a puzzling phenomenon for most Americans. Much criticism has been directed at it for its clownish atmosphere, the use of pressure tactics and secret bargains, and the lack of popular participation in the candidate-selection process. Yet conventions seldom ignore public opinion and have chosen many distinguished candidates. Today, conventions remain wholly free from federal regulation.

Nepotism.   Granting of political favors to relatives.
• *Significance:* Nepotism has been carried on by various kinds of public officials on all levels of government throughout American history. It may contribute to efficiency in government if the official's relatives are qualified and cooperative, but it is generally frowned upon by the voting public.

Nineteenth Amendment.   An amendment to the Constitution, adopted on August 26, 1920, which prohibits any state from denying the right to vote to any citizen because of sex. Wyoming took the initiative, in 1869, in granting suffrage to women, but only a few states followed this lead. Suffragette agitation during the early part of the twentieth century culminated in the Amendment, which was adopted in time for women to participate in the presidential election of 1920.
• *Significance:* Like the 15th Amendment, the 19th does not grant the right to vote to anyone, but it does restrict the states from discriminating on the basis of sex. Since 1920, there have been no attempts to interfere with the voting rights of women. Some observers believe that the Amendment has had no appreciable effect on elections since "women vote the way their husbands tell them to," but some evidence exists to contradict this thesis. Because women voters considerably outnumber eligible male voters today, campaigns have acquired more of a feminine touch, and candidate qualifications now include that of "sex appeal."

Nomination.   The official designation of an individual as a candidate for public office. Methods for selecting such candidates in the United States have included the rank and file party caucus, legislative and congressional caucuses, the mixed caucus (legislators and party representatives), the party convention, the primary, and petition. Nomination also signifies the first step in the appointment of an executive or judicial official.
• *Significance:* Today, the direct primary is the most widely used nominating scheme, being mandatory or optional in all 50 states. The convention system, discredited and largely replaced by the direct primary by 1910, is once again gaining acceptance on the state and local levels. Some disillusionment with the primary system exists, and the convention method is credited with giving greater emphasis to party responsibility and selection of able candidates. The selection of the candidates for the presidency remains in the hands of each party's quadrennial convention.

Nonpartisan Election.   An election in which candidates have no party designations and political parties are prohibited from running candidates or seeking to influence the outcome. Nonpartisan elections are typically used to elect state and local judges and municipal officials. They are often preceded by nonpartisan primaries in which the number of candidates for each office is reduced to two.

• *Significance:* A progressive movement early in the twentieth century proposed to eliminate party corruption by eliminating political parties and partisan elections. Many nonpartisan electoral reforms were introduced, especially on the local levels. Most nonpartisan systems, however, have not produced the anticipated results. Political parties have been weakened by severance from their grass roots. At the local level, however, nonpartisan elections have the major advantage of reducing the impact of irrelevant national partisan issues.

Office Block Ballot.   A type of ballot in which the candidates for elective office are grouped together under the title of each office. The "office block" or "office group" is in contradistinction to the other common type of ballot, the "party column," or "party line," in which all candidates of a particular party are arranged in one column.

• *Significance:* The office block is now used, in some form, in 20 states. Politicians dislike it because it places more emphasis on the office than on the party and it tends to discourage "straight ticket" voting. Studies have shown that it definitely encourages voters to "split their ticket" in general elections, compared with voter performance on party column ballots.

Open Primary.   A direct primary voting system which permits the voter to choose the party primary in which he wishes to vote without disclosing his party affiliation or allegiance, if any. In an open primary, the voter makes his choice in the privacy of the voting booth. However, he is still limited to casting votes for candidates of only one party.

• *Significance:* Today 11 states use the open primary system. Unlike the closed primary, it permits independents to vote in primaries and does not require public disclosure of party affiliation, regarded distastefully by many voters. The open primary is criticized because it reduces party responsibility and permits "raiding" by voters of one party who cross over and seek to nominate the weaker candidates of the opposing party. Studies have indicated, however, that little "raiding" actually occurs in open primary states.

Party Column Ballot.   A form of ballot in which the candidates for various offices are arranged in one column under their respective party names and symbols. The "party column" or "party line" is in contradistinction to the other common type of ballot, the "office block" or "office group," in which candidates are grouped under each elective office.

• *Significance:* The party column ballot permits the voting for all of a party's candidates by marking a single "X" or by pulling a single lever. Some variation of this kind of ballot is used in 30 states today. Politicians generally prefer the party column type of ballot because it simplifies and encourages "straight ticket" voting. This is particularly true of a party which has an exceptionally strong presidential or gubernatorial candidate to head the list of party candidates.

Patronage.   The power to make partisan appointments to office or to confer contracts, franchises, honors, or other special favors. Patronage powers are vested primarily in the President, in governors and other state elective officials, in mayors, and in various county officers. Through senatorial courtesy and similar practices, legislators on all levels of government also share in patronage disposition.
• *Significance:* An era of unrestricted patronage was ushered in on the national level, in 1829, by the Jackson Administration's spoils system. Presidential patronage reached a high water mark during Abraham Lincoln's first term (1861–1864), but began to lose ground progressively after the enactment of the Civil Service Act of 1883 (Pendleton Act). Patronage is often defended as an essential feature of the party system to provide inducements and rewards for party workers. It also enables a chief executive to surround himself with loyal subordinates who support his views and who will strive to help him redeem his campaign pledges. Antipatronage forces counter these arguments by pointing to the long, disreputable history of the spoils system. Intelligent and well-trained personnel, it is argued, can work effectively with administrations of either party. Today, the county is the major remaining stronghold of the patronage system in the United States.

Periodic Registration.   A system requiring the voter to register at the appropriate local official's office annually or at fixed intervals.
• *Significance:* Periodic registration is intended to help maintain the honesty and accuracy of elections by keeping lists of eligible voters up to date. It is more expensive to local government and more troublesome to voters than the permanent type of registration. Periodic registration is most useful in large cities where the mobility of population is high.

Permanent Registration.   A system in which the voter, once enrolled, remains on the eligible list until he dies, moves, or fails to vote in several consecutive elections.
• *Significance:* Forty-seven states now use some form of permanent registration, although in 15 of these states it does not have state-wide application. Permanent registration is more economical and less bothersome to voters, but it involves the problem of keeping voting lists up to date by enrolling new voters and deleting those who die, move, or are otherwise disqualified. Partisan or lackadaisical administration of these functions can, and often has, resulted in fraudulent voting.

Petition.   A method of placing a candidate's name on a primary or general election ballot by submitting a specified number, or percentage, of signatures of registered voters to an appropriate state or local official for certification. Petitions may also be used to commence the initiative and referendum procedures in several states.
• *Significance:* The petition requirement to get an aspirant's name placed on a primary ballot is intended to help restrict the election to serious candidates.

In general elections, the petition method provides a means for political independents to get their names on the ballot. Petitions frequently become matters of political controversy, involving charges of invalid signatures.

Pivotal States.   Those states with large electoral votes where the outcome is doubtful, and which are crucial in winning a presidential election.
• *Significance:* The major efforts in organization, spending, and candidate appearances are usually concentrated by each major party upon the seven most populous states which aggregate over 200 electoral votes—California (40), Illinois (26), Michigan (21), New York (43), Ohio (26), Pennsylvania (29), and Texas (25). In recent elections, all of these states were also given "doubtful" status, adding to the attention given them during the campaign by both parties and their candidates. The nomination of presidential and vice presidential candidates is most likely to be of popular leaders from pivotal states.

Platform.   A statement of principles and objectives espoused by a party or a candidate which is used during a campaign to win support from voters. Platforms are, typically, written at national, state, and county party conventions by platform committees and adopted by the conventions.
• *Significance:* American party platforms consist, for the most part, of generalities and platitudes. They extol the vast accomplishments of their party while indicting the opposition party for its failures. In areas where the party stands united, however, the language will be precise and the commitment clear. Party platforms are variously supplemented and modified by candidates and party leaders, but few consider themselves bound by platform commitments when elected.

Plurality.   The winning of an election by a candidate who receives more votes than any other candidate when none has received a majority of the total vote.
• *Significance:* Most American electoral laws for national, state, and local elections provide for winning by a plurality vote. Whenever there are more than two strong candidates running for an office, the winner usually secures a plurality rather than a majority vote. An exception is found in the runoff primary system used in several southern states whereby, if no candidate receives a majority vote, a second, runoff election is held between the two highest vote getters.

Political Machine.   A well-entrenched party organization headed by a boss or small group of autocratic leaders. Political machines usually operate at the city or county level and occasionally on a state-wide basis. They often use ruthlessly efficient methods in maintaining themselves in power through such techniques as bribery, patronage, "honest graft," control over nominations, and the rigging of elections.
• *Significance:* Political machines have flourished throughout American history, although their number and effectiveness have been reduced in recent years. The direct primary was instituted in the early twentieth century largely as a reform to clean up politics by wresting power from political machines, but new techniques were developed by the bosses to control primaries. A high level of

interest, participation, and civic spirit in an aroused community is the best answer to machine politics, but reform movements which incorporate these attributes are often short-lived in their vigor and interest, resulting in a return to power of the machine.

Poll.   An attempt to uncover public opinion or to forecast a future election. Public-opinion polling has developed from the early newspaper straw vote poll of its subscribers to the personal interview technique, based on "scientific" quota sampling of the voting population, developed during the 1930's. New polling methods in use today involve probability sampling in which representative precincts are used as barometers to indicate prevailing opinions. Poll results are checked against the actual voting records of the precincts.
• *Significance:* The best-known polls today include those conducted by Dr. George Gallup, Elmo Roper, A. M. Crossley, and the Princeton Research Service. Most polling interest is directed to predictions of presidential elections, a field in which pollsters have often accurately predicted voting behavior. In the 1948 presidential election, however, all of the polling groups failed to predict the Truman victory, resulting in considerable public skepticism of polling techniques and suspicion of pollsters' objectives. New techniques developed since 1948 have resulted in much greater predictive accuracy. Polls have also become increasingly significant as a means of keeping elective officials aware of public opinion on important issues, and in the selection of presidential nominees by the major parties. Supporters of polling regard it as a major democratic advance, whereas opponents fear the rigging of polls to influence elections and the restrictions polls may place on policy makers.

Poll Tax.   A special head tax which must be paid as a qualification for voting in five southern states—Alabama, Arkansas, Mississippi, Texas, and Virginia. Several states since 1920 have repealed their poll tax laws or have made numerous exceptions to the requirement.
• *Significance:* The poll tax requirement in southern states has reduced voting participation of both whites and Negroes. The tax works a greater hardship upon Negroes because of their lower income status in these states and because unequal enforcement of the requirement is common. On the average, in national elections poll tax states have had turn outs of only one half the size of those in states not using the poll tax. In some states, the poll tax has also been used to maintain political machines in power by the payment of the tax by political leaders for many of their supporters. Attempts to eliminate poll taxes have taken the form of congressional bills, state legislative consideration, and unsuccessful litigation in federal and state courts to test their constitutionality.

Poll Watcher.   An individual appointed by a political party to be present at a polling place on election day to ensure the honesty of the election. In many states both major parties have poll watchers present at all polling places during partisan elections. In primary elections, poll watchers may also be appointed to prevent "raiding" by the opposition party.
• *Significance:* Poll watchers can play a significant role in maintaining the

honesty of elections, and, in this way, keep American voters from losing confidence in the democratic process. Poll watching is essential when a party challenges an entrenched political machine.

Precinct.   The basic unit in the United States in the election process and for party organization. Cities and counties are divided into precinct polling districts, each containing from 200 to 1000 voters and a polling place. In political organization, each party usually elects or appoints a precinct captain or committeeman who functions as a party leader within the precinct. Precinct leaders in the cities may represent their precincts in some form of party ward committee. The precinct also serves for the election or appointment of delegates to city or county party conventions.

• *Significance:* The precinct, being a small voting district, provides easy access to the polls for voters on election days. In politics, the precinct organization of the parties is the key to election success, especially in the metropolitan areas. An effective precinct leader is expected to work tirelessly the year around gaining party converts, getting voters registered, carrying on routine party business, and, most significant for his political future, turning out large majorities for his party on election days.

Presidential Primaries.   The election of delegates to a major party's national convention. About one third of the states hold some form of presidential primary in the weeks or months preceding the conventions; delegates are selected in the others by political party conventions or committees. Delegates selected in the primaries may or may not be "pledged" to vote for a presidential aspirant. In a few states, delegates are selected by the party organization but are bound to support the candidate designated by the voters in a so-called popularity contest.

• *Significance:* The presidential primary was pioneered by Wisconsin in 1905 and, although by 1916 both parties selected a majority of their national convention delegates by this method, it has since lost considerable ground. The main controversy surrounding the presidential primary concerns the "preferential" problem—i.e., should pledged or unpledged delegates be elected. Popular influence is reduced because pledged delegates are under no legal, and little moral, obligation to honor such pledges beyond the first ballot. For these reasons and because fewer than one half the delegates are selected from primary states, the presidential primary is not usually of great significance in choosing presidential nominees. In 1952, for example, Estes Kefauver won most of the delegates in the preferential primary states but was not selected for the presidential nomination by the Democratic convention; Adlai Stevenson, conversely, did not enter any presidential primaries and yet won the Democratic nomination. Presidential primaries, however, may be significant in eliminating those who lack vote-getting ability and in building the stature of those who demonstrate widespread popular support. Supporters of preference primaries argue that they prevent bosses from dominating conventions, build interest for the presidential election, and expand democratic influence. Those who oppose them point out that they are indecisive because voter opinion often is split in many directions, that they prolong the presidential election spectacle until voters get weary, and that only a convention free from voter pledges can reconcile party differences and unite the party behind a candidate. Although popular demands have increased in recent years for a nationwide preferential primary system, most professional politicians regard such a system as too costly in money, energy, and confusion.

Pressure Group.   An organized interest group in which members share common views and objectives and actively carry on programs to influence government officials and policies. Unlike political parties which seek to win control of and operate the government, pressure groups are mainly interested in determining public policies which directly or indirectly affect their members. They vary considerably in size, wealth, power, and objectives. Their methods, however, are quite similar and include lobbying, electioneering, and propagandizing to influence public opinion. They seek to influence decisions in the legislative, executive, and judicial branches.

• *Significance:* In America's pluralistic society, groups rather than individuals exercise most political influence. The most powerful interest groups are those which have emerged out of the three basic economic areas: agriculture, business, and labor. Other significant groupings which carry on pressure activities include professional societies, women's groups, patriotic and veterans' organizations, and religious and reform groups. Pressure group efforts are directed toward an identification of their particular interests with the general interest. The countervailing theory of pressure politics holds that the major interest groups, powerful as they may be, tend to counteract and balance out each others' power, which keeps any one from exercising a dominant influence. Congress in 1946 sought to regulate the lobbying activities of pressure groups through the Federal Regulation of Lobbying Act. The Act is largely concerned with publicizing lobbying groups and their activities, but its vague and confusing language and the absence of an enforcement agency have encouraged much noncompliance. The enactment of stiffer laws involving extensive regulation of pressure groups and their activities might involve serious questions of constitutionality concerning basic rights of assembly and petition.

Property Qualification.   A qualification for voting which requires the ownership of property, usually real estate.
• *Significance:* When the Constitution was adopted, voting was generally restricted to white, male, property owners. By 1850, most state property qualifications had been eliminated in the democratic reforms which characterized the era of Jacksonian Democracy. Today, six states retain some measure of property qualifications for voting on local bond issues or special assessments.

Proportional Representation (PR).   An electoral system which allocates seats in the legislative body to each party or group approximately equal to its voting strength. For example, a minority party which receives approximately 5 percent of the total vote in an election will win about 5 percent of the legislative seats. The most commonly used systems of PR are the list system based on voting by party, and the Hare system based on voting for individuals using the single transferable vote. *See* HARE PLAN, page 100.

• *Significance:* Several American cities, including New York, have experimented with the Hare system to provide some measure of minority representation. Most democratic countries use the continental European PR list system in preference to the Anglo-American, single-member district system. Proponents of PR point out that it provides representation for minority parties, reduces or eliminates machine politics, and is more democratic. Opponents argue that PR tends to proliferate parties, is too complicated for the average voter, and inevitably results in unstable coalition governments.

Public Opinion. An aggregate of individual views, attitudes, or beliefs shared by a significant portion of a community. No single public opinion in the sense of a general will exists; a number of publics hold various opinions on a host of issues. Public opinion can be made known in a democracy through elections, referendums, lobbying and pressure group activities, public opinion polls, and by elected representatives who "sound out" grass roots sentiment.
• *Significance:* A common problem of democracies involves the question of how responsive elected representatives should be to public opinion. Should they, for example, exercise their own best judgment in voting on issues, or rather should they follow the public opinion positions of their constituents? If the latter, there remain the difficult problems of how to determine the existence of public opinion and how to measure it. Although public opinion is a vague concept, it continues to play a major role in the decision-making processes of democratic government. In dictatorships, public opinion is recognized as a significant factor to be stimulated and shaped in the interests of the state.

Recall. A procedure enabling voters to remove an elected official from office before his term has expired. The required number of valid signatures on petitions results in the calling of a special election. If the majority of voters favor recall, the official is replaced by a successor who is either chosen on the recall ballot or in a subsequent election. Eleven states and numerous local units of government provide for the recall of elected officials.
• *Significance:* The recall enables the voters to hold their public officials continuously responsible. It is used infrequently, but the threat of recall is ever-present, and does not go unnoticed by elected officials. No provision is made for the recall of federal officials.

Referendum. An electoral device available in 22 states by which voters can "veto" a bill passed by a legislature. Bills passed by the legislature do not take effect during a specified period, usually 90 days, during which the bill may be suspended by obtaining the required number of voters' signatures on petitions, usually 5 percent of total votes cast in a preceding election. Emergency and financial bills are commonly excluded from referendum action. The bill is then voted upon by the electorate and, if disapproved by a majority, it is killed. The *constitutional referendum* gives voters an opportunity to approve or reject amendments or revisions of state constitutions. Many state and local governments may also use the *optional referendum* by which a legislative body may voluntarily refer a measure to the voters for an expression of popular sentiment.

• *Significance:* The referendum was adopted by many states in the early part of the twentieth century as an ultrademocratic weapon to check the objectionable enactments of the legislatures. It is not intended for regular use but rather remains a "gun behind the door" by which the people hold a continuing veto power. The referendum has been used infrequently in most states which provide for it. Supporters of the referendum regard it as a useful check on ill-considered or dangerous actions by the legislature and as an expansion of democracy. Those who oppose it regard it as an unnecessary check on representative government which weakens legislative responsibility, gives great power to organized groups, and provides for the making of decisions on complex or technical issues by the average citizen who is incapable of voting intelligently on them.

Republican Party.   A major American party which emerged in the 1850's as an antislavery party. The Republican party is the successor to two earlier major parties, the Federalist and the Whig. It became firmly established in American politics when its candidate, Abraham Lincoln, won the presidency in 1860 and successfully prosecuted the Civil War. The period from 1860 to 1932 was characterized largely by Republican dominance of the American political scene.
• *Significance:* The Republican party today draws heavy voter support from New England, the Northern Great Plains, the West, and the rural areas, small towns, and suburbs of the Middle West and Northern Atlantic. Studies have shown that Republican support among the voters increases as income and educational levels rise. Traditionally, manufacturing, business, financial, and farming interests have been influential in the party except in the Deep South. The Republican party has consistently advocated individual initiative, free enterprise, fiscal responsibility, and sound money policies. Its policies have generally been more conservative than Democratic party policies, although both include a coalition of conservatives, moderates, and liberals. Historically, Republicans have supported a high protective tariff and isolationism, although in recent years the party has supported lower tariffs and various American international commitments. It has generally opposed the ideas of the welfare state and big government although it has given some support to social welfare programs in recent years.

Residence.   A qualification for voting in the United States. State laws require that a person live in the state for a specified period of time, commonly one year, although several states in the North and East require only six months and a few in the South demand two years residence. Additional residence requirements include living within a county and a voting precinct, typically 90 days for the former and 30 days for the latter.
• *Significance:* Residence requirements are intended to prevent the importing of "floaters" to win elections and to ensure that the individual is acquainted with state and local problems and candidates before he becomes eligible. The qualification, however, serves to disfranchise temporarily large numbers of voters as the American people become increasingly mobile. Students of government have recommended the adoption of a constitutional amendment to

eliminate or reduce state residence requirements for voting in presidential elections.

Runoff Primary. A nominating system used in 11 southern states in which a second primary election is held between the top two candidates if the leading candidate in the first primary fails to poll a majority vote.
• *Significance:* The runoff primary is particularly advantageous in one-party states where winning the primary is tantamount to election. It guarantees that the nominee will have the majority support of the voters rather than a mere plurality when three or more candidates are in the running.

Sectionalism. The influence of local or regional loyalties on state or national elections, issues, or party unity.
• *Significance:* Traditionally, national unity has been seriously challenged by sectional cleavage on such vital issues as slavery, civil rights, "free silver," and the tariff. Most deep-rooted sectional loyalties of the early American period have given way, in the course of a century and a half, to nationalizing and unifying forces, but the position of the South on civil rights' issues, for example, remains a major factor of sectional separatism.

Short Ballot. A ballot containing relatively few offices to be filled by election. It is differentiated from the long ballot which contains numerous elective offices, especially in the executive and judicial branches. Several states, such as New Jersey and Alaska, have reduced the number of elected executive officials to a governor and lieutenant governor and have considerably reduced the number of judicial elections. The national government ballot is already a "short" one, providing only for the casting of a single vote for President and Vice President and the election of a single representative, and, in two out of three elections, of a senator. The longest ballots, typically, are found on the local government level, especially in the county.
• *Significance:* During the era of Jacksonian Democracy, the view that "the more numerous the elective offices, the more democratic the system" gained widespread acceptance. In the twentieth century the short ballot movement was established to try to reverse this situation. Advocates of the short ballot have called for patterning the state, county, and municipal ballots after the national by providing for the election of one or two executive officials and legislators, with other executives and judges to be appointive. Underscoring the short ballot movement is a belief that not only do shorter ballots simplify elections but they also make them more democratic by securing larger and more intelligent voter participation. Opponents adhere to the older doctrines that democracy thrives on numerous elections and that responsibility of officeholders can only be secured through the ballot.

Single-Member District. An electoral district from which a single legislator is chosen by a plurality vote. The single-member district voting system is used in the United States and Britain, and differs from the multimember districts typical of continental European electoral systems based on proportional representation.
• *Significance:* The single-member district is usually regarded as the most in-

fluential factor contributing to the development of a two-party system. It provides for elections based on the principle of "winner take all." Minor parties as a result are usually unable to win any share of political power and become parties of principle. A few American states depart from the single-member district principle in holding elections for one house of the legislature, and a few cities have instituted the Hare system of proportional representation. Other than these exceptions, American elections are based on single-member districts. Supporters of the single-member district principle argue that it avoids confusion, helps guarantee a majority party, and avoids the pitfalls of government by coalition. Those who oppose it point out that the votes of defeated parties and candidates are wasted, that it distorts the final election results, and that it fosters a false majority which does not democratically reflect voter sentiment.

Socialist Party.   A minor party, moderately Marxian in doctrine, which was active in American politics, particularly presidential elections, from 1900 to 1956. The Socialist party nominated Eugene V. Debs in five successive presidential elections in the early part of the twentieth century, and from 1928 through 1948 it nominated Norman Thomas for six successive elections. In 1952 and 1956 its standard bearer was Darlington Hoopes, but in 1960 the party offered no presidential candidate.

• *Significance:* The Socialist party has been a fairly influential minor party in American politics, polling nearly a million votes in presidential elections in 1912, 1920, and again in 1932, but gathered only 20,000 votes in 1956. It has been particularly influential in pushing for the adoption of social legislation which the major parties have extensively put into effect during and since the great depression. Ideological schisms continued to sap the strength of the party throughout its history until it became a victim of disunity and frustration in the early 1950's. The extremist element among its members helped form the Communist party in 1918, whereas the remaining liberal element eventually accepted the reforms of the New Deal and welfare state as a new approach.

Solid South.   A term which denotes the tendency of the people of the southern states to vote for Democratic party candidates. States which have made up the Solid South since Reconstruction include Alabama, Arkansas, Florida, Georgia, Louisiana, Mississippi, North Carolina, South Carolina, Texas, and Virginia. Historically, this phenomenon is attributable to the fact that the Republican party prosecuted the Civil War and carried out the Reconstruction programs.

• *Significance:* In recent years, the Solid South has abandoned its Democratic party unity for an anti–civil rights "Dixiecrat" or "States' Rights" revolt in 1948, and for the personal popularity of Dwight Eisenhower in the 1952 and 1956 presidential elections. Although Dixiecrat candidate Strom Thurmond carried four southern states and won 39 electoral votes in 1948, the revolt did not block the election of Democratic candidate Harry Truman. The loss of status in the Democratic party resulting for the Dixiecrats has largely prevented further defections, despite the clashes over school integration and other civil rights' issues. Southern voters, however, gave Eisenhower four southern states in 1952 and again in 1956, the first times since 1928 that a Republican candidate had carried a single southern state. In 1960, Richard M. Nixon also cracked the Solid South, winning 22 electoral votes from Florida and Virginia. Kennedy won all remaining states of the Solid South except for the election of eight unpledged electors in Mississippi.

Split Ticket.   The marking of a ballot by a voter for candidates of two or more parties for different offices. Split ticket voting is not permitted in primaries.
• *Significance:* Split ticket voting is encouraged by the "office-block" ballot which emphasizes individual choice for each office rather than straight ticket party voting. Some observers regard split ticket "voting for the best man, not the party" as the most desirable approach to politics. Political scientists generally oppose it on the grounds that the voter can too easily be fooled by personality and glibness, that issues rather than individuals are most important, and that it tends to weaken party and governmental responsibility. A frequent result of split ticket voting is a government in which different parties control the executive and the legislature and deadlocks and stalemates are common, with the voters unable to fix clearly responsibility for action or inaction.

State Central Committee.   The principal committee of a political party within a state. State central committees are composed of members representing congressional districts, state legislative districts, or counties.
• *Significance:* The state central committee has responsibility for carrying out policy decisions of the party's state convention. During political campaigns the committee makes decisions concerning strategy and the use of party campaign funds. It also may give direction to the party's state chairman, but, typically, has little influence with the party's state legislators or executive officials after they are elected.

Straight Ticket.   The marking of a ballot for all candidates of a single party for all offices.
• *Significance:* Straight ticket party voting is encouraged by the use of "party column" ballots which require the marking of a single "X" or the pulling of a single lever to vote for all party candidates for all offices. Students of government tend to prefer straight ticket voting because it reduces the impact of personality, places major emphasis on issues, and promotes party and governmental responsibility. The case against straight ticket voting is based on the assumption that intelligent voters should "vote for the man, not the party."

Third Party.   A new party, usually comprised of independents and dissidents from the major parties, which, typically, is based on a protest movement and often rallies sufficient voter support to affect a presidential election. Most students of government distinguish it from a *minor* party, a long-standing party of principle which seldom affects a specific election outcome.
• *Significance:* Third parties have played an important role in American politics by influencing the adoption of reforms and by keeping the major parties from becoming too similar in their approach to issues, or too indifferent. When a political, economic, or social consensus breaks down, third-party move-

ments have their best opportunity to present voters with a new and different approach. For example, in 1856 the Republican party was a third party which took the initiative away from the Whig party with a forthright antislavery program and replaced it as a major party. Another significant third-party movement was Theodore Roosevelt's "Bull Moose" party which split the Republican vote and enabled Woodrow Wilson to win in 1912. The Dixiecrat party in 1948 was a sectional third party which failed to influence the election results because of a lack of sympathy outside the Deep South for its protest position.

Twelfth Amendment.   Provides for the use of separate ballots by the electors in voting for the President and Vice President. The Amendment, which was ratified in 1804, also reduces the range of choice of the House of Representatives from the five highest to the three highest candidates when none has received an electoral vote majority. The Senate's choice of Vice President under these circumstances is limited to the two highest candidates.

• *Significance:* The 12th Amendment developed out of the confusion in the election of 1800 in which party-pledged electors were chosen for the first time. Since each elector voted for two candidates, the result found Thomas Jefferson, the presidential candidate, tied with his own vice presidential candidate, Aaron Burr. The election was thrown into the House where the lameduck Federalist party majority finally elected Jefferson as President after toying with the idea of electing Burr President to embarrass the Jeffersonian Republican party. To avoid such confusion in subsequent elections, the 12th Amendment specified that electors "name in their ballots the person voted for as President, and in distinct ballots the person voted for as Vice President." The Amendment adapted the Electoral College to the new political party system which had not been anticipated by the Founding Fathers.

Twenty-Third Amendment.   The most recently adopted amendment to the United States Constitution which enables the people of the District of Columbia to participate in the election of President. The Amendment was proposed by the Congress on June 16, 1960, and became effective when Kansas became the 38th state to ratify it on March 29, 1961.

• *Significance:* The 23rd Amendment allots the District of Columbia three electoral votes, which increases the size of the Electoral College to 538 electors beginning with the 1964 presidential election. Although President Kennedy proposed that voting eligibility in the District be established by 90 days residence and at the age of 18, the Congress, in 1961, prescribed a residence of one year and a minimum voting age of 21. Various groups in the District are continuing their agitation for congressional representation and local self-government.

Two-Party System.   Division of voter loyalties between two major political parties resulting in the virtual exclusion of minor parties from sharing in political power. The two-party system is the traditional British system which has been adopted in many Commonwealth countries and by the United States.

• *Significance:* Although tradition and the Anglo-American tendency to view problems in terms of black-or-white alternatives are important, the really significant factor in maintaining a two-party political system is the use of the single-member district system. The two-party monopoly on governmental power has, on several occasions in American history, been seriously challenged by the rise of a third party. However, under a single-member district electoral system, the third party cannot compete effectively for political power unless it displaces one of the major parties, as when the Republicans took over the major party status of the Whigs in 1860. Americans support the two-party system because it assures the election of legislative majorities, provides an effective and cohesive opposition, simplifies the role of the voter, and generally provides stability in government. Some opponents of the two-party system, however, charge that it creates artificial legislative majorities, narrows the voter's choice to two alternatives when there may be many, and makes a fetish out of stability while denying minority parties and groups representation in the government.

Unit Rule.   A rule applicable in Democratic national conventions which provides that state delegations may cast their total votes in a block for a single presidential candidate when so instructed by the state party convention. The unit rule is not imposed by the national convention; it is merely recognized when properly invoked by state party authorities. Each state delegation not instructed to use the unit rule may, by a majority vote of its delegates, adopt the procedure.

• *Significance:* Permission to invoke the unit rule in Democratic national conventions reflects the states' rights tradition of the party. It increases the influence of such states in nominating the presidential candidate in contrast to those states which may split their strength among several candidates. Southern state delegations have made effective use of the unit rule in maintaining a significant voice in the selection of Democratic presidential candidates. The Republican party does not recognize the unit rule and permits each delegate to cast his ballot individually.

Voting Qualifications.   Requirements which prospective voters must fulfill to become eligible to vote in a state. Qualifications imposed in all of the states include citizenship, age (21 in all but four states), and residence (commonly, one year). Special qualifications involving tax payments and literacy are imposed in a minority of the states. Additionally, most states disqualify mental incompetents, prison inmates, election law violators, and vagrants. No person may be disqualified by a state from voting because of race or sex, as provided by the 15th and 19th Amendments.

• *Significance:* Fewer than 50 percent of the potential voters actually participate in most elections, and the best turnouts in presidential contests have only slightly exceeded 60 percent. Many potential voters are denied the ballot because of failure to qualify. Suggestions for improving voter participation include (1) reducing residence requirements for most elections and eliminating them for presidential contests; (2) reducing the voting age to 18 or 19 through state action or by federal constitutional amendment; (3) eliminating poll taxes at least in federal elections through state or federal action; and (4) increasing federal oversight of national elections to prevent disfranchisement because of color or race. Although much could be accomplished by such reforms, many observers believe that simple inertia and lack of interest by millions of people remain the major difficulties.

Whig Party.   A national party which evolved in the early 1830's in reaction to the programs and policies of Jacksonian Democracy. The party combined National Republicans, Anti-Masons, and various anti-Jackson elements in an alliance of southern slave owners with northern manufacturing, financial, and commercial interests.
• *Significance:* The Whig Party contested national offices with the Democratic party from 1832 to 1856, electing two military heroes, William Henry Harrison in 1840 and Zachary Taylor in 1848, to the presidency. The Whig party disintegrated during the 1850's in conflict over the slavery question and a new party alignment developed. Southern, slave-owning Whigs joined the Democratic party, and northern Whigs helped to create the new Republican party.

White Primary.   An attempt by several southern states to exclude Negroes from primary elections by leaving primary voting qualifications up to a political party acting as a private organization. The objective of this maneuver was to evade the restrictions against governmental discrimination found in the 15th Amendment. The theory behind the white primary was that if the Negro could be excluded from the Democratic primary, which is the significant election in southern states, he could then be permitted to vote in the general election without affecting the results.
• *Significance:* The white primary was the most effective device for barring Negroes from casting a meaningful ballot for many years in several southern states. The Supreme Court, after much vacillation, finally declared the white primary unconstitutional in *Smith v. Allwright,* 321 U.S. 649 (1944). The Court held that the Democratic party acted as an agent of the state in holding a primary, which is an integral part of the election process, and that this constituted state action within the meaning of the 15th Amendment.

IMPORTANT CASES

Gomillion v. Lightfoot, 364 U.S. 339 (1960): Upheld a suit against an Alabama law that changed the city of Tuskegee's boundaries to exclude all Negro voters from participating in city elections. The Court found the law to be a violation of the right to vote as guaranteed by the 15th Amendment.
• *Significance:* The Supreme Court has been reluctant to interfere in the manner in which states organize their voting districts. However, the Court has sought to restrict any activities which have as their fundamental purpose the denial of the right to vote on the basis of race or color.

Guinn v. United States, 238 U.S. 347 (1915): Declared "grandfather clauses" to be unconstitutional under the 15th Amendment. These clauses had been used by many southern states to bestow the franchise upon white voters who had been disfranchised by state tax and literacy requirements intended to keep the Negroes from voting. The grandfather clauses granted the franchise to persons whose ancestors had voted prior to 1867.

• *Significance:* Although the grandfather clause might have appeared to be a means of expanding the electorate, a creditable endeavor, the Court uncovered the subterfuge by recognizing the intent behind it. The decision put the Court on record as regarding any attempt, direct or roundabout, effectively to disfranchise any group because of its color or race as a violation of the 15th Amendment.

Smith v. Allwright, 321 U.S. 649 (1944): Established, finally and conclusively, that the "white primary" was a violation of the 15th Amendment. The case arose over the denial of a ballot to Smith, a Negro resident of Houston, Texas, in the Democratic primary of 1940 for nominating candidates for congressional and state offices. The Court recognized that its earlier decision, allowing the exclusion of Negroes from "private" party primaries, in the case *Grovey v. Townsend,* 295 U.S. 45 (1935), had been "in error." The Court reasoned that the party was actually performing a state function in holding a primary election and was not acting as a private group. Moreover, the Court pointed out that a primary is an integral part of the election process.

• *Significance:* In the Solid South, nomination in the Democratic primary is usually tantamount to winning the election. By being denied a vote in the primary, the Negro was prevented from effectively participating in the selection of public officials. By invoking the 15th Amendment against a private group (political party), the Court closed a loophole which it had opened with its earlier interpretation. This case stands as an important landmark in the continuing legal battles to ensure voting rights for all. This decision resulted in more vigorous use of other techniques by southern states to keep the Negroes from the polls, such as literacy tests and difficult registration procedures.

United States v. Classic, 313 U.S. 299 (1941): Upheld the power of the Congress to supervise the holding of state primary congressional elections to ensure the right of the people to vote and to have their ballot counted. Classic, a Commissioner of Elections in Louisiana, was convicted for vote fraud under a federal criminal law prohibiting interference with constitutional rights. The Court based its decision on Article I, Section 4, which establishes the regulatory powers of the Congress over congressional elections, holding that the primary is an integral part of the election process.

• *Significance:* The Court's position, that the Congress might validly regulate congressional primary elections in the states, overturned its earlier precedent established in *Newberry v. United States,* 256 U.S. 232 (1921). The Court recognized that the "times, places and manner" clause of the Constitution would be meaningless, especially in the one-party states of the South, if it were applied only to general elections and not to the primaries. In 1880, in *Ex parte Siebold,* 100 U.S. 371, the Court had upheld the power of the Congress to regulate the conduct of general elections for national office.

IMPORTANT STATUTES

Electoral Count Act.   An act of Congress of 1887 which provides for settlement of disputes over the election of presidential electors. When more than one set of electors are certified by different authorities of a single state, the Congress, voting as two separate houses, decides which to accept. If the Congress fails to agree, the electors certified by the governor are accepted.

• *Significance:* The Electoral Count Act resulted from the great confusion in the election of 1876. Hayes finally won the presidency over Tilden, 185 electoral votes to 184, after 20 contested electoral votes were awarded to Hayes on a strictly partisan basis by a hastily created Electoral Commission. The establishment of regular procedures is important not only because the outcome of such disputes within one or a few states may affect the outcome of a close presidential election, but also because the effectiveness of the democratic process depends upon the acceptance of election results by both winners and losers.

Hatch Acts (Political Activities Acts of 1939, 1940).   Two of the important corrupt practices acts enacted by the Congress. The first Hatch Act of 1939 forbids a political committee to spend more than $3 million in any campaign and limits individual contributions to a political committee to $5,000. Federal civil service personnel may not be pressured in any way to make political contributions, and they are forbidden to participate actively in politics. The second Hatch Act of 1940 imposed similar restrictions on state and local employees working on projects supported by federal funds.

• *Significance:* The Hatch Acts were intended to reduce the increasing influence of heavy campaign funds in winning elections and to free government employees from pressures exerted by political superiors upon them during campaigns. The intent of the Congress has not been fully realized. The $3 million spending limitation placed upon any party committee has been easily evaded through the creation of additional committees and by decentralization of expenditures in state bodies. The provision that no one individual may contribute more than $5,000 to a political committee has been circumvented by making several contributions to different committees, and by letting other members of a family make contributions. The section of the law which forbids solicitation of government employees for contributions has been fairly effective, but many make "voluntary" contributions. In general, the Hatch Acts, like most corrupt practices legislation, have proved to be ineffective in correcting the weaknesses in the financing of American political campaigns.

7

The Legislative Process: Congress and the State Legislatures

Act.   A term used to describe statutes enacted by the Congress and by state legislatures. Simple, concurrent, and joint resolutions adopted by the Congress are not considered to be acts.
• *Significance:* At the close of each session of the Congress all acts of Congress enacted during the session are published chronologically in the *Statutes at Large of the United States.* Those applicable today can be found in the *Code of Laws of the United States,* which is revised and supplemented annually. The *Code* is organized on a subject matter basis. State laws are published but not codified regularly.

Adjournment.   To terminate a session of a legislative body. Adjournment sine die means to end the session without definitely fixing a day for reconvening. It is used to end a congressional session officially. Neither house of the Congress can adjourn for more than three days without the concurrence of the other.
• *Significance:* Under existing rules, the Congress adjourns no later than the last day of July, unless it specifically provides otherwise. Under the Constitution, if the two houses of the Congress cannot agree on an adjournment day, the President can determine it. This has never occurred.

Advice and Consent.   The power vested in the United States Senate by the Constitution (Art. II, sec. 2) to give its advice and consent to the President in treaty-making and appointments. A two-thirds vote of the senators present is required for treaties. The Senate may give its advice through consultations between Senate leaders and the President, by resolutions setting out its position, or by delegating some of its members actually to sit in on the negotiations.
• *Significance:* Although the Constitution's phraseology seems to associate the Senate with the President throughout the treaty-making process, President Washington, after several attempts to consult with the entire Senate, found it impractical, and initiated the tradition of consulting with the Senate only

after a treaty had been negotiated and signed. Since World War II, however, presidents have increasingly expanded the "advice" rule of the Senate by inviting influential senators to participate in the negotiation of such significant treaties as the treaty which created the United Nations and several which established military alliances. The Senate generally accepts the nominees of the President for high-level positions, but in the case of many presidential appointments within states, the rule of "senatorial courtesy" applies.

Agenda.   A list of specific items of business to be considered at a legislative session or at a conference or meeting.
• *Significance:* The agenda sets out in itemized form the subjects to be taken up. Hence, by keeping an item off the agenda it can be killed through inaction. In the Congress, the House Rules Committee and the Senate Majority Leader exercise considerable control over the agenda in their respective chambers.

Amendment.   A proposal by a member of a legislative body to delete, alter, or revise the language of a bill or an act. Bills in Congress may be amended at any one of a number of stages in the legislative process. Generally, amendments are printed, debated, and voted upon in the same way as a bill.
• *Significance:* Through the amending process, a bill may undergo such extreme revision or modification as to lose much of its original character. Often, legislators will seek to render bills innocuous through amendments rather than by attempting to kill the bills outright. Legislators may, furthermore, seek to kill a bill by attaching amendments to it which are unacceptable to the majority of that house or the other chamber. In the Congress, the responsibility for reconciling the various amendments of the two houses falls upon the conference committees. State legislatures have similar arrangements for adjusting conflicting versions of a bill.

Apportionment.   Article I, section 2 provides that representatives "shall be apportioned among the several states . . . according to their respective numbers." After each decennial census, the House seats are redistributed among the 50 states on the basis of population shifts. Under the 1960 reapportionment, 16 states lost, and nine states gained, seats in the House. California led with an increase of eight seats.
• *Significance:* Because of the mobility of the American people, gross under- or overrepresentation of states in the House is avoided through the "automatic" reapportionment by the Bureau of the Census, following each ten-year census. However, within each state the responsibility for redistricting is then placed upon the majority party in the state legislature. Here, the use of gerrymandering can result in serious over- and underrepresentation problems.

Appropriation.   A legislative grant of money for a specific purpose. First, authorization bills are enacted by the Congress establishing a specific program. Then, an appropriation bill is usually passed to provide the money to carry out the program. All appropriation bills originate in the House of Representatives by custom.
• *Significance:* In the national government, no expenditure of public money can be made unless authorized by law. Thus, the Congress (and in the states,

the legislatures) exercises full "control over the purse strings." This is one of the most important powers exercised by a legislative body.

Bicameralism.   The division of a legislative body into two houses. At the Philadelphia convention of 1787, the Founding Fathers adopted a compromise solution in the battle over representation in the Congress. This "Connecticut Compromise" established a balanced bicameral legislature with one house (House of Representatives) based on population and the second (Senate) based on equality of states. In the states, the Nebraska legislature is the only one-house (unicameral) legislature. *See* UNICAMERALISM, page 151.
• *Significance:* A two-house legislature provides opportunity for two different types of representation and response to varying interests, such as population, area, and existing political units. Also, the second house can function in a capacity of revising and correcting mistakes made by the first chamber. Bicameralism is consistent with the principle of checks and balances. All bills must pass both houses before becoming law.

Biennial Session.   A regular meeting of a legislature held every two years. Thirty-three state legislatures convene in regular session once every two years, with 17 meeting annually. In biennial session states, typically, legislatures hold their sessions in the odd-numbered years.
• *Significance:* The biennial session was established for the state legislatures by constitution framers early in our nation's history, partly from a desire to save money, and partly because of suspicions that if the legislature convened too frequently it might engage in mischievous doings. Biennial sessions have proved inadequate to meet the vast number of complex problems facing state governments today, necessitating frequent special sessions.

Bill.   A proposed law. Most legislative proposals before Congress are in the form of bills. All bills introduced during a two-year congressional term are designated "HR" in the House and "S" in the Senate, with consecutive numbers assigned in the order in which they are introduced in each chamber. Each bill must have three readings in each house, be approved by a majority vote in each house, and, normally, be signed by the President to become law. Public bills deal with matters of general concern and may become public laws. Private bills are concerned with individual matters and become private laws if approved.
• *Significance:* Thousands of bills are introduced into every Congress. They are drawn up by pressure groups, interested citizens, congressional committees, individual congressmen, and by members of the executive branch. However, only members of the Congress can introduce them in their respective chambers. The great majority of these bills are killed because the committees in each house do not act upon them.

Bill Drafting.   The Congress and many state legislatures are provided with staff agencies which render aid to members in the process of formulating bills. In the Congress, members seeking assistance in study and research have access to a Legislative Reference Service in the Library of Congress. Aid in drawing up bills is supplied by the Office of the Legislative Counsel.

• *Significance:* Bills must be drafted with precision in correct legal language. If enacted, the courts may refuse to sanction their enforcement if drawn up in vague language or in a way which allows too much discretion to be exercised by enforcement officers.

Bloc.   Members of a legislative body, not necessarily of the same party, who have common aims or goals. Some examples include the "farm bloc," the "high tariff bloc," the "silver bloc," and the "anti-civil rights bloc."
• *Significance:* Bloc voting in Congress and in state legislatures is an effective means by which a sizable segment of the population can be effectively represented. It is basically a bipartisan approach. The danger inherent in voting blocs results from the hard and fast positions taken by them on specific issues with the result that rivalry is intensified and the legislative body may be split into warring factions. There is also a tendency to reduce party responsibility as a result of bloc voting.

Calendar.   An agenda or list which contains the names of bills to be considered before committees or either chamber of the legislature. When a standing committee of the House of Representatives reports a bill out it is placed on one of the five possible calendars: *Consent* (noncontroversial bills), *Discharge* (discharge petitions), *House* (nonfiscal public bills), *Private* (private bills), and *Union* (appropriation and revenue bills). In the Senate, all bills reported out go on a single calendar, although nonlegislative matters (treaties and confirmations) are placed on the *Executive* calendar.
• *Significance:* Because a bill is placed on a calendar is no guarantee that it will be considered by that chamber. Decisions as to which bills will be debated and voted on are made in the House by the Rules Committee and by the House party leaders, and in the Senate by the Majority Leader. In the Senate, the Minority Leader is consulted frequently in order to ensure unanimous consent agreement to consider bills. Many bills are killed because they are still on the calendars at the end of a two-year Congress.

Calendar Wednesday.   In the House of Representatives, Wednesdays may be used to call the roll of the standing committees for the purpose of bringing up any of their bills for consideration from the House or the Union Calendars. General debate on each bill called up in this way is limited to two hours. Calendar Wednesday is not observed during the last two weeks of a session and, by a two-thirds vote, may be eliminated during the entire session, which usually is the case.
• *Significance:* It is a device by which the committee chairmen in the House of Representatives can, when the rule is operative, bypass the Rules Committee and place a controversial bill before the House for debate and a vote.

Caucus.   A meeting of party members in one of the houses of a legislative body for the purpose of making decisions on selections of party leaders and on legislative business. Republicans in the Congress prefer to call their party meeting a "conference."
• *Significance:* The majority caucus in each house makes important decisions regarding the organization of its chamber, which then become official when

ratified by that house in regular session. In the Congress, the Democrats provide for "binding" caucus decisions on party stands on bills, with a two-thirds vote of the caucus required. No member is bound, however, if the party position involves a question of constitutional construction or a measure contrary to a pledge given by the member to his constituents. Republicans operate their conference on a majority vote basis but do not seek to bind their members on voting positions. Some observers have recommended that the role of party caucuses in Congress be strengthened by providing for *binding* decisions on important legislative proposals. This, it is suggested, would strengthen the democratic process by making the parties more responsible.

Censure.   A judicial type of power vested in each chamber of a legislative body by which the chamber can discipline its own members. Under the Constitution, "Each house may . . . punish its members for disorderly behavior, and, with the concurrence of two-thirds, expel a member." (Art. I, sec. 5).
• *Significance:* Cases of either house censuring a member are rare. It has occurred on a few occasions, the most recent having been the Senate's motion to "condemn" Senator Joseph McCarthy in 1954–55. Disciplinary measures can range in severity from adoption of a simple motion of censure to withdrawal of privileges and, in extreme cases, the expelling of a member.

Census.   A decennial enumeration of the total population of the United States, conducted by the Bureau of the Census. The Constitution provides that the population count be used for the purposes of apportioning direct taxes and representatives among the several states (Art. I, sec. 3). The first census was taken in 1790 and new ones, every ten years since. Approximately one half of the states also conduct a mid-decade census along the same lines as the federal census.
• *Significance:* The American people have become extremely mobile, with considerable shifts in population occurring within the ten-year periods. The flow of population today is toward the West, and this is resulting in a shift of political power in the same direction. After each census, the Census Bureau reapportions the seats in the House of Representatives on the basis of the new population statistics. No direct taxes are now levied by the federal government. States use census figures in apportioning grants and allowances for local governments.

Cloture (or Closure).   A rule in the Senate under which debate might be limited and a filibuster broken. One sixth of the Senate membership can initiate action under cloture by petitioning the Senate to close debate on a pending measure. If such a petition is approved by two thirds of the senators voting, thereafter no senator may speak for more than one hour on the bill being considered. Hence, in a short time the measure will come up for a vote and the attempt of the minority to "talk the bill to death" by filibuster will have been defeated.
• *Significance:* In theory, the cloture is important because it provides a means of safeguarding majority rule by limiting the power of the Senate minority to kill bills by parliamentary maneuvers. In practice, however, on only four

occasions from 1917 to 1962 has cloture been successfully invoked—on none since 1927. Many important bills have been killed by minority action using the filibuster or the threat of filibuster.

Committee of the Whole.   An informal procedure used by a legislative body for expediting business by resolving the official body into a committee for the consideration of bills and other matters. In the Congress, it is used only by the lower house which becomes "The Committee of the Whole House [of Representatives] on the State of the Union." A temporary chairman is appointed to supplant the Speaker and the formal rules are suspended.

• *Significance:* Advantages of this procedure include (1) only 100 members need be present to constitute a quorum; (2) business is expedited through relaxed procedures; (3) time-consuming roll call votes are not permitted, nor are members' votes put on record; (4) the full House retains control in that it must act upon all decisions made by the Committee of the Whole.

Committee on Committees.   Party committees which determine the assignments of party members to standing committees in the House of Representatives. The Republican Committee on Committees consists of one representative from each state having Republican members in the House. In voting within the Committee on Committees, each member casts the number of votes equal to the number of Republican members his state has in the House. The Democrats in caucus first choose their party's members of the House Ways and Means Committee and this group then determines the party's standing committee assignments. In the Senate, where only one third of the seats are filled in each biennial election, a Committee on Committees of each party (Democrats use their Steering Committee) makes the necessary adjustments for each committee. In the State legislatures, committees in the lower house are appointed by the Speaker of the House. In the upper house, the procedure varies from selection by the presiding officer, by the chamber as a whole, or by a committee on committees.

• *Significance:* Selections of committee personnel made unofficially in these ways are, typically, approved by the respective party caucuses and thence by their respective chambers. The power to assign committee members is significant because it will largely determine the role that an individual legislator will play as well as have a substantial influence on the fate of any bill which a committee might consider during that session.

Concurrent Resolution.   A special measure, designated "H Con Res" or "S Con Res," which requires approval by both houses of the Congress but does not need the President's signature.

• *Significance:* Concurrent resolutions of the Congress are used to make or amend joint rules or to express the sentiment of the Congress on some issue or event. Specific examples might include fixing the time for adjournment, the creation of joint committees, and special greetings welcoming official foreign visitors to the United States.

Conference Committee.   When a bill passes the two houses of Congress in different forms, a conference committee may be called to try to reconcile the differences. This special committee is comprised of "managers" appointed by the Speaker of the House and the President of the Senate. Efforts are directed toward a compromise version of the bill which must be approved by a majority of the managers for each house voting separately. It then goes in the form of a "conference report" to each house, where it cannot be amended, and if rejected by either may go back to conference for further negotiation.

• *Significance:* The most important bills frequently end up in conference committees; differences over bills of lesser importance are usually ironed out by securing the agreement of each chamber to the other's amendments. Frequently, great power is wielded by these committees. Many important bills are substantially rewritten in conference or are killed through failure to achieve a compromise agreement. Meetings of the committees are always secret. Finally, their power is reflected in the large number of times that the two houses accept conference reports and enact them into law.

Confirmation.   The power of a legislative body to approve nominations made to fill executive and judicial positions. Nominations for such offices made by the President must be confirmed by the Senate with a majority vote. Many of the appointments made by the governors in the various states must also be approved by the upper houses of the legislatures.

• *Significance:* All federal judges are appointed subject to senatorial confirmation. Most important diplomatic and administrative positions not under civil service or other merit systems also come under senatorial scrutiny. Often a President will confer with the Senate leaders before nominating an individual for a cabinet position, to determine in advance that he is *persona grata* (acceptable). In the case of appointments to federal positions located in the several states, the senior senator of the President's party from the state in which the appointment is to be made actually selects the appointee, thus reversing the constitutional procedure. This is known as "senatorial courtesy."

Congressional Directory.   A handbook published annually containing information regarding the organization of the Congress and its committees and brief biographical sketches of the senators and representatives.

• *Significance:* This is a useful reference guide for citizens and students of government.

Congressional District.   A geographical division of a state from which one member of the House of Representatives is elected.

• *Significance:* Districts generally are drawn up by the partisan majorities in state legislatures in such a way as to favor their party's candidates in congressional elections (gerrymandering). Until 1929, a law of Congress specified that state legislatures draw up these districts as "compact and contiguous" areas, substantially equal in population. Since 1929, the Congress has not tried to specify criteria for redistricting with the result that partisan advantage remains a major consideration in most states.

Congressional Record.   A verbatim record of the proceedings (debates, speeches, and votes) in both the House and the Senate, printed daily. Members may edit their remarks and speeches before printing, and they also may insert material, called "extension of remarks," which was not actually delivered on the floor of their chamber.

• *Significance:* The *Congressional Record* is an invaluable source of data and resource materials for the student of Congress. The inclusion of committee reports enhances its utility.

Congressman.   A member of the Congress of the United States, but colloquially used to describe a member of the House of Representatives.

• *Significance:* In speaking to a member of the House of Representatives, he should be addressed as "Congressman," or "Congressman Jones." In addressing a member of the Senate, protocol calls for the use of either "Senator," or "Senator Smith."

Congressman at Large.   A member of the House who is elected by the voters of the entire state rather than of a specific district. If a state gains seats following a decennial reapportionment and fails to redistrict, the new seats will be filled by election at large. If a state loses seats and fails to redistrict, then all of the state's congressmen will be elected at large. States with only one member of the House will, of course, always elect that one at large. Decisions concerning redistricting are made by the majority party in the state legislatures.

• *Significance:* Election of congressmen at large permits a state to fail to redistrict congressional seats in order that the existing district system not be disturbed. The existing system has usually been drawn up in such a way as to favor the election of members of the majority party of the state legislature.

Constituent.   A resident of a legislator's district. The district itself is sometimes referred to as the member's constituency.

• *Significance:* Legislators must act in the capacity of a go-between in the relationship of the average citizen and his "big government" in far away Washington, D.C., or in the state capital. Much of a legislator's day must be spent in answering letters, running errands, showing the sights to visitors, and similar activities on behalf of his constituents. This is useful in that it keeps a congressman in close contact with the voters. On the other hand, there has been a tendency for constituents to regard their representatives as mere errand boys. This may result in the overburdening of the legislator to the extent that he is unable to devote sufficient time to dealing with the important law-making function.

Constituent Power.   The power to participate officially in the process of constitution making, amending, or revising. The constituent power of the Congress consists of its authority to propose amendments to the United States Constitution by a two thirds vote of both houses, or to call a national convention for this purpose. Amendment proposals must be submitted for ratification by three fourths of the state legislatures or by specially elected conventions in three fourths of the states. In the states, the legislatures are usually empowered to propose specific amendments to their state constitutions. Extensive revisions of state constitutions are generally done by special constitutional conventions or commissions established solely for that purpose.

Ratification of state constitutional changes is vested in the people of the state.
• *Significance:* Under a system of limited government the fundamental law found in the constitution provides for the regulated exercise of power by the three branches of government. To the extent that the legislature exercises some considerable powers of a constituent nature, it can affect and change the nature of the limitations placed upon itself as well as those placed upon the other two branches of government.

Contempt of Congress.   The authority vested in both houses of the Congress and in their investigating committees to cite for contempt of Congress any subpoenaed witness who refuses to appear, or to give testimony under oath. The United States Supreme Court has upheld this power by asserting: "It is unquestionably the duty of all citizens to cooperate with the Congress . . . to respond to subpoenas . . . and to testify fully with respect to matters within the province of proper investigation." (*Watkins v. United States,* 354 U.S. 178 [1957]). Under existing interpretation of the courts, valid contempt citations may not be issued for refusal of a witness to testify when (1) the subject under examination is beyond the proper scope of authority of the committee; (2) questions directed to a witness are not pertinent to the subject being investigated; and (3) answers of the witness might tend to provide evidence which might be used against him in a criminal case.
• *Significance:* The contempt power of the Congress, though it might occasionally be misused, is essential if Congress is to have the authority to conduct meaningful investigations to learn facts on which to base legislative decisions.

Contested Elections.   Article I, section 5 states: "Each house shall be the judge of the elections, returns, and qualifications of its own members. . . ." When the election of a member is contested, the chamber concerned sets up a committee to conduct an investigation.
• *Significance:* The Constitution makes the Congress the exclusive judge of the qualifications of its members, and, therefore, there can be no appeal to the courts. Thus, the House and the Senate on occasion have refused to seat elected members for reasons other than those provided in the Constitution. Examples of this include the barring of a polygamist in 1900, of a socialist in 1919, and, in 1926, of two senators because they had exceeded lawful campaign expenditures.

Deficiency Bills.   These are special bills appropriating funds to make up the difference between an agency's appropriation for the fiscal year and the amount deemed necessary to enable it to continue to operate for the full fiscal year.
• *Significance:* Deficiency bills become necessary because of miscalculation in the budget process or because of new developments requiring greater activity by the agencies concerned. Unlike regular appropriations, which are made for the next fiscal year, deficiency appropriations are for the same fiscal year period in which they are passed.

Dilatory Motion.   The introduction of an irrelevant or nongermane motion in a legislative body. This is a delaying action, used especially for the purpose of preventing action on a bill.

• *Significance:* Dilatory motions are not allowed under the rules of either house of the Congress, but considerable discretion is left to the presiding officers in enforcement of these rules. They are potentially most useful in the hands of the minority to force concessions by disrupting the time schedule of the majority.

Direct Legislation.   Methods used in many states which enable the voters to participate directly in deciding upon governmental policies. Direct methods include the initiative and the referendum.

• *Significance:* The initiative enables the people of the state to circumvent the inaction of the state legislature. A new law may be proposed by securing the legally required number of signatures on initiatory petitions. If approved by the voters in an election, the proposal becomes law. The referendum is a means by which the people can "veto" laws passed by the state legislature before they become effective. An initiatory petition with sufficient signatures suspends the law until it can be voted on by the people. In both the initiative and the referendum, the legislature may not repeal the action of the people. There are no provisions for their use in the national government.

Discharge Rule.   A procedure by which a bill in the House of Representatives may be forced out of a committee (discharged) that has refused to report it out for consideration by the House. Bills not reported out within 30 days after referral to a committee may be subject to discharge. The discharge motion must be signed by an absolute majority (218) of the House membership. If the motion to discharge the bill carries by a simple majority vote, consideration of the bill then becomes a matter of high privilege. The Rules Committee may be discharged of a bill after it has held it for only seven legislative days.

• *Significance:* One of the very considerable powers of legislative committees is that of killing bills by refusing to report them out for consideration. The discharge rule is one means by which the majority of the House can overcome this "minority" power. Yet it is used only on rare occasions, since members are reluctant to challenge the prerogatives of committees and their chairmen. Similar to the discharge rule is the discharge resolution in the Senate, which may be initiated by an ordinary motion. Many state legislatures also vest discharge powers in the majority of each house.

Division.   A method of voting used in a legislative body. Members voting for or against the motion alternately rise, and are counted by the presiding officer.

• *Significance:* No record is made of how individual members vote in a division or "standing" vote. It has the advantage of enabling an accurate count to be made without delay. Its disadvantage lies in the way members may successfully hide their vote from their constituents, with the result that there is a weakening of democratic responsibility.

Engrossed Bill.   The final authoritative copy of a bill passed by one house of a legislative body.

• *Significance:* The text contains all amendments and is certified by the clerk of the House or the secretary of the Senate. Engrossment of joint resolutions follows the same procedure as bills. Engrossment is one of the many steps in the lawmaking process.

Enrolled Bill.   The final authoritative copy (printed on parchment) of a bill passed by both houses of a legislative body. In the Congress, an officer of the chamber in which the bill originated must certify its authenticity. The signatures of the Speaker of the House and the President of the Senate are then affixed to it.

• *Significance:* Enrolled bills and joint resolutions are forwarded to the executive for signature, which completes the lawmaking process. If vetoed, enrolled bills and joint resolutions are returned to the house of origin.

Executive Session.   A session of a legislative body or committee which is closed to the public.

• *Significance:* Although most committee decisions are made in closed sessions in the Congress and in state legislatures, frequently the vote of individual members is made available to the public. The advantage of holding secret sessions lies in the greater freedom of members to express themselves knowing they will not be put on record. The main disadvantage is that it may tend to encourage irresponsible action which can be hidden from public view. City commissions and councils and other local policy-determining bodies often make important decisions in executive committee of the whole sessions prior to the public meeting. Thus, in the formal meeting the group may give the impression of consensus and agreement, when, in reality, major battles had already been fought out at the earlier secret session.

Expulsion.   The power of a legislative body, usually exercised by each chamber separately, to expel a member as an extreme disciplinary measure. Typical grounds for expulsion include conduct unbecoming a member, disloyalty, and moral turpitude. By Article I, section 5 each house is empowered to expel a member with the concurrence of two thirds of the members of that chamber. State constitutions generally vest similar powers in state legislatures.

• *Significance:* Expulsion is a rarely used power of legislative bodies. Members usually try to reconcile differences and, if absolutely necessary, to mete out punishment in the form of censure or denial of privileges.

Extension of Remarks.   Material incorporated into the *Congressional Record* by a member of the Congress, although not delivered verbally on the floor of either chamber. Permission to extend remarks is required by the member's house and is ordinarily granted. Material which elaborates on remarks made by the member on the floor follows the text of his speech; other insertions are printed in the appendix.

• *Significance:* The extension of remarks privilege enables a member to record his position on legislative matters even though he had not been able, or did not wish, to do so orally on the floor of his chamber. Many such insertions are aimed at influencing a congressman's constituents and not other members.

Farm Bloc.   A group made up of both Democratic and Republican representatives and senators from the farm states, who put aside party differences to pass legislation favorable to the farmers. The creation of this voting bloc in the early part of the twentieth century followed the attempts of the farmers to achieve their aims through the creation of various farmers' parties which had been unsuccessful in challenging the two major parties.

• *Significance:* The farm bloc is considered to be one of the most consistent and successful voting alignments in the Congress and in most state legislatures. Much of the continuing success of the bloc stems from the overrepresentation of farm areas in both houses of the Congress and in most state legislatures. Today, the farm bloc has lost some of its effectiveness because of the failure of farmers and farm organizations to agree on solutions to farm problems. Increasing urban representation is also modifying the power of the farm bloc.

Filibuster.   A means by which a minority of senators in the Congress seek to frustrate the will of the majority by literally "talking a bill to death." Senators are proud of their chamber's reputation for being the world's greatest forum for free discussion. Rule 22 of the Senate Rules provides for unlimited debate on a motion before it can be brought to a vote. A filibuster is a misuse of this freedom of debate, since full exploration of the merits and demerits of the pending measure is not its objective. Rather the minority of senators seeks to gain concessions or the withdrawal of the bill through delaying tactics. These include prolonged debate and speeches on relevant and irrelevant topics, parliamentary maneuvers, dilatory motions, and other tricks of the legislative game. The objective of the minority is to delay action on the measure interminably, until the majority is forced by the press of other business to withdraw it from consideration.

• *Significance:* Over the years, many important bills have been filibustered to death. Many more have been killed by using the threat of a filibuster to force withdrawal of a bill. Until the enactment of the Civil Rights Acts of 1957 and 1960, the filibuster or threat of it had been successful for many years in the hands of a minority of senators from the South in foreclosing any successful action in this area. Strom Thurmond holds the record for the longest individual filibuster. He spoke almost continuously for more than 24 hours against enactment of civil rights legislation in 1957. Filibusters may be defeated by the use of cloture or round-the-clock sessions of the Senate.

Franking Privilege.   Enables members of the Congress to send materials through the mail free by substituting their facsimile signature (frank) for postage. Free mail privileges have also been accorded by the Congress to other officials and agencies of the national government.

• *Significance:* The franking privilege provides a means by which members of the Congress can keep their constituents informed on issues before it, voting records, and other business. It is a recognition that the "representative" function of the Congress requires that means be provided by which the individual congressman can keep in contact with his constituents.

Freedom of Debate.   The right of members of a legislative body in a democratic system of government freely to discuss, to deliberate, and to act upon matters of policy without fear of legal action or recrimination. The Constitution, Article I, section 6, provides that "for any speech or debate in either House, they [Senators and Representatives] shall not be questioned in any other place." Utterances which might otherwise constitute slander are privileged, therefore, when made in the Congress. Immunity to suit does not ordinarily apply to statements made outside of the Congress. In all cases, however, whether in or out of the Congress, members can be held to account through the disciplinary powers of their own house. State legislatures generally provide similar immunity for the members. Freedom of debate is sometimes used to describe the right to speak indefinitely on a pending measure. Only members of the United States Senate enjoy this right under Rule 22 of the Senate Rules. • *Significance:* The purpose of ensuring maximum freedom of debate is to guarantee that decisions made by the legislative body will be freely made after thorough debate. Without such a guarantee, members might become too restricted in their deliberations to do a good job of legislating. On occasion, however, a member can abuse this right by using it unjustly to slur the reputation of a citizen, who has no recourse in the courts.

Gerrymandering. The drawing of legislative district boundary lines with a view to obtaining partisan or factional advantage. The practice is engaged in frequently by partisan majorities in state legislatures when drawing up congressional and state legislative districts. The objective is to spread the support for one's own party over many districts and to concentrate the support for the other party into as few districts as possible. Gerrymandering is possible because of the pattern of consistency in voting behavior of most Americans. • *Significance:* Most redistricting laws enacted by state legislatures show evidence of varying degrees of manipulation of boundaries for partisan advantage. The courts, in 1962, began to intervene to curb this practice. Attempts by the Congress in the past to force the state legislatures to abide by a "compact and contiguous" rule were largely ineffective and have been dropped. Gerrymandering has resulted in gross overrepresentation of rural areas in the House of Representatives and in most state legislatures. This means that, in elections, one citizen may cast one vote equal to several of those cast by several citizens in more populous districts. For example, in a recent Congress this "misrepresentation" resulted in a congressman from one of the largest districts having eight times the number of constituents that a congressman from one of the smallest districts had. "Misrepresentation" in some state legislatures goes far beyond this 8–1 disparity. Gerrymandering may result in the election of a majority of the state's congressional delegation and of a majority in both houses of the state legislature by a minority of the state's voters.

Hearing. A public session of a committee of a legislative body to obtain information and to hear arguments pro and con on a proposed law. In the Congress, public hearings are commonly functions of subcommittees which report their findings to the full committees. The theory behind public hearings is that out of the "combat" between contestants using every ethical means to convince committee members of the wisdom of their positions will emerge the "true facts." The members can then make their decisions, much like a judge and jury in a judicial proceeding. The hearings thus serve as a means by which American citizens can "petition" their elected representatives and seek to influence their decision making.

• *Significance:* Most hearings involve only professional lobbyists. Commonly, administration officials are pitted against private lobbyists. In recent years there has been an increasing tendency for committees to use the hearings to try to influence public opinion or executive action, as in the areas of communism and crime. Public hearings are used extensively and are considered to be a valuable legislative aid. All state legislatures also provide for public hearings on important measures.

High Crimes and Misdemeanors.   The Constitution provides in Article II, section 4, that the President, Vice President, and all civil officers of the United States are subject to impeachment and removal from office upon conviction for "treason, bribery, or other high crimes and misdemeanors." There has been no attempt to spell out what acts might constitute high crimes and misdemeanors. Discretion is vested completely in the Congress.

• *Significance:* In practice, probably based on English historical precedent, the grounds on which impeachment action is taken are usually restricted to unethical conduct and criminal offenses. Congress has not regarded incompetence or political disagreement as grounds for invoking its impeachment powers. Yet, because so much discretion is vested in the Congress by the Constitution, the threat of its use may sometimes constitute a potent weapon.

Hopper.   The box situated on the desk of the clerk of the House of Representatives. Members may officially "introduce" a bill simply by dropping it into the "hopper." Thereafter, it is given a consecutive number and is referred to one of the standing committees.

• *Significance:* The House's procedure is in contrast to the Senate's wherein a member must first be recognized by the presiding officer to make a verbal announcement of the introduction of a bill.

House of Representatives.   The lower house of the bicameral Congress, in which representation is based on population. The upper house, the Senate of the United States, is based on the principle of state equality. The House was intended by the Founding Fathers to be the popular chamber of the Congress, and it was made larger and more responsive to the public will than the Senate, which was intended to be the more deliberative body. Each state is guaranteed at least one representative. Since 1910, the House has had a permanent membership of 435. The ratio of population to representatives has been steadily increasing until now it is more than 400,000 per representative. The Constitution vests certain powers exclusively in the House, among them (1) the impeachment power; (2) the initiation of revenue bills; (3) the election of a President if no candidate obtains a majority in the Electoral College; (4) the determination of its own rules of procedure; and (5) the discipline of its members.

• *Significance:* Some critics reject the assertion that the House is the more representative of the two houses of Congress. They point out that because of gerrymandering and failure to redistrict seats on a population basis in many states, the House today may be less responsive to the public will than the Senate. Moreover, they assert that because of its unwieldy size, and the inordinate power vested in the Rules Committee, it is less able than the Senate to cope with contemporary legislative problems. Nevertheless, the American voter tends to regard his representative as his most direct contact with the national government.

Impeachment.   A formal accusation rendered by the lower house of a legislative body which commits the accused civil official for trial in the upper house. Impeachment is, therefore, merely the first step in a two-stage process. In the national government, constitutional authority to impeach is vested in the House and the power to try impeachment cases in the Senate. All civil officers of the United States are subject to impeachment, excluding military officers and congressmen. The impeachment process begins with the preferring of charges by a representative, followed by referral to either the Judiciary Committee or to a special investigating committee. A simple majority vote of the House is sufficient to impeach. "Articles of impeachment" are drawn up, setting forth the basis for removal. The House appoints managers who prosecute the case in a trial before the Senate. If a President is on trial, the Chief Justice of the United States presides. The procedure during the trial closely resembles that of a court of law. A two-thirds vote in secret session is necessary for conviction. The only punishments that may be meted out are removal from office and disqualification from holding any office in the future. Once removed, however, the individual may be tried in a regular court of law if he has committed a criminal act. The President's pardoning power does not apply to impeachment convictions.
• *Significance:* In the course of American history, only 12 officers have been impeached and only four convicted, all of them judges. President Andrew Johnson was acquitted by the margin of a single vote in 1868. Few state officials have been convicted and removed by state legislatures. Occasionally, partisan politics may influence the exercise of the power as was true in the Johnson case and in the removal of several state officials by their legislatures.

Initiative.   An electoral device by which interested citizens can propose legislation or constitutional amendments through initiatory petitions signed by the required number of registered voters. The number of signatures varies from 5 to 15 percent of the voters in the different states. The proposition is then voted on by the people. Constitutional amendment proposals usually require a greater number of signatures on the petitions. The "direct" initiative involves a vote of the people following the filing of petitions; the "indirect" provides that the proposal, after being filed, be sent to the legislature. If not approved, it then goes before the voters.
• *Significance:* Fewer than one half of the states provide for the initiative in either form. In 1962, 20 states permitted its use for ordinary laws and 13 for constitutional amendments. Only one state, Alaska, has adopted the initiative

since 1918. The national government does not employ the initiative, but groups have, from time to time, advocated its adoption.

Investigating Committee.   A committee engaged in investigating legislative subjects. Investigations have become one of the most important adjuncts of the legislative process. They are conducted by both the regular standing committees and by special committees created for that purpose by resolution or statute. The purposes behind investigations include (1) finding of facts on which to base legislation; (2) discovering or developing of public opinion; (3) overseeing of administrative agencies; (4) uncovering the questionable activities of public officials and private individuals; and (5) sometimes securing personal or partisan political gain. In time, effort, and publicity, the investigatory activities of Congress and some state legislatures have in recent years rivaled their legislative functions. A legislative body may investigate any subject which is properly within the scope of its legislative powers.

• *Significance:* Many important topics have been investigated in over 600 congressional investigations in our nation's history. Some have been mere "fishing expeditions" and others were politically motivated by attempts to embarrass the rival party. Increasingly, the Congress has relied on investigations as a means of seeking to regain its position of power vis-à-vis the executive branch, which has steadily been gaining in relative power during this century. Serious questions have been raised concerning the scope of congressional inquiries, the rights of witnesses who appear before committees, fair procedures, and the extraction of testimony from unwilling witnesses and executive officials. Congress has sought to deal with some of these problems through the study and correction of procedures and the setting up of a "fair play" guarantee for witnesses.

Joint Committee.   A legislative committee composed of members of both houses. The number appointed to a joint committee is usually divided equally between the two houses with each member having one vote. On some, such as conference committees, each chamber may determine the size of its membership on the committee, and the two groups vote separately on measures. Joint committees are usually select (special) committees appointed for a specified purpose: typically, to conduct investigations. Congress has created a few standing (permanent) joint committees, such as the Joint Committee on the Economic Report, and the Joint Committee on Atomic Energy.

• *Significance:* Joint committees make it possible for the two houses of a legislative body to work out compromises on bills or mutual problems. They tend to encourage greater cooperation and co-ordination between the activities of the two chambers. Some observers have recommended that all standing committees of Congress be joint committees so that time-consuming duplication of the existing dual-committee system could be eliminated. Supporters of this proposal believe that it would result in quicker and more effective action on most bills and it would eliminate the need for two appearances before separate committees by persons wishing to testify for or against a bill. Opponents point out that such a change would eliminate much of the effectiveness of the checks and balances system inherent in a bicameral legislative body.

Joint Resolution.   A measure similar to a bill, which must be approved in both chambers and by the executive. In the Congress, joint resolutions are designated "H J Res" and "S J Res" and, if passed by a simple majority in both houses, must be signed by the President to become law. The procedure is identical to that used in passing a bill into law except when the joint resolution is used to propose an amendment to the Constitution. Then the President's signature is unnecessary. About half of the state legislatures also employ the joint resolution in enacting laws and proposing constitutional amendments.

• *Significance:* Joint resolutions are employed by the Congress to approve of executive actions in foreign affairs or to take the initiative in foreign policy. They have occasionally proved useful in circumventing the two-thirds vote requirement in the Senate on treaty matters, as in the annexation of Texas and of Hawaii. Joint resolutions are also used for such limited matters as the passing of a single appropriation bill for a designated purpose.

Joint Session.   The meeting together of the members of both chambers of a legislative body.

• *Significance:* The Congress meets in joint session to count the electoral votes and certify the election of the President, and when addressed by the President or a foreign dignitary. A joint session is never used to consider specific bills. Most state legislatures meet in joint session to receive the governor's annual message.

Legislative Council.   An interim committee employed by some legislatures to study state problems and to plan a legislative program. In some states, legislative councils have pursued extensive fact-finding research programs. The councils range in size from five members to the entire legislature. Usually, membership is selected from the two houses of the legislature, but, in several states, the governor is authorized to include representation from the executive branch.

• *Significance:* Legislative councils are one means by which the legislatures of three fourths of the states have sought to develop leadership and planning facilities staffed by their own members. In this way, dependence on the executive to formulate a comprehensive program for consideration by the legislature is reduced. Moreover, as the workload becomes heavier and more complex, legislatures are becoming more dependent upon well-prepared programs worked out carefully in advance of their typically intermittent and brief sessions. The fear that power might become too concentrated in the hands of those legislators making up the councils has not been justified in the experience of the states that have adopted the plan.

Logrolling.   An arrangement by which two or more members of a legislative body agree in advance to support each other's bills. The technique pertains especially to the trading of votes among legislators in order to gain support for appropriations beneficial to each legislator's home district (pork barrel legislation).

• *Significance:* Over the years, billions of dollars have been spent on the improvement of rivers and harbors and other local projects. Much of this has been spent wisely, but much also has been appropriated on the basis of congressional logrolling. To the extent that logrolling exists, it probably results from the American belief that a representative should seek to "deliver the goods" for his home district, which encourages "horse trading."

Majority Floor Leader.   The chief spokesman and strategist of the majority party who directs the party's forces in legislative battles. In the House, only the Speaker is considered to be more influential. In the Senate, the Majority Leader is the undisputed leader of his party. He seeks to carry out decisions of his party's caucus and Policy Committee, and is aided by party whips. His counterpart in the other party is the minority floor leader. Floor leaders are selected by their respective party caucuses. Similar party leadership positions exist in most state legislatures.
• *Significance:* Much of the success of a floor leader depends on his ability. If he is an able organizer and possesses personal characteristics of real leadership, he can exercise considerable influence on legislation. In the Senate, he must work closely with the minority leader because much business is transacted through unanimous consent.

Pair.   An understanding in advance between two legislators, holding opposing views on a bill, to withhold their votes on a yea-and-nay roll call. In this way, each is assured that his absence from the chamber during the vote will not affect the outcome. In effect, each member of the pair cancels out the other's vote. A "special" pair applies to one or several votes taken on the same subject. A "general" pair, occasionally used in the Senate, applies to all votes taken over a specified period of time. On a question requiring a two-thirds vote, two members must be "paired for" the measure to balance off one "paired against" it.
• *Significance:* The advantage of pairing lies in the nature of the "gentlemen's agreement" between the two lawmakers. Neither can show up unexpectedly and vote in the roll call without breaking the agreement. Each, in effect, casts a vote by cancelling out the other's vote, although they are not counted in vote totals. Members of Congress frequently find it necessary to be absent from their chamber, and pairing enables them to put their position on bills on record.

Pigeonhole.   To kill a bill in committee by putting it aside and not reporting it out for consideration by the chamber. The term relates to the old-time desks in committee rooms of the Congress which had open "pigeonholes" rather than drawers with handles. To pigeonhole a bill means, figuratively, to open the desk and file the bill away and forget it. This usually kills the bill.
• *Significance:* More bills die in committee each congressional session than are rejected before the two houses. The same is true in the state legislatures. The chances for a pigeonholed bill to be enacted into law are slight because members of the chamber are reluctant to use the extraordinary procedures required to discharge bills from committee.

Policy Committee.   Party committees in the United States Senate which formulate majority and minority party plans and strategy. They were created in 1946 as part of the general reorganization of the Congress. Though membership is fixed by law at seven, both parties have added additional members so as to give representation to all major regions of the nation and important factions in the party.

• *Significance:* The policy committees have substantially superseded the Democratic and Republican steering committees in the Senate as the basic party strategy organs. Both meet frequently, and the majority policy committee plans its party's legislative program to determine when and how bills will be considered.

Pork Barrel Legislation.   Appropriations made by a legislative body providing for expenditures of sums of public money on local projects not critically needed. The term is closely related to logrolling, in that members of the legislative body usually do not question each other's pet projects for fear that their own may be voted down. It is frequently a simple matter of *quid pro quo*—that is, "You scratch my back and I'll scratch yours."

• *Significance:* Pork barrel legislation results in the expenditure of large sums of money each year. Basically, the problem relates to the theory of representation. The American representative goes to his legislature or to the Congress as the representative of the people of his district rather than of the state or nation. This means that he will be expected by his constituents to perform creditably on their behalf. If he can obtain "pork" (appropriations for local highways, river and harbor construction projects, etc.) by raiding the pork barrel (the state or national treasury) he is likely to improve his chances for re-election.

Power of the Purse.   The historic power of democratic legislative bodies to control the finances of government. The power extends to both revenue and appropriation functions. In the national government, the Constitution specifies that "No money shall be drawn from the Treasury, but in consequence of appropriations made by law." (Art. I, sec. 9). New programs must be twice approved, first, through authorization and, second, through appropriation to finance them. Expenditures by the executive must be validated by the General Accounting Office to ensure that such outlays fall within the limits of appropriations made by the Congress. Additional checks are carried on through the "watchdog" oversight committees of Congress.

• *Significance:* The "power of the purse" remains a major power of all legislative bodies. The power can be used in an affirmative manner to force positive action by government as well as in a negative way to stop action. The threat of budget cutting is usually enough to elicit cooperation from executive officials. Historically, legislative bodies first succeeded in limiting executive absolutism through control of the purse. One of the major grievances leading to the American Revolution was the taxation of the colonists without their consent.

President pro Tempore.   The temporary presiding officer of the Senate. He is elected by the Senate following his nomination by the majority party caucus. He is eligible for the presidency of the United States following the death or disability of the President, Vice President, and Speaker of the House.

• *Significance:* Like the Speaker of the House, the President pro tempore is a partisan office, used when possible to aid the program of the majority party. Although the office is usually overshadowed by that of the majority floor leader, it is one of considerable prestige.

Previous Question.   A motion in a legislative body to cease debate and force a vote on a pending measure. In the Congress, the rules permit its use in the House but not in the Senate. The motion itself cannot be debated nor laid on the table. If the motion carries before any debate on the bill has occurred, each side is allowed 20 minutes to present its case. State legislatures use similar rules to limit debate.

• *Significance:* The "previous question" rule in the House makes it possible to avoid unlimited discussion such as occurs during a filibuster in the Senate. With 435 members in the House, such a rule is necessary to prevent the chamber from bogging down in endless debate. It is also used as a parliamentary device to prevent amendments which might cripple a bill.

Private Bill.   Bills introduced into a legislative body which deal with specific matters and individuals rather than general legislative affairs. In the Congress, although the number of private bills was considerably reduced by the Reorganization Act of 1946, thousands are still introduced at each session. The main categories today include (1) immigration and naturalization bills applying to specific individuals; (2) claim bills not subject to administrative resolution; and (3) land bills assigning title to individuals. Private bills are introduced by congressmen who are petitioned by their constituents to right a government-inflicted wrong or to deal with a matter not covered by general statute. If enacted, they become private law and apply only to specific individuals named in the act. All state legislatures allow introduction of private bills.

• *Significance:* Many observers believe that it would add considerably to the efficiency of Congress to reduce further the categories of private bills. Their complete elimination is unlikely. Private bills tend to force the legislative body into performing a judicial-like function in determining the merits of particular claims made by individuals. They are time-consuming and detract from the general lawmaking function of the Congress as well as of the legislatures in the states. Further use of administrative agencies to handle these matters could serve to lighten the burden on the legislative body.

Quorum.   The minimum number of members of a legislative chamber who must be present in order to transact business. The Constitution specifies that "a majority of each [house] shall constitute a quorum to do business." (Art. I, sec. 5). This means 218 in the House and 51 in the Senate. In the House, the quorum for the Committee of the Whole is 100. Typically, state legislatures also require a majority of members to be present for the transaction of business.

• *Significance:* The House frequently escapes the quorum requirement of 218 by dissolving into the Committee of the Whole. Decisions reached, however, must be ratified by the duly constituted House. Both chambers often proceed with fewer than a quorum present unless challenged by a point of order. When this occurs, either the chamber must adjourn or the Sergeant at Arms is instructed to round up the absent members.

Ranking Member. That member of the majority party on a legislative committee who ranks first after the chairman in number of years of continuous service (seniority) on the committee.
• *Significance:* In the Congress, the ranking member automatically succeeds to the chairmanship of a committee if that post is vacated while his party has majority control of that house. The ranking member is often accorded the chairmanship of one of the committee's important subcommittees. Most state legislatures follow the same procedures.

Ranking Minority Member. The minority party member of a legislative committee with the longest continuous service (seniority) on the committee.
• *Significance:* In the Congress, the ranking minority member succeeds to the chairmanship of the committee when his party wins control of that house. Most state legislatures also follow the rule of seniority. The ranking minority member also provides some leadership for the minority members on the committee.

Ratification. A power vested in a legislative body to approve (or reject) agreements entered into with other states and constitutional amendment proposals. In the states, interstate compacts negotiated by the governors of several states must be approved by the state legislature of each before becoming effective. Amendments proposed to the United States Constitution must be ratified by legislatures or conventions in three fourths of the states to become effective. Amendments proposed to state constitutions, however, must be ratified by a vote of the people of that state. The term, ratification, is also popularly used to describe the "consent" function of the United States Senate regarding treaties negotiated by the United States with foreign nations, although here the term more properly applies to the role of the President in accepting or rejecting the Senate version of a treaty.
• *Significance:* The power to ratify is important because it includes the power to reject as well as to approve. It gives the legislative body an effective check over agreements entered into with other states and over changes made in the fundamental law. Often, important agreements and amendment proposals are killed by the failure of legislatures to bring them to a vote.

Readings. The three readings of a bill required at different stages of the legislative process. In the Congress, the first reading occurs when the bill is introduced and printed by title in the *Congressional Record*. The second, often a reading in full, takes place when the bill is brought out of committee for consideration before the chamber. The third reading, usually by title only, comes after amendments have been voted on and the bill is up for a final vote. State legislative procedure is quite similar.
• *Significance:* The required three readings of a bill, based on traditional parliamentary law, is expected to ensure careful consideration of all bills and to prevent any from sneaking through almost unnoticed. The procedure is of

little significance today in the legislative process of either the Congress or the state legislatures. On occasion, full reading of a bill may be demanded, and used, as a delaying tactic.

Recommittal.   The action of a legislative body to send a bill back to the committee which had reported it out for consideration. A motion to recommit may instruct the committee to report the bill out again with certain amendments or at a later date. Most motions for recommittal, however, simply call for further study by the committee.

• *Significance:* In most cases, the adoption of a motion to recommit a bill to committee is considered a death blow. Often legislators prefer not to alienate constituents who support a bill by directly voting it down. Recommittal can accomplish the same purpose without giving the appearance of killing the bill.

Record Vote.   A "yea or nay" roll call vote in a legislative body in which each member's vote is required to be recorded. Those members not voting for or against the measure will either be "paired" or "present." In the Congress, the Constitution requires a record vote on overriding a presidential veto, and whenever one fifth of the members demand it. Record votes are not taken in Committee of the Whole. State constitutions also require record votes on important measures before the state legislatures.

• *Significance:* In the Congress, a roll call vote is demanded on almost all important bills. In a representative system of government it is essential that the voters have an opportunity to examine a legislator's voting record. In the House of Representatives, a record vote is frequently used as a delaying tactic to allow time for absent members to participate in the vote. Some state legislatures have installed electronic voting devices so that a complete record of the vote can be made instantaneously.

Redistricting.   The action of a legislative body in redrawing legislative electoral district lines following a new population census. After each decennial federal census, congressional seats are reapportioned among the 50 states. In each state that gains or loses seats, the state legislature usually draws up new districts. Additionally, state legislatures are required by most state constitutions to redraw district boundary lines for electing state representatives and senators to the legislatures following each federal census.

• *Significance:* The power to redistrict or to refuse to redistrict is one of the most important exercised by state legislatures. Redistricting decisions, typically, are made by partisan majorities in the legislatures, and the partisan nature of the undertaking is usually reflected in the final results. Large cities are especially underrepresented and rural areas tend to be grossly overrepresented, reflecting the rural dominance in the state legislatures today. The failures to redistrict or to redistrict on a population basis tend in many states to result in continuing political conflicts between the rural dominated and conservative-minded legislative majorities and the urban dominated and liberal-minded executives elected by state-wide votes.

Refer to Committee.   The sending of a bill introduced into one of the houses of a legislative body to a standing committee. In the Congress, public bills are assigned to committees by the parliamentarian under the scrutiny of the presiding officer in each house. Private bills are usually referred to the committee requested by the senator or representative who introduces the bill.

• *Significance:* Referral of bills to the proper committee is generally a routine matter. Some bills may include subject matter pertinent to several committees. In such cases, the presiding officer in each house may exercise some discretion in assigning bills, which may have a significant effect on whether specific bills are killed in committee or reported out. For example, the Speaker of the House would be likely to refer a bill to a committee favoring such legislation if he personally favored it, whereas if he opposed such legislation, he would likely refer it to a committee hostile toward such legislation. In each house, the majority of members can overrule the decision of the presiding officer by removing a bill from one committee's jurisdiction and assigning it to another. This is a rare occurrence.

Report.   The action of a legislative committee in sending out its findings and recommendations to its chamber following consideration of a bill or investigation of some matter. The report explains the reasons for the committee's action. Most committee reports are favorable, but on rare occasions a committee will report out a bill with a recommendation that its parent chamber kill the bill. In any case, many reports are not unanimous, and those members of the committee who dissent may file a minority report. If a bill has been amended in committee, the majority report will provide an explanation for this action.

• *Significance:* Typically, the great majority of bills introduced each session in a legislative body fail to become law because they are not reported out by the various committees to which they have been assigned. In the House of Representatives, a committee's refusal to report out a bill for consideration can be overridden only by the rarely used discharge rule, and in the Senate the discharge resolution can be used. Most bills and resolutions reported out with recommendations to the chamber that they be passed are acted on favorably. Recommendations on bills of a controversial political nature are of lesser importance in influencing action in the chamber. In the House, bills reported out by committees are sent first to the Rules Committee, which also has the power to kill bills by refusing to report them out for floor consideration.

Rider.   A provision, unlikely to pass on its own merits, added to an important bill so that it will "ride" through the legislative process. Riders become law if the bills to which they are attached are passed.

• *Significance:* In the Congress, most riders are attached to appropriations bills, although this procedure is technically banned under the rules of the House and Senate. Opponents of the rider, and the President, are forced to accept it if they want the bill to become law. In several states, the governors have been given the item veto power which permits them to veto only those sections of a bill with which they disagree, allowing the remainder to become law. Such power vested in the President would go far toward meeting the problem of riders.

Rules Committee.   A standing committee of the House of Representatives that can provide special rules under which specific bills will be debated, amended, and considered by the House. The Rules Committee functions as a valve or sifting device to control the flow of bills from the committees to the floor for consideration.

• *Significance:* Because more bills are reported out of committees than the House has time to consider, the Rules Committee functions as a legislative traffic control officer. In this role it can exercise a virtual veto power over bills reported out by other committees. It can, conversely, send out bills to be considered under favorable procedures. Much depends on the attitudes of the chairman and members toward such legislation. If the majority of the Committee favor a bill, this will likely be reflected in the rule specified for consideration of that bill. The Committee may also provide a "gag" rule by which amendments to the bill may be forbidden or limited to specified areas. Because of these powers, the Rules Committee exercises almost a life or death power over legislation in the House. Under the House procedure, a bill can be pulled out of the Rules Committee by means of a discharge petition signed by a majority of the House members. This method has not proved satisfactory because of a reluctance of congressmen to challenge committee leadership and prerogatives. In 1961, under pressure from the new Kennedy administration, the membership of the Rules Committee was enlarged by three to a total of 15. This was an attempt to offset the conservative control of the Committee through the addition of liberals who would help to prevent the Committee from sitting on some of the major presidential legislative proposals. The Rules Committee remains the most powerful in the House today.

Select Committee.   A legislative committee established for a limited time period and for a special purpose. Select committees may be created by either house or may include members from both houses (joint committee).

• *Significance:* Select committees are given assignments which do not fall within the jurisdiction of any standing committee, or which the latter may prefer not to carry on. Most special committees have been given investigatory duties, although others have been assigned supervisory, housekeeping, and co-ordination responsibilities. The Legislative Reorganization Act of 1946 reduced the need for select committees by placing responsibility for investigations in the standing committees.

Senate.   The upper house of the United States Congress and of 49 state legislatures. Representation in the United States Senate is based on the principle of state equality, and the Constitution specifies that no state may be deprived of its equal representation in the Senate without its consent. Today, the Senate is comprised of 100 Senators from 50 states. State senates are generally chosen on an area basis and many are small in size. In the Congress, the Vice President is the presiding officer over the Senate, and in the state legislatures, the lieutenant governor normally presides. In the absence of a presiding officer, a president pro tempore elected from the membership assumes that role.

• *Significance:* In the Congress, the Senate shares the lawmaking function with the House. Many observers believe that because of the Senate's greater prestige, it plays a more important role than the lower house in making laws. Also, contrary to popular myth, many observers regard the Senate as being more responsive to public opinion than the House because it tends to represent more accurately the large urban majorities of the nation. Aside from the lawmaking and representational functions, the Senate is also vested with special powers, including the power to try all impeachments and to give its advice and consent to treaties and appointments. If no candidate for the vice presidency receives a majority of the electoral vote, the Senate then elects the Vice President from the two candidates with the highest electoral votes. State senates tend to be less representative in nature than their lower houses, but in many cases they, too, exercise special powers, such as confirmation of appointments and trial of impeached officials.

Senator.   A member of the United States Senate or of the upper house in state legislatures. United States senators have been directly elected by the people of their respective states since the adoption of the 17th Amendment in 1913. Their term of office is for six years, with one third of the Senate seats up for election every two years. Vacancies are usually filled by appointment by the state's governor, although the legislature may provide for a special election. The Constitution provides that a senator must be at least 30 years of age, a citizen for nine years, and a resident of the state from which he is elected. In the state legislatures, senators are in all cases elected by the people.
• *Significance:* In the Congress, senators generally are regarded as more capable and as having greater prestige than their colleagues in the lower house. Many representatives aspire to achieve election to the Senate. Most senators represent more constituents than do House members, and the smaller size of the chamber makes more thorough deliberation on measures possible. In state legislatures, the average senator represents more constituents than does a member of the lower house and usually exercises considerable power in state matters.

Senatorial Courtesy.   An unwritten agreement among senators which requires the President to confer with the senator or senators of his party from a state before he makes a nomination to fill a federal office in that state. The Senate will almost invariably reject a presidential nominee when the senator involved raises a personal objection. When neither senator of a state is of the President's party, the President is apt to consult state party leaders.
• *Significance:* Senatorial courtesy has resulted in the transferring from the President to senators of his party the patronage distribution within a state. This means that such senators normally choose the appointees and give their names to the President. Federal positions affected by senatorial courtesy include judges, district attorneys, customs officials, postmasters, and field service officials of most important agencies. Presidents may reject senatorial recommendations, but this rarely occurs. An example arose in 1951, when President Harry Truman nominated two persons to fill vacant judgeships in Illinois without consulting Democratic Senator Paul H. Douglas. The latter called upon his Senate colleagues to show him "courtesy" by voting down the two appointees. President Truman, however, remained adamant and refused to nominate the two choices of Senator Douglas. The end result was that these positions were finally

filled by President Dwight Eisenhower several years later with two Republicans. The case illustrates the importance of senatorial courtesy to the Senate, to the President, and to the political party involved.

Seniority Rule.   A custom nearly always followed in both houses of the Congress of awarding chairmanships of committees to the majority party member who has the longest number of years of continuous service on the committee. On committees, each party, majority and minority alike, lists its members strictly according to the seniority rule. When a high-ranking member leaves the committee, all members of that party move up one notch on the seniority list. Most state legislatures follow the seniority rule.

• *Significance:* The seniority rule has been a source of much controversy inside and outside the Congress. Supporters of seniority argue that (1) it guarantees chairmen will have had long experience in committee matters; (2) it avoids intrigues, conflicts, and deadlocks within the party organizations which would inevitably occur whenever a new chairman was chosen; (3) it makes possible the rise to positions of importance of the congressmen from small states; and (4) it has produced men of ability and stature in the chairmanships of the important committees. Opponents of seniority argue that (1) it tends to hold back men of ability while often it moves mediocre men steadily ahead; (2) it requires nothing more of a man than that he continue living and getting re-elected; (3) it tends to favor the stagnant, one-party voting areas of the nation over the two-party competitive areas which reflect changes in public opinion; and (4) it reduces party responsibility by filling most key power positions in both houses with members from the conservative wings of either party. Likelihood of changing the seniority rule is remote.

Session.   The period during which a legislative body assembles and carries on its regular business. Each Congress has two regular sessions based on the requirement in the Constitution that the Congress assemble at least once each year. In addition, the Congress may be summoned into special session by the President. The first session of a Congress usually begins on January 3 of odd-numbered years, with the start of the terms of all representatives and one third of the senators. The second session begins January 3 of the even-numbered years. The Congress which assembled in January 1961, for example, was the 87th Congress, 1st session. Adjournment is left up to the Congress, although the Constitution provides that if the two houses cannot agree on a date, the President may adjourn them at his discretion. No president has exercised this authority. In the states, most legislatures convene in regular session every two years, although 17 have regular annual sessions. Most state constitutions limit the length of legislative sessions either by specifying the number of days or by cutting off pay and allowances for legislators after a certain date.

• *Significance:* To cope with the many complex problems of modern society, a legislative body must be in session regularly and not only at widely separated intervals. Because the Constitution leaves sessions pretty much up to the discretion of Congress, this problem does not exist in the national government. In most of the states, however, sessions are generally short and infrequent.

Constitutional revision is needed in most states to free the legislatures from restrictions that date back more than a century.

Seventeenth Amendment.   An amendment to the Constitution of the United States, proclaimed May 31, 1913, which provides for the direct election of United States senators. The amendment changed those sections of Article I which authorize senators to be chosen by the legislatures of the states. It also provides that, when a vacancy occurs, the legislature may authorize the gover- nor to make a temporary appointment until a special election can be held. Most legislatures have so authorized their governors.
• *Significance:* Prior to the adoption of the 17th Amendment, selection of senators frequently resulted in lengthy distractions from normal state legis- lative business. Deadlocks in the selection process often resulted in states going unrepresented in the Senate for many months. Although popular election is no guarantee of fitness, most observers believe that senatorial abilities, stature, and responsiveness to the public will, have all tended to increase since 1913.

Simple Resolution.   A measure adopted by one chamber of a legislative body. It does not require approval either by the other house or by the Presi- dent. Simple resolutions are designated either "H Res" or "S Res."
• *Significance:* Simple resolutions do not have the force of law. They are usu- ally adopted for the purpose of making or amending rules of procedure. In the Congress, one chamber may adopt a resolution to express its sentiment on a current issue or to give advice to the President on foreign policy or in other areas of executive responsibility.

Sine Die.   Adjournment of a legislative body without fixing a specific day for reconvening. It differs from "adjournment to a day certain" wherein the exact time of the next meeting is set in the adjournment resolution.
• *Significance:* Adoption of a resolution for adjournment sine die marks the end of a session of Congress. The Legislative Reorganization Act of 1946 provides that the two houses shall adjourn sine die each year by the end of July, unless the Congress provides otherwise.

Speaker of the House.   The presiding officer in the House of Representatives and in the lower chamber of state legislatures. His election by the House is a formality which follows his selection by the majority party caucus. As a mem- ber of the House, the Speaker may engage in debate and vote on measures.
• *Significance:* The Speaker is the most powerful and influential member of the House. As presiding officer, he recognizes members wishing to speak, interprets and applies the rules, and decides questions of order. Although he can be overruled by the House itself, this rarely occurs. He appoints select and con- ference committees and refers bills to committee. His real importance lies in the fact that, in exercising all of the foregoing powers, the Speaker may use his own discretion and political acumen. He is thus placed in a strategic position whereby he can influence the passage or rejection of bills at almost every stage in the legislative process in the House. As the leader of the majority party in the House, the Speaker also exercises considerable power in shaping and im-

plementing party decisions on pending legislation. Most Speakers have been men of ability, stature, and tact, able to provide the kind of leadership needed by the majority party. The role and powers of speakers in the various state legislatures are analogous to those of the Speaker in the House of Representatives, with the additional power to appoint members of standing committees as well.

Special Session.   An extraordinary session of a legislative body convoked, usually, on the initiative of a chief executive. The Constitution grants power to the President to summon the Congress or either house into session "on extraordinary occasions" (Art. II, sec. 3). Although the House has never been called into special session, the Senate has been convoked to act upon executive appointments or treaties. In all 50 states, the governors are empowered to call special sessions of the legislatures. In several states, a stipulated number of legislators may petition the governor to call the legislature into session. In a few others, the legislature can call itself into special session.
• *Significance:* The Congress when called into special session possesses full constitutional power to legislate. In about one half the states, legislatures convened in special sessions are similarly free to act, whereas in the other half they are limited to acting upon what the governor specifies in his call. Calling of special sessions of the Congress may be useful in meeting a sudden crisis or new problem. In 1939, when Europe went to war, President Franklin D. Roosevelt called such a session for the purpose of securing the repeal of the Neutrality Acts. In two instances, angry state legislators, called into unwanted special sessions, have retaliated by impeaching and removing the governor. Although executive officials may summon legislative bodies into special sessions, they cannot exercise appreciable control over legislative action or inaction once convened.

Split Session.   A session of a legislative body which is divided into two parts with a recess period between them. Under a split session arrangement, the legislature meets for a short period, usually less than a month, to organize, introduce bills, and pass urgent measures. Then the legislature adjourns for a month or more, during which time members study pending legislation and consult their constituents. The legislature then reconvenes to consider the bills introduced in the first part of the session, with the introduction of new bills severely restricted.
• *Significance:* Several states, including California, have experimented with the split session. Its objective is to provide fuller consideration of legislation by giving legislators more free time to study bills, by enabling public opinion to develop and be heard, and by reducing the last minute rush at the end of a session.

Standing Committee.   A regular committee of a legislative body which considers bills within a subject matter area. In the Congress, there are 19 House and 15 Senate standing committees. House committees range in size from 9 to 50 members and Senate committees from 9 to 23 members. Representatives are normally assigned to only one standing committee, senators to two. In the

House, the leading standing committees include Rules, Ways and Means, Appropriations, Foreign Affairs, Commerce, and Agriculture. In the Senate, influential committees include Foreign Relations, Appropriations, Finance, Judiciary, Armed Services, and Banking and Currency. The majority party in each house holds a majority vote on each committee and the chairmanship. Positions of importance on the committees are determined under the rules of seniority.

• *Significance:* The standing committee system operates on the principle of specialization secured through a division of labor. Members of Congress usually respect the decisions and recommendations made by the standing committees on pending legislation. This has resulted in the fate of most bills being decided in committee rather than on the floors of the two chambers. This great power led Woodrow Wilson to describe American government as "government by the standing committees of Congress."

Steering Committee. A party committee in a legislative body entrusted with the responsibility of achieving party goals. With the floor leader as chairman, the majority party steering committee often determines the order in which measures will be considered. Acting as an agent of the party caucus, its members seek to rally partisan support for or against bills. In the House of Representatives, the Democratic Steering Committee has 15 members representing geographical areas, selected by Democratic congressmen from those areas, and six ex officio members. The Republican Steering Committee in the House consists of ten members chosen by the committee on committees, four members ex officio, plus the Republican members of the Rules Committee.

• *Significance:* In the Senate, the steering committees have been overshadowed by the policy committees. In recent sessions, the Senate Republicans have not bothered to organize their steering committee, and the Democrats use their committee solely for assigning members to other committees. In the House, the steering committees of both parties have remained active in directing party activity and strategy. Party organizations in most state legislatures also seek to carry out party decisions through steering committees. The importance of steering committees to the legislative process varies, depending upon the degree of party unity, the power of the rules committees, and the personalities and drive of the individuals on the committees.

Supplementary Appropriation. An appropriation of public money authorized by a legislative body after the regular appropriation bills have been enacted. It differs from a deficiency appropriation in that it is passed prior to the fiscal period in which it will be spent.

• *Significance:* Supplementary appropriations are useful in correcting miscalculations in the budget process, in meeting new problems, and in reacting to changes in public opinion.

Suspension of Rules. A time-saving procedure used by a legislative body to bring a measure to a vote. In the House of Representatives, a motion to "suspend the rules and pass the bill" requires a two-thirds vote of members present for passage. Debate on the bill is limited to 40 minutes and no amendments are permitted.

• *Significance:* Because of the size of the House, a means by which debate can be closed and a measure brought to a vote quickly is necessary to the flow of business. The Senate, with its rules for unlimited debate, can obtain these results only through unanimous consent.

Teller Vote.   An unrecorded vote in which the members of a legislative body are counted as they file past tellers. In the Congress, the House, but not the Senate, uses teller votes, which can be demanded by one fifth of a quorum (44 in the House, 20 in Committee of the Whole). When a teller vote is called, two tellers, one for and one against, stand in front of the Speaker's desk and count the votes as the members file past. The Speaker then announces the results, but individual votes are not announced.

• *Significance:* A teller vote offers a means of securing an accurate vote quickly. However, by not recording the individual congressman's vote his accountability to his constituents is weakened.

Twentieth Amendment.   Provides that a new Congress elected in November of even-numbered years start work on January 3 of the following year. Prior to its adoption, a newly elected Congress did not convene in regular session until December of the following year, a lapse of 13 months. The old Congress, meanwhile, with many members who had failed to win re-election ("lame ducks"), met in perfunctory session for four months following the election. A decade of agitation against this anachronism, led by Senator George W. Norris of Nebraska, was capped with the adoption of the 20th Amendment in February 1933. The Amendment also changed the presidential term to start a month and one half earlier, on January 20 instead of on March 4. *See* TWENTIETH AMENDMENT, page 167.

• *Significance:* The Amendment provides for more democracy and greater efficiency. By reducing the interim period between an election and the assumption of office by newly elected congressmen, the people's mandate may be more quickly and accurately realized. By changing the President's term to start at an earlier date, a new President has the opportunity to present his legislative and budgetary programs to the Congress to coincide with the start of the legislative session. Some observers, including former Presidents, have suggested that the interim period be still further reduced so as to enable a new Congress and President to come to grips with pressing problems of government at an even earlier date following the election.

Unanimous Consent.   A time-saving procedure used by a legislative body to adopt noncontroversial motions, amendments, and bills without submitting them to a vote. Both houses of the Congress use the procedure to expedite business. In the House, an objection from a single member results in the bill or motion being tabled for two weeks.

• *Significance:* Unanimous consent can be useful in rapidly disposing of a host of minor matters which are cluttering up a legislature's docket. By expediting noncontroversial measures, more time is made available for dealing with the really crucial issues.

Unicameralism.   The principle of a one-house legislature, as contrasted with bicameralism or a legislature based on two houses. One state legislature—Nebraska's—is unicameral, as are local governmental policy-determining bodies, such as county boards, city councils, township boards, and school boards.
• *Significance:* The merits of unicameralism include (1) greater economy and efficiency of operation; (2) greater prestige which attracts outstanding citizens; (3) elimination of deadlocks resulting from rivalry and friction between two houses; (4) elimination of the need for conference committees; and (5) more accurate fixing of responsibility of elected representatives by the public. Arguments against unicameralism include (1) hasty, careless, ill-considered legislation may result; (2) special interest lobbies can concentrate their influence more effectively against one house; (3) one house may be more susceptible to aroused popular passions and other democratic excesses; (4) only one basis of representation, such as population, can be followed; and (5) control over a one-house legislature may be focussed in a single major interest group or in a small geographical area.

Vice President.   The presiding officer of the United States Senate. Unless he assumes the presidency, the Vice President remains primarily a legislative official. *See* VICE PRESIDENT, page 169.
• *Significance:* Unlike the Speaker of the House, the President of the Senate is not the chosen leader of the majority party in the Senate, nor is he a member of the Senate. He cannot speak from the floor on issues and, as presiding officer, he must not show his partisanship. He can cast a vote only in case of a tie. Although the vice president's powers are negligible, he may, as some have, exercise considerable influence in the Senate's decision making by reason of his ability and personal powers of persuasion. Also, if he is a leader of high standing in the majority party of the Senate, his potential influence is increased. In recent years, a succession of vice presidents selected from the Senate—John N. Garner, Harry Truman, Alvin Barkley, Richard M. Nixon, and Lyndon B. Johnson—have proved to be valuable liaison agents between the President and the Congress. The vice presidency appears to be moving in the direction of bridging the gap between the executive and legislative branches.

Viva Voce Vote.   A voice vote in a legislative chamber in which the presiding officer determines the outcome from the volume of response from those for and against the measure.
• *Significance:* Viva voce votes on important measures are often challenged because it is difficult to determine voice volume with precision. Much discretion can be exercised by the presiding officer if left unchallenged. Its main advantage lies in the speed with which it permits great quantities of business to be transacted. A defect of this procedure is that individual votes are not recorded.

Watchdog Committee.   A committee established by a legislative body for the purpose of overseeing the administration of the laws. In the Congress prior to 1946, each house created a number of select committees to perform this oversight function. In the Legislative Reorganization Act of 1946 the Congress vested the "watchdog" responsibility in the standing committees, each responsible for overseeing the execution of laws within its jurisdiction.

• *Significance:* In its report in 1946 that led to the Reorganization Act, the Joint Committee stated: "Without effective legislative oversight of the activities of the vast executive branch, the line of democracy wears thin." The Committee recommended "a continuous review of the agencies administering laws originally reported by the committees." The Government Operations Committees of the House and the Senate have been given the special responsibility of "studying the operation of government activities at all levels with a view to determining its economy and efficiency." Congressional oversight can be distinguished from congressional investigations in that the former is more of a continuing scrutiny of executive operations whereas the latter involves a more intense digging for facts within a limited problem area.

Ways and Means Committee.   A standing committee of the House of Representatives to which all bills for raising revenue are referred. Its 25 members study tax and tariff bills and make recommendations to the full House. Occasionally, the Committee itself writes new tax measures.

• *Significance:* The Ways and Means Committee is usually regarded as second in importance only to the House Rules Committee. Democratic members of the Committee are chosen by the Democratic caucus. These members then assign the Democratic members to all other House committees, subject to caucus approval. Republican members do not exercise this power. When the Ways and Means Committee holds public hearings on tax and tariff measures, large numbers of citizens and lobbyists testify before the Committee, reflecting the importance of the revenue raising function today.

Whip.   An assistant floor leader who aids the majority or minority leaders of each party in each house of Congress. Whips are selected in party caucuses, usually on the recommendation of the floor leaders. Each whip in the House appoints several assistants to aid him, whereas the Senate whips are aided by the secretaries to their respective party policy committees.

• *Significance:* The duties of the whips include (1) canvassing fellow party members so as to inform party leaders of the number of votes which can be counted on; (2) taking action to bring full voting power of their party to bear on key issues; (3) acting for the floor leaders when they are absent from the chamber. On crucial issues, when close votes are anticipated, much depends on the party organization and the effectiveness of the whips' operations.

IMPORTANT AGENCIES

Legislative Reference Service.   A staff agency of the Congress established to provide research data for congressmen to aid them in their legislative duties. It was set up in the Library of Congress in 1914 and has been progressively strengthened to include a professional staff of specialists in a variety of fields of legislative interest. Each year, studies, statistics, and charts are furnished to congressmen and committees in response to thousands of inquiries. Many state legislatures have created similar staff facilities.

• *Significance:* The creation and expansion of the Legislative Reference Service has resulted somewhat from the reluctance of Congress to be dependent upon "experts" in the executive branch for information. The Service not only performs essential staff functions but, because of the nature of its work, has a considerable effect on the end product of legislation.

Library of Congress.   The national library of the United States which serves the entire national government and state and local governments as well as the public. The Library of Congress was created in 1800 by the Congress and is headed by the Librarian of Congress, who is appointed by the President with Senate approval. Two important divisions of the Library are the Copyright Office and the Legislative Reference Service.

• *Significance:* The Library of Congress is particularly useful to the Congress and the executive branch because it is a vast storehouse of official records and documents. Much legislation involves extensive studies and research, and the role of the Library has grown as governmental activities have increased and grown more complex.

Office of Legislative Counsel.   A staff agency of the Congress specializing in the drafting of bills. Each house provides its members with technical bill-drafting service through the Office. The staff consists of trained bill writers, many of whom are specialists in areas of legislation.

• *Significance:* Bill drafting is a difficult and highly technical job. Few members of the Congress, not even many lawyers, are capable of putting legislative ideas into precise statutory language. Bills must be carefully drafted because the courts will invalidate statutes that are vague.

IMPORTANT CASES

Baker v. Carr, 82 S. Ct. 691 (1962): Ruled, in an epic Supreme Court decision, that federal courts have jurisdiction over lawsuits challenging the apportionment of legislative districts on the ground that malapportioned districts may violate the equal protection clause of the 14th Amendment. The case had the effect of overturning *Colegrove v. Green,* 328 U.S. 549 (1946) in which the Court held that the issue of malapportioned legislative districts was a political question and relief should be sought through the political process. The *Baker* case involved a suit to compel the Tennessee legislature to redistrict state legislative districts on a population basis as provided in the Tennessee Constitution, a provision which the legislature had ignored for over 60 years.

• *Significance:* Many state legislatures have refused for long periods to provide for equitable apportionment for state legislative and congressional election districts. The decision reflected the new view of the Court's majority that it is unrealistic to seek to achieve a fair system of representation through the ballot box, since state legislators often maintain themselves in power through gerrymandering and refusals to redistrict. What kind of districting would meet the requirements of equal protection of the laws and how specific decisions might be enforced are the basic problems facing the federal courts in seeking to implement this decision.

McGrain v. Daugherty, 273 U.S. 135 (1927): Decided that the Congress has the right to compel testimony from private individuals as an aid to its power to pass laws. This investigation arose out of the Teapot Dome scandal involving bribery and other illegal acts by public officials. The Court held that the Congress could subpoena a private individual as well as a public official when this action is pertinent to a proper legislative function.

• *Significance:* This case established the constitutional justification for legislative investigations. Although courts have always had the power to compel testimony and production of papers and other materials, such action by a legislative body must be justified. So long as the investigation is being conducted for gathering facts for legislation, the courts will not inquire into the motives of Congress.

Pacific States Telephone and Telegraph Co. v. Oregon, 223 U.S. 118 (1912): Involved the question of whether the initiative and referendum provisions of the Oregon Constitution destroy the republican form of government guaranteed to all states by the United States Constitution in Article IV, section 4. The Court held it to be a political question not open to judicial inquiry.

• *Significance:* Although no provision is made by the United States Constitution for direct action by the people in the lawmaking process, the Court, in effect, here recognized that the states may validly adopt such measures. About one third of the states and numerous cities have adopted the initiative and referendum, most of them during the first two decades of the twentieth century.

United States v. Harriss, 347 U.S. 612 (1954): Upheld the constitutionality of the Federal Regulation of Lobbying Act of 1946 against charges that it violates due process, freedom of speech and press, and freedom of petition.

• *Significance:* The Court narrowly construed the application of the Lobbying Act by holding that it applies only to lobbyists who directly seek to influence members of Congress concerning pending or proposed federal legislation. Lobbyists who seek to influence federal legislation indirectly through public opinion do not fall within the scope of "lobbying activities" regulated by the Act. Chief Justice Earl Warren, speaking for the majority of the Court, emphasized that the intention of the Lobbying Act was to enable the Congress to discover "who is being hired, who is putting up the money, and how much." This is information which the Congress is entitled to know.

Watkins v. United States, 354 U.S. 178 (1957): Established that a person may refuse to answer a question put to him by an investigating committee of the Congress if the question is not pertinent to the inquiry. The Court upheld Watkins' refusal to answer questions of the House Committee on Un-American Activities regarding certain persons who had at one time been members of the Communist party. For refusing to answer, Watkins was cited for contempt of

Congress. The Court reversed his conviction on the ground that the Committee had failed to demonstrate that the questions were pertinent.

• *Significance:* Many rights guaranteed in the Constitution apply to congressional investigations as well as to judicial proceedings. In the same way that an individual is entitled to know the precise charges against him when charged with a crime, so he is entitled to know how any particular question asked of him at a legislative investigation pertains to the matter under investigation. Congress may not conduct a "fishing expedition" in the hopes of uncovering information. This case illustrates one of the limitations on the investigatory powers of Congress.

IMPORTANT STATUTES

Legislative Reorganization Act of 1946.   Enacted to strengthen the Congress in its organization and operations. The Act was based on the studies of a bipartisan joint committee which was charged with recommending plans "with a view toward strengthening Congress, simplifying its operations, improving its relations with other branches of the United States Government, and enabling it to meet its responsibilities under the Constitution." The Act provided for structural and procedural changes, including (1) reorganization of the committee system; (2) strengthening the operations of the committees; (3) provisions for a legislative budget system; (4) reduction in the workload of Congress; (5) increases in the professional assistance available to each congressman; (6) increases in congressional salaries and fringe benefits; and (7) regulation of lobbying activities.

• *Significance:* Committee functioning has been definitely strengthened as a result of the Act, although the number of subcommittees has been increased. Claims legislation has been reduced, but many minor matters remain under congressional responsibility. The legislative budget proposal has proved unworkable and has been discarded. Lobbying has been brought under a measure of public and congressional oversight. Congressional salaries have since been increased to $22,500. Staff assistance for each congressman has been improved in quantity and quality. Two persistent problems—the seniority system in committee organization and the filibuster in the Senate—were excluded from any consideration by the joint committee.

Regulation of Lobbying Act (Title III, Legislative Reorganization Act of 1946).   The first attempt by the Congress to control interest groups, lobbyists, and lobbying activities through legislation. The Act provides for a minimum of *regulation* and a maximum of *publicity.* Specific provisions include (1) persons or organizations receiving money to be used principally to influence passage or defeat of legislation before the Congress must register; (2) the persons or groups registering must, under oath, give their name and address, employer, salary, amount and purpose of expenses, and duration of employment; (3) each registered lobbyist must report full information quarterly on his activities which are published at quarterly intervals in the *Congressional Record;* and (4) severe penalties are prescribed, ranging up to $10,000 fine and a five-year prison term, and including a three-year ban against further lobbying.

• *Significance:* The Lobbying Act has been criticized on the ground that its language is confusing and vague, resulting in much noncompliance. No enforcement agency has been created by the Congress. The public generally has ignored the publicity given in quarterly reports. It is doubtful whether the Act has had any appreciable effect on lobbyists or their activities. Congress must be careful in enacting lobby control legislation to avoid regulations which might abridge freedom of speech, press, or petition.

8

The Executive:
Office and Powers

Amnesty.   Power exercised by the President to grant a blanket pardon to all members of a group who have violated national law. Amnesties have also been occasionally granted by Congress.

• *Significance:* Amnesties have been used generally to absolve groups from legal accountability for political offenses. For example, President Thomas Jefferson granted a general amnesty to all persons convicted under the Alien and Sedition Acts. The best known amnesties in American history were those granted by Presidents Abraham Lincoln and Andrew Johnson to all Confederates who had participated in rebellion against the United States. An attempt by the Congress to limit the effect of Johnson's amnesty proclamation was found by the United States Supreme Court to be an invalid interference with the President's constitutional pardoning powers (*Ex parte Garland,* 4 Wall. 333 [1867]).

Budget Message.   Early in each legislative session, usually in February, the President sends to the Congress his annual budget message as required by the Budget and Accounting Act of 1921. Unlike the State of the Union message which precedes it, the budget message is not usually delivered in person by the President but is sent to the Congress in writing to be read to each chamber by its clerk. The budget message contains the receipt and expenditure estimates recommended by the President for the next fiscal year. In the states, many governors, especially of those which have undergone recent reorganization, also deliver or send to the legislature annual or biennial budget messages.

• *Significance:* The importance of the budget message is that it places responsibility for the initiation of the financial plan for government in the executive. Legislative bodies begin their consideration of financial matters only after the budget message, with its detailed itemization of fiscal recommendations, has been laid before them. Although the Congress or state legislature is free to modify or reject the proposals found in a budget message, its size and specificity tend to reduce legislative discretion. The executive may also use his budget message as a means of arousing public support for certain programs, even though immediate enactment is unlikely.

Cabinet.   An advisory group selected by the President to aid him in making decisions. President Washington instituted the Cabinet idea when he began regularly to call together the heads of the four executive departments and the Vice President to consult with him on matters of policy. The Cabinet remains an informal group today with its membership determined by tradition and presidential discretion. By custom, the heads of the major departments (State, Treasury, Defense, Justice, Post Office, Interior, Agriculture, Commerce, Labor, and Health, Education, and Welfare) are members of the Cabinet and the President may also invite the Vice President and other officials to sit in on Cabinet meetings.

• *Significance:* The Cabinet may be a highly influential staff agency or relatively insignificant, whichever the President decides to make it. The members of the Cabinet individually are often far more influential in advising the President than is the Cabinet as a body. Some Presidents, such as James Buchanan and Warren G. Harding, placed great reliance on their Cabinets, whereas others, such as Woodrow Wilson and both Theodore and Franklin D. Roosevelt, assigned their Cabinets an insignificant role. Abraham Lincoln is reported to have summarily rejected a unanimous vote of his Cabinet, which illustrates the advisory nature of Cabinet decisions. In making Cabinet appointments, Presidents, typically, seek to obtain broad geographic and interest group representation and to give some representation to the different political wings of their party. For these reasons Presidents usually prefer to seek advice elsewhere and to confine Cabinet meetings to matters of party policy or routine matters. President Dwight D. Eisenhower in 1954 sought to strengthen the Cabinet's role by establishing a Cabinet secretariat to prepare the agenda and follow up Cabinet decisions.

Chief Legislator.   The role of the President in influencing the making of laws. Constitutional powers available to the President to affect legislation include the recommending of legislative programs through messages to the Congress, the veto, and some control over sessions. Informal methods of influencing legislation include the President's personal contacts with congressional leaders, his use of patronage, his ability to arouse public opinion in support of his program, his efforts to influence the election of congressmen sympathetic to his views, and the continuing efforts of executive officials acting as a "presidential lobby" before congressional committees. In addition, the President's legislative powers include the issuing of rules and regulations having the effect of law under powers delegated to him by the Congress.

• *Significance:* An evaluation of a President's administration is based considerably upon his success or failure in his role as chief legislator. Presidents who have initiated broad legislative programs and successfully pushed them through Congress, using a variety of constitutional and informal political methods and weapons, are generally classified as "strong" Presidents; those who have failed to provide effective legislative leadership, through unwillingness or inability, have generally been relegated to the category of "weak" Presidents.

The Congress, because of its size and diffusion of interests, lacks the means of formulating broad legislative programs and of enacting them into law without the continuing leadership and goading of the President and his aides.

Chief of State. The role of the President as ceremonial head of the government of the United States. Duties of the chief of state include greeting foreign dignitaries, acting as host at state dinners, throwing out the first baseball at the start of the season, and bestowing honors.

• *Significance:* The President serves in a dual capacity as chief of state and as chief executive. In most other countries, these roles are split, as in Britain where the Queen is the ceremonial head of state and the Prime Minister and Cabinet head the government and formulate policies. Many students of government believe that the role of chief of state detracts from the ability of the President to give sufficient time and energy to his many other, significant responsibilities. His role as chief of state, however, has blended with his political and executive roles enabling him to stand as a symbol of national unity, especially during times of crisis.

Delegation of Power. The transfer of authority from one government or branch of government, which has been constitutionally assigned the power, to another branch, or specific agency. Generally, delegations of power have involved the transfer of legislative power by the Congress to the President, to an executive department or official, or to independent regulatory commissions.

• *Significance:* The tendency of the Congress and state legislatures to delegate legislative powers has increased as legislative workloads have become burdensome and highly technical. Involved in all such delegations, however, is the constitutional question of the legality of the transfer. The United States Supreme Court, for example, struck down the National Industrial Recovery Act of 1933 in two significant cases in 1935, holding that the Congress could not constitutionally transfer its legislative power to the President or to an executive agency (*Panama Refining Co. v. Ryan*, 293 U.S. 388 [1935]; *Schecter Poultry Corp. v. U.S.*, 295 U.S. 495 [1935]). In another case, the Supreme Court held that Congress may not delegate its constitutional powers to the states (*Knickerbocker Ice Co. v. Stewart*, 253 U.S. 149 [1920]). In the field of foreign affairs, however, the Supreme Court upheld a sizable delegation of power to the President by the Congress on the ground that the President has a special responsibility in foreign affairs (*United States v. Curtiss-Wright*, 299 U.S. 304 [1936]). The Supreme Court has also laid down the general rule that, if delegations of legislative powers are to be considered valid, the Congress must determine the general policies and establish clear standards to guide the President or agency in making detailed applications of the general law.

Economic Message. An annual message from the President to the Congress which embodies an "economic report" concerning employment levels, production, purchasing power, trends of the nation's economy, and recommendations to the Congress on maintaining or improving economic activity. The economic message, typically, is sent to the Congress in writing, and is read to each house by its clerk. It is prepared by the President with the advice and assistance of the Council of Economic Advisers (CEA), comprised of three leading economists. A joint congressional Committee on the Economic Report, of seven members from each house, studies the message and makes recommendations on implementing it.

• *Significance:* The President's annual economic message is required by the Employment Act of 1946 and it reflects an acceptance by the national government of responsibility for maintaining stability in the nation's economy through monetary and fiscal policies. Like other messages, it adds to the President's role as chief legislator by charging him with responsibility to initiate and recommend a broad legislative program and to give it nationwide publicity through the message technique.

Emergency Powers.   Seldom used powers exercised during a period of crisis by the national government, or those powers conferred by the Congress upon the President for a limited period of time. The term is also popularly (and erroneously) used to describe an alleged reservoir of national powers not specified in the Constitution which has been drawn upon during depression and war crises.

• *Significance:* The Constitution does not recognize the need for additional national powers during an emergency. The Supreme Court has made this clear in stating that "emergency does not create power" (*Home Building and Loan Assoc. v. Blaisdell,* 290 U.S. 398 [1934]). Yet, emergencies have helped to develop the use of otherwise dormant powers and the novel application of ordinary powers. Moreover, the President's exercise of inherent powers in the field of foreign affairs, does provide some additional source of power for use during emergencies.

Executive Agreement.   An international agreement, reached by the President with foreign heads of state, which does not require senatorial approval. Such agreements are concluded under the President's constitutional power as commander in chief and his general authority in foreign relations, or under power delegated to him by the Congress. *See* EXECUTIVE AGREEMENT, page 308.

• *Significance:* Executive agreements contribute to the President's position of leadership in foreign affairs. Quick, decisive action can be taken during a crisis without having to follow the difficult and time-consuming route of treaty making. President Roosevelt's destroyers-for-bases agreement with Britain in 1941 illustrates this advantage. Secrecy can be maintained through executive agreements when open debate in the Senate would be dangerous or provocative. Moreover, by possessing the executive agreement alternative the President is placed in a better bargaining position with the Congress on foreign policy matters.

Executive Order.   A rule or regulation, issued by the President, a governor, or by some administrative authority, which has the effect of law. Executive orders are used to implement and give administrative effect to provisions of the Constitution, to treaties, and to statutes. They may be used to create or modify the organization or procedures of administrative agencies or may have general applicability as law. Under the national Administrative Procedure Act of 1946 all executive orders must be published in the *Federal Register*.

• *Significance:* The use of executive orders has greatly increased in recent years as a result of the growing tendency of legislative bodies to delegate discretionary powers to the executive branch by statute. This trend will likely continue as government continues to concern itself with highly complex and technical matters in its regulatory and promotional functions. The increasing use of executive orders to implement statutes contributes to the importance of the executive's role as chief legislator.

Item Veto.   The power exercised by the governor in a majority of the states (41, in 1962) to veto sections or items of an appropriation bill while signing the remainder of the bill into law. Governors in several states can reduce appropriation items and in two states may veto sections of nonfinancial bills. The legislature may override the vetoed items. The President does not exercise the item veto power.

• *Significance:* It is often suggested that the item veto power should be given to the President. Many constitutional amendments have been introduced into the House and Senate to this effect, but none has passed. Congress might delegate a limited item veto to the President by inserting such a provision into each appropriation bill. The item veto power is consistent with growing executive responsibility in fiscal affairs. With it, the executive is able to curtail riders, reduce pork barrel legislation, and generally fight legislative extravagance. Those who oppose the item veto regard it as a serious impairment of legislative authority and as an unwarranted increase in executive powers.

Minority President.   An elected President who has received fewer than 50 percent of the total *popular* votes cast for all candidates although obtaining a majority of the *electoral* votes. A winning candidate is most likely to be a minority president when there are several fairly strong minor party candidates in the presidential contest.

• *Significance:* Many American Presidents have been "minority presidents," including Abraham Lincoln, Woodrow Wilson, Harry Truman, and John F. Kennedy. Two Presidents, Rutherford B. Hayes in 1876 and Benjamin Harrison in 1888, won election even though their opponents polled more popular votes than they. So long as more than two candidates run for the office, there is always the possibility of electing a minority president. The election of a minority president acquires new significance during times of crisis when the new President needs to have the majority of voters in support of him and his policies.

New Deal.   A comprehensive program of liberal social and economic reforms instituted during the 1930's by the administration of Franklin D. Roosevelt. The New Deal included currency reform, social security, business regulation, wage and hour legislation, trade union rights, resource development, banking reform, freer trade, and civil rights.

• *Significance:* Much of the early New Deal program was declared unconstitutional by the Supreme Court, but most of the later New Deal remains today as basic social legislation. Although the New Deal proposals led to one of the most controversial domestic political battles in American history, they have come to be accepted generally by both major parties. Most social welfare legislation enacted since the 1930's has merely tried to expand or improve upon the basic New Deal legislation.

Pardon.   The granting of a release from the punishment or legal consequences of a crime by the proper executive authority before or after conviction. An absolute pardon restores the individual to the position he enjoyed prior to his alleged commission of a crime. A "conditional pardon" requires that certain obligations be met before the pardon becomes effective. The President exercises the complete pardoning power for federal offenses except for convictions in impeachment cases. Thirty states entrust the governor with the full authority for granting pardons. In the remainder, the governor typically shares the power with a pardon board or with the state senate. Pardons are granted usually to provide a remedy for mistakes made in convictions or to release offenders who have been properly rehabilitated. Executives also have the power to grant *reprieves* which postpone the execution of a sentence for humanitarian reasons or to await new evidence.

• *Significance:* Controversies concerning the extent of the presidential pardoning power have arisen concerning its application to a person held in contempt of Congress and another in contempt of court. In the former instance, the pardon was not contested but the latter was upheld by the Supreme Court (*Ex parte Grossman,* 267 U.S. 87 [1925]). Most governors regard the pardoning power as among their most bothersome and distasteful tasks. Relatives and friends of offenders besiege governors with applications and pressures for pardons. The trend in the states is toward vesting greater responsibility in recommending or deciding pardons in full-time boards staffed by correctional experts.

Pocket Veto.   A special veto power exercised at the end of a legislative session whereby bills not signed by a chief executive die after a specified time. Under the Constitution, if the President holds a bill for ten days without signing or vetoing it, the bill becomes law if the Congress is in session and is pocket vetoed if the Congress adjourns during the ten days. In about one third of the states, the governors exercise a similar pocket veto power if they do not approve the measure during a stated period after legislative adjournment. This period varies in these states from 3 to 30 days.

• *Significance:* The pocket veto provides a chief executive with a major legislative power. Unlike the ordinary veto which is merely suspensive in nature and can be overridden, the pocket veto is absolute. Whereas the regular veto requires an explanation from the chief executive, the pocket veto does not, although some Presidents have chosen to defend their inaction. Most significant, the pocket veto is available at the crucial period at the end of the legislative session when large numbers of bills are enacted in a last-minute legislative rush. In some states, it is the practice of the legislature to recess rather than adjourn when work is completed. They then reassemble briefly before the pocket veto becomes effective and thereby prevent its use by the governor.

President.   The chief executive of the United States and the key official in the American system of government. The Constitution in Article II vests the complete executive power in the President. The President is elected every four years through the Electoral College machinery, and is eligible under the 22nd Amendment to one additional term. His chief official advisers are found in the Executive Office and the Cabinet. The President exercises a broad array of powers, some provided by the Constitution, some based on custom and tradition, some delegated to him by the Congress, and others which are simply inherent in the nature of his office. Foremost are those broad and largely undefined powers which he exercises in his role as chief of foreign policy. These include the leadership of the armed forces, the recognition of foreign states and governments, the conduct of diplomacy, the making of international agreements and of treaties with the Senate's approval, the initiation of new foreign programs, and providing leadership for the United States and the free world. In his role of chief administrator, the President exercises broad appointing and removal powers, directs and supervises the operations of the executive branch, directs the formulation of the annual budget, and sees that the laws are faithfully executed. As chief legislator, the President initiates comprehensive legislative programs, delivers regular and special messages to the Congress, summons the Congress into special sessions, wields a broad veto power, and influences the course of much legislation in his relations with legislative leaders and by arousing public opinion to support his programs. As chief of party, the President dispenses patronage, influences the direction and nature of party policies, provides leadership to his party's delegation in both houses of Congress, and generally influences and determines party actions and policies. In his role as chief of state, the President maintains relations with other nations and performs numerous ceremonial functions in the United States. The prestige of his office contributes much to the effectiveness of the President in his many roles. His easy access to the mass media of communications aids him in molding public opinion. His many sources of information keep him well-informed on the complex problems facing the nation.

• *Significance:* The office of President has been shaped and molded by the experiences of the various Presidents who have held the office during American history. Much has depended upon the personalities of the individual Presidents, their political, economic, and social philosophies, and their conceptions of the office itself. Often, the man and the office have been shaped by the times, were they quiet and peaceful or hectic and crisis-filled. Some Presidents, such as William H. Taft and Calvin Coolidge, have viewed the presidency largely in terms of administration and law enforcement. Others, like Abraham Lincoln, Woodrow Wilson, and the two Roosevelts, have regarded the presidency as a position which allows and demands strong leadership and the exercise of broad, undefined powers whenever necessary for the security and well-being of the country. The former group has been labeled as "weak," and the latter as "strong," Presidents. All indications are that the nation is moving in the direction of stronger executive leadership for the future, toward what has often been called "presidential government."

President-Elect.   The candidate selected by the Electoral College to be the next President. Following the November popular election, the winning candidate is unofficially called the "President-designate" until the electors are able to ratify the people's choice. Under the 20th Amendment, the President-elect is sworn into office at noon on the 20th day of January, and if the President-elect fails to qualify at that time, the Vice President-elect then acts as President until a President qualifies.

• *Significance:* The status of President-elect is an important one because it enables the new chief executive to prepare for his assumption of the duties and responsibilities of the office. From the November election until the inauguration on January 20, the President-elect may meet periodically with the outgoing President to be briefed on special continuing problems, especially those in the foreign affairs field. The President-elect may also begin unofficially to select his top appointees, prepare some of his legislative messages, study the new budget which he inherits, and make other preparatory efforts.

Presidential Succession.   The Constitution in Article II, section 1 stipulates that "In case of the removal of the President from office, or of his death, resignation, or inability to discharge the powers and duties of the said office, the same shall devolve on the Vice-President. . . ." The Congress is empowered by the same section of Article II to provide for the officer to act as President in case both the President and Vice President are unable to serve. Congress has from time to time provided by statute for the line of succession, the present order based on the Presidential Succession Act of 1947. This law provides for the following order: Speaker of the House, President pro tempore of the Senate, Secretary of State, Secretary of the Treasury, Secretary of Defense, Attorney General, Postmaster General, and the Secretaries of the Interior, Agriculture, Commerce, and Labor. In addition, the 20th Amendment provides that the Vice President-elect shall become President if the President-elect is unable to assume his office on inauguration day.

• *Significance:* Seven Vice Presidents have succeeded to the office of President as a result of the deaths of Presidents in American history. No President, however, has resigned, been removed, or been incapacitated to the extent of turning the office over to the Vice President. The question of disability has arisen on several occasions, but the Constitution makes no provision for making such a determination other than for the disabled President to step down voluntarily. As a result of two serious illnesses suffered by President Dwight Eisenhower, attempts were made to establish a statutory remedy to this problem, but to no avail. Following his second illness, Eisenhower entered into a pact in 1958 with Vice President Richard Nixon, which provided that the Vice President could determine presidential inability if the President were unable to communicate with the Vice President. President Kennedy entered into a similar agreement with Vice President Johnson. These arrangements are, of course, not binding on future administrations, and the knotty problem of determining inability remains.

Ratification.   The approval by the President of the version of a treaty which has been consented to by the Senate by a two-thirds vote. Ratification may involve the problem of whether a president will accept amendments and reservations to the treaty affixed by the Senate, which would entail reopening of negotiations with other signatory nations.

• *Significance:* Ordinarily, presidential ratification of a treaty requires the exchange of ratification documents with other signatories to the treaty and an official proclamation putting the treaty into effect. When significant amendments or reservations are made by the Senate, the President must decide whether to try to gain their acceptance by the other parties to the treaty or to drop the matter, which kills the treaty as far as the United States is concerned. For example, when President Wilson refused to accept crippling reservations to the Versailles Treaty in 1919, this action contributed to the eventual defeat of the Treaty and the refusal of the United States to join the League of Nations. By leaving the last word with the President so far as American approval of treaties is concerned, the ratification power serves to enhance his role in foreign affairs.

Recess Appointment.   An appointment of a federal official made by the President to fill a vacancy which has occurred while the Senate is not in session. To prevent the President from postponing appointments until the Senate has adjourned, the Congress has by statute prohibited the payment of salary to an officer appointed to fill a vacancy that existed while the Senate was still in session. Recess appointments expire at the end of the next congressional session unless the Senate has confirmed the appointed official by a majority vote. Most state constitutions provide for recess appointments by the governors.

• *Significance:* Recess appointments have often been a matter of contention between the President and the Senate. The provision denying salary to an official who was given a recess appointment, although the position became vacant while the Senate was in session, is an obvious attempt to limit the President's use of recess appointments to circumvent the Senate's approval. Presidents usually refrain from straining relations with the Senate by not giving recess appointments to highly controversial persons or to those previously rejected by the Senate. In the states, recess appointments may be more contentious because of the typical lack of harmony between governors and state senates, and because such appointments are often for long durations owing to the sizable interims between legislative sessions.

Recognition.   The power exercised exclusively by the President to establish diplomatic relations with foreign states. Recognition powers are vested in the President by the Constitution which grants him the power in Article II, section 2 to send and receive ambassadors. *See* RECOGNITION, page 318.

• *Significance:* The President's recognition power is particularly significant because it involves the ability to refuse to recognize a new state or government as well as to grant recognition. Thus, the act of accrediting foreign diplomats, perhaps intended by the framers to be a mere ceremonial function, has become a significant discretionary power in the day-to-day conduct of foreign relations.

In deciding whether or not to recognize a new state or government, the President may be influenced by his advisers, by the Congress, and by public opinion, but the final decision is his alone. Important recognition controversies in American history have involved the question of whether revolutionary regimes, or states created by conquest, should be recognized. In cases such as those of the Soviet Union and Communist China, the President faces a dilemma: should he recognize the new state or regime and thereby help stabilize it with some degree of international respectability or, should he refuse to recognize it and hope thereby to hasten its collapse? Also involved is the question of whether the President considers it advantageous to maintain direct communication with and observation of the regime. Presidents have used their own discretion in such cases and no consistent American recognition policy has been developed.

Removal.   The authority of an executive official to dismiss appointed officials from office. Although the Constitution is silent on the subject, the President has from the beginning exercised the power to remove executive and administrative officials. As a general rule, all officials appointed by the President serve at his pleasure. Federal judges, however, have life tenure, on good behavior, while members of "independent commissions," and merit system employees can be removed only for cause. The removal power of state governors generally compares unfavorably with that of the President because of the number of elective officials in most states and the sharing of the governor's removal power, in many states, by the state senate or executive council.

• *Significance:* The ability of the President to get the vast national administration to follow his leadership and direction depends to a considerable degree on his authority to dismiss those who disobey his orders, are unsympathetic toward his program, or neglect their duties. Unless the President can surround himself with loyal subordinates who will strive to carry out his program, the system of democratic accountability, focused in the President as the only elected executive official, breaks down. Congress has, on occasion, sought by statute to gain a share of the power to remove executive officials, but the matter was finally decided by the Supreme Court in favor of unrestricted presidential removal power (*Myers v. United States,* 272 U.S. 52 [1926]). This decision, however, was modified by the Supreme Court in holding that members of independent regulatory commissions can be dismissed by the President only for cause as specified by Congress (*Rathbun v. United States,* 295 U.S. 602 [1935]). In the states, the recent trend has been in the direction of strengthening and expanding the governor's removal powers.

State of the Union Message.   An annual message to the Congress in which the President sets out the legislative program which he wants considered by the Congress. It is based on the constitutional directive that the President "shall from time to time give to the Congress information of the state of the Union, and recommend to their consideration such measures as he shall judge necessary and expedient. . . ." (Art. II, sec. 3). Some Presidents have delivered the message personally before joint sessions of the Congress; others have merely sent their messages to be read by a clerk. Although the President may choose his time for the message, it has become customary to transmit it at the beginning of a legislative session.

• *Significance:* The importance of the state of the union message lies primarily in its placing the initiative for developing a broad, comprehensive legislative program in the hands of the President. At the opening of a new legislative session, members of Congress busy themselves with routine organizational matters and minor legislative proposals until the President presents them with his legislative program. In his message, the President discusses the major problems facing the nation and recommends statutory solutions. His message is followed up in subsequent months by scores of bills drawn up in the executive departments and introduced in the Congress by "administration" congressmen. Over the past three decades, all Presidents have delivered their state of the union messages in person. Radio and television have greatly increased the importance of these messages, and the President now speaks not only to the Congress but to the American people and, in a sense, to the world as well. It offers him an opportunity to dramatize his policies and objectives and to gain support for them by arousing public opinion.

Stewardship Theory.   The view of presidential powers which holds that the President has not only the right but the duty to do anything needed to safeguard the nation and to protect the American people, unless such action is specifically forbidden by the Constitution. The stewardship theory is usually ascribed to Theodore Roosevelt.

• *Significance:* The stewardship theory is one of several conceptions of the President's powers which has contributed to the shaping of that office. Strong presidents have often acted on the stewardship assumption without theorizing. The theory is closely related to the doctrine of inherent powers. President Taft and others rejected the stewardship view and emphasized the contractual and limiting nature of our constitutional system.

Twentieth Amendment.   The "lame duck" Amendment which changed the beginning of the presidential and vice-presidential terms from March 4 to January 20, and of congressional terms from March 4 to January 3. The Amendment was proposed by Congress on March 2, 1932, and was proclaimed on February 6, 1933. Other provisions are (1) if the President-elect dies before taking office, the Vice President-elect shall become President; (2) if a President-elect has not been chosen or fails to qualify by January 20, the Vice President-elect shall act as President until a President is chosen; (3) if neither qualifies, then the Congress shall decide who shall act as President until a President or Vice President qualifies; and (4) if the election of the President and Vice President is thrown into the House and the Senate and a candidate dies, the Congress shall determine by law what shall be done.

• *Significance:* The 20th Amendment reduced the "lame duck" period for the outgoing President, enabling the newly elected President more quickly to usher in a new administration with its new policies. The change reflects a disposition to make the office more responsive to democratic influences and enables a newly elected President to proceed to develop his policies and programs with little delay. The provisions in the Amendment regarding the inability of the President-elect and Vice President-elect to serve are designed to close a gap in the original Constitution which failed to provide for these eventualities.

Twenty-Second Amendment. The limiting of the presidential tenure to two terms for an individual. The Amendment was proposed by the Congress in March 1947, and was proclaimed February 26, 1951. A Vice President who succeeds to the office may serve as long as ten years as President, provided he has not served more than two years of the uncompleted term of his predecessor. The incumbent President, Harry S. Truman, was excluded from the limitations of the Amendment, but he chose not to run for a third term.

• *Significance:* The 22nd Amendment was proposed by the Republican-controlled 80th Congress in reaction to the four terms of Franklin Roosevelt. Roosevelt had shattered the strong "no-third-term" tradition started by Washington and followed thereafter until 1940. The Amendment was also a reaction to the growth of executive power that had resulted from war and depression crises and reflected a yearning to return to the "normalcy" of congressional domination of weak presidents. Supporters of the Amendment defend it as a useful safeguard against the dangers of executive tyranny and self-perpetuation in power. Opponents argue that it tends to reduce further a second-term President's already weak position as political leader and exhibits a fundamental distrust of the democratic process. During Dwight Eisenhower's second term, the Amendment set the presidential race in motion earlier than had been customary, reduced his capacity to bargain politically, and tended to undermine his political leadership.

Veto. A legislative power vested in a chief executive enabling him to return an unsigned bill to the legislative body with reasons for his objections. The Constitution provides that every bill which passes the House and the Senate must be sent to the President for his signature before it becomes law. When the President receives a bill, he may (1) sign it, and it thereupon becomes law; (2) not sign it, and it then becomes law after ten congressional working days; (3) veto it, and send it back to the house of its origin; or (4) not sign it, and if the Congress adjourns within ten days the bill is killed (pocket veto). The President vetoes a bill by writing "veto" (I forbid) across the face of the bill; he then sends it back to the Congress with a message setting forth his objections. Congress may amend the bill according to the President's demands and then repass it, or it may reject the President's objection and override the veto by repassing the bill with a two-thirds roll call vote in each house. Governors, in all states except North Carolina, exercise the veto power and, in 39 states, the governors may veto items of appropriation bills, a power denied to the President. In the states, the number of votes needed to override a gubernatorial veto varies from a simple majority in each house to a two-thirds vote of all members elected to the legislature.

• *Significance:* Presidents employed the veto power infrequently and with great caution until the post–Civil War administration of Andrew Johnson. Since 1865, the veto power has been used with increasing vigor by most presidents; Grover Cleveland with 414 regular and pocket vetoes, and Franklin Roosevelt, with 631, were its most persistent users. The scope of the veto power has also expanded since 1865. The earlier view that the veto should be used to block unconstitutional or technically imperfect laws has been supplemented by its employment to express disapproval of any kind. Although the veto is merely suspensive, few are overridden by the Congress. The *threat* of the veto can also be used effectively by a President to shape and change legislation while it is still in the hands of the Congress.

Vice President.   The constitutional officer assigned to preside over the Senate and to assume the office of President in case of the death, resignation, removal, or disability of the President. The Vice President is elected on the same ballot with the President and, in case no candidate receives a majority of the electoral vote, the Senate chooses from the two candidates with the highest number of electoral votes. Although President of the Senate, the Vice President is not considered to be a member, participating only informally, if at all, in its deliberations, and voting only when a tie occurs. He is regarded as a legislative officer and only potentially as an executive officer.
• *Significance:* During most of American history, the vice presidency has been regarded as an insignificant office and as a political graveyard to be avoided by promising politicians. The low repute of this potentially significant office perhaps results mainly from the method of selecting vice-presidential candidates—to balance the party ticket or to reward or appease party wings. Recent Presidents have sought to make more effective use of their Vice Presidents as intermediaries between the President and the Congress and as roving ambassadors of good will in foreign affairs. Vice Presidents customarily attend Cabinet meetings, and Presidents Eisenhower and Kennedy have assigned their Vice Presidents additional responsibilities in the executive branch. The trend is in the direction of developing the office into an assistant presidency. Seven Vice Presidents have assumed the office of President.

IMPORTANT AGENCIES

Executive Office of the President.   The top staff agencies which give the President help and advice in carrying out his major duties. Congress created the Executive Office in the Reorganization Act of 1939. It consists of the Bureau of the Budget, the White House Office, the National Security Council, the Council of Economic Advisers, the National Aeronautics and Space Council, and the President's Advisory Committee on Government Organization.
• *Significance:* The objective in the creation of the Executive Office was to provide the President with a "general staff" to give him the help needed to direct effectively the far-flung activities of the executive branch. The President has been hampered, however, by the refusal of the Congress to place some key agencies within the Executive Office, such as the Civil Service Commission and the General Accounting Office. All indications point to a growth in the importance of the Executive Office as the President's tasks become more extensive and complex and he is forced to place increasing dependence upon

his staff. The White House Office in particular contains the close confidential advisers whom the President leans on for day-to-day operations of the executive branch.

Secret Service.   A law-enforcement division of the Treasury Department which has full responsibility for protecting the life and security of the President and his family. The Secret Service also performs security functions concerned with treasury matters.

• *Significance:* Like the "G-men" of the FBI, the "T-men" of the Treasury Department are carefully selected, rigorously trained, and are devoted to duty. Each year the Secret Service agents check out thousands of "crank" and threatening letters sent to the President and investigate numerous threats made against the life of the President or members of his family. Whenever the President travels at home or abroad, all security arrangements are handled by the Secret Service, with the cooperation of the police of the area or country which the President is visiting.

IMPORTANT CASES

Ex parte Grossman, 267 U.S. 87 (1925): Upheld a pardon granted by the President to Grossman who had been convicted of contempt of Court. It was alleged that the independence of the judiciary depends upon the authority of judges to try without jury individuals who violate court orders, and to sentence them for contempt of court free from interference by other departments of government. The Court rejected this argument and upheld the President, holding that he "can reprieve or pardon all offenses after their commission, either before trial, during trial or after trial, by individuals, or by classes, conditionally or absolutely, and this without modification or regulation by Congress."

• *Significance:* The effect of the case was to extend the President's pardoning power to all federal cases regardless of which branch of government is involved. Only conviction of a public official through impeachment proceedings is beyond the President's power to grant pardons.

Mississippi v. Johnson, 4 Wallace 475 (1867): Rejected an attempt by the State of Mississippi to enjoin President Johnson from enforcing the Reconstruction Acts of 1867. It held that the President cannot be restrained by injunction from carrying out his official duties of a political nature, such as the enforcement of an act of the Congress.

• *Significance:* The decision enhanced the position of the President under the separation of powers by freeing him from judicial interference with his law-enforcement duties. Laws which are alleged to be unconstitutional may be struck down by the courts only after the President has begun to enforce them.

Myers v. United States, 272 U.S. 52 (1926): Upheld the President's removal from office of a postmaster without securing the approval of the Senate to the removal. The Court held that the Congress cannot limit the President's power to remove executive officials, and the provisions of a law of 1876 requiring the Senate's concurrence in presidential removals was held to be unconstitutional.

• *Significance:* The *Myers* case, with the Court's majority speaking through

Chief Justice (former President) Taft, asserted a broad presidential removal power which had been in some doubt during much of American history. However, in *Rathbun v. United States*, 295 U.S. 602 (1935) the Court upheld the power of the Congress to limit the President's authority to remove members of the independent regulatory commissions.

Rathbun (Humphrey's Executor) v. United States, 295 U.S. 602 (1935): Upheld the provisions of the Federal Trade Commission Act providing that members of the Commission may be removed from office only for causes specified in the Act. President Roosevelt had removed Humphrey for political reasons, and in this case, decided after Humphrey's death, the Court held that the Congress clearly had the authority to limit the President's removal power to instances of "inefficiency, neglect of duty, or malfeasance in office." The Court pointed out that the broad removal powers accorded to the President in *Myers v. United States*, 272 U.S. 52 (1926), pertained only to purely executive officers, whereas members of the Federal Trade Commission exercise legislative and judicial powers as well.

• *Significance:* The *Humphrey* case resulted in a general acceptance of the independence of the regulatory commissions, such as the FPC, the FTC, the SEC, the ICC, and others. The Court, in recognizing the need for statutory requirements concerning tenure of commissioners, cited the character of their work, the need to develop expertness through experience, the need for freedom from political domination or control, and the threefold nature of their duties (administrative, quasi-legislative, quasi-judicial).

Youngstown Sheet and Tube Co. v. Sawyer, 343 U.S. 579 (1952): Struck down the President's Executive Order which had authorized seizure of the steel mills and their operation by the national government. The President had acted, under his inherent power as chief executive and commander in chief to safeguard the nation's security during the Korean War, when a strike in the steel mills had threatened the supply of weapons. The Court held that the President has no authority under the Constitution to seize private property unless the Congress had authorized the seizure, and that the Constitution does not permit the President to legislate.

• *Significance:* The immediate result of the seizure case was the return of the steel mills by the government to their private owners and the resumption of the strike by the United Steelworkers Union. More fundamentally, the case established for the first time that limits exist in the exercise of the President's inherent powers in seeking to safeguard the security of the nation. It reaffirmed the inviolability of private property rights under the Fifth Amendment, and that legislative powers can only be exercised by the Congress.

IMPORTANT STATUTES

Presidential Succession Act. The Act provides for the line of succession to the presidency beyond the Vice President, in the following order: Speaker of the House, President pro tempore of the Senate, the Secretaries of State,

Treasury, Defense, the Attorney General, the Postmaster General, and the Secretaries of Interior, Agriculture, Commerce, and Labor. Only those meeting the qualifications of the Office of President are eligible, and they must first resign from their positions to accept the presidency.

• *Significance:* The Presidential Succession Act of 1947 changed the old line of succession under which Cabinet officials in the above order followed the Vice President. The Speaker of the House is in a preferred position under the Act, not only because he is first in line after the Vice President, but because the line of succession is unlikely to go beyond him. Under the Act, Cabinet members serve only until a Speaker or President pro tempore qualifies to succeed to the presidency. The Act was supported by those who believed that it would be more democratic to place two leaders of Congress in the first two succession slots. Some students of government, however, have opposed the change, holding that the prestige and ability needed for the presidency are more likely to be found in the Secretary of State or of the Treasury than in the congressional leadership.

9

Public Administration:
Organization and Personnel

Administration. The procedure by which laws are enforced and public policy is carried out. *Public* administration, as distinguished from private or business administration, is largely the function of the executive branch of government. It carries out the policies established by the legislative branch subject to the oversight and review of both the legislative and judicial branches. Administration is the art or science of managing public affairs with emphasis on such factors as organization, personnel, and finance.
• *Significance:* All organizations are faced with the problem of efficient administration. Public administration, however, is increasingly complex because of the tremendous range of responsibilities which modern government has undertaken, the need for organizing and directing millions of employees, and the problem of controlling the expenditure of billions of dollars. The traditional view that administration and policy formation are separate has given way to recognition of the policy-making aspects inherent in administration. This results from the assignment of rule-making and adjudicating functions to many agencies. In recent years, much scholarly attention has been paid to developing sound principles and practices of administration in order to ensure the responsibility and accountability of administrative personnel to the people.

Administrative Order. A directive issued by an administrative agency which has the force of law. An order is generally distinguished from a "rule" or "regulation" in that an order is specifically directed to an individual or group to correct infractions of a rule. An example would be an order of the National Labor Relations Board (NLRB) to a union or an employer to cease violation of a labor practice which the Board had declared to be unfair. Orders are issued after a hearing conducted by the agency which resembles the procedures of a court of law. Appeals may be brought to the regular courts. Orders of federal agencies are published in the *Federal Register*.
• *Significance:* Administrative orders are part of the over-all development of the administrative process. Legislative bodies have vested control over complex

173

economic and social problems in various administrative agencies which have been granted broad powers to prescribe rules and regulations and to enforce these rules through orders. In this way, the legislature is saved the impossible job of determining in advance all the aspects of complex matters, and the courts are freed from deciding disputes over technical subjects in which they lack competence. The administrative agency can develop the necessary expertness to handle specialized cases. An increasing number of businesses and individuals are subject to administrative orders.

Administrative Reorganization.   The reform of administrative agencies and procedures for better efficiency, economy, and responsibility. Reorganization movements have generally had as their major purposes the concentration of authority and accountability by (1) integrating agencies with similar functions to eliminate overlapping and waste; (2) fixing of responsibility in some hierarchical arrangement; (3) establishing advisory and centralized housekeeping agencies to aid the chief administrator; (4) eliminating multiheaded boards or commissions, and elective officers engaged in purely administrative work; and (5) improving personnel, budget, and auditing procedures.
• *Significance:* The twentieth century has witnessed increased interest and activity in administrative reorganization at all levels of American government. For the most part, it has resulted in increased authority for the President, governors, and mayors, the shortening of the ballot, and the adoption of the council-manager plan at the municipal level. Official reorganization studies are underway in many areas and the President and some governors have been given authority to reshuffle agencies. Budgetary and personnel practices have been improved. Reorganization movements frequently meet resistance from legislatures which fear executive power, from interest groups which seek to protect the position of agencies which serve them, and from the agency personnel who fear loss of status.

Auxiliary Agency.   A governmental unit which services other governmental agencies. Typical auxiliary agencies include central purchasing, personnel, and accounting. They perform what is sometimes called housekeeping or technical services.
• *Significance:* Auxiliary agencies not only provide a centralized and less expensive means of providing technical services but also provide the department head or the chief executive with an important mechanism for control. Previously, it had been the practice for each agency to do its own hiring or purchasing, for example, but improved administration generally results from assignment of such functions to auxiliary units.

Board.   A group of persons, usually three or more, who are charged with responsibility for directing a particular governmental function. The term "commission" is frequently used interchangeably with board.
• *Significance:* Multiheaded versus single-headed directorship is one of the most controversial problems of administrative organization. Both forms are found at all levels of government. It is generally agreed that a board is best when the agency has quasi-legislative and quasi-judicial functions, particularly

in the area of regulation of the economy. It permits the use of bipartisan personnel for controversial matters and, where overlapping terms are held, continuity of policy. However, a board makes it difficult to locate responsibility and conflict may develop within the board itself. A single head makes for well-defined responsibility and unity of purpose. Administrative experts recommend the single director for purely administrative tasks, but boards or commissions are frequently used for this purpose. A compromise proposal which has found favor is to retain plural bodies for regulatory and adjudicatory functions but to assign administrative responsibility to the chairman of the board. This has been done, for example, in the Federal Trade Commission and the Civil Service Commission.

Bureau.   The major working unit of a department or agency. It is generally assigned a specific function and its head is responsible to the head of the entire department. Leading examples include the Federal Bureau of Investigation (FBI) in the Department of Justice and the Census Bureau in the Department of Commerce. A bureau may be broken down into various divisions, branches, or sections, each with responsibility for specialized activities.

• *Significance:* While the nomenclature assigned to various parts of an agency is by no means uniform, it is considered useful for the development of scientific principles of administrative organization. The Hoover Commission which studied the organization of the federal executive branch, and the "little Hoover commissions" in the states, suggested a standard nomenclature for all administrative units. In this way, responsibility is more clearly fixed within a major department and persons working within a department better understand their role.

Bureaucracy.   A system wherein excessive growth of administrative agencies is accompanied by concentration of power in administrative officials, excessive red tape, dedication to routine, and resistance to change. The term bureaucracy is also used to designate the administrative or executive branch of the government.

• *Significance:* All modern governments have extensive administrative units. The problem in a democracy is to keep the government employees responsive to the law and to the elected representatives of the people. Safeguards against the development of irresponsible bureaucracy include congressional oversight of administrative agencies through investigations and the power of the purse, presidential direction of the administration, and judicial review of administrative actions. The increased growth and power of administrative agencies makes imperative strong control over their actions, lest administrative officials obstruct rather than further the policies established by the people's representatives.

Career Service.   A professionalized civil service wherein employment is based on merit, opportunity is afforded for advancement, and guarantees are provided against arbitrary dismissal.

• *Significance:* It is only since the 1930's that the concept of a government career service has taken hold. Employment by merit has made large inroads on the spoils system with stress now placed on a career service which emphasizes the opportunity to spend a satisfying lifetime in government service and to reach high positions of honor and prestige. In recent years, the national government and some states have attempted to recruit talented college graduates into government careers. In the federal government, major opportunities are made available to those college graduates who pass the Federal Service Entrance Examination and the Management Internship Examination. The concept of a career service has been most successfully applied in the Foreign Service.

Cease and Desist Order.   An administrative order directed to an individual, firm, or labor union to refrain from violating the law or the rules and regulations established by an administrative agency.
• *Significance:* The cease and desist order has become the major instrument of economic regulation through administrative agencies. The power was first given to the Interstate Commerce Commission (ICC) and has since been given to most independent regulatory commissions, state and national. Violation of a cease and desist order may result in prosecution or in the loss of benefits which the agency administers, such as a license to do business.

Centralized Purchasing.   Vesting authority in one agency to purchase and handle supplies and materials for government agencies. This is now done for the national government by the General Services Administration, and the practice has been adopted by most states and many local units of government.
• *Significance:* Centralized purchasing has replaced the system whereby each department or agency purchases its own supplies. The advantages include savings through large purchases, standardization of equipment and record keeping, reduction of possibilities of corruption, and centralization of responsibility. The major disadvantage is that standardized purchases may not meet specialized needs of specific agencies, but this problem is easily worked out by mutual arrangements or by exempting certain items from central purchase.

Certificate of Public Convenience, Interest, and Necessity.   Permission granted by a regulatory agency to an individual or group to conduct a particular type of business. The standard of "public convenience, interest, and necessity" has been established by the Congress and state legislatures to guide regulatory agencies in the issuance of licenses and permits to public utilities and communication media.
• *Significance:* The public interest is rarely served by the presence of several telephone companies in one community, or by competing railroads or buses. Limited channels for television and radio make regulation essential lest the airways be jammed. Thus, the determination of which company will be given the right to a television channel or to engage in a public utility enterprise is a major problem facing regulatory agencies. A company granted such a privilege is subject to continuing regulation of the quality of its service and the rates it may charge. Many agencies, state and national, have been charged with favoritism in the granting of certificates, necessitating constant oversight by the legislature and the public.

Certification of Eligibles.   The practice by which a civil service commission provides a hiring officer of an agency with the names of persons who have qualified for a position. This is usually done in accordance with the ranking of individuals on test scores. The practice in most jurisdictions is to certify the top three names, often called the "rule of three."

• *Significance:* Certification is the initial step in the hiring process. The rule of three is designed to give the hiring officer a chance to weigh intangible factors, such as personality, in making a final decision. In some jurisdictions, only the name at the top of the list may be certified, while in others, five or more are required. Personnel experts differ over what constitutes the best practice. Certification rules may be further complicated by limiting certain positions to veterans or by the availability of two or more suitable lists from which a position might be filled. A person whose name is certified but is not selected is returned to the eligible list, but there is no guarantee that an appointment will result.

Civil Service.   A collective term for most persons employed by government who are not members of the military services. It is more generally understood to apply to all those who gain government employment through a merit system which is more correctly called the "classified civil service." Elective officials and high ranking policy making officers who are appointed by elected officials, and members of the judiciary are not considered to be civil servants.

• *Significance:* The civil service has gained prestige in recent years. The merit system in particular has made substantial headway in the national government and in some states and cities. County and township government, however, still retain the spoils system to a large degree. Marked interest has arisen in professionalizing civil service employment and in applying sound principles of personnel management. In the United States, civil servants are restricted in the scope of their political activities and, though permitted to join labor organizations, are not permitted to strike. One of the essential ingredients of modern civil service is the loyalty of the civil servants to whatever administration is in power.

Classified Service.   Those positions of government employment which are under the jurisdiction of a civil service commission and which are filled by merit. The term is erroneously confused with the actual classification of positions for assignment of duties and salary known as "position classification." Congress has permitted some agencies to establish their own merit systems, such as the Foreign Service, TVA, FBI, and CIA.

• *Significance:* Under federal law, the President may exempt certain positions from the classified service. This includes top-ranking administrators as well as positions of a confidential or highly technical nature. In the states, exemptions may be determined by statute or by a civil service agency. It is generally left to the civil service agency to determine which classified positions will be filled by competitive exam and which by noncompetitive exam or which are exempt from examination. The latter categories include technical or top-ranking positions, and positions for which there is no suitable examination procedure, such as laborers or part-time employees.

Decentralization.   An administrative concept which deals with the need for large organizations or departments to assign decision-making responsibility to subunits on a geographical or subject matter basis.

• *Significance:* It is impossible for the chief executive or the head of a large department to make every decision relative to the services of a particular agency. Decentralization encourages responsible participation by lesser officials and permits adaptation to local needs in field-service operations. Major policy decisions, however, should be limited to top officials who are more directly responsible to the people.

Delegation of Authority.   The assignment of decision-making responsibility to subordinate officials. The heads of large agencies find it essential to delegate some of their authority to others, but this must be done within clearly defined standards, subject to review by the head.

• *Significance:* In establishing a public agency, the Congress often assigns a wide range of power to the agency head. He, in turn, must delegate some of his authority if he is to maintain adequate control over the agency and not have to handle every detail alone. Successful administration requires that delegations of authority be made ungrudgingly and that authority be commensurate with responsibility. Many top officials overburden themselves out of fear of losing power or out of fear that others will make the wrong decisions. Proper delegation of authority, under standards of policy established at the top, enables the settlement of many matters at lower levels of the administrative hierarchy. Personnel and administrative experts point out that departmental morale is improved by delegation of authority, through giving others a sense of participation.

Department.   A major administrative unit with responsibility for the conduct of a broad area of government operations. In the national government, the departments are headed by officers who comprise the President's Cabinet. These departments include State, Treasury, Defense, Justice, Commerce, Labor, Agriculture, Interior, Post Office, and Health, Education, and Welfare. State and local governments also departmentalize major functions. Departments are generally subdivided into bureaus, divisions, sections, and other units.

• *Significance:* Most of the work of government is conducted through major departments. Departmental status generally indicates a permanent interest on the part of the government to promote a particular function. The Departments of the Army, Navy, and Air Force retain the title but have been incorporated into the Department of Defense. A number of major functions are vested in agencies outside the regular departments, such as independent regulatory commissions and corporations, in order to remove them from direct presidential supervision. Many administrative authorities feel that all functions should be assigned to one of the major departments to prevent diffusion of responsibility. The creation of a department of urban affairs at the national level has been urged by President Kennedy.

Ex Officio.   A Latin term for "by virtue of office." Many persons hold a position on a board or agency by virtue of their holding some other related

position. For example, a governor, typically, is a member of numerous state boards and commissions by virtue of his position as governor.
• *Significance:* The ex officio principle is designed to involve important officials in the decisions of major agencies. It serves to coordinate the efforts of related agencies and to strengthen responsibility.

Federal Register.   A government publication initiated by law in 1935 requiring publication of presidential proclamations and executive orders. The Administrative Procedure Act of 1946 requires every public agency to publish a statement of its organization, authority, methods of operation, and statements of general policy in the *Federal Register*. Notice of proposed rules and regulations and administrative orders resulting from the adjudicatory functions of the agency must also be published. The *Federal Register* is published five times each week. The documents are codified in the *Code of Federal Regulations* (CFR). Some states have similar publications.
• *Significance:* The increasing growth of executive orders and administrative rules and regulations has made the *Federal Register* one of the most important and widely read government publications. Prior to its publication, the citizen and business interests in particular had no way of knowing what and how new rules applied to them. Publication of proposed rules and regulations is designed to assure interested parties an opportunity to be heard prior to enforcement of the rule.

Federal Service Entrance Examination.   A federal civil service examination open to college juniors, seniors, and graduates with broad educational backgrounds who are interested in securing junior management positions in federal service upon graduation from college. The examination tests general intelligence and aptitudes and is designed to find promising career servants who can move into management positions in the future. Persons who take the examination have the option of taking an additional examination called the Management Internship Examination which, if passed, offers greater opportunity for employment.
• *Significance:* Unlike most civil service examinations which test specific skills, the Federal Service Entrance Examination is part of the government's effort to attract persons who possess outstanding qualities essential for supervisory and administrative positions. Many college graduates who are ineligible to take examinations for specific skills may qualify under this program. A few states have similar examinations.

Field Service.   Local or regional branch offices of a federal or state agency. Operations, personnel, and finance are under the control of the central office in Washington, D.C. or the state capital.
• *Significance:* Most government work is conducted through field offices. Only about 10 percent of federal employees work in Washington, D.C., with the remaining 90 percent distributed in field-service offices around the nation. Field-headquarters relationships pose a continuing problem for sound administration in securing co-ordination of activity and responsibility. Field offices

provide the citizen with close-to-home services and make possible the settlement of most problems at the point at which they arise.

Functional Consolidation.   Combining several administrative units which do related work into one major department. *See* FUNCTIONAL CONSOLIDATION, page 348.

• *Significance:* Functional consolidation is a basic principle of administrative organization. The tendency on the part of legislative bodies is to create a new agency to meet new problems. The result often has been diffusion of responsibility over similar problems and the existence of too many agencies for the chief executive to direct and control. Administrative experts have suggested that, on the state level, all agencies should be consolidated into from 10 to 20 departments. The New Jersey Constitution of 1947 places a limitation of 20 departments within the executive branch. The Hoover Commission suggested, in 1949, that some 1800 federal agencies could be logically consolidated into 22 major departments.

Government Corporation.   An agency of government which administers a business enterprise. The corporation form is used when an activity is primarily commercial in nature, produces revenue for its continued existence, and requires greater flexibility than the Congress normally permits regular departments. Corporations are used at the national level for such enterprises as electric power distribution (Tennessee Valley Authority) and insuring of bank deposits (Federal Deposit Insurance Corporation). At the state level, corporations (often called "authorities") are used to operate airports, turnpikes, and harbors, the best known being the Port of New York Authority.

• *Significance:* The corporation device is generally used to provide a business service which no private enterprise could undertake. Prior to 1945, the Congress permitted corporations a great degree of independence but the Government Corporation Control Act of 1945 subjects them to annual budgetary and auditing controls and civil service controls. Corporations are generally run by a board of directors and many are attached to one of the major departments for administrative purposes. The government corporation has presented the problem of how to balance the corporation's need for flexibility with the need for legislative and executive controls.

Hearing.   Adjudication by an administrative or regulatory agency of alleged violations of the law or of the rules and regulations of the agency. Hearings are also held to give interested parties an opportunity to be heard prior to the promulgation of a rule.

• *Significance:* Hearings may be initiated by the agency itself or by any aggrieved party. They are conducted in a manner similar to, but less formal than, a court of law, under rules established by the Administrative Procedure Act of 1946. Decisions result in the issuance of administrative orders having the force of law. Appeals may be made to the courts which generally limit themselves to a review of the overall fairness of the hearing and to whether the record substantiates the findings of the agency. The quasi-judicial power of administrative agencies is one of the major developments of the twentieth century. The requirement of a hearing prior to the promulgation of a rule is designed to permit parties likely to be affected by a rule to have a part in its formulation.

Hearing Examiner.   An official who conducts hearings for a regulatory agency and makes recommendations to the heads of the agency for issuance of administrative orders. By virtue of the Administrative Procedure Act of 1946, hearing examiners are appointed under civil service rules, and are protected against arbitrary dismissal and loss of salary. They are generally attached to a specific agency, hear cases in rotation, and may not be assigned other duties.
• *Significance:* Hearing examiners were created in response to the pre-1946 concern that regulatory agencies were both prosecutor and judge of those who violated their rules. By giving a degree of independence to hearing examiners, the Congress sought to overcome the major weaknesses of administrative adjudication of private rights. Decisions of hearing examiners are generally presented to the agency heads who make the final determination, but if no appeal is made from the examiner's recommendations, his decision is final. Hearing examiners have become the central locus of "administrative justice."

Hoover Commission.   A commission appointed in 1947 to study the organization of the executive branch. The group of 12 persons (four appointed by the President, four by the President pro tempore of the Senate, and four by the Speaker of the House), known as the Commission on Organization of the Executive Branch, was headed by former President Herbert Hoover. It filed its report in 1949. A second Hoover Commission, similarly appointed in 1953, was charged with the function of suggesting which federal functions might be discontinued.
• *Significance:* The first Hoover Commission submitted a voluminous but highly regarded series of reports and made almost 300 specific recommendations, approximately 70 percent of which have been adopted. Basically, the Commission proposed greater consolidation of agencies, greater authority and assistance for the President, and improved budget, personnel, and administrative procedures. The Commission inspired the creation of "little Hoover commissions" in about half the states, many of which have met with some success. The second Hoover Commission's concern with policy matters rather than organization has limited the influence of its report.

Independent Agency.   A federal agency which is not part of the ten executive departments. The term may include independent regulatory commissions, but is generally used to describe agencies which perform service rather than regulatory functions. Examples of independent agencies are the Civil Service Commission, the Veterans Administration, and the General Services Administration. Many independent agencies are organized like regular departments and are headed by persons responsible to the President. Others take the form of boards or commissions, such as the Tariff Commission and the Atomic Energy Commission.
• *Significance:* A large number of agencies have independent status. In many instances, either they do not fit into any particular major department or else

they service all departments. In other cases, the Congress has wanted to keep a tighter rein on an agency than its departmental status permits or has responded to the pressures of interest groups which seek autonomy for a given function. A few have been given independent status to shield them from partisan politics, as is the case with the Tariff Commission and the Atomic Energy Commission. Terms of officials frequently overlap to avoid control by any one President, and the removal power of the President may be limited. The existence of large numbers of independent agencies complicates the organizational pattern and lines of responsibility of the executive branch.

Independent Regulatory Commission.   An agency established outside the major executive departments and charged with the regulation of important aspects of the economy. They include (1) the Interstate Commerce Commission, (2) Federal Trade Commission, (3) Federal Power Commission, (4) Securities and Exchange Commission, (5) Federal Communications Commission, (6) National Labor Relations Board, (7) Civil Aeronautics Board, and (8) Federal Reserve Board. All of these agencies are empowered to establish rules for the particular industries they regulate and to prosecute violators. All are multiheaded, with five or seven members, except for the 11-member Interstate Commerce Commission.

• *Significance:* The independent regulatory commission represents one of the most important developments in American government in recent years. Vast authority to determine individual and property rights has been vested in such agencies. This has been necessary because of the sheer complexity of modern economic problems and the desirability of having agencies which could develop expertness and continuity of policy with regard to these problems. Neither the Congress nor the courts are equipped with the talent or the time necessary. The agencies have been made independent of the President in order to withdraw their legislative and adjudicatory functions from partisan politics. Though members of the commissions are appointed by the President with the Senate's consent, they may be removed only for cause, and terms of office are lengthy and overlapping to avoid dominance by appointees of one President. Further, no more than a majority of commissioners may be from one party. A problem has arisen from the tendency of these commissions to become captives of the industries they are supposed to regulate, since many officials are necessarily drawn from the particular industries. Further, the independence of the commission may result in policies which are contrary to those of the party in power. These commissions have often been called "the headless fourth branch" of government because of their peculiar place in the organization of the government and lack of continuing supervision from the President or the Congress.

Line and Staff.   An administrative concept that categorizes the work of an agency in accordance with whether the agency has an operating or advisory function. The line is concerned with carrying out the legislative programs, and deals directly with the people. The executive departments such as Agriculture or Labor are typical line departments. The staff serves in an advisory capacity and directs its efforts toward aiding the chief executive and the line officials through such activities as planning, co-ordinating, and budgeting. The Bureau of the Budget is a major staff agency of the federal government. *See* AUXILIARY AGENCY, page 174.

• *Significance:* The distinction between line and staff serves the purpose of administrative organization and convenience, and attempts to prescribe the division of labor in large organizations. However, the distinction is by no means a precise one. Line officials may engage in staff or advisory work, as members of the Cabinet generally do, and some staff agencies may engage in operating tasks as some budgeting or planning offices do.

Merit System.   The selection, retention, and promotion of government employees on the basis of demonstrated fitness. Though the term is often used interchangeably with "civil service," the merit system emphasizes positive programs of sound personnel management rather than the mere placing of restraints upon the spoils system.

• *Significance:* The merit system has by no means been universally adopted in the United States, particularly when viewed as a thoroughgoing personnel program. While much headway has been made at the national level, much remains to be done on the state and local levels, particularly in counties and townships. Originally, the concept of civil service was limited to keeping unfit persons out of government service. The merit system represents a more positive approach looking toward the development of a career service and in-service training, position-classification, pay standardization, and retirement programs.

Organization.   The arrangement of persons for the most effective achievement of a purpose or objective. Public administration experts are consistently concerned with the problem of the best way to organize the government or a particular agency to eliminate friction and to best accomplish the task assigned. This involves decisions as to the nature of line, staff, and auxiliary agencies, the location of responsibility, and the over-all co-ordination of efforts. Activities may be organized according to major purpose (e.g., the Department of Agriculture), process or skills (e.g., central purchasing), area (e.g., fire and police protection), or clientele (e.g., Veterans Administration). The use of a single head or a board is another concern of organization.

• *Significance:* Organization concepts and techniques tend to be the concern of administration specialists but are important to all citizens who seek to understand the nature of administrative organization and problems of reorganization. All agencies contain all or some of the organizational patterns, and one is rarely used to the exclusion of others. Much depends on the purposes to be served and, in government in particular, on the desires and influence of legislative bodies and pressure groups.

Position Classification.   The grouping of government employment positions on the basis of duties, responsibilities, and qualifications. A position is classified in accordance with the nature of the job rather than in terms of the person holding the position.

• *Significance:* Position classification is regarded as an essential ingredient of a sound merit system. The benefits include (1) simplification of recruitment and selection of personnel through administration of similar tests for similar positions; (2) establishment of equal pay for equal work, an important goal of public personnel administration and essential for high morale; (3) clearer lines of responsibility for the individual worker and top management; (4) establishment of clear avenues of promotion and transfers. The over-all objective of position classification is equitable treatment of government employees which benefits both the employee and the public. It is necessary, however, that classification schemes be reviewed from time to time, lest they act as a straightjacket on effective administration, and optimum utilization of employees. Position classification is in effect in the national government and in several state and local governments.

Quasi-judicial.   Powers exercised by administrative agencies which have the characteristics of a judicial act. Independent regulatory commissions as well as other administrative agencies exercise quasi-judicial powers when they conduct hearings and make decisions having the force of law.
• *Significance:* Under the doctrine of the separation of powers, only courts and judges may exercise judicial power. The highly technical nature of modern economic regulation has necessitated the delegation of "quasi-" (Latin for "seemingly" or "resembling") judicial power to expert administrators. Thus, the Congress has empowered the Federal Trade Commission to determine what constitutes an unfair trade practice, for example. Concern over the inherent violation of the separation of powers led to the passage of the Administrative Procedure Act of 1946 which required the use of hearing examiners, more judicial-like procedures, and broadened the power of judicial review of administrative adjudications.

Quasi-legislative.   Powers exercised by administrative agencies which have the characteristics of legislation. Numerous administrative agencies have been authorized to issue rules and regulations having the force of law. These include not only the independent regulatory commissions but a host of other agencies as well, such as the Department of Agriculture which issues rules relative to crop quotas and other agricultural practices.
• *Significance:* Under the doctrine of the separation of powers, all legislative power is vested in the legislative body. But the Congress and the state legislatures cannot legislate in sufficient detail to cover the great range of problems likely to arise in a complex society. Thus, the legislature delegates power to administrative agencies to "fill in the details" under the standards established by the legislature. The Administrative Procedure Act of 1946 requires administrative agencies to give notice and hold hearings on proposed rules and regulations and to publish all rules and regulations in the *Federal Register*. Congress retains a check on "quasi-" (Latin for "seemingly" or "resembling") legislation by being able to change the basic law of the agency. The courts, too, maintain a check over abuse of powers delegated to agencies. A substantial number of rules which govern the individual emanate from administrative agencies rather than the legislature.

Schedules A, B, and C.   Three classes of positions in the federal service which are filled without the usual competitive examinations. Schedule A positions are those for which no practical examination is possible, such as federal attorneys. Schedule B includes positions filled by a noncompetitive examination, which includes a survey and evaluation of a candidate's experience and qualifications. Schedule C, established by President Dwight Eisenhower in 1952, includes positions of a confidential and policy-making character.

• *Significance:* Schedules A, B, and C are designed to give flexibility to civil service rules since it is impracticable to fill all jobs by competitive examination. The Civil Service Commission determines which positions fall into the exempted schedules. The most controversial classification is Schedule C since it is possible to utilize this classification in order to increase patronage appointments and to remove career servants. Yet, it is recognized that the President should have a number of confidential and policy-making positions which he can fill as he wishes. The Civil Service Commission has been reluctant to grant too many exemptions and has approved about 1000 Schedule C positions while turning down an equal number which were requested by President Eisenhower.

Secretary.   The title of most of the heads of the major executive departments in the national government and a few major state officials.

• *Significance:* The secretaries of the executive departments are part of the President's Cabinet, and serve at the pleasure of the President. They serve as legal and administrative heads of their departments and have broad powers over expenditures and personnel. Several have quasi-legislative and quasi-judicial powers. They set the tone with which a department operates and act as advisers to the President. Generally, they are chosen more for their political acumen and acceptability than for their training in the subject area of the department. State government secretaries may have similar powers and duties but are generally elected. The title is most commonly used in the states for the office of secretary of state.

Separation from Service.   Termination of employment in the classified service. Separation may be voluntary, as by resignation, or may be the result of retirement laws, a reduction in force, or disciplinary action for conduct unbecoming a public employee.

• *Significance:* A public employee may resign at any time without prejudice, and liberal retirement allowances are made for those who serve a long period of time. When a reduction in force is ordered because of a cut in appropriations or a lessened need for employees, as after a war or crisis period, due weight is given to such factors as seniority, performance, and, in large measure, veterans are given preference over nonveterans. Dismissal from service is permitted under the law "for such causes as will promote the efficiency of said service," and procedures are established by law. Contrary to popular assumption, civil servants may be, and are, dismissed without elaborate procedures. Basically, the head of an agency may hire and fire employees. In order to avoid dismissal for racial, religious, or political reasons, the department head must inform the employee in writing of the causes for his dismissal and give him an opportunity to respond. No hearings are held unless the employee is a veteran and appeals his case to the Civil Service Commission. Those in sensitive positions may also be discharged as "security risks" and all government employees are given security checks. Similar procedures are followed in many states, while, in others, more formal appeal procedures, to a commission or court, are in effect.

Span of Control.   An administrative concept which is concerned with the number of agencies or subordinates which one person can effectively supervise. Experts are far from agreement on the proper span of control, but a figure of about 20 appears to be the maximum.

• *Significance:* The President and almost all governors have far more agencies under their supervision than they can effectively supervise. The same is true for many persons with top-level jobs in government. The Hoover Commission and most reorganization plans have sought to minimize the span of control by drawing as many functions as possible into as few departments as possible. In this way, a hierarchy of responsibility can be developed in which no individual has more than a few persons reporting directly to him.

Spoils System.   The award of government jobs to political supporters and friends. The term derives from the expression, "to the victor belongs the spoils." The spoils system is generally associated with President Andrew Jackson.

• *Significance:* The spoils system is usually defended on the grounds that it is essential for the maintenance of a party system since people are not likely to work for a party without some reward, and that victorious candidates should have as employees those who are devoted to them and to their policies. President Jackson took the view that government work is so simple that anyone could handle it and that rotation in office is necessary and healthy for vigorous administration. Few people today consider government work simple but many still support the principle of rotation in office since civil service tenure may result in an administration having unsympathetic employees. Vestiges of the spoils system remain at the local government level and many federal jobs are filled by patronage. The merit system has made large inroads on the spoils system but spoils are still an important factor in American politics.

Tenure.   The right to hold a position or office free from arbitrary dismissal. Public employees in the classified service have tenure after serving a probationary period.

• *Significance:* Tenure is essential for the operation of a merit system of employment whether applied to professional persons or others. It encourages freedom of thought and action on the part of the employee and frees him from fear of dismissal for purely personal, political, or arbitrary reasons. Safeguards have been established by law to assure tenure for government employees who are in the classified service.

United States Government Organization Manual.   A government publication which lists all the departments and agencies of the national government with detailed descriptions of their powers, duties, and activities.

• *Significance:* The *Manual* is a useful resource for students of government and citizens generally. Information is provided about the major agencies of government and the various units within the agencies. A list of agencies which have been discontinued in recent years is also included. Similar information about state agencies can be found in state manuals.

Unity of Command.   An administrative concept which holds that no person should be subject to the orders of more than one superior. It is related to the idea of "chain of command" which is common to the military services.
• *Significance:* Unity of command is difficult to put into practice in the public service because of the variety of tasks which the government has undertaken and the large numbers of persons employed. Reorganization studies have revealed a wide dispersion of authority and responsibility which accounts for frequent recommendations to integrate agencies with similar functions and to establish a hierarchical arrangement of responsibility. The problem is most acute in areas of technical specialization where a clash might occur between general administrators and the specialists as to the best approach to a problem. A number of informal chains of command tend to develop in an agency wherein certain individuals may command more respect than the actual head. Further, government agencies may be independent of the chief executive and more responsive to the legislature or a pressure group. Authority for final decisions must rest in one individual to avoid irresponsibility and confusion.

Veterans' Preference.   Special consideration given to veterans in various aspects of the civil service. These include (1) the addition of five points to the test scores of veterans, ten points to disabled veterans; (2) the waiver of age, physical, and education requirements in some instances; (3) the competition for some positions is limited to veterans; (4) veterans are given extra rights with regard to layoffs and dismissals; (5) veterans' preference extends to wives, widows, and mothers of disabled or deceased veterans. These preferences are provided by almost all civil service jurisdictions in the United States.
• *Significance:* Veterans' preference has resulted in filling a majority of civil service ranks with veterans and has, therefore, become a major concern of public personnel administration. All of these special considerations are based on the idea that the country owes a debt to the veteran, and veterans' preference is vigorously supported by veterans' interest groups. Yet, personnel experts view veterans' preference as a derogation of the merit principle and an obstacle to qualified nonveterans seeking a government career.

IMPORTANT AGENCIES

Civil Service Commission.   The central personnel agency of the national government, established in 1883. It is composed of three members appointed to six-year terms by the President with the Senate's consent. Its principal activities include the recruitment, examination, and preparation of eligible lists of prospective government employees. The Commission also administers a variety of laws pertaining to government employees with regard to veterans' preference, classification, security checks, political activity, retirement, and insurance programs.
• *Significance:* The Civil Service Commission is largely concerned with providing leadership in federal personnel administration by establishing standards

of good practice and stimulating improvements in personnel methods in the operating agencies. The Commission employs over 4500 people and has regional offices in major cities. Day-to-day personnel matters are handled in individual departments and agencies, with the Commission playing a policy-making and supervisory role. Though conflicts often arise between the various government agencies and the Commission over personnel policies, the Commission has managed to maintain a strong, independent position in the executive branch. Civil service commissions are also found in most states and in many local units of government.

General Services Administration.   An independent agency established in 1949 to centralize purchasing and property and records management for the national government. The General Services Administration, operating through ten regional offices, is assigned responsibility for the procurement, supply, and transportation of property and services for the executive agencies, the acquisition and management of federally owned or leased property, disposal of surplus property, and records management.

• *Significance:* The General Services Administration gathers under one agency a number of functions formerly performed by separate units. It is headed by a director who is responsible to the President. The General Services Administration was created upon the suggestion of the Hoover Commission which noted the need for centralized purchasing and property management in order to avoid waste and duplication in the world-wide operations of the national government. In addition to its service activities, the General Services Administration publishes the *Statutes at Large,* the *Federal Register,* and the *United States Government Organization Manual.*

IMPORTANT CASES

Opp Cotton Mills v. Administrator of Wage and Hour Division, 312 U.S. 126 (1941): Declared that the provisions of the Fair Labor Standards Act authorizing an administrative determination of minimum wages in a particular industry do not constitute an unconstitutional delegation of legislative power.

• *Significance:* This was one of the last in a long series of cases which challenged the right of the Congress to vest rule-making power in an administrative agency. The Court pointed out that in a complex society, the Congress could not be expected to fill in the details of all public policies. So long as a standard is established within which the administrative agency must operate, the delegation of authority is permissible. The Court noted further that the Constitution does not demand the impossible and the Congress could not be expected to set every wage rate, railroad rate, or every other rule which a business must follow. For all intents and purposes, the *Opp* case put an end to the delegation of power issue in American constitutional law.

Railroad Comm'n of Texas v. Rowan and Nichols Oil Co., 311 U.S. 570 (1941): Refused to overturn a ruling of the Railroad Commission relating to the amount of oil that could be taken from wells in Texas. The Court noted that the issue was too complex for judges to determine and that the Commission's order must stand in the absence of a showing that it was based on insubstantial evidence.

• *Significance:* In this, as in numerous cases which have come before it challenging specific rulings of state and national administrative agencies, the Court has taken the view that administrative decisions will stand if supported by "substantial evidence." Otherwise, the Court would be substituting its judgment for that of an expert administrative agency. Congress, in the Administrative Procedure Act of 1946, has supported the Court's stand by providing that the scope of judicial review of administrative rulings be limited to determining relevant questions of law and by approving the substantial evidence rule.

United Public Workers v. Mitchell, 330 U.S. 75 (1947): Ruled that the Congress may prohibit federal employees from participating in political activities. The Court upheld the Hatch Act of 1939 which authorizes the removal of a person from civil service employment for taking an "active part in political management or political campaigns."

• *Significance:* The Court found no invasion of the constitutional rights of public employees in the Hatch Act. In another case, the Court applied this ruling to state government employees working on projects financed by federal grants-in-aid (*Oklahoma v. United States Civil Service Commission,* 330 U.S. 127 [1947]). Critics of these rulings claim that they literally bar millions of persons from active participation in the democratic process. However, the Court agreed with the Congress that the Hatch Act contributes to the efficiency of the public service and prevents the growth of bureaucratic political machines.

IMPORTANT STATUTES

Administrative Procedure Act of 1946.   A major law governing the procedures of regulatory agencies and providing for standards of judicial review of administrative determinations. The Act requires that every agency publicize its operations, give advance notice of proposed rules, and permit persons to testify, to be accompanied by counsel, and to cross-examine witnesses. The Act provides further that the same official may not act as both prosecutor and judge and that persons may appeal decisions of these agencies to the courts. The courts are authorized to set aside any agency ruling which is arbitrary or unsupported by substantial evidence.

• *Significance:* The Administrative Procedure Act was passed in response to growing criticism of the lack of procedural safeguards in administrative legislation and adjudication. Since so many private rights are now affected by administrative agencies, the Congress sought to regulate the internal procedures by which rights are determined and to provide broad standards for judicial review. In many respects, the Act codified a number of procedures which the agencies themselves had undertaken in response to growing criticism, but it has served to make these practices more uniform. The standards for judicial review are largely those established by the courts themselves in earlier cases.

Pendleton Act (Civil Service Act of 1883).   This law, as amended over the years, forms the basis for the personnel policies of the national government. The law established the principle of employment on the basis of open, competitive examinations, and created a Civil Service Commission to administer the personnel service. The Pendleton Act extended the merit principle to only 10 percent of national employees, but later laws and executive orders have extended coverage to more than 90 percent of employees.

• *Significance:* The Pendleton Act was a direct result of the assassination of President James Garfield by a disappointed office seeker. The Act brought to a close the period of Jacksonian spoils which made government employment a reward for political activity. The Pendleton Act turned the tide in favor of employment by merit, which, despite occasional lapses, has spread to all levels of government.

Ramspeck Act (Civil Service Act of 1940).   Authorizes the President to place, by executive order, nearly all federal positions under the civil service system. Exemptions include those positions filled by presidential appointment requiring the Senate's approval, and certain special agencies, such as the Tennessee Valley Authority and the Federal Bureau of Investigation, which have merit systems of their own.

• *Significance:* The Ramspeck Act is considered to be the culmination of the civil service reforms initiated in 1883 by the Pendleton Act. Presidents Franklin Roosevelt, Harry Truman, and Dwight Eisenhower all used this authority to broaden the coverage of the civil service laws. As a result, most national government positions are covered. At first, this power was used to "freeze" political appointees into their positions, but the net effect has been to strengthen civil service in the United States.

Reorganization Act of 1949.   A grant of power to the President to reorganize the executive branch of the government. Plans for reorganization must be submitted to the Congress, and either house may veto the proposal within 60 days.

• *Significance:* A vast enterprise needs continuing reorganization to ensure efficiency of operation. The Reorganization Act places the initiative in the hands of the President who bears major responsibility for administration. The veto in the hands of the Congress is designed to prevent any reshuffling which may threaten the status of any "pet" agencies of members of Congress or major pressure groups. A sustantial portion of the recommendations of the Hoover Commission have been put into effect through procedures established by the Reorganization Act.

10

The Judicial Process:
Courts and Law Enforcement

Activism versus Self-Restraint.　　Two approaches to the proper role of the Supreme Court in the American political system. Activists hold that a judge should use his position to promote desirable social ends. Self-restrainers hold that a judge should, in deciding cases, defer to the legislative and executive branches, which are politically responsible to the voters, and submerge his personal philosophy. Both schools of thought recognize the policy-making nature of the Supreme Court's decisions on major social questions, but they differ on how that power should be used.

• *Significance:* Today, as in the past, the Supreme Court is divided between activists and self-restrainers. Justice Hugo L. Black is the leading spokesman for the activists and Justice Felix Frankfurter for the restrainers. This division underscores the policy-making role of the Supreme Court in its decisions on questions of broad policy which are framed in legal terms. Most observers take the view that judges cannot help but inject their personal views into decisions and that one is apt to refer to a judge as an activist or self-restrainer depending upon one's view of the outcome of a particular case. For example, during the New Deal period of the 1930's, liberals opposed the "activism" of the Court in striking down social welfare programs, whereas many of these same liberals today favor Court "activism" on behalf of civil rights.

Administrative Court.　　Courts established outside the regular judicial system to hear cases between private persons and government agencies. Such courts are found on the European continent but, technically speaking, do not exist in the United States. However, a number of courts established by the Congress, such as the Court of Claims and the Court of Customs, are sometimes referred to as administrative courts in that they are authorized to hear suits between individuals and government agencies on specialized administrative matters.

• *Significance:* The extensive growth of administrative agencies in the United States has been accompanied by an increasing body of rules and regulations made by these agencies (such as the Federal Communications Commission)

191

which affect individual conduct. The second Hoover Commission recommended, in 1955, that special administrative courts be established to hear cases related to taxation, business regulation, and labor-management problems. Such courts could not only relieve the work burden of the regular courts but also develop expert competence to deal with new legal concepts.

Administrative Law. That branch of law which creates administrative agencies, establishes their methods of procedure, and determines the scope of judicial review of agency practices and actions. The term is also used to describe the rules and regulations which are made by administrative agencies. Administrative law deals with rate making, operating rules, the rights of persons and companies regulated by administrative agencies, and the power of the courts to review.
• *Significance:* The widespread use of administrative agencies to regulate important aspects of economic and social life has resulted in a great flow of law coming from these agencies governing individual conduct. Correspondingly, a body of law has evolved controlling the operations of administrative agencies to assure fair procedures that protect the rights of persons affected by these operations. Increasingly, more people are affected by administrative agency rulings than by legislative statutes.

Admiralty Jurisdiction. Authority vested in federal courts to hear cases involving problems connected with shipping and commerce on the high seas and on the navigable waters of the United States. It is a highly technical body of law based on tradition, congressional statutes, and international law. Typical cases involve maritime contracts, collisions, and crimes committed on vessels.
• *Significance:* The federal courts have exclusive jurisdiction over admiralty and maritime cases as provided in Article III, section 2. This assures maintenance of national supremacy over foreign and interstate commerce over water routes.

Advisory Opinion. An opinion given by a court, though no actual case or controversy is before it, as to the constitutionality or legal effect of a law. No advisory opinions are rendered by federal judges. Ten states, however, do authorize the highest state court to give such opinions upon the request of the legislature or governor. An advisory opinion is not binding except in the state of Colorado, though in all cases they carry great weight.
• *Significance:* The advisory opinion is designed to avoid the confusion which might result from a declaration of unconstitutionality after a law has been in effect for a long period of time. Such an opinion serves as a guide to the legislature, particularly when a statute appears to break new ground, and to governors in deciding whether to sign or veto legislation. However, when rendering an advisory opinion, the courts lack the benefit of opposing arguments by adverse parties.

Amicus Curiae. A legal term meaning "friend of the court." It refers to those who are not actual parties to a lawsuit but who may aid the court in reaching its decision. The court may at its discretion give permission to persons seeking to appear as *amicus curiae.* Oftimes, a party will seek to appear as *amicus curiae* when the decision in the case will affect his rights as well as the rights of those directly involved. In some states, a friend of the court is permanently attached to a court to help it reach decisions in cases involving minors, divorce, or criminal offenders.

• *Significance:* Many lawsuits have implications reaching far beyond the interests of the litigants involved in the case. For example, in a case involving the rights of a labor union, several other unions may seek permission to testify or file documents to demonstrate to the court the implications of any decision which might be reached.

Appeal. The carrying of a case from a lower court to a higher tribunal. The term is also used to identify those types of cases which may be carried to the United States Supreme Court as a matter of right; these include cases from federal courts and highest state courts when state or federal laws are declared in conflict with the Constitution or a treaty. Such cases are brought to the Supreme Court "on appeal."

• *Significance:* An ordinary appeal is designed to serve as a check upon any errors committed in lower tribunals. The Supreme Court's duty to take cases on appeal assures that controversial questions of constitutionality and national supremacy are decided in the highest court in the land.

Appellate Jurisdiction. Authority of a court to review decisions of an inferior court. In the federal court system, the courts of appeals and the Supreme Court have power to review decisions of district courts as well as other tribunals. All states have courts of appellate jurisdiction to review decisions of lower state courts. The losing party in any lawsuit generally has the right to appeal the decision to an appellate court.

• *Significance:* Courts of appellate jurisdiction serve as a check upon errors of law or fact which might arise in the course of trials in lower courts. They also serve to give the losing party a second chance to win his case. The scope of appellate jurisdiction, that is, the types of cases and questions which may be appealed, is determined by rules of procedure established by the courts or by the legislative body.

Arbitration. A method of settling disputes wherein the parties to the dispute agree to accept the decision of a third party as binding. A number of states have authorized arbitration and make the decision enforceable by the courts.

• *Significance:* Arbitration serves to provide an informal forum for settlement of disputes, while saving the time and expense of court action. It also serves to relieve the burden of crowded court dockets. Technical matters can be arbitrated by experts in the field of the dispute. The American Arbitration Association, a private organization, provides a panel of available arbitrators.

Attorney General. The head of the Justice Department and a member of the President's Cabinet. He serves as legal advisor to the President and to all agencies of the executive branch and is the chief law-enforcement officer of the United States. The Attorney General directs the work of federal district attorneys, United States Marshals, and federal penal institutions. Criminal investigations and the conduct of lawsuits involving the United States fall under his charge. An attorney general is also found in each of the states, where he is frequently an elected official. He, too, serves as legal advisor and law-enforcement officer.

• *Significance:* The Attorney General ranks as one of the most powerful individuals in government. Opinions of the Attorney General on legal matters have the force of law unless overturned by a court. The emphasis to be given to particular kinds of law enforcement, such as antitrust or civil rights laws, rests largely in the discretion of the Attorney General. At the national level, broad discretion has been vested in the Attorney General in the areas of immigration, citizenship, and subversion.

Blue-Ribbon Jury.   A system of jury selection which makes use of special panels of jurors to try difficult, complex, or important cases. Such juries are impaneled upon request of a party to the suit with the consent of the presiding judge. This method of juror selection is in contrast to the ordinary, random selection of jurors from voting or tax lists to represent a cross section of the community. The use of the blue-ribbon jury has been approved by the Supreme Court (*Fay v. New York,* 332 U.S. 463 [1947]).

• *Significance:* Blue-ribbon juries represent an attempt to meet the objection that many jurors are incompetent to try complex cases. In widely publicized cases, it may be difficult to get an unbiased jury and the blue-ribbon jury may serve to speed the administration of justice. However, some see it as an attempt to exclude all but the "best citizens" from jury duty.

Capital Punishment.   The death penalty for conviction of a serious crime, such as murder, rape, kidnaping, or treason. Electrocution is the most commonly used method of execution; lethal gas and hanging are also employed. In Utah, the condemned person may choose to be hanged or shot. Nine states bar capital punishment: Alaska, Hawaii, Delaware, Maine, Michigan, Minnesota, North Dakota, Rhode Island, and Wisconsin; Puerto Rico and the Virgin Islands do likewise. Several states have reinstated the death penalty after having once voted to abolish it. In many states, the jury may recommend life imprisonment instead of the death penalty.

• *Significance:* Capital punishment has long been debated on both moral and legalistic grounds. Many authorities question its utility as a deterrent to crime, while others abhor it for religious or other moral reasons. In recent years, legislation has been frequently introduced in the Congress and in numerous states to abolish the death penalty. The number of executions has decreased in recent years, due in part to the reluctance of judges and juries to assign the death penalty. In the decade of 1930–1939, 1666 persons were executed; 716, in the decade 1950–1959.

Certiorari.   An order issued by a higher court to a lower court to send up the record of a case for review. Most cases reach the United States Supreme Court through the writ of certiorari, which is issued at the discretion of the Court when at least four of the nine justices feel that the case should be reviewed.

• *Significance:* Though it is commonly assumed that anyone may bring his case to the Supreme Court, only a limited number of cases may be appealed as a matter of right. In all other cases, the party must petition the Court to issue a writ of certiorari. The net effect of this procedure is that it vests in the Supreme Court complete discretion over the cases it will consider. Due to the press of work, only about 20 percent of petitions for certiorari are granted, thereby leaving the lower court decision as final. Only cases of importance reaching far beyond the interests of the particular parties to the suit tend to be heard. Oftimes, the Court will limit its grant of certiorari to specific questions rather than review all elements of the trial or of lower court decisions.

Challenge.   Objection to having a prospective juror serve on a jury. A juror may be challenged by either party. A challenge may be for "cause" or "peremptory."An unlimited number of challenges may be made for cause with approval of the presiding judge. Peremptory challenges, for which no reason need be given, are limited to a specific number, which varies from state to state, depending upon the nature of the offense involved. For crimes punishable by death, as many as 40 peremptory challenges may be allowed; as few as five may be permitted for minor offenses.
• *Significance:* Both parties to a case are entitled to a trial by an impartial jury. The challenge permits counsel to remove prospective jurors who show bias or, for any reason, appear unfit to sit in judgment. The limit placed on peremptory challenges prevents unreasonable delay in filling the jury panel.

Charge.   A statement by the judge to the jury at the conclusion of a trial to aid the jury in reaching its verdict. The judge instructs the jury in the law governing the case and reviews the evidence. The authority of the judge to comment on the facts of a case, as distinguished from the law involved, varies from state to state, although federal judges have wide latitude.
• *Significance:* The charge to the jury serves to refresh the minds of the jurors, particularly after a lengthy trial, and provides instructions as to the law applicable to the case. It is for the jury to weigh the truth or falsity of the evidence, but the jury is bound by the law as interpreted by the judge. If the judge is careless in his charge or demonstrates bias, the case may be overturned by a higher court. Nevertheless, the charge to the jury may play a major role in the verdict which the jury eventually reaches.

Chief Justice.   The highest judicial officer of the United States or of a state. The Chief Justice of the United States Supreme Court is appointed for a life term by the President with the consent of the Senate. He presides over sessions of the Court and over meetings of the justices for reaching decisions, assigns the writing of opinions, and performs a variety of administrative duties as head of the federal court system. In the states, the chief justices are chosen in a variety of ways—appointment, election, seniority—usually for a limited term. Their duties are similar to the Chief Justice of the United States, although in many states they lack control over lower court administrative matters.
• *Significance:* Aside from administrative duties and a slightly higher salary, chief justices have no more power than other members of highest courts in deciding cases. However, the position does carry considerable prestige and the

chief justice may be in a position to use his post as presiding officer to influence the course of decision making.

Circuit Court.   A general trial court in the states, sometimes called a district court or a superior court. In many states, the court serves several counties and the judges go on "circuit" from one county to another according to a schedule. In most states, the judges of these courts are elected by the voters of that particular county or circuit, with terms varying from two to six years. These are courts of "original jurisdiction" where important civil and criminal cases begin, trials are held, and juries are frequently used. Cases from minor courts, such as justices of the peace or municipal courts, may be appealed to the circuit court. From circuit courts cases may be appealed to higher state courts.

• *Significance:* For most people, the circuit court represents their main contact with the judicial branch of the government. This includes not only parties to a suit but witnesses and jurors as well. Hence, it is vital that trial courts be efficiently administered in order to maintain respect for the law. Competent judges and juries and simplified procedures, frequently lacking in these courts, are goals of proponents of state judicial reform.

Civil Law.   The code regulating conduct between private persons. It is to be distinguished from criminal law which regulates individual conduct and is enforced by the government. Under civil law, the government merely provides the forum for the settlement of disputes between private parties in such matters as contracts, domestic relations, business relations, and auto accidents. The government may be one of the parties in a civil suit but, in a criminal case, the government is always the prosecutor. Most civil cases in both state and federal courts are tried without jury. Where juries are used, state law may authorize trial by a jury of less than 12, and decision by less than unanimous vote.

• *Significance:* Civil law serves to provide stability in private arrangements. Thus, a person who enters into a legal contract can seek the aid of the civil law and the courts to enforce the contract. Civil law provides a substitute for private duels as a means of settling private disputes. The government not only provides an impartial tribunal but will see that any judgment reached (a money award, for example) is enforced.

Code.   A compilation of laws in force, classified according to subject matter. Federal laws currently in force are collected in the *Code of the Laws of the United States,* which is kept up to date with annual supplements. The *Code* may be found in most libraries. Many states have collected and classified their statutes, including pertinent judicial decisions, under the title *Compiled Laws.*

• *Significance:* Without the code, one would have to search through the annual statute books for laws relating to a particular subject. The code collects all related laws under a subject heading for easy reference use. The failure of some states to keep their codes up-to-date works a hardship on professional legal personnel and laymen alike who want to know "what the law is."

Common Law.   Judge-made law which originated in England from decisions shaped according to prevailing custom. Decisions were reapplied to similar situations and, thus, gradually became common to the nation. Common law forms the basis of legal procedures in American states, except in Louisiana where certain French legal traditions are preserved. There is no federal common law, since the national government is one of delegated powers; however, federal judges do apply state common law in certain cases involving citizens of different states, where there is no applicable federal statute. A statute overrides the common law, but many statutes are based upon the common law and are interpreted according to the common-law tradition.

• *Significance:* Many important matters, such as the idea of a 12-man jury, are part of the common law. Moreover, the common law results in giving vast power to judges and accounts for heavy reliance on precedents (previous judicial decisions) in determining legal rights and duties. The common law permits great flexibility to judges to adjust the law to community needs. In countries not having the common law tradition, judges are bound to a greater degree by legislative acts.

Conciliation.   A method by which a third party attempts to settle a controversy between disputants outside the courtroom. It is similar to arbitration, except that the decision is not binding upon the parties nor enforceable in court. A number of large cities have established a conciliation branch in their judicial structure.

• *Significance:* This is another method which looks toward less formal proceedings for settlement of disputes in the hope of easing the burden on courts and lessening expenses for litigants. Conciliation has proved to be particularly effective in divorce proceedings.

Concurrent Jurisdiction.   Authority vested in two or more courts to hear cases involving the same subject matter. The term is generally used to indicate those instances in which both federal and state courts may hear the same kind of case. For example, the Congress has conferred concurrent jurisdiction upon state and federal courts in suits between citizens of different states where the amount in controversy exceeds $10,000. The parties to such a suit may choose to have their case heard in either a federal or state court. Suits involving less than $10,000 must be heard in state courts.

• *Significance:* Concurrent jurisdiction may serve to ease the burden on a court if a certain type of case tends to crowd the court dockets. For example, auto accidents between citizens of different states have become quite common. By sharing this kind of case with state courts, federal courts have been freed to handle other federal cases.

Concurring Opinion.   An opinion of one or more judges, usually of an appellate court, which supports the conclusions of a majority of the court but which offers different reasons for reaching that conclusion. Concurring opinions are quite common in the United States Supreme Court.

• *Significance:* A concurring opinion is of no legal force or effect. Yet, by offering alternative approaches to the interpretation or application of the law, it frequently serves as a guidepost for future decisions. Thus, a concurring opinion may become the majority view of the court in a similar case in the future. A concurring opinion signed by a substantial minority of a court may reduce the impact of the majority position.

Constitutional Court. A federal court established under the provisions of Article III. Constitutional courts are limited to the jurisdiction conferred by Article III and their judges are protected as to tenure and compensation. These are to be distinguished from "legislative courts" which are created by the Congress under its delegated powers. The major constitutional courts are the district courts, courts of appeals, and the Supreme Court. Congress has conferred constitutional status upon certain specialized courts, such as the Court of Claims, the Customs Court, and the Court of Customs and Patent Appeals.
• *Significance:* Constitutional courts enjoy a greater degree of independence than do legislative courts. Congress has somewhat confused the distinction by conferring constitutional status upon judges of certain specialized or legislative courts while not giving these courts jurisdiction under Article III. In effect, constitutional status today refers mainly to the selection and tenure of judges.

Constitutional Law. Law which involves interpretation and application of the Constitution. It is concerned largely with defining the extent and limits of governmental power and the rights of individuals. Final decision as to the meaning of the Constitution is in the hands of the United States Supreme Court. In the case of state constitutions, the highest court of the state renders final decisions, with appeal possible to the United States Supreme Court if conflict with the national Constitution, laws, or treaties can be shown.
• *Significance:* Constitutional law represents the highest law, and the Constitution, as interpreted by the Court, is the supreme law of the land. American constitutional law is noted for its flexibility, with the judiciary acting to maintain its vitality to meet changing social and economic conditions. Typically, constitutional law involves interpretation of such vague phrases as "interstate commerce" or "due process of law." Judges wield their greatest power when they are called upon to interpret the Constitution.

Contempt of Court. Disobedience of a court order, or any action which operates to impair the authority of a court or to interfere with its proper functioning. Contempt may be civil or criminal. Civil contempt involves a refusal to honor a court judgment in a civil case. Criminal contempt involves any interference with court proceedings. Both may be punished by fine or imprisonment or both. Usually, contempt is punished summarily (without trial), when committed in the presence of the court.
• *Significance:* If a court order is to have any meaning, the court must have power to enforce its order and to punish disobedience. Similarly, courts may not be obstructed in the performance of their duties so that the ends of justice may be served. Major difficulties arise in connection with criminal contempt. Some judges may act too hastily to punish overemotional lawyers or observers. More serious is the conflict with freedom of speech and press which may arise when a judge punishes a person for remarks or publication which, in the judge's view, obstructs the administration of justice.

Coroner. A county official who investigates deaths that occur by violent means and certifies the cause of deaths unattended by a physician. In the case of violent death, the coroner may conduct an investigation, called an "inquest," to determine if death resulted from a criminal act. A jury of six persons is chosen to hear evidence presented by the county prosecutor. If the verdict is death by criminal act, the coroner may order the arrest of suspected persons. Most coroners are elected, although a number of states have substituted an appointed medical examiner to perform the duties of the coroner and have transferred his judicial functions to the prosecutor.

• *Significance:* Most students of government oppose the elected coroner system. The office requires extensive medical knowledge as well as knowledge of criminal investigation and judicial proceedings. Often, the coroner is a layman with no medical or legal training; in some cases, he is an undertaker who may profit personally from his position. The trend is toward the appointment of an expert medical examiner to perform medical functions, the abolishment of the coroner's jury, and the use of the prosecutor for the legal and judicial aspects of the office.

Court of Appeals.   In the national court system, the appellate court below the Supreme Court. A few states also have an intermediate court of appeals, although in Kentucky, Maryland, and New York, the highest state court is called the Court of Appeals. On the national level, there are 11 courts of appeal. The country is divided into 11 "circuits" including the District of Columbia. Prior to 1948, these courts were known as the Circuit Courts of Appeals. The United States Courts of Appeals have only appellate jurisdiction, being empowered to hear appeals from the district courts in their particular circuit and to hear appeals from decisions of independent regulatory commissions, such as the Federal Trade Commission or Interstate Commerce Commission. Each court normally hears cases in panels of three judges but, on occasion, a full court of nine judges will sit. All judges are appointed for life by the President with the Senate's consent.

• *Significance:* For most cases, decisions of the courts of appeals are final since few cases reach the Supreme Court. Hence, they relieve the Supreme Court of a large burden of work. Review of decisions of independent regulatory commissions gives the Washington, D.C. circuit, in particular, an important role in development of administrative law.

Court of Claims.   A court established in 1855 to hear claims of private individuals against the government for breach of contract, for injuries caused by negligent behavior of government employees, or for recovery of other claims, such as back pay. The Court of Claims has five judges who sit "en banc" (together) in Washington, D.C. Any awards made by the Court cannot be paid unless the Congress appropriates the money, which it usually does. Its decisions may be appealed to the Supreme Court by writ of certiorari. Since 1953, it holds the status of a constitutional court, and its judges are appointed for life by the President with the Senate's consent.

• *Significance:* The national government may not be sued without its consent. However, it would be grossly inefficient if the Congress had to consider each claim. The Court of Claims serves as a clearing house for legitimate claims against the government. In most instances, its decisions are final since the Supreme Court rarely accepts a case from the Court of Claims.

Court of Customs and Patent Appeals.   A court created by the Congress in 1910 which reviews appeals made from decisions of the Customs Court, the Patent Office, and the Tariff Commission. The Court has five judges who sit in Washington, D.C. They are appointed for life terms by the President with consent of the Senate. Congress designated it a constitutional court in 1958. Decisions may be appealed to the Supreme Court by writ of certiorari.
• *Significance:* A large body of specialized law has been developed in the subject areas assigned to the Court of Customs and Patent Appeals. The expertness developed by this court has served to take an immense burden off the regular federal courts.

Court of Military Appeals.   A court established by the Congress in 1950 to review court-martial decisions. It is composed of three civilian judges appointed for 15 years by the President with consent of the Senate. The court is obligated to review decisions affecting top military personnel as well as those imposing the death penalty. It has discretion to review certain other cases upon petition, such as bad conduct discharges or those involving lengthy prison terms. The court applies military law, a special body of rules developed by the Congress, rather than ordinary federal criminal law. Appeals may be made to the Supreme Court by writ of certiorari.
• *Significance:* Recent events, resulting in military service for millions of Americans and the continuation of the military draft, caused great concern over the standards and procedures of military justice. The Uniform Code of Military Justice, passed in 1950, attempts to strengthen rights of persons in court-martial proceedings while meeting the needs of military discipline. The Court of Military Appeals is part of this reform effort. By requiring that its judges be civilians and by permitting appeal to the Supreme Court, the Congress has assured civilian control over military justice.

Criminal Law.   The code which regulates the conduct of individuals, defines crimes, and provides punishment for violations. In criminal cases, the government is always the prosecutor, since all crimes are against public order. The major body of criminal law is enacted by states although the list of federal crimes is growing. Criminal law falls into two categories, felonies and misdemeanors, the former being the more serious.
• *Significance:* Criminal law is designed to protect the public against wrongdoing as defined by law. The law which defines the crime must be clear so that people are put on notice as to what they may or may not do. Violators must be prosecuted under procedures established by the Constitution or other law to assure fair treatment. Government prosecution and punishment for crime serves as a civilized substitute for personal vengeance.

Customs Court.   A special court created by the Congress in 1926 to decide disputes that arise over tariff laws and duties levied on imported goods. The Court consists of nine judges appointed for life terms by the President with the

Senate's consent. It sits in divisions at principal ports of entry, with its main office in New York City. In 1956, the Customs Court was given constitutional status by the Congress. Its decisions may be appealed to the Court of Customs and Patent Appeals.

• *Significance:* The Customs Court relieves the regular courts of the burden of hearing the many disputes arising over the classification and valuations placed by customs officers on imported goods. This court has developed a high degree of expertness in this field.

Declaratory Judgment.   A legal procedure used to declare the rights of parties under a contract, will, or other dispute, before any damage occurs. It is a method of preventive justice contrary to the traditional procedure of suing for damages after the damage results. The national government and most of the states permit the use of this procedure.

• *Significance:* Declaratory judgments are relatively new on the legal scene, reflecting the view that the power of the courts should be made available to prevent the doing of a wrong as well as to redress a wrong. It differs from an advisory opinion in that the parties to the suit must have an actual controversy in which loss or injury is likely to occur. Expensive legal entanglements are often forestalled.

Dissenting Opinion.   An opinion of one or more judges, usually of an appellate court, which disagrees with the decision reached by a majority of the court. Such opinions are frequently presented on the United States Supreme Court.

• *Significance:* A dissenting opinion has no legal force. Oftimes, however, a dissenting view has eventually become the law. If a court is sharply divided —for example, a 5–4 vote on the Supreme Court—a dissenting opinion may weaken the force of the majority view.

District Attorney.   A county official, elected in all but six states for two or four year terms, who represents the state in prosecutions against violators of criminal laws. In some states, he is called the county attorney, county prosecutor, or, simply prosecutor. Prosecutions for the national government are handled by United States Attorneys. District attorneys also conduct proceedings before grand juries. In states where grand juries are not used, the district attorney brings charges in the form of an information. In addition, the district attorney acts as legal advisor to the county and represents the county in lawsuits.

• *Significance:* District attorneys wield great power in local government. Whether or not prosecutions are brought rests largely on their discretion. Recommendations which they make to the court regarding bail or sentences are generally given serious consideration. The office has been used as a political steppingstone by many young attorneys. The conduct of the office may well depend upon the political climate of a given county, resulting in an uneven application of criminal law within the state.

District Court.   The lowest level of the federal court system. This is the court of "original jurisdiction," where most federal cases begin. It is the only federal court where trials are regularly held, juries are used, and witnesses are called. Both criminal and civil cases arising under federal law are heard. Each state has at least one district court; a few have as many as four. District courts are also found in Washington, D.C., Puerto Rico, Guam, the Virgin Islands, and the Panama Canal Zone. Each court has from one to 18 judges depending on the volume of business, but each judge holds court separately. Certain cases are heard by a three-judge panel. All judges are appointed for life terms by the President with the Senate's consent.

• *Significance:* The bulk of judicial work in federal courts is conducted by the district courts. About 100,000 cases a year are tried, mostly civil cases involving such matters as admiralty law, bankruptcy proceedings, copyright and patent disputes, and postal laws. A small proportion of cases are appealed to courts of appeals and an even smaller number reach the Supreme Court. Thus, for most people, contact with federal justice is limited to district courts.

Diversity of Citizenship.   Lawsuits involving citizens of different states. The Constitution (Art. III, sec. 2) confers jurisdiction in such cases on the federal courts which, generally, apply relevant state law. Congress has conferred exclusive jurisdiction on state courts for suits between citizens of different states if the amount in controversy is less than $10,000, and concurrent jurisdiction if more than $10,000 is involved.

• *Significance:* A very complicated body of law has developed in diversity of citizenship cases. Originally, the purpose of the constitutional provision was to prevent bias by state courts against out-of-state litigants. The net effect is that federal court dockets are filled with such cases due to the increasing mobility and interrelationships of the American people. Automobile accidents between citizens of different states, for example, could be cause for a federal case. This accounts for congressional action to give state courts jurisdiction over diversity of citizenship cases. The federal courts have tried to cut down on these cases by applying relevant state law.

Eleventh Amendment.   An amendment to the Constitution, adopted in 1798, which provides that federal courts do not have authority to hear cases brought against a state by an individual citizen of another state or of a foreign state. The Amendment overruled a decision of the Supreme Court in *Chisholm v. Georgia,* 2 Dallas 419 (1793), which upheld the right of a citizen of one state to sue another state in federal court.

• *Significance:* Although Article III did confer jurisdiction upon federal courts to hear cases between a state and citizens of other states, the states were alarmed by the *Chisholm* decision which denied the necessity for the state's consent to be sued. The states feared the possibility of many suits against them for defaulting on their debts, as well as the loss of "states' rights." The 11th Amendment applies only to suits against the state itself; a suit may be brought against an officer of the state.

Equity.   A branch of law which supplements the common law to provide a remedy where the common law does not apply. The common law is concerned largely with granting of damages after a wrongful action. Equity is designed to provide substantial justice where damages may come too late to be meaningful. In an equity case, the court may order that something be done (specific performance) or forbid certain actions (injunction). In a typical case the court may order a person to fulfill a contract or forbid a union to go on strike under certain conditions. Equity procedures are less formal than regular court procedures and no juries are used.

• *Significance:* Equity is a legal inheritance from England which grew out of petitions to the king to redress wrongs for which the law provided no remedy. It was largely based on abstract principles of justice, but has developed its own body of rules and precedents. A few states have separate courts for equity proceedings, sometimes called chancery. The courts have a wide area of choice in equity cases to provide solutions to impending conflicts. Irreparable damages are thereby avoided.

Ex Parte.   A judicial proceeding by or for one party without contest by an adverse party. In an ex parte proceeding, there may be no adverse party, or a possible adverse party has had no notice of the case. The term "in re" is sometimes used in place of ex parte.

• *Significance:* Individuals frequently bring actions in their own behalf seeking the aid of the court. A typical ex parte proceeding may be one brought by a prisoner seeking a writ of habeas corpus. Such cases are reported under the name of the person bringing the suit preceded by the term "ex parte": *Ex parte Milligan,* for example.

Felony.   A serious crime punishable by death or by imprisonment in a penitentiary for a year or more. The precise character of a felony varies from state to state and is defined by law. Less serious violations of law are called misdemeanors. Felonies generally include murder, arson, robbery, aggravated assault, and forgery.

• *Significance:* Persons accused of felonies are accorded the full protection of constitutional guarantees, such as indictment by grand jury or information, trial by jury, etc. Misdemeanors are generally tried by "summary process," without indictment or trial by jury. Minor state courts rarely have jurisdiction to try felonies, which are usually heard by district or circuit courts. On the national level, felonies are tried in the district courts.

Five to Four Decision.   A decision of the United States Supreme Court in which the judges divide sharply over the decision or interpretation of the Constitution or law. Such decisions tend to attract wide notice and it is sometimes said that one judge, in effect, decided the case.

• *Significance:* Many important cases have been decided by a 5–4 vote. When this results in a declaration of unconstitutionality, as happened frequently during the New Deal period in the 1930's, it may have a significant effect on social or economic conditions. Since a 5–4 vote casts serious doubt upon the validity of such decisions, it has been suggested that a minimum of six or seven, or even all nine judges, must agree when a law is declared unconstitutional.

Hearing.   In an equity case, a hearing is a trial. In a criminal case, a hearing is an examination of the accused to determine if he should be held for trial; this is generally referred to as a "preliminary hearing" or "preliminary examination." If a preliminary hearing is held in an equity case, it is called an interlocutory hearing.

• *Significance:* The term "hearing" has a technical meaning in law. Whereas in an equity case it is technically the trial of the case, in a criminal proceeding, the hearing is not a trial to determine guilt or innocence but a procedure to protect the accused from unwarranted detention.

Indeterminate Sentence.   A sentence of imprisonment with minimum and maximum limits set by the court or by statute. Once the prisoner serves the minimum sentence he may be released upon approval of a parole board or a special commission. This is the procedure now used in most states in place of the fixed sentence.

• *Significance:* The indeterminate sentence reflects present policy to reform and rehabilitate criminals rather than to exact revenge for wrongdoing. It provides hope to the prisoner of eventual release for good behavior and demonstration of fitness to return to society.

Injunction.   An order issued by a court in an equity proceeding to compel or restrain the perfomance of an act by an individual or government official. A "mandatory" injunction demands that something be done, although the term "injunction" generally refers to a restraining order. Violation of an injunction constitutes contempt of court, punishable by fine or imprisonment.

• *Significance:* The injunction serves to prevent irreparable damage to one's personal or property rights. Its use is indicative of the power of courts to issue orders and to compel obedience without the necessity of a lawsuit after damages are done. Judges enjoy a great deal of freedom to determine the scope of an injunction.

Intermediate Court.   A court of appeals below the level of the highest court, as found in about one fourth of the states. In about half the states, there are county courts just above the level of justice of the peace courts, with limited jurisdiction, which are also referred to as intermediate courts. In both cases, "intermediate" refers to the fact that these courts fall somewhere between the lowest courts, courts of general trial jurisdiction, and the state supreme court.

• *Significance:* The use of the term "intermediate" reflects the great variety in court organization, structure, and jurisdiction, found in the several states. An intermediate court of appeals serves to lighten the burden on state supreme courts. Lower intermediate courts, however, tend to confuse the administration of justice with multiplicity of courts and overlapping jurisdiction. Proponents of judicial reform seek a simplified organization of courts.

Judicial Council.   An investigative and advisory agency composed of judges, lawyers, and laymen to promote more efficient administration in state courts. Councils are found in about three fourths of the states. Though their composition and authority vary from state to state, they are generally charged with the duty of collecting statistics on court operations and recommending changes in court organization, court procedure, assignment of judges, and other matters to improve the handling of court business.

• *Significance:* Little attention has been paid to the efficient administration of court business as compared with concern over the outcome of particular cases. The judicial council is a relatively recent innovation, recognizing the importance of applying sound administrative techniques to the operations of courts. The judicial council acts as a unifying force to counteract the lack of unity resulting from extreme decentralization of most state court systems and the independence of locally elected judges. On the national level, the Administrative Office of the United States Courts performs duties similar to those of a judicial council.

Judicial Review. The power of the courts to declare acts of the legislative and executive branches unconstitutional. All courts, both state and national, may exercise this authority, though final decision is usually made by the highest state or federal court. Though the United States Constitution is silent on this matter, the Supreme Court asserted the power of judicial review in the famous case of *Marbury v. Madison,* 1 Cranch 137 (1803). Judicial review is based on the assumptions that the Constitution is the supreme law, that acts contrary to the Constitution are void, and that the peculiar province of the judiciary is to act as guardian of the Constitution.

• *Significance:* Judicial review is one of the most important features of the American system of government. It places in the judiciary, and the Supreme Court in particular, vast power to determine the meaning of the Constitution and to act as final arbiter over questions involving the power of governmental officials at both the state and national levels. Several hundred state laws and about 80 federal laws have been declared unconstitutional by the Supreme Court. Though this number is small when compared to the total number of laws passed, a declaration of unconstitutionality may deter a long line of similar legislation. Courts are reluctant to exercise this vast power, since due respect must be accorded the other branches of government and the Constitution is susceptible to varying interpretations. A court decision on the Constitution can be changed only by amending the Constitution or by a change of view by the court itself. The exercise of judicial review invariably generates widespread comment from those who are dissatisfied with the decision, particularly when the court is divided in its decision. Throughout American history, courts have played a major role in the development of public policy through the exercise of this power. Since 1937, the Supreme Court has used considerable self-restraint in exercising the power of judicial review.

Judiciary. A collective term for courts and judges, considered to comprise the third branch of government. In the United States, the judiciary is divided into the national and state judiciary. Each is independent of the other with the exception that the United States Supreme Court may, under special circumstances involving federal questions, review a state court decision. Jurisdiction of particular courts or judges is determined by either the national or state constitutions and laws.

• *Significance:* An independent judiciary, coequal with the legislative and executive branches, is one of the cornerstones of the American system of government. The judiciary serves to protect the people against excessive exercise of power by the legislature and executive and to provide an impartial forum for the settlement of civil and criminal cases.

Jurisdiction.   Authority vested in a court to hear and decide a case. The term literally means power "to say the law." The jurisdiction of national courts is controlled by the Constitution and by the Congress. State court jurisdiction is similarly determined by state constitutions and statutes. Jurisdiction may be assigned according to such things as the amount of money involved or the type of offense. Courts may exercise original or appellate jurisdiction, or both.
• *Significance:* Lawsuits must be brought to the court which has authority "to say the law" with regard to that lawsuit. A case brought to the wrong court will either not be heard or be cause for overruling by an appellate court. It is common practice in lawsuits for the attorney to show immediately that the court has authority to hear the case. The differing jurisdiction of state and national courts is an important element in preservation of the federal system, since each government maintains control over the application of its law. Within any court system, specialized jurisdiction tends to promote expertness in the courts.

Justice of the Peace.   A judicial officer empowered to try minor civil and criminal cases, such as traffic violations or breaches of peace. In some areas, he may hold preliminary hearings to determine whether a person should be held for trial in a higher court. The justice of the peace is usually elected in rural areas and small towns for a two-year term. He is generally paid through fees.
• *Significance:* The office of justice of the peace has been under attack in recent years. Few justices are learned in the law, and the fee system, it is charged, leads to corruption and biased judgment. Supporters argue that the justice of the peace provides an inexpensive method of dispensing justice in petty cases. In many urban areas, the justice of the peace is being replaced by municipal courts.

Law.   A rule of conduct prescribed by or accepted by the governing authority of a state and enforced by courts. The law may derive from the constitution, legislative acts, and administrative rules, or may develop through custom, as have common law and equity. The law controls relations among men, and between men and their government. Penalties are imposed for violation of law.
• *Significance:* Democracy is distinguished from totalitarian government largely in terms of the place of law in society. A totalitarian system operates under the whim of the rulers. In a free society, law provides advance notice of what legally is right and wrong. Conflicts are resolved by application of pre-existing rules. Law must emanate from and be enforced only by duly constituted authority.

Legislative Court.   A court established by the Congress under its delegated powers rather than under the authority granted in Article III. The judges of these courts need not have life tenure, may be assigned nonjudicial functions, and have only that jurisdiction which the Congress assigns. For example, the Territorial Courts of Guam, Virgin Islands, and the Panama Canal Zone were created under congressional power to govern the territories. The judges have limited terms and the courts have regular federal jurisdiction as well as jurisdiction over matters which ordinarily belong in state courts. Another example is the Court of Military Appeals, created under the power to make rules for the armed forces.

• *Significance:* Courts established under Article III are limited in jurisdiction to those matters delegated in that Article. By establishing specialized courts, Congress can provide flexibility to the court system and, at the same time, relieve the regular courts and the Congress, itself, of some burdens.

Magistrate.   A minor judicial officer, usually elected in urban areas, with jurisdiction over traffic violations, minor criminal offenses, and civil suits involving small amounts of money. Magistrates may also conduct preliminary hearings in serious criminal cases and commit the offender for trial in a higher court. In some areas, the magistrate court is called a police court, and its authority is similar to that of a justice of the peace serving in a rural area. Juries are rarely used in magistrate courts.

• *Significance:* Magistrate courts have been established to handle the large number of cases which arise in urban communities. Unlike the justice of the peace, a magistrate is usually paid a salary rather than a fee. The magistrate can dispose of large numbers of petty offenses, thereby relieving the burden on higher courts and facilitating matters for offenders. Increasingly, cities are turning to specialized courts, such as traffic courts and domestic relations courts, to handle the large volume of work.

Mandamus.   An order issued by a court to compel performance of an act. A writ of mandamus may be issued to an individual or corporation as well as to a public official. In the case of public officers, a writ will be issued only to compel performance of a "ministerial" act—one which the officer has a clear legal duty to perform. If he has discretion to determine whether he will perform an act, the court will not order him to do so.

• *Significance:* The authority of the court may be brought to bear upon anyone who threatens to or fails to perform an act which someone has a legal right to expect. Thus, a contract must be fulfilled as agreed upon, or a court order will be issued. Similarly, a public officer who refuses to issue a marriage license to someone authorized to have one may be ordered to do so by the court. Failure to obey the court order is contempt of court.

Marshal.   An official of the federal Department of Justice who is attached to each federal district court. The duties of United States Marshals correspond to those of the sheriffs in county governments. They make arrests in federal criminal cases, keep accused persons in custody, secure jurors, serve legal papers, keep order in the courtroom, and execute orders and decisions of the court. Marshals are appointed by the President subject to the Senate's confirmation, for four-year terms.

• *Significance:* Marshals are part of the executive, not the judicial branch, and perform federal police duties. Although the job is not quite as glamorous as portrayed on television westerns, modern day United States Marshals perform important functions in enforcement of federal law. Deputy marshals are also attached to most district courts.

Misdemeanor.   A minor criminal offense. The precise nature of a misdemeanor varies from state to state where it is defined by law. It may include such things as traffic violations, petty theft, disorderly conduct, and gambling. Punishment is usually limited to light jail terms or fines. Minor courts such as justices of the peace or municipal courts usually hear such cases without a jury.
• *Significance:* Most violations of law are misdemeanors and constitute the bulk of judicial business in the United States. Many such cases are handled by "summary process," without indictment or trial, and are settled by payment of a fine. Misdemeanors are to be distinguished from "felonies" which are more serious violations of law, requiring more formalized proceedings in arrests and trials.

Missouri Plan.   A method of selecting state judges which combines both appointment and election. In Missouri, judges of the Supreme Court, of courts of appeals, and of courts in St. Louis and Kansas City are appointed by the governor from a list of three names prepared by a commission composed of lawyers and laymen. The judge serves one year and then stands for election on the basis of his record. There is no opposition candidate. If the voters approve, he serves for 6 to 12 years, depending on the court. If he is defeated, the procedure is started anew. Other communities in the state may come under the plan if the voters approve. A similar plan exists in California, where, however, the governor nominates the candidate subject to approval of, rather than from a list prepared by, the commission.
• *Significance:* The issue of appointment versus election of judges is one of the "great debates" of American politics. The Missouri Plan has been hailed as a satisfactory compromise in that it retains power in the electorate while freeing the judges from the necessity of campaigning for office.

Obiter Dictum.   A statement in a court opinion on an issue not precisely involved in the case. Since such statements are not relevant to the conclusions reached in the decision, they are not binding as precedents.
• *Significance:* Obiter dicta provide clues to the thinking of the court on issues related to the case at hand and may influence the decisions of the court in similar cases.

Original Jurisdiction.   The authority of a court to hear a case in the first instance. Generally, courts of original jurisdiction are minor courts or trial courts. They are to be distinguished from courts of appellate jurisdiction which hear cases on appeal from courts of original jurisdiction. A court which is primarily appellate may have some original jurisdiction. The United States Supreme Court, for example, has original jurisdiction over suits involving ambassadors and those to which a state is a party.
• *Significance:* Original jurisdiction is often "final" jurisdiction since few cases

are heard on appeal by higher courts. Even if a case is appealed, the determination of the facts in the case by the judge or jury in the court of original jurisdiction is generally considered to be final, with questions of law heard by the appellate court.

Panel.   The list of persons summoned for jury duty. A trial jury is "impaneled" when the parties to the case have agreed to the selection of the jurors from the panel. Panels are selected in a variety of ways in different states by jury commissioners or county or township clerks or other officials. Names are usually selected from voting or taxpayer lists.
• *Significance:* The major problem in selecting jury panels is to assure fair trials by impaneling representative cross sections of the community. State laws frequently exempt public employees, professional persons, and those who will suffer financial hardship while serving. As a result of these exemptions, it is often difficult to get a representative panel to enable an accused person to be tried by a jury of his peers. No persons may be systematically excluded from jury panels because of race, religion, or color.

Parole.   Release from prison prior to the expiration of a sentence. The release is based on the good behavior of the parolee who may be returned to prison if he violates the conditions of his parole. In the national government, paroles are administered through the Department of Justice by the Board of Parole, consisting of eight members appointed by the President. In the states, paroles are generally administered by parole boards or by the governors.
• *Significance:* The possibility of parole provides a stimulus to prisoners to be on their good behavior and to demonstrate fitness to return to a normal life. In this way, correction rather than punishment is emphasized in prison administration. A major criticism of parole practice is that parole boards are often composed of political appointees rather than properly qualified persons. Well-qualified parole officers who supervise the parolee while he is out of prison are vital for successful parole administration.

Political Question.   A doctrine enunciated by the Supreme Court which holds that certain constitutional issues cannot be decided by the courts but by the executive or legislative branches. The doctrine has generally been invoked when the issue would place the courts in serious conflict with other branches, involve the courts in political controversies, or raise serious enforcement problems. Examples of "political questions" include presidential power to recognize foreign governments, congressional power to determine whether constitutional amendments have been ratified within a reasonable time, and congressional and presidential power to determine whether states have a republican form of government.
• *Significance:* The doctrine of the political question is a self-imposed restraint on the Court's power of judicial review. Thus, it is for the Court to decide which issues are "political" and which are "justiciable." Few cases have involved "political questions," and it is impossible to predict with certainty what issues will be considered to be "political." Much depends upon the political climate of the day and the viewpoint of the majority of the Supreme Court.

Precedent.   A legal decision which governs subsequent decisions in similar cases, or which is relied upon to substantiate a ruling on a case. The common law is based primarily upon reasoning from precedents.
• *Significance:* Legal disputes in the United States are fought out largely over the application of precedents to a particular controversy. A lawyer will try to convince the court that the precedents serve to prove his case. Judges, in turn, must decide between competing precedents in reaching a decision. If a precedent appears to be unreasonable or unjust, a court may specifically over-rule it and establish a new precedent.

Pretrial Procedures.   An informal conference prior to the formal trial of a case in which the judge and opposing attorneys attempt to clarify the issues and eliminate irrelevant witnesses or evidence. An attempt is also made to reach a settlement without going to trial.
• *Significance:* Pretrial conferences have come into wide use in recent years due to the considerable saving of time and expense for both courts and litigants. The conference serves not only to narrow the differences between the parties but helps to familiarize the judge with the case. Costly appeals are often thereby avoided.

Probate Court.   A court, found in about one half the states, with jurisdiction over wills, estates, guardians, and minors. Probate courts are found at the county level; in states without separate probate courts, such matters are handled by regular county courts. In some areas, probate courts are called surrogate courts. Much of the work connected with probate courts is administrative in nature, being concerned largely with ensuring proper handling of minors and estates by guardians and administrators. Juries are rarely used. Probate judges are generally elected.
• *Significance:* Probating, or proving, the authenticity of a will and the subsequent administration of an estate is an important element of American law, which reflects concern with property rights. The rights of minors, too, are zealously protected. Probate courts exist, in the main, to help people rather than to punish wrongdoers. One major problem is that separate probate courts tend to proliferate an already complicated court system in the states. In a more simplified court system, probate duties would be assigned to regular courts within an integrated court system.

Probation.   A suspension of the sentence of a person convicted of a crime, permitting him to remain free, subject to good behavior. Persons on probation are subject to supervision by an agent of the court. If the person's conduct justifies it, he will be released from probation after a period of time determined by the court. Failure to observe the terms of probation subjects him to possible imprisonment.
• *Significance:* Imprisonment may do more harm than good to numerous offenders. Probation permits the offender to demonstrate to the court that he can become a good citizen. This technique has been particularly effective with juvenile delinquents. A competent probation office staff is essential for successful administration of probation.

Public Defender.   An official whose duty it is to act as attorney for persons accused of crime who are unable to secure their own counsel. A few counties and cities make use of the public defender system. In some jurisdictions, the public defender acts only on behalf of those accused of serious crimes, while in others he has general responsibility for defense of indigent defendants.

• *Significance:* The use of a public defender is considered to be superior to the more common practice of assignment of counsel by the court or by a private legal aid association. Assigned counsel not only vary in ability but in willingness to devote attention to the defendant's interests. Moreover, private counsel frequently lack the resources available to the public prosecutor. The public defender tends to equalize the differences between the public prosecutor and the defendant by assuring the latter adequate counsel regardless of his financial resources. In short, the public defender system is designed to assure greater "justice for the poor."

Referee.   A person, ordinarily an attorney, appointed by the court to conduct a hearing on a particular matter and report to the court. In federal courts, referees are used often in bankruptcy proceedings to collect information and to present it to the court for final disposition of the case.

• *Significance:* The referee relieves the judge of attention to routine matters or matters of detail. Preliminary consideration is given to questions which eventually require judicial decision. This is particularly useful when accounting or administrative detail is involved, as in a bankruptcy case.

Sheriff.   The chief law enforcement officer of the county. He is elected in all states except Rhode Island, where he is chosen by the legislature. His duties pertain to both civil and criminal actions. In addition to general law enforcement, the sheriff, as an officer of the court, serves papers, enforces orders, maintains the jail, and collects taxes, with particular functions varying from state to state. In many jurisdictions, the sheriff is paid through fees for each job performed rather than on a regular salary basis. Law enforcement activities are generally limited to areas outside cities and to patrol on county highways.

• *Significance:* The office of sheriff has had a long history, dating back to ninth-century, Anglo-Saxon England. Though the office has declined in power and prestige, it remains strongly entrenched as part of American law enforcement. In many areas, the office has proved to be highly lucrative because of the fee system, but it rarely excels as a police agency. With the growth of population in suburban areas, sheriff offices have been faced with increased responsibilities which untrained sheriffs and appointed deputies have not been able to meet. Many critics advocate the substitution of a professional, county-wide police system.

Small Claims Court.   A court found in many large cities designed to expedite minor cases between individuals at low cost. Disputes over such things as fuel or grocery bills or wages are quickly settled by a judge.

• *Significance:* Thousands of small claims are settled each year in small claims courts without the necessity for cluttering the dockets of regular courts and without need for the parties to hire attorneys or go to other great expense.

Where small claims courts are not found, such cases are generally heard by justices of the peace who receive a fee for their service.

Solicitor General.   An important official in the Department of Justice who conducts cases on behalf of the United States before the Supreme Court. In addition, his approval is necessary before any appeal may be taken on behalf of the federal government to any appellate court.
• *Significance:* As chief counsel for the government, the fate of many important programs may rest upon the Solicitor General's conduct of cases. In his role as supervisor of appeals, he is in a position to affect the administration of federal criminal and civil law by determining which issues or cases are worthy of appeal. His decisions and the general conduct of his office may be important keys to the policies of the administration in power in Washington, as reflected in the types of cases in which appeals are brought and in the arguments made before the Supreme Court.

Stare Decisis.   A legal term which means "let the decision stand." It is an important element of the common law whereby a decision applies in similar cases and is binding upon lower courts. Precedents thus established stand until overruled.
• *Significance:* The rule of stare decisis lends stability to the law and to legal arrangements among individuals. Thus lawyers, judges, and the public at large, are bound by what has gone before unless compelling reasons call for establishing new precedents.

Statute of Limitations.   A state or federal legislative act which establishes a time limit within which lawsuits may be brought, judgments enforced, or crimes prosecuted. The time limit varies among different jurisdictions and with the nature of the case, although for certain major offenses, such as murder, no limits are placed on prosecution.
• *Significance:* Statutes of limitations are designed to prevent endless harassment of individuals by other persons or by the government. Though certain violations of law may go unchallenged, it is considered desirable that at some point, the threat of prosecution be ended.

Subpoena.   An order of a court, grand jury, legislative body or committee, or of any duly authorized administrative agency, compelling the attendance of a witness. A subpoena duces tecum requires the witness to produce specific documents. Failure to honor a subpoena subjects the person called to prosecution for contempt.
• *Significance:* Public agencies could not properly perform their functions without the power of subpoena. Persons called to testify or to bring with them certain documents must comply, unless they can demonstrate that such action will result in self-incrimination. The power of subpoena is of special importance in judicial proceedings where both sides of a case have the right to compel testimony of witnesses.

Summons.   A complaint made by an individual or a police officer and signed by a judicial officer requiring a person to appear before the court to answer charges made against him.

• *Significance:* The summons is usually the first step in civil suits or minor criminal cases which gives formal notice to the defendant of the charges made against him. In more serious criminal matters, charges are made through indictment by grand jury or through a prosecutor's information. The summons satisfies the requirement that a person not be brought to trial without some formal complaint and proper notice of the charges against him.

Supreme Court.   The court of last resort in the federal and in most state judicial systems. In a few states, the highest court is called by another title. The Supreme Court of the United States is composed of a chief justice and eight associate justices. The number of judges is established by the Congress and has varied from five to ten, but the figure has been set at nine since 1869. Cases are decided by majority vote. It is the only court specifically provided for in the Constitution, and its original jurisdiction is set thereby to include cases affecting ambassadors, public ministers and consuls, and those to which a state is a party. Its appellate jurisdiction is determined by the Congress. Certain cases involving federal questions may be appealed to the Supreme Court from the highest state court. With the exception of certain specified cases involving questions of constitutionality, the Supreme Court determines which cases it will hear through the writ of certiorari. The Supreme Court sits from October to June and its decisions are reported in the *United States Reports.* State supreme courts vary in size and jurisdiction in accordance with state constitutions and laws but, except for cases which may be brought to the United States Supreme Court, they are the courts of last resort in the state. Justices of the United States Supreme Court are appointed by the President, with the Senate's consent, for life terms subject to impeachment. Most state supreme court judges are elected.

• *Significance:* Courts of last resort, particularly the Supreme Court of the United States, wield tremendous power and play a major role in the development of public policy. In the final analysis, these courts determine the meaning of the Constitution and of statutes, the scope of legislative and executive power, and the scope of their own power. Decisions as to the meaning of constitutional phrases have lasting impact, unless overruled by the court itself (as in the segregation cases), or overturned by constitutional amendment (as in the case of the income tax). Decisions are binding upon all lower courts. Because of the importance of the questions which, typically, reach the United States Supreme Court, it has often been involved in major economic, political, and social controversies. Appointments to the Court are watched with avid interest to ascertain in which way the new justices may influence the interpretation of the Constitution and laws.

Supreme Court Packing Plan.   A proposal made in 1937 by President Franklin D. Roosevelt that the President be authorized to appoint an additional justice of the Supreme Court for each justice over the age of seventy who did not retire after ten years of service. The maximum number of appointments was to have been six, thereby possibly increasing the size of the Supreme Court from nine to fifteen. The President claimed that this plan would increase the efficiency of the Court, but it was defeated in the Congress on the ground that Roosevelt was trying to "pack" the court to overcome unfavorable decisions on New Deal programs.

• *Significance:* The idea of packing the court so as to affect the nature of decisions is not novel in American history. The size of the Court was altered on six different occasions by the Congress, either to prevent appointments by a President or to affect decisions. These instances, plus the Roosevelt plan, point up the significance of the Supreme Court in the formulation of public policy. The plan met with strong resistance from members of the Court and the Congress as well as the public at large, demonstrating general support for the Court as an institution which should not be tampered with. In the course of the debate, the Court reversed its previous position, handing down new interpretations of the Constitution which gave free rein to the New Deal. It is said that President Roosevelt "lost the battle but won the war."

Taxpayer's Suit.   A suit brought by a taxpayer to prevent the expenditure of public funds for a given purpose. Such suits are permissible in most of the states but not in federal courts.

• *Significance:* The taxpayer suit is based on the theory that each taxpayer has an interest in how public funds are spent, regardless of the amount of his contribution. Such suits are not heard in federal courts because the Supreme Court has held that no taxpayer has a sufficient personal interest in the vast expenditures of federal funds.

Territorial Court.   Courts established by the Congress in the territories of the United States, namely, Guam, Puerto Rico, the Virgin Islands, and the Panama Canal Zone. Congress has established a district court in each of these areas, under its power to govern the territories, and has authorized minor courts in some cases. With the exception of Puerto Rico, the federal district courts of the territories also hear cases ordinarily heard in state courts. Judges of these courts are appointed for four- to eight-year terms rather than life terms. Some people consider the courts of the District of Columbia to be territorial courts since they, too, exercise special jurisdiction other than that held by regular federal courts.

• *Significance:* Residents of Guam, Puerto Rico, and the Virgin Islands are citizens of the United States. Though statehood is not in the offing, Congress has seen fit to provide these areas with regular district courts, thereby establishing the American legal tradition. A territorial court is recognition of the basic rights of the inhabitants of a territory. Some American territories, such as Samoa, have no courts and are administered by military officials.

Tort.   A wrongful act involving injury to persons, property, or reputation but excluding breach of contract. The injured party may bring suit against the wrongdoer. This is an important and often used branch of law. A major tort problem concerns the responsibility of governmental units for torts committed by government employees against individuals.

• *Significance:* Tort law serves as a substitute for private duels and assures that for most wrongs there will be a remedy. The issue of the tort liability of government has not been definitely resolved. Generally, no one may sue the government without consent. Many states and the national government have authorized suits for certain kinds of torts. At the municipal level, the law varies from state to state but as a general rule, municipalities are not responsible for torts committed by their employees when engaged in purely "governmental" functions. However, there may be liability for torts committed in the course of "proprietary" functions (such as gas supply, transportation, and other business-like functions). The Federal Tort Claims Act of 1946 permits claims of $1,000 or less against the national government to be settled by administrative officials.

Trial. The examination of a civil or criminal action in accordance with the law of the land before a judge who has jurisdiction over it. A trial must be public, conducted fairly before an impartial judge and, in the case of criminal trials, started without unreasonable delay.
• *Significance:* A speedy, impartial, and public trial conducted in conformity with established procedures of the law is one of the major hallmarks of a free and civilized people. Knowledge that disputes will be settled in this manner gives the people confidence in the law and makes unnecessary private feuds and duels for settlement of grievances. Under American trial procedures, adequate opportunity is given to both sides to present their case for examination by the judge or jury.

Unified Court System. A proposal for judicial reform at the state and local level which has been put into effect in New Jersey and in some municipalities. The essence of the plan calls for an integrated state-wide or area-wide court system, organized into divisions for more efficient distribution of caseload and judges. A chief judge, aided by a judicial council or business manager, supervises the operations of the courts, shifts judges about to meet case load demands, and, through collection of significant data, promotes the efficient administration of justice.
• *Significance:* Most proponents of judicial reform endorse the unified court plan. Under present conditions, courts are organized on a geographic basis, with many types of cases heard in each jurisdiction by the same judge. The unified plan, its proponents claim, will encourage specialization among judges, relieve the situation in which some court dockets are crowded while others are not filled, and promote uniformity in decision making. Overall supervision by a chief judge will result in more efficient use of manpower and money, and expedite the business of the courts.

United States Attorney. A federal official whose principal function is to prosecute violations of federal law. A United States Attorney is assigned to each district in which a federal district court is located. He is appointed for a four-year term by the President with the Senate's consent, and is under general supervision of the Department of Justice and the Attorney General of the United States.
• *Significance:* The functions of the United States Attorney underscore the

divided nature of law enforcement. Though he may cooperate with local law enforcement officials, he is responsible only for violations of federal law. The position is considered to be a choice political plum and is, frequently, a step toward appointment to the federal judiciary.

United States Commissioner.   An official of a federal district court, appointed by the judge for a four-year term, who holds preliminary hearings in criminal cases. Commissioners issue arrest warrants, determine if the accused shall be held for the grand jury, and may set bail.

• *Significance:* Commissioners relieve regular judges of routine and preliminary matters, thereby freeing the judge for full-time attention to his major trial duties. Where district courts serve a large area or an entire state, commissioners make it unnecessary to bring federal law violators to the seat of the district court immediately.

United States Reports.   The official record of cases heard and disposed of by the United States Supreme Court, including the full opinions of the justices. The volumes are issued at the conclusion of the term of the Court but opinions are available in "advance sheets" prior to issuance of the volumes. Two or three volumes of the *Reports* may emerge each year, depending on the volume of business and length of opinions. The volumes are numbered consecutively but, prior to 1874, at which time the *Reports* totaled 90 volumes, they were identified by the names of the official court reporters. These include: Dallas, Cranch, Wheaton, Peters, Howard, Black, and Wallace. Thus, a case cited as 1 Cranch 137 (1803), means that the case, decided in 1803, can be found on page 137 of the first volume compiled by Cranch. Since 1874, the volumes are simply numbered, beginning with 91. A case cited as 345 U.S. 123 (1953) will be found on page 123 of volume 345 of the *United States Reports,* and was decided in 1953. All recorded legal decisions in any court may be found in similar fashion by locating the title, volume, and page of the *Report* in which it is given. Reports are available from federal courts of appeals (*Federal Reporter*), district courts (*Federal Supplement*), and highest state courts which are identified by the name of the state, for example, 156 Michigan 124. Commercial companies also put out volumes reporting these cases.

• *Significance:* The reports of cases are available for use by lawyers, legal scholars, and for all citizens. The report of Supreme Court cases, in particular, provides some of the best material available on American political and legal thought and practice. Major social and political issues are apt to find their way to the Supreme Court and the opinions are important social documents.

Venue.   The county or district in which a prosecution is brought for trial and from which jurors are chosen. Venue refers to a particular area, not to the court which has jurisdiction.

• *Significance:* Under American law, trials are held in the area in which the wrong is done. The Sixth Amendment to the Constitution provides that, in federal criminal prosecutions, trials are to be held in the state and district in which the crime was committed. Similar provisions are found in state constitutions. This is designed to give the defendant the benefit of a court and a jury familiar with the problems and people of the area. However, a defendant may ask for a "change of venue," a transfer of the trial to another locality, on the grounds that the people of the locality are prejudiced against him and that an impartial jury could not be drawn. It is for the judge to determine whether a change of venue is justified.

Writ.   An order in writing issuing from a court ordering the performance of an act or prohibiting some act. A wide variety of writs exist, ranging from orders to appear in court to orders regarding the execution of the court's judgment.
• *Significance:* Courts exercise their power largely through the issuance of writs which are essential for the orderly progress of judicial functions. The right to enforce a decision is as necessary as the right to hear and decide cases. Failure to honor a writ subjects a person to a fine and/or imprisonment for contempt of court.

IMPORTANT AGENCIES

Administrative Office of the United States Courts.   An agency which handles administrative matters for all federal and territorial courts except the Supreme Court. The Office, established in 1939, is headed by a director who is appointed by the Supreme Court. Its functions include supervision of administrative personnel of the courts, the fixing of compensation of such personnel, preparation of the budget for the operations of the court system, and care of court funds, books, equipment and supplies. The Office also gathers statistics on dockets, and supervises administration of bankruptcy and federal probation.
• *Significance:* The Administrative Office of the United States Courts has established centralized control over court administration. In the past, little attention had been paid to the administrative problems involved in maintaining an effective judiciary. In many of the states, similar duties are carried on by judicial councils. Information on court dockets is of particular importance to assure speedy and efficient administration of justice.

Department of Justice.   A major department of the executive branch concerned with the enforcement of federal laws. The Justice Department is headed by the Attorney General who is a member of the President's Cabinet. The Department furnishes legal counsel in cases involving the national government, interprets laws under which other executive agencies operate, supervises federal penal institutions, directs United States Attorneys and Marshals, supervises immigration laws, and directs paroles of federal prisoners. The Department includes the famed Federal Bureau of Investigation (FBI), which is the major police agency for the national government.
• *Significance:* The Department of Justice maintains a close relationship with all other units of the national government because of its widespread responsibility for law enforcement. Its functions also put it into frequent contact with the judicial branch at all stages of judicial proceedings, from the apprehension of law violators to their imprisonment and parole. However, the Department

is not a part of the judicial branch, as is sometimes erroneously thought, since to be so would constitute a violation of the separation of powers by uniting prosecutor and judge.

IMPORTANT CASES

Ableman v. Booth, 21 Howard 506 (1859): Established that a state court may not issue a writ of habeas corpus to a prisoner in federal custody.
• *Significance:* The *Abelman* case underscores the independence of state and federal courts from each other in their proper spheres of authority. No judicial order can have any effect outside the lawful jurisdiction of the court. Neither the states nor the federal courts can intrude into the domain of the other unless the nature of the case demands the exercise of the supreme federal authority.

Ashwander v. TVA, 297 U.S. 288 (1936): Upheld the right of the TVA to sell surplus electric power. Furthermore, the case is well-known for the concurring opinion by Justice Louis D. Brandeis in which he attempted to sum up the rules which the Court had developed in considering the constitutionality of the acts of the legislative and executive branches. Among these were the following: (1) The Court will not decide questions of a constitutional nature, unless absolutely essential to dispose of the case. (2) The Court will not pass upon a constitutional question if the case can be disposed of on some other ground. (3) The Court will not formulate a constitutional rule broader than is required by the precise facts of the case. (4) The Court will try to construe a statute so as to avoid ruling on constitutional questions, even if serious doubts exist as to its constitutionality.
• *Significance:* The Court's self-denying rules, as formulated by Justice Brandeis for handling constitutional issues, have governed its course in recent years. The Court has shown great reluctance to rule on constitutional questions, and only a few, minor statutory provisions have been declared unconstitutional since 1937. Through these rules, the Court has sought to avoid controversy with the legislative and executive branches.

Cohens v. Virginia, 6 Wheaton 264 (1821): Ruled that state court decisions are subject to review by the Supreme Court if the case involves a question of federal law, treaties, or the Constitution, even though a state is a party to the suit. An appeal brought to a federal court by a defendant who has been convicted in a state court does not constitute a suit against the state contrary to the 11th Amendment.
• *Significance:* The question of whether the Supreme Court had appellate jurisdiction over cases appealed from state courts was crucial to the development of federal judicial power. Prior to the *Cohens* decision, the Supreme Court held, in *Martin v. Hunter's Lessee,* 1 Wheaton 304 (1816), that it had the right to review state court decisions involving suits between private individuals when a federal question is involved. The *Cohens* decision extended this principle to cases in which a state is a party. In both cases, the Court pointed out that federal jurisdiction is essential to establish uniformity of decision throughout the United States on the interpretation of the Constitution,

federal law, or treaties. Otherwise, each state, rather than the national government, would be supreme.

Dred Scott v. Sanford, 19 Howard 393 (1857): Held, in a famous case, that Negroes could not become citizens of the United States nor were they entitled to the rights and privileges of citizenship. The Court also ruled that the Missouri Compromise, which had banned slavery in the territories, was unconstitutional.

• *Significance:* The *Dred Scott* decision is considered to be one of the most disastrous handed down by the Supreme Court. The Court, itself, was badly divided and muddled in its views. The case failed to resolve the slavery issue and contributed to making inevitable the Civil War conflict. Both the Civil War and the provisions of the 14th Amendment on citizenship were needed to overcome the *Dred Scott* ruling. The *Dred Scott* case is also noted for being the second in which a federal law was declared unconstitutional, following the Supreme Court's exercise of judicial review in *Marbury v. Madison,* 1 Cranch 137 (1803). The crucial role of the Supreme Court in American life and politics is underscored by the *Dred Scott* case.

Eakin v. Raub, 12 S. & R. 330 (1825): Decided by the Supreme Court of the State of Pennsylvania, this case is famous for an opinion by Judge John B. Gibson discussing the power of judicial review. Judge Gibson disagreed with the logic of Chief Justice John Marshall's opinion in *Marbury v. Madison,* 1 Cranch 137 (1803) in which Marshall argued that judges had a special duty to interpret the Constitution and to declare any law in conflict with the Constitution null and void. Judge Gibson argued that the judges had no such duty. Rather, the legislature bore the responsibility for unlawful acts and the people should hold them responsible.

• *Significance:* Judge Gibson's opinion is the best known argument by a judge against the principle of judicial review. Although it never overthrew that principle, the position which he took is still held by many persons. The student of government may find the complete opinion of Judge Gibson reproduced in many casebooks or textbooks on constitutional law.

Erie Railroad v. Tompkins, 304 U.S. 64 (1938): Ruled that, in diversity of citizenship cases heard in federal courts, the law to be applied is the state law as declared by the state legislature or courts. There is no federal common law.

• *Significance:* The *Erie* case overruled *Swift v. Tyson,* 16 Peters 1 (1842), which had held that in the absence of a state statute controlling a case, the federal courts could apply their own principles of the common law. After almost a century of confusion resulting from several versions of the common law, particularly in commercial cases, the Court declared in the *Erie* case that the *Tyson* rule was not only incorrect but unconstitutional as well, since there is no general federal common law.

Ex parte McCardle, 7 Wallace 506 (1869): Declared that the Supreme Court may not exercise appellate jurisdiction over a case when the Congress prohibits such jurisdiction. This case arose when the Congress repealed an 1867 law which had authorized appeals to the Supreme Court in certain cases involving enforcement of the post-Civil War Reconstruction Acts.

• *Significance:* It is generally recognized that the Congress withdrew jurisdiction from the Supreme Court in this case for fear that the Court would declare the Acts unconstitutional. Nevertheless, the Court dismissed the case on the ground that it lacked jurisdiction. The *McCardle* case demonstrates the veto power of Congress over the appellate jurisdiction of the Supreme Court. The Constitution in Article III, section 2, provides that the Supreme Court has appellate jurisdiction in all cases heard in federal courts "with such exceptions, and under such regulations as the Congress shall make." Congress does not grant appellate power but may make exceptions to its exercise.

Frothingham v. Mellon, 262 U.S. 447 (1923): Held that a taxpayer may not bring suit in a federal court to restrain the expenditure of federal funds. Mrs. Frothingham had protested a federal grant-in-aid to the states for maternity benefits.

• *Significance:* An important element of judicial procedure is that a party to a suit must have standing to sue. That is, a party must be able to show "some direct injury . . . and not merely that he suffers in some indefinite way in common with people generally." Although taxpayer suits are common in state and local courts, the Supreme Court has taken the view that an individual's interest in federal taxation and expenditures is too minute. As an important consequence, the *Frothingham* rule relieves the federal courts of a tremendous burden of taxpayer suits.

Marbury v. Madison, 1 Cranch 137 (1803): Struck down, for the first time in our history, an act of Congress as unconstitutional. The Court, speaking through Chief Justice John Marshall, held unconstitutional a portion of the Judiciary Act of 1789 which had added to the original jurisdiction of the Supreme Court. The case was essentially a political controversy between the defeated Federalist party and the incoming Jeffersonian party over last-minute Federalist party appointments to the federal courts.

• *Significance:* Few cases have had the impact upon American governmental development as has *Marbury v. Madison,* in which Chief Justice Marshall struck a decisive blow for judicial supremacy. Marshall argued that the Constitution was the supreme law, and that judges were bound by their oath and the nature of their positions to act as guardians of the Constitution. Any law in conflict with the Constitution cannot be enforced by the courts. The logic of Marshall's opinion has never been successfully refuted. Although the Constitution fails to mention judicial review, the American people have accepted its exercise by the courts as an integral part of the American constitutional system.

Muskrat v. United States, 219 U.S. 346 (1911): Ruled that the federal courts will not issue advisory opinions. Federal judicial power extends only to "cases and controversies" between opposing parties and not to "friendly" suits to test the law. In this case, the Congress had authorized certain Indians to bring suit to test the validity of a law relating to Indian lands.

• *Significance:* Although some state courts issue advisory opinions, this is not done by federal courts. This is based on the theory that, in a hypothetical case, the courts lack the advantage of arguments by opposing sides. Since advisory opinions are not binding, the court would be put in an embarrassing position should a genuine controversy arise over the same issue. The refusal of federal courts to issue advisory opinions helps to maintain their high prestige by avoiding premature embroilment in controversial issues.

IMPORTANT STATUTES

Judiciary Act of 1789.   A law passed by the first Congress to establish the federal court system. The Act determined the organization and jurisdiction of the courts. Over the years, the Judiciary Act has undergone numerous changes, adding and deleting courts, changing jurisdiction of courts, establishing rules of procedure, and providing for a variety of court officers and employees. The last major revision of the law took place in 1948.
• *Significance:* The Judiciary Act of 1789 and its subsequent amendments demonstrate congressional authority over federal court organization, jurisdiction, and procedure. The only constitutional limit placed on the Congress is that a Supreme Court must exist with specified original jurisdiction. A portion of the Judiciary Act of 1789 was declared unconstitutional in the famous case of *Marbury v. Madison,* 1 Cranch 137 (1803), because, in it, the Congress had unconstitutionally added to the original jurisdiction of the Supreme Court. Recent changes of significance include the Act of 1925 which authorized the Supreme Court to issue writs of certiorari, and the 1948 provision which changed the name of the circuit courts of appeals to, simply, "courts of appeals."

11

Finance and Taxation

Ability Theory.   The belief that taxes should be based upon the individual's ability to pay, as indicated by income, property, or wealth.
• *Significance:* The ability theory has often been challenged, particularly by the benefit theory which holds that taxes should be paid by those who derive benefit from them. The income tax is generally regarded as that tax which most nearly approximates the ideal of the ability theory because of its progressive increases in rates as income (and, hence, ability to pay) rises. The federal individual income tax is based on the ability theory, although many exemptions, and other favored treatments, have reduced its progressive nature.

Auditor.   An official, usually an agent of a legislative body, who checks on the expenditure of appropriated funds to determine that they have been spent for the purposes approved by the legislature in its appropriation acts. The federal auditor, the Comptroller General, is appointed by the President with the Senate's approval; state and local auditors are either appointed, or elected by the voters.
• *Significance:* Proper auditing of disbursed funds is essential to fiscal responsibility. In many state and local governments, only a preaudit in the form of a spending authorization is required, with no proper postaudit after expenditures to check their validity. In other cases, the same officials who authorize the expenditures are later called upon to check upon the authenticity of their own work. Effective auditing procedures require careful examination of the validity of accounts and payments *after* the expenditures have been made, and competent auditors who have complete independence from the executive branch.

Banking Systems.   The national and state banking systems which exist side by side in the United States. Congress was not granted the specific power to charter banks, but the power is implied from granted powers which can best be carried on through banks, such as the borrowing and currency powers. Both national and state chartered banks are privately owned financial institutions which are regulated and have their accounts audited by the respective chartering government. National banks, chartered by the national government since 1863, are supervised by the Comptroller of the Currency in the Treasury Department, and are required to join the Federal Reserve System. Most state banks accept Federal Reserve membership and, thereby, come under a measure of national as well as state regulation. The citizen can usually distinguish between a national and state chartered bank by their names, such as First National Bank or Industrial State Bank.

• *Significance:* Federal and state regulation of their respectively chartered banks controls such matters as issuance of stock, stockholder liabilities, assets and investments, organization and management, reserves, loans, and depositor security. The public is protected through periodic inspections and audits by examiners, and by deposit insurance, up to $10,000 for each account, guaranteed by the Federal Deposit Insurance Corporation. The dual national-state banking system provides some measure of financial flexibility, although state banks have lost much of their autonomy through membership in the Federal Reserve System.

Benefit Theory. The belief that individuals should be taxed in proportion to the benefits they derive from government services.

• *Significance:* The benefit theory has largely been superseded by the ability theory which is regarded as more equitable and easier to determine in a complex society where benefits derived from taxes often go unnoticed. The benefit theory is still applied in special areas where the benefits can be directly or easily assessed. The 1956 Federal Highway Act, for example, provides for financing of the vast interstate highway system with federal gasoline excise taxes levied on highway users. On the local level, special assessments on improvements which benefit the property owner are used extensively.

Bond. A certificate of indebtedness, tendered by a borrower to a lender, which constitutes a written obligation for the borrower to repay to the lender the principal plus accrued interest on the loan. A public bond is issued by the national government or by a state or local government as a means of borrowing money for public needs which cannot be financed out of current revenues.

• *Significance:* Various types of bonds, such as savings bonds, are issued by the United States government to help finance its huge expenditures. State and local governments commonly make use of either serial bond or sinking fund issues to finance new projects. Sinking fund bonds are paid from a separate fund set aside from revenues over a period of time until the bonds are due for payment. Serial bonds, which are becoming more popular than the sinking fund type, come due at different dates over a period of years, with each series paid off by the borrowing authority from current revenues.

Borrowing Power. The authority of a government to finance those expenditures which exceed its income. The Constitution provides the Congress with the full borrowing power, entirely free from restrictions. Most state constitutions, however, severely limit the authority of state governments to incur indebtedness, permitting state borrowing only when authorized by constitutional amendment (18 states), or by a vote of the people (18 states). Local units of government are restricted by state constitutional or statutory limitations on their borrowing power.

• *Significance:* The borrowing power is essential in enabling governments to meet short and long term crises and in financing major projects which could not be paid for out of current income. The national government, for example, used its borrowing power extensively in financing the prosecution of World War II and in meeting the economic crisis of the 1930's. Deficit spending to counteract economic recessions has become a standard weapon in the arsenal of federal fiscal policy. Most state and local borrowing, conversely, is used to finance major building projects. Some citizens support borrowing for capital improvements as an investment in the future, similar to borrowing by a family to purchase a home. Others view extensive use of the borrowing power as fiscal irresponsibility.

Budget.   An estimate of the receipts and expenditures needed by government to carry out its program in some future period, usually a fiscal year. The President is responsible for formulating the national budget under the Budget and Accounting Act of 1921, and the governors of most of the states likewise operate under an "executive budget" system. The budget process begins with the lengthy and detailed process of preparing estimates, followed by a central review in which budget officers hold hearings for agency officials who defend the estimates. In the third step, the budget is approved by the chief executive and submitted to the legislative body in a "budget message." After study and the holding of hearings by appropriations committees, the budget is enacted as an appropriation act. The fifth step is budget execution, the actual spending of the money during the fiscal period by executive officials, which is followed by the final step of a postaudit check on the validity of expenditures. Some states and cities use a separate capital budget for financing major public works projects, which are often paid for on a long-term bonding or self-liquidating basis.

• *Significance:* A budget is a work plan which gives direction to the execution of government policies. The budget process has undergone a major change in the twentieth century with the adoption of the executive budget to replace the formulation of budgets by legislative committees. The executive budget gives the chief executive—President, governor, or mayor—extensive control over fiscal affairs.

Comptroller General.   The federal official responsible for auditing the accounts of all national government agencies. He heads the General Accounting Office (GAO), and is appointed by the President with the Senate's approval for a 15-year term. The Comptroller General (pronounced con-troller) also has power to validate all payments to ensure that they fall within the purposes and limits of congressional appropriations acts and to standardize accounting systems of government agencies. He can be removed from office by impeachment or by joint resolution of the Congress.

• *Significance:* The Comptroller General acts as an agent of the Congress in controlling and auditing the budget execution process in the executive branch. Without his approval, money cannot be validly withdrawn from the Treasury.

Controversy has developed on occasion when the Comptroller General has been charged with letting his personal views influence the validation of expenditures. For example, President Franklin Roosevelt became involved in many controversies with the Comptroller General because the latter's open hostility to the New Deal was regarded as the reason for his holding up many emergency spending programs. Many observers, including the first Hoover Commission, have recommended that the Comptroller General's "preaudit" validation of payments be transferred to an executive official, leaving the Comptroller General with responsibility for a "postaudit." In recent years, the Comptroller General has expanded his operations by sending his GAO investigators abroad to check on foreign aid and other types of overseas spending.

Corporation Income Tax. A national tax levied on corporations, based on their annual net income. The corporation income tax rate in recent years has been a flat 30 percent for the first $25,000 of net income and 52 percent on all net income over that figure.
• *Significance:* The federal corporation income tax is probably the most complicated tax levied by the national government, resulting from efforts by the Congress to determine with fairness what constitutes "net income" and what are "legitimate" expenses for a corporation. It ranks next to the individual income tax in the amount of its annual yield. In recent years, it has produced between $17 and $22 billion annually. It has been vigorously attacked by some who regard it as fostering "double taxation," that is, the taxing of corporation income through the corporation income tax, followed by the taxing of shareholders' dividends through the individual income tax. Others have criticized the corporation income tax for its lenient rates and loopholes.

Debt Limit. A constitutional or statutory limitation upon the ability of a government to incur indebtedness. In the national government, the debt limit is fixed by the Congress and can be changed to meet new debt needs. All but a few states, however, are restricted by constitutional provisions which usually limit state indebtedness to a specified figure. Debt limitations on local governments usually take the form of restricting total debt to a percentage of assessed valuation or involve state approval of bond issues.
• *Significance:* Self-imposed statutory debt limits established by legislative bodies, as by the Congress, are useful only psychologically, if at all. Over the past three decades, the Congress has altered the public debt limit on numerous occasions, raising it to more than $300 billion in a change made in 1962. On the state and local levels, cumbersome constitutional restrictions have produced many new techniques for evasion. Although debt limits can ordinarily be exceeded by favorable referendum votes in the state and local governments, voter apathy or conservatism has made this increasingly difficult. Devices which have been used to incur indebtedness beyond state or local limits include borrowing by state agencies instead of the state, per se, and borrowing on a self-liquidating basis without state certification of bonds. For example, state toll road authorities borrow large sums to construct highways, and repay the debt out of income from tolls. Despite efforts to keep debt limited on the national, state, and local levels, new demands for government functions and

services beyond the means of current income keep debt rising in the United States.

Deficit Financing. A technique of fiscal policy which utilizes government spending beyond income to combat an economic slump. The use of deficit financing to "prime the pump" of the free enterprise economy was popularized by the British economist, John Maynard Keynes, in the 1930's. *See* FISCAL POLICY, page 229.

• *Significance:* The objective of deficit financing is to inject new purchasing power into the economy in order to stimulate an upturn in economic activity when the economy is in a period of stagnation resulting from overproduction or underconsumption. Deficit financing is accepted today by most economists and politicians, on the assumption that deficits incurred during economic slumps will be paid off with budget surpluses during periods of prosperity. Conservatives generally oppose it on the grounds that it involves fiscal irresponsibility and is ineffectual, and they usually demand government cutbacks in spending as the best means of stimulating the free economy. The national government used deficit financing extensively during the depression of the 1930's and has employed it to combat four post–World War II recessions.

Deflation. An economic condition in which the price level is decreased and the value of money in terms of purchasing power is consequently increased.

• *Significance:* Proponents of stable monetary policies regard deflation and inflation, its opposite, as twin evils to be equally avoided. Deflation is characteristically associated with economic depressions, just as inflation tends to accompany prosperity. Most economists believe that deflation can be prevented or controlled through proper use of monetary policy by the Federal Reserve Board and the Treasury and by the use of fiscal policy, such as deficit financing. A policy of deflation is sometimes adopted by a nation which is suffering from an adverse balance of payments, with the objective of reducing prices to make exports more attractive to other countries and imports from them more expensive.

Devaluation. A policy undertaken by a nation to reduce the value of its monetary unit in terms of gold or its exchange ratio with other national currencies. The United States devalued the dollar by about 59 percent in 1934, increasing the price of gold to $35 an ounce, at which it has since remained fixed.

• *Significance:* Although American devaluation of the dollar in 1934 was based largely on domestic reasons, ordinarily the objective of devaluation is to improve a nation's balance of international payments by reducing imports and expanding exports. These results are likely to occur because devaluation increases the cost of foreign products and decreases the cost of domestically produced items in foreign markets. Devaluations are often matched by equal or greater devaluations by competitor states in an effort to maintain their position in international trade. Although successive rounds of devaluations were carried on by many states during the 1930's, the only major devaluations in the postwar era occurred in 1949 when Britain and most sterling bloc countries

depreciated their currencies by about 30 percent. In recent years, much specula-
tion has concerned the possible devaluation of the dollar because of the imbalance in the American balance of payments and the resulting outflow of gold.
One of the major responsibilities of the International Monetary Fund (IMF) of
the United Nations is to try to eliminate competitive unilateral devaluation as
an international trade weapon.

Direct Tax.   Any tax paid directly to the government by the taxpayer. An
indirect tax, conversely, is paid to private business persons who then remit
it to the government, such as a sales or excise tax. The Constitution in Article
I, section 9 states: "No capitation, or other direct tax shall be laid, unless in
proportion to the census or enumeration hereinbefore directed to be taken."
This provision means that, for example, the people in a state containing 10
percent of the nation's population would pay 10 percent of any direct tax
levied by the national government.
• *Significance:* The question of which taxes are direct and, therefore, to be
apportioned according to the population of the states, has been the subject of
much legal controversy. In 1796 (*Hylton v. United States,* 3 Dallas 171), the
Supreme Court interpreted "direct taxes" to include poll taxes and taxes on
land. In 1895 (*Pollock v. Farmers' Loan and Trust Co.,* 158 U.S. 601), the
Court struck down an income tax as a direct tax which the Congress must ap-
portion among the states. This decision was overcome by the 16th Amendment
which granted the Congress the power to tax incomes "without apportionment
among the several states, and without regard to any census or enumeration."
Congress has generally refused to levy direct taxes because apportionment involves many administrative complications and because of inequities which
would result since tax-paying ability is not divided equally among the people
of the 50 states.

Estate Tax.   A tax, usually with progressive rates, levied on the property of
deceased persons. Estate taxes apply to the total estate, whereas inheritance
taxes are levied on the portions of the estate received by the beneficiaries. The
national government has regularly levied an estate tax since 1916, and all
states except Nevada have an estate or inheritance tax, in most instances, the
latter.
• *Significance:* The federal estate and gift taxes together have averaged over
$1.3 billion annually in recent years. The gift tax, having rates nearly as high
as the estate tax, is used to plug the loophole by which money was given to
relatives and friends before death in order to avoid estate taxes. A high percentage of state death taxes may be offset as a credit against payment of the
federal estate tax, which has served as an encouragement for the states to enact
such levies. State inheritance taxes are also progressive, with rates increasing
sharply as the beneficiary's share rises, and increasing also as the relationship
of the beneficiary of the deceased becomes more distant. Estate and inheritance
taxes are aimed at preventing excessive concentrations of wealth in a few families.

Excess Profits Tax.   A special tax levied during wartime to supplement the corporation income tax. The excess profits tax is calculated on the difference between business earnings in normal years and earnings during the war years when profits soar. An excess profits tax was levied by the Congress during World Wars I and II, and during the Korean action from 1951 to 1953. In the last case, the tax was fixed at 30 percent of the excess profits, with the limitation that the combined corporation income tax and excess profits tax should not exceed 70 percent of net income.

• *Significance:* The excess profits tax is designed primarily to recapture abnormal profits and to help finance military expenditures. It also is psychologically motivated to quiet public fears of wartime business profiteering. The opposition of businessmen to the tax, usually quiescent during the war period, has always forced an early repealing of the tax at the war's end.

Excise.   A tax levied upon the manufacture, transportation, sale, or consumption of goods within a country or a state. Federal excise taxes are permitted by the Constitution, and such levies have been placed on a variety of consumer goods, mostly luxuries and amusements. The main excise taxes used by the states are sales and use taxes.

• *Significance:* Federal income from excise taxes, averaging about $10 billion annually in recent years, has been exceeded only by the individual and corporation income taxes. The excises on liquor and tobacco provide the greatest yields. State excise taxes, unlike the federal, are often criticized for their regressive character in taxing necessities, with the tax burden falling proportionately heavier on low-income families. Many of the federal excises were first levied during wartime as emergency income measures, but the Congress has provided for few reductions since.

Federal Reserve Notes.   Currency issued by Federal Reserve banks, backed by deposits with the government of discounted commercial paper (promissory notes, bills of exchange, etc.), government bonds, and gold certificates.

• *Significance:* Federal Reserve notes are the most important kind of currency in circulation in the United States today. A small volume of silver certificates, treasury notes, Federal Reserve bank notes, and national bank notes still circulate, but, except for the silver certificates, are being slowly retired. Since going off the gold standard in 1934, the United States has had a "managed" currency. Elasticity in the supply of Federal Reserve notes is provided by its commercial paper backing; when borrowing is heavy, more currency can be issued, and when demand for loans shrinks, the issue of currency can be reduced. Gold backing of Federal Reserve notes is fixed by statute at 25 percent, but the gold reserve has consistently remained at more than that amount.

Federal Reserve System.   The private-public banking regulatory system in the United States which establishes banking policies and influences the amount of credit available and the currency in circulation. The Federal Reserve System was created by Congress in 1913. It consists of 12 Federal Reserve banks, each located in one of the 12 Federal Reserve districts into which the country is divided, and a central Board of Governors of seven members appointed by the President and confirmed by the Senate. Each of the 12 Federal Reserve banks is headed by a board of nine Directors, six of whom are chosen by the member banks in the district and three by the Federal Reserve Board in Washington. Membership in district Federal Reserve banks is required of all national banks and permitted to state banks, and most of the latter have joined. The Federal Reserve banks are actually privately owned "bankers' banks," with all member banks required to hold stock in them. Buying and selling of commercial paper and government securities is carried on through an Open Market Committee.

• *Significance:* The Federal Reserve System determines the nation's general monetary and credit policies through decisions made by the Board in Washington, D.C., and by the regional Directors. The policies are carried out through the Reserve banks and by the thousands of member banks across the country. The System has played an increasingly significant role in meeting the nation's major economic problems of inflation and recession. In trying to control inflation, the System has tried to carry out "hard" money policies during economic boom periods when inflationary pressures are greatest. In fighting recessions, the System has carried out more liberal monetary and credit policies designed to stimulate investment and purchasing power.

Fiscal Policy. The use by government of its financial powers to influence the nation's economy. Decisions on fiscal policy are made largely by the President and the Congress, and are concerned with revenue, expenditure, and debt. John Maynard Keynes, the British economist, was one of the first to develop the theoretical basis and sophisticated applications of fiscal policy in combating economic slumps.

• *Significance:* Fiscal policy is usually aimed at using governmental financial programs to maintain economic stability by arresting and reversing violent downswings or upswings in the economy. The objective is to maintain a viable economy while steering a middle course between inflation and recession. Fiscal policies available to fight a serious downturn or recession include compensatory (deficit) spending, public works projects, and tax reductions. To combat inflation, reverse policies of reduced government spending, surplus budgets and debt retirement, and increased taxes are called for. Although the application of government fiscal policies to effect changes in the nation's economy is generally accepted as a proper function for government, some opposition exists. Most controversy, however, involves conflicts over the choice of specific policies, and arises, particularly, from groups adversely affected.

Fiscal Year. The 12-month financial period which is used by a government for record keeping, budgeting, appropriating, revenue collecting, and other aspects of fiscal management. The fiscal year of the national government runs from July 1 to June 30, but some state and local governments use the calendar year from January 1 to December 31, while a few states use a two-year fiscal period.

• *Significance:* It is important for the student of government to differentiate between those statistics which apply to the calendar year and to the fiscal year. The national government's fiscal year was selected to conform with the flow of governmental actions involved in budgeting and appropriating.

General Welfare Clause.   The clause in Article I, section 8, which authorizes the Congress to lay and collect taxes to provide for the common defense and general welfare of the United States.
• *Significance:* The general welfare clause appears to give the Congress an unlimited spending power, but it has been a source of extensive constitutional controversy. The issue is whether the Congress can spend tax monies only for purposes authorized in other sections of the Constitution, or whether the general welfare clause gives the Congress an unlimited power to spend for whatever might contribute to the "common defense and general welfare." The former position has been held by the strict constructionists, the latter by the loose or liberal constructionists. The liberal constructionist view of the interpretation of the general welfare clause has prevailed, and the spending power as such has never been successfully challenged in the courts. The only limitation suggested by the Supreme Court (*United States v. Butler,* 297 U.S. 1 [1936]), was that taxes levied by the Congress be spent for *national* welfare and not for the welfare of particular groups. The general welfare clause has enabled the national government to carry on programs in fields not specifically granted to it by the Constitution.

Gold Standard.   A monetary system in which a nation's currency is backed by gold, has a standard of value measured in gold, and can be exchanged for gold. An international gold standard provides for free convertibility of currencies into gold and the unimpeded movement of gold bullion from one nation to another to pay international debts. The gold standard became universally accepted during the nineteenth and early twentieth centuries; the United States adopted it in 1900. In the world-wide depression of the 1930's, the nations of the world discarded it, the United States going off the gold standard in 1934.
• *Significance:* The gold standard provided stability in domestic monetary systems, and an "international currency" and self-regulating payments system in international trade and finance, for many years. The severe depression of the 1930's, however, forced the major industrial countries, including the United States, to adopt flexible fiscal and employment policies based on "managed" paper currencies which were incompatible with the gold standard. In discarding the gold standard, the Congress provided for calling in gold and gold coin in circulation and fixed the price at $35 for a fine ounce.

Income Tax.   A tax levied on income received from profits, salaries, rents, interest, dividends, and other sources, less deductions permitted by law. The national government's income tax includes both a tax on individual income and on corporation income, with different rates applicable to each. More than 30 states also levy income taxes, most being applicable to both individual and corporate income.
• *Significance:* The individual income tax is based on ability to pay and provides for progressive or graduated tax-rate increases as income increases. The federal tax rate currently starts at 20 percent for the first $2,000 in income and increases progressively to a high of 91 percent on taxable income over $200,000. The income tax also permits flexibility in providing greater or lesser yields simply by adjusting a few rates. Its major weakness results from its complicated nature

and the successful efforts of various pressure groups to riddle it with exemptions and loopholes. Over 40 million persons pay some income tax today, the majority through the payroll withholding system. The individual income tax is by far the major source of revenue for the national government, with, typically, twice the receipts of the next most important source, the corporate income tax. The two together provide well over one half of total national tax receipts. In the states, the income tax, including both individual and corporate, is the third largest source of state revenue. Increased use of income taxes by the states or by local governments is hampered by the extensive pre-emption of the field by the national government and public opposition to additional taxes on incomes.

Inflation.　An economic condition in which the price level is increased and the value of money in terms of purchasing power is consequently decreased. Inflation may result from either an increase in the amount of money and credit available or a decrease in the supply of consumer goods.
• *Significance:* The traditional definition of inflation—too many dollars chasing too few goods—has been supplemented by the "cost-push" explanation of the phenomenon. This view holds that when typical conditions for inflation do not exist, but inflation does, it is then a product of rising costs of production, or of imperfect competition reflected in "administered prices" whereby business-men reduce production and set artificially high prices. Mass psychological factors may be a significant ingredient of inflation. Most economists believe that serious inflation can be prevented through proper use of monetary policy by the Federal Reserve Board and the Treasury, and by the use of fiscal policy, such as providing for surplus budgets and increased taxes. Although the effects of inflation are largely internal, a nation suffering from a serious inflation may jeopardize its foreign markets and suffer consequently from a disequilibrium in its balance of international payments. Within a country, persons living on a fixed income typically suffer most from inflation.

Legal Tender.　Any medium of exchange which by law must be accepted in payment of a debt. The Constitution gives the national government full control over the nation's money, and it forbids the states to "make anything but gold and silver coin a tender in payment of debts. . . ." (Art. I, sec. 10).
• *Significance:* A major legal controversy developed over the first century of American history as to whether the national government could issue fiat notes not backed by the precious metals as legal tender. A series of cases was climaxed in 1884 by *Juilliard v. Greenman,* 110 U.S. 421, in which the Supreme Court declared that the Congress has full power to issue notes as legal tender in the payment of debts. The states for many years authorized state chartered banks to issue notes for circulation as currency, but not as legal tender. Although these issuances did not violate the Constitution, the Congress regarded them as a danger to monetary uniformity and stability. In 1865, the Congress levied a 10 percent tax upon state notes which was sustained by the Supreme Court (*Veazie Bank v. Fenno,* 8 Wallace 533 [1869]), and which drove all state notes out of circulation.

Monetary Policy.　A policy which aims at affecting the amount of currency in circulation and the availability of credit. The Federal Reserve Board uses "tight money" monetary policies to restrain and prolong boom periods in the nation's economy and to fight inflation. "Loose money" policies are used to check deflation and to fight recessions by making money and credit more freely available.

• *Significance:* In the post-World War II period, continuing reliance for fighting recessions and restraining booms has been placed upon the Federal Reserve Board and its employment of monetary policies. The use of such policies must be delicately and expertly handled lest a serious deflationary or inflationary spiral be touched off. In pursuing a tight or hard money policy, the Federal Reserve Board decreases the availability of money and credit by raising member banks' reserve requirements, by raising the rediscount rate, and by selling government securities through its Open Market Committee. The Federal Reserve Board pursues policies exactly the opposite of these when loose or soft money policies are called for. Monetary policy is particularly effective when used in conjunction with fiscal policies initiated by the President and the Congress and aimed at the same objectives.

Open Market Committee.   A committee composed of the Board of Governors of the Federal Reserve System, and five Directors of the Federal Reserve banks chosen annually by the boards of directors. The Federal Open Market Committee carries on "open market operations" in buying and selling government securities, bills of exchange, and other commercial paper.

• *Significance:* The Federal Open Market Committee operations are designed to facilitate commerce and business and to stabilize credit in the United States. Its functions are particularly useful in implementing the monetary policies determined by the Federal Reserve Board. For example, during a period when inflation threatens, the Committee sells government securities and commercial paper in the open market to restrict the availability of credit; when deflation or recession threatens, the Committee buys so as to make credit more easily available through member banks. The Committee's open market operations are supplemented by other instruments of monetary policy, such as the fixing of the rediscount rate and the reserve requirements for member banks.

Performance Budget.   The drawing up of a plan for anticipated expenditures based on the activities, services, and functions performed by government, rather than allotting funds on the basis of items to be purchased and salaries to be paid by each department and agency.

• *Significance:* Based on the recommendations of the Hoover Commission, the Congress adopted the principle of the performance budget in the Budget and Accounting Procedures Act of 1950. Since 1951, the Bureau of the Budget has drawn up much of the general budget for the national government on a performance basis. The major advantage of the performance budget is that by detailing how and for what government funds are expended it gives a clearer picture than did the itemization system.

Personal Property.   The ownership of things of value other than real property. Personal property is usually classified as tangible or intangible, the former including valuables of substance, such as automobiles, jewelry, and household goods, and the latter a right, claim, or interest of value, such as found in bonds, stocks, and bank accounts.

• *Significance:* Property is usually classified for tax purposes, the tax on personal property being applied at a rate ordinarily lower than that on real property. Personal property tax collection involves considerable administrative work, particularly that of getting the owners to declare their property for tax purposes or, if they do not, of finding it. This becomes an almost hopeless task when levying the tax on intangible properties which can easily be concealed from the assessors' eyes. Often, the value of such intangibles as stocks and bonds exceeds the value of real estate and tangibles, yet the taxes levied upon them depend almost entirely on the personal honesty of the individual taxpayer.

Progressive Tax.   Any tax in which the tax *rates* increase as the amount to be taxed increases. It is the opposite of a regressive tax in which tax rates remain uniform or decline as the tax base increases.

• *Significance:* Progressive taxes levied by the national and state governments include the individual and corporate income taxes and the estate and gift taxes. Progressive taxes are based on the principle of ability to pay, as reflected, for example, in the federal individual income tax where percentage rates range from 20 percent on $2000 to 91 percent on income over $200,000. Supporters of progressive taxation regard it as an equitable means of securing necessary government income. Opponents criticize it mainly on the ground that it penalizes initiative and success.

Property Tax.   An ad valorem tax levied on real or personal, tangible or intangible property. The general property tax is levied by local units of government throughout the country, and most states make limited use of some form of the tax. The tax process includes assessment of property valuations, determination of tax rates (millage), tax computation, and tax collection. To correct injustices, boards of review on the local level adjust inequalities in assessments. Where the taxing jurisdiction crosses political boundaries, central assessment or equalization is provided to avoid geographical inequities.

• *Significance:* The general property tax provides the fiscal foundation for local units of government across the nation. In recent years, it has provided about 85 percent of the tax revenue for cities, counties, school districts, towns, townships, villages, and other local units. For many years, the general property tax was the nation's major source of revenue, exceeding all state and national levies until the twentieth century's many crises boosted income and sales taxes. The general property tax has come increasingly under attack in recent years because of difficulties and conflicts involved in assessment, equalization, and exemptions. The flexibility of the tax as a source of revenue has nearly reached exhaustion in many localities because of constitutional or statutory limitations, popular rejections of tax increase referendums, and heavy tax loads resulting from failure to find other tax sources.

Public Debt.   The total indebtedness, including accrued interest, of a government or of a country, the latter case embracing the indebtedness of all units of government. The public debt of the United States government is usually referred to as the national debt. Whenever expenditures exceed revenue during a fiscal year, the deficit is added to the public debt; when revenue exceeds expenditures, the public debt is reduced by the amount of the surplus.

• *Significance:* Over a period of three decades of frequent unbalanced budgets, the United States has built up a national public debt of huge proportions. The national debt rose from about $16 billion in 1931 to almost $49 billion in 1941, as a result of deficit financing to stimulate the stagnated economy; by 1946, it had risen to $269 billion through the financing of World War II; from that point, it rose to a level of more than $300 billion in 1962 as a result of financing cold war defense programs and combating four postwar recessions. Much controversy has arisen concerning the rapid rise of the national debt in recent years. Some economists view the debt as a useful governmental weapon for stabilizing the economy, adding to it by "pump priming" (deficit spending) during economic downturns, and retiring portions of it through surpluses during periods of prosperity to reduce the threat of inflation. Some students of finance are relatively unconcerned about the size of the debt, pointing out that "we owe it to ourselves," that much of the debt constitutes an investment for the future of the American people, and that the debt has actually grown smaller in recent years if measured on a per capita basis or in relation to national income. The concerned, on the other hand, regard the "owe it to ourselves" argument as specious, and contend that future generations of Americans will suffer from our excessive spending, and that the size of the debt threatens not only our economic solvency but our national security as well. In recent years, state and local debt has increased at a more rapid rate than the national debt.

Rediscount.   A loan made by a Federal Reserve bank to a member bank on negotiable instruments which had already been discounted when the member bank made loans to its customers.

• *Significance:* The Federal Reserve System uses the rediscount rate as a tool of monetary policy. By lowering the rediscount rate, the Federal Reserve Board can encourage member banks to liquidate their holdings of commercial paper by having the Federal Reserve banks buy them at a discount of their face value. This frees funds of the member banks and enables them to make additional loans to the public, thus stimulating purchasing power and, thereby, the nation's economy. By raising the rediscount rate, the Federal Reserve banks can obtain the opposite result of contracting the availability of credit in the country. The rediscount rate, therefore, is, typically, lowered during a recession to stimulate an upturn in the economy (loose money policy), and is, typically, raised during a boom period when serious inflation threatens (tight money policy).

Regressive Tax.   Any tax in which the burden falls relatively more heavily upon the low-income groups than upon the more wealthy taxpayers. It is the opposite of a progressive tax in which tax rates increase as ability to pay increases.

• *Significance:* Regressive taxes are used mainly by the state and local governments and include, for example, the sales tax and the uniform or declining rate income tax. Such taxes take a higher percentage of the total income of low-income groups than of the total income of the high-income groups, even though the rates are uniform. Sales taxes on the necessities of life are probably the most regressive in nature, since a major portion of the expenditures of low-income families are for such commodities.

Reserve Ratio. The percentage of liquid assets held by a bank as a reserve for its deposits. The *legal* reserve ratio is that percentage set by government to ensure that banks will maintain a safe proportion of ready cash to meet depositors' demands for their money. Under the Federal Reserve System, the legal reserve requirement is set for the member banks within each district by the Federal Reserve Board of Governors. Reserve requirements for state banks are usually set by law in each state.

• *Significance:* Legal reserve requirements are set by government to protect the rights of individual depositors. Through the Federal Reserve System, the government additionally obtains a powerful means of carrying out monetary policy and maintaining stability with flexibility in the monetary system. When deflation or economic recessions threaten, the Federal Reserve Board can free money and credit to stimulate business by lowering the reserve requirements of member banks. When inflation threatens, or it is desirable to restrain an economic boom, the Board reduces the availability of money and credit to business and consumers by raising reserve requirements. Along with its open market operations and its rediscount function, the setting of reserve ratio requirements is a major monetary tool which helps the Board set the general direction and tone of the American economy.

Revolving Fund. An operational fund established for a government agency carrying on proprietary (business-type) functions which make the agency financially self-supporting, or nearly so. Income from the agency's operations is not turned in to the Treasury Department but is spent directly by the agency. For example, the Tennessee Valley Authority (TVA) uses its revenue from electric power sales to finance its continuing operations and its expansion programs.

• *Significance:* A revolving fund gives a public business enterprise the financial flexibility to carry out significant long-range programs. Agencies ordinarily cannot plan operations beyond those approved by the Congress in its annual appropriations, and a revolving fund frees the agency from this kind of dependence. The revolving fund principle has been followed especially in setting up federal lending agencies.

Sales Tax. A tax levied upon the sale of commodities, usually paid by the purchaser. The sales tax may apply generally to all commodities or it may be restricted to certain classifications or specific commodities. Typically, the sales tax is levied on retail sales, but in some cases it is imposed on sales by manufacturers and wholesalers as well. Closely related to the sales tax is the "use" tax, which applies to purchases made outside the taxing jurisdiction and is designed to prevent state residents from avoiding the sales tax through out-

of-state purchases. Thirty-eight states levy sales taxes of from 2 to 4 percent.
• *Significance:* Most of the states which levy a sales tax adopted it during the depression of the 1930's when they were under heavy obligation to meet rising welfare and general governmental costs. The sales tax has become the single most important source of state revenue. Most opposition to the sales tax centers around its regressive character, which places a heavy tax burden upon the low-income groups. Some states have sought to reduce its regressive impact by exempting food, clothing, or other necessities. Support for the sales tax is based on the idea that all citizens should contribute to the support of government and the sales tax makes this possible because all persons are consumers.

Severance Tax.   A tax levied upon natural resources at the time they are taken from the land or water.
• *Significance:* Severance taxes are used by many states for both revenue and conservation purposes. Conservation objectives can be achieved by adjusting tax rates to control the "severing" of timber, minerals, and other resources from the soil. Some states accomplish the same purpose without a severance tax, per se, by, for example, exempting timberland from the general property tax until the timber has been harvested.

Sixteenth Amendment.   An amendment to the Constitution adopted in 1913 which grants the Congress the power to levy taxes on incomes without apportioning them among the states according to population. The individual and corporation income taxes of the national government are based on the power granted in this Amendment.
• *Significance:* The 16th Amendment resulted from a Supreme Court decision which held that a federal income tax is a direct tax and, under Article I, section 9, must be apportioned among the states according to population (*Pollock v. Farmers' Loan and Trust Co.*, 158 U.S. 601 [1895]). Although a Civil War income tax levy had been upheld by the Supreme Court as an indirect tax, the 1895 decision reversed this view. The controversy, however, continued. The 16th Amendment put aside the question of whether income taxes are direct or indirect by giving the Congress blanket power to lay and collect taxes on incomes "from whatever source derived," and without any apportionment or regard to any census. Without this Amendment, income taxes apportioned among the states according to population would have been manifestly unfair and inequitable because of the vast differences in income among the states, and the Congress refused to levy such a tax. Since 1913, the individual and corporation income taxes have become the major sources for federal revenue.

Special Assessment.   A charge made by a government against a property owner for that part of the cost of public improvements made adjacent to his property which are especially useful or beneficial to his property. Special assessments are different from taxes in that they are levied for a specific purpose which has been petitioned for by the landowners concerned.
• *Significance:* Special assessments are used mainly by local units of government in providing facilities for homeowners, such as paved streets, sewers, and

sidewalks. A portion of the cost of such public improvements is, typically, borne by the local government out of taxes, which recognizes that they are generally beneficial to the community as well as to the individual landowner. Such projects are financed through special assessment bonds which are backed by the government's power to assess for public improvements.

Tax Exemption.   The privilege granted by a government legally freeing certain types of property, sales, or income from general taxpaying obligations.
• *Significance:* Most of the states have established constitutional or statutory exemption of educational and religious properties from the general property tax. Income from certain national, state, or local bonds may be exempted from taxation, and cooperatives from income tax levies. Most state sales taxes exempt certain classes of commodities. Tax exemptions may be used to encourage activities as well as to recognize that exceptions within general taxpaying categories must be acknowledged in the interest of fairness. Often, tax exemptions may merely illustrate the political power of special interest groups.

Tax Incidence.   The point at which the actual burden of paying a tax falls, regardless of whom the tax is formally levied upon. Those taxes in which the burden cannot be shifted to someone else by the taxpayer are sometimes classified as *direct* taxes; those in which the burden can be passed on are *indirect* taxes.
• *Significance:* The incidence of almost all taxes which are levied at some point in the production and consumption of goods is, typically, shifted to consumers through higher prices for commodities. The price of a loaf of bread, for example, may include scores of national, state, and local taxes which, having been paid by different farmers, processors, distributors, etc., are passed on to the ultimate consumer. Direct taxes in which the burden cannot ordinarily be shifted include income levies, poll taxes, and taxes on land, although when the land is rented the owner can shift the burden of his tax to the renter. The incidence of taxation brings into serious question the fairness of taxes which are eventually paid by others than those who make the formal tax payments.

Tax Offset.   A device used by the national government to induce states to adopt certain types of taxes or programs by permitting individuals to deduct such state taxes from the amount of federal tax which they would otherwise pay.
• *Significance:* The tax offset has been used effectively by the national government in prodding the states into adopting such tax programs as unemployment compensation and state inheritance taxes. To induce the states to adopt unemployment compensation programs, for example, the national government levies a 3 percent payroll tax on employers, but permits them to offset 90 percent of that tax if they contribute to a state unemployment compensation fund. The effect of this tax offset was to secure a nationwide, but state administered, program of unemployment compensation. Some economists regard the tax offset as the best means of inducing all of the states to adopt

uniform tax programs to meet growing revenue needs, without any state losing ground in the fierce competition among states to attract and hold industry by means of low taxes.

Tax Sharing.   The levying and collecting of a tax by one unit of government and its turning over a certain portion of the tax yield to another unit of government, according to a formula established by law.
• *Significance:* Most shared taxes involve state and local governments. Many state governments, for example, levy and collect sales or income taxes with a constitutional or statutory requirement that a certain percentage of these collections be turned over to local governments. Common examples of taxes collected by the states and shared with their local governments are motor fuel taxes, license taxes, income taxes, liquor and cigarette taxes, and sales taxes.

Treasurer of the United States.   An official of the Treasury Department, not to be confused with the Secretary of the Treasury, who is responsible for the receipt and disbursement of public monies, the redeeming of government bonds, and the issuance of currency and coin.
• *Significance:* The Treasurer of the United States does not hold a significant policy-making position, although the administrative responsibilities of the office are numerous and complex. In recent years, Presidents have tended to appoint women to the office who have played a leading role in their party's campaigns and other activities.

Valuation.   The determination of assessments, taxes, charges, rates, or profits based on an appraisal of the value of the property or service.
• *Significance:* In governmental regulatory and taxation functions, the equitability of the rates or taxes often depends upon the skill and honesty with which government officials estimate the value of property or services. For example, the property tax paid by an individual is determined by the assessed valuation placed on his property by an assessor, as well as the tax rate determined by his elected representatives. Rates charged consumers of utility services likewise depend considerably on the valuation placed upon the assets of the public utility in determining a fair return for its operations. Because valuation cannot be made into a precise scientific or mathematical function, it leads to innumerable controversies over estimated valuations.

Withholding Tax.   Provisions of an income or payroll tax system by which the employer deducts a specified percentage from an employee's wage or salary and remits it to the government's tax bureau. Amounts withheld by employers constitute a credit against the employees' total tax liability.
• *Significance:* Under the Current Tax Payment Act of 1943, the national government has provided for the payment of federal income taxes through employer-withholding of wages and salaries and the payment of an estimated tax in quarterly installments on income derived from other sources. The individual taxpayer must still file a return on the day of reckoning, April 15 each year, at which time he must pay any amount owed over his total withholdings or file a refund claim if his tax is less than his withholdings. The

withholding system was adopted by the Congress during World War II to help finance the military effort. The main advantages of the system are that it makes tax collections more certain and it facilitates payment of taxes through relatively "painless" deductions from paychecks. It also provides the Department of the Treasury with sizable funds coming in regularly during the year. Most opposition has come from employers who dislike the extensive bookkeeping involved and from other groups who oppose the singling out of wage and salary incomes for withholding. In recent years, the Congress has considered extending the withholding principle to other categories of income, such as interest and dividends.

IMPORTANT AGENCIES

Board of Governors, Federal Reserve System. A board composed of seven members which determines general monetary and credit policies and oversees the operations of the 12 district Federal Reserve banks and member banks throughout the country. Board members are appointed for 14-year terms by the President with the Senate's confirmation, with consideration given to geographical and major business interests in the selection process.
• *Significance:* The Board of Governors determines monetary policies through its control over the issuance of Federal Reserve notes by Federal Reserve banks, its fixing of the rediscount rate and, through its Open Market Committee, the regulation of the purchase and sale of government and other securities. All of these activities have a profound effect on the amount of money in circulation and the credit available through Federal Reserve member banks, which in turn influences general economic conditions in the country. The Board also sets the margin requirements for purchases of securities, and conducts periodic examinations of Federal Reserve and member banks. Some students of government and finance would like to have its activities brought under the direct supervision of the President because of the close, important relationship of its activities to the role of government and the stability of the economy. Others consider it essential that the Board retain its independence from presidential control in order that its decisions be free from politics.

Bureau of the Budget. An agency in the Executive Office of the President which has primary responsibility under the President's direction for budget preparation and administration. The Bureau of the Budget operates under a Director and five Assistant Directors. Each of the latter is at the head of a major office which describes the nature of his responsibility: budget review, legislative reference, management and organization, statistical standards, and accounting.
• *Significance:* The Director of the Bureau of the Budget is empowered, under the Budget and Accounting Act of 1921, to "assemble, correlate, revise, reduce, or increase" the estimates from executive agencies. Broad fiscal powers flow from this grant, both in the planning and estimate stage and, following congressional approval of the budget, in the budget execution stage, when agency heads must obtain Bureau approval in financing their programs. In addition to its budgeting function, the Bureau carries on duties directed toward improving organization and management within the executive branch and acts

as a clearinghouse for legislative proposals originating in the executive agencies. Since 1939, when the Bureau of the Budget was transferred from the Department of the Treasury to the Executive Office, it has become the President's major staff agency in fiscal and related matters.

Department of the Treasury.   A major department of the national government, responsible for fiscal management and headed by a Secretary with Cabinet status. The Department of the Treasury is one of the original departments established in 1789; today, it carries on a variety of significant functions, employing over 75,000 persons.

• *Significance:* Major responsibilities of the Department include (1) collection of internal revenue taxes and customs duties; (2) administration of the public debt; (3) keeping central accounts for the entire national government; (4) coining and printing money and protecting against counterfeiting; (5) registration and licensing of ships engaged in foreign and interstate commerce; and (6) administration of the narcotic control laws. Important administrative units include the Internal Revenue Service, Bureau of Customs, Bureau of Accounts, Secret Service, Bureau of Public Debt, and the Coast Guard. The Secretary of the Treasury is usually regarded as second only to the Secretary of State as a Cabinet adviser to the President. The Department plays a broad and significant role in formulating both monetary and fiscal policies for the national administration.

General Accounting Office (GAO).   An independent agency which controls and audits national government expenditures as an agent of the Congress. The GAO is headed by the Comptroller General who is appointed by the President with the Senate's approval for a 15-year term and can be removed only through impeachment or by a joint resolution of the Congress.

• *Significance:* The major functions carried on by the GAO include (1) prescribing accounting systems for federal agencies; (2) authorizing federal agencies to make specific expenditures (preaudit); and (3) making extensive investigations to determine the validity of the receipt and disbursement of public funds (postaudit). In short, the Congress by law determines in general how public money shall be spent, and the GAO acts as an agent of the Congress, checking on specific expenditures to ensure that each falls within the intent of the Congress. Students of finance object to the system whereby the GAO makes both the preaudit authorization and the postaudit check, holding that the President cannot reasonably be held responsible for executive spending activities if the GAO can determine the validity and reasonableness of expenditures before they are paid.

Internal Revenue Service.   A unit in the Department of the Treasury which has major responsibility for the collection of taxes except customs duties. The Internal Revenue Service is headed by a Commissioner and operates through 64 district offices, each headed by a director.

• *Significance:* The Internal Revenue Service collects over $90 billion each year, mostly in individual and corporation income taxes. Collection costs average less than 50 cents for each $100 of tax collected. Because of its discretionary powers in making decisions in specific tax cases, it has become an important agency in the lives of millions of Americans.

Tax Court of the United States.   A special agency which hears controversies between taxpayers and the Commissioner of Internal Revenue, and has jurisdiction over excess profits proceedings. It is, in fact, not a court but a quasi-judicial administrative agency. The Court consists of 16 "judges" appointed by the President with the Senate's consent, for 12-year terms. Each judge heads a division and court is held in various places throughout the country.
• *Significance:* The Tax Court provides a relatively easy and inexpensive means for taxpayers to appeal decisions made by tax officials. It relieves the regular courts of the tremendous burden of suits resulting from the far-reaching effect of federal tax programs. All decisions of the Tax Court, except those involving excess profits, may be appealed to a court of appeals and, by writ of certiorari, to the Supreme Court.

IMPORTANT CASES

Legal Tender Cases (Knox v. Lee; Parker v. Davis), 12 Wallace 457 (1871): Recognized the power of the Congress to make Treasury notes (paper money) legal tender in place of gold or silver in payment of debt.
• *Significance:* The case grew out of a wartime debt but, a few years later, the Court also upheld the issuance of paper money as legal tender in time of peace in *Juilliard v. Greenman,* 110 U.S. 421 (1884). In the *Legal Tender Cases* the Court recognized a new category of "resulting powers"—those powers which are not expressly granted nor implied from a single enumerated power but which arise from the aggregate powers of government.

Massachusetts v. Mellon and Frothingham v. Mellon, 262 U.S. 447 (1923): Rejected claims by a state that the federal grant-in-aid program to protect the health of mothers and infants was an unconstitutional invasion of the reserved powers of the states guaranteed by the 10th Amendment. In a companion case (*Frothingham v. Mellon*), the Court rejected the claim of Mrs. Frothingham that the grant-in-aid program would take her property under the guise of taxation.
• *Significance:* Three important rules were established by these cases: (1) A state cannot validly seek to protect its citizens who are also citizens of the United States from the enforcement of laws of the United States. (2) A grant-in-aid system based on voluntary acceptance of programs by the states is a political and not a judicial question. (3) An individual taxpayer who cannot show suffering and injury different from that of the general taxpaying public has no standing in court to challenge the constitutionality of tax laws (Frothingham rule). Today, under this rule, it continues to be impossible for an individual to test the constitutionality of a tax law in the federal courts.

Pollock v. Farmers Loan and Trust Co., 158 U.S. 601 (1895): Held the federal income tax law of 1894 unconstitutional on the ground that it was a direct tax and, therefore, the Congress should have apportioned it among the several states according to population as provided in Article I, section 9.

• *Significance:* The *Pollock* decision was a reversal of earlier decisions by the Court in which the validity of income taxes not apportioned according to the population had been upheld. The inequity of levying income taxes on a population basis restrained the Congress from enacting a new income tax law until 1913, when the 16th Amendment was adopted. The Amendment sidestepped the dispute of whether an income tax law is a direct or indirect tax simply by ruling out the necessity of apportionment.

South Carolina v. United States, 199 U.S. 437 (1905): Upheld a federal tax levied upon wholesale and retail liquor sales by the state of South Carolina on the ground that exemption of states from federal taxes applies only when a state carries on strictly governmental functions, not when it engages in business of a private nature. The state had argued that because all profits from liquor sales went into the state treasury, it was exercising the sovereign power of the state and should be immune from federal taxes.

• *Significance:* The *South Carolina* case laid down the fundamental rule that state immunity from federal taxation does not apply when a state enters a commercial or proprietary field. Since this decision, however, much controversy has arisen concerning the determination of what does and does not constitute an "ordinary private business" function by government. The case, along with many related decisions of more recent origin, has served to modify substantially the intergovernmental tax immunity rule laid down in *McCulloch v. Maryland,* 4 Wheaton 316 (1819).

Veazie Bank v. Fenno, 8 Wallace 533 (1869): Upheld the validity of a 10 percent tax levied by the Congress in 1866 upon notes issued by state banks for the purpose of driving them out of circulation.

• *Significance:* The *Veazie Bank* decision gave judicial acceptance to the use of a federal tax primarily for a nonrevenue regulatory purpose and it sanctioned the action of the Congress in providing a uniform currency for the United States. The objective of the tax sustained in this case has been realized, and state bank notes have been out of circulation for many years.

IMPORTANT STATUTES

Budget and Accounting Act of 1921. A law which established a national budget system and created the Bureau of the Budget and the General Accounting Office. It provides for the formulation of an annual executive budget by the Bureau under direction of the President, and for the auditing of all government expenditures by the General Accounting Office under the direction of the Comptroller General as an agent of the Congress.

• *Significance:* Prior to the enactment of the Budget and Accounting Act of 1921, the budget process was a loose and haphazard affair in which various executive agencies submitted requests to as many as 24 different House and Senate committees. No attempt was made to look at the financial picture from an over-all viewpoint, and the President had little or no voice in the entire process. Under the Act, a budget is prepared by fiscal experts under the direction of the President and is submitted as a single-package budget to the Congress, where it is assigned to revenue and appropriations committees for study. Congress can now consider the budget in the total picture of all requests for the fiscal period and in the relationship between anticipated income and proposed expenditures. Execution of the budget by the spending agencies is done under the watchful eyes of the General Accounting Office which carries on both preaudit and postaudit functions. The Budget and Accounting Act of 1921 is probably the most significant piece of fiscal control legislation to come out of the Congress, and has served to bring considerable order out of former budgetary chaos.

12

Government and Business

Antitrust Laws. Laws intended to regulate or prohibit combinations in restraint of trade, including monopolies, cartels, trusts, and interlocking directorates.

• *Significance:* The objective of antitrust action by the government is to maintain and strengthen the free enterprise system by ensuring the continuation of competition in business. Responsibility for the enforcement of antitrust laws is vested in the Antitrust Division of the Department of Justice and in the Federal Trade Commission. Since the enactment of the Sherman Act in 1890, the national government's antitrust policy has been vigorously enforced at times, while at other times it has been sporadically enforced or ignored. Enforcement has been greatly influenced by Supreme Court decisions limiting or expanding the scope of enforcement authority, by the antitrust philosophy of particular presidents and the "trust busters" of the Antitrust Division, and by the views and pressures of public opinion calling for action or accepting inaction. Much also has depended upon the circumstances of the times, antitrust action having been reduced during periods of war, defense programs, or strenuous foreign competition.

Bankruptcy. A procedure for discharging unpaid obligations through a court action which frees the individual from further liability for his debts. Bankruptcy proceedings may be initiated either by the insolvent debtor (voluntary bankruptcy) or by a required number of his creditors (involuntary bankruptcy). Such cases are usually handled by federal district courts under equity jurisdiction. The court appoints an officer who sells the bankrupt's assets and pays his creditors on a prorated basis.

• *Significance:* Bankruptcy proceedings enable persons, both human and corporate, to wipe clean a slate of hopeless debt and start anew. Some provisions of this kind are indispensable to protect the credit structure of modern business enterprise. Major federal bankruptcy acts have been passed by Congress in 1898 and 1933, and, although state legislation in this field is possible, the federal law is comprehensive and takes precedence over state enactments.

244

Some critics of bankruptcy proceedings charge that it encourages financial irresponsibility and recommend more restrictive measures concerning voluntary bankruptcy.

Blue Sky Laws.   State laws to protect investors in securities from misrepresentation and outright fraud. Blue sky laws commonly require that companies selling securities be certified by a state agency and furnish detailed information concerning their financial position.
• *Significance:* The term "blue sky" refers to the gullible investor who discovers that the securities he has purchased represent nothing of value but the blue sky above. Blue sky laws have been enacted in almost all states since the early part of the twentieth century. Although most states continue to offer some protection to buyers of securities, most of their functions have been taken over by the Securities and Exchange Commission, created by the Congress in 1934.

Bond.   A certificate of indebtedness issued by a borrower to a lender as a legal promise to repay the principal of the loan plus accrued interest. Bonds are issued by private corporations, by all levels of government, and by many government agencies and corporations. Most bonds have limited negotiability in the security markets.
• *Significance:* In recent years, bonds have greatly exceeded new stock issues in their importance in financing business expansion in the United States. Like stocks, the issuance of private corporation bonds is regulated by the Federal Securities and Exchange Commission and by regulatory agencies in most of the states. Unlike stockholders, bondholders are not part owners of the corporation but have merely lent their money to it for investment purposes.

Business Affected with a Public Interest.   Any privately owned and operated selling or service activity which as a matter of public policy has been brought under the regulatory power of government. Businesses affected with a public interest, such as public utilities, are regulated by government boards and commissions in regard to their services and rates.
• *Significance:* Many regulatory bodies have been created by national, state, and local governments when policy makers have determined that the free competition of the marketplace has become an insufficient means of protecting the right of the public to obtain satisfactory products or services at reasonable rates. Through such regulation, Americans have decided that business may operate under conditions of monopoly or near monopoly without danger to the public interest. The doctrine of "business affected with a public interest" was developed by the Supreme Court in *Munn v. Illinois,* 94 U.S. 113 (1876).

Business Cycles.   The rhythmic fluctuation of a free economy as changes occur in business activity. Business cycles, typically, involve movements from prosperity to recession or depression, followed by economic recovery and the completion of the cycle by a return to the previous high point of economic activity. A new cycle then begins.
• *Significance:* Business cycles were considered to be natural economic phe-

nomena by classical economists, and their recurrence was regarded as inevitable. Since the 1930's, however, it is no longer considered to be politically feasible to allow the cycles to run their course because of the heavy costs in unemployment and economic stagnation at low points in the cycles, and the ever-present dangers of inflation at the high points. Today, the national government increasingly employs fiscal and monetary policies to control the extremes of business cycle activity and inactivity and to promote general and continuing stability for the economy.

Caveat Emptor.   A term meaning literally, "let the buyer beware." The idea of *caveat emptor* grew out of the laissez faire doctrine that business should be free from governmental regulation and restraints, and that each consumer had a responsibility to ensure that the products he purchased were of sound value.
• *Significance: Caveat emptor* characterized American business operations during the nineteenth century when the consumer had little or no government protection and was frequently defrauded by products which were misrepresented, worthless, or dangerous.

Caveat Venditor.   A term meaning literally, "let the seller beware." *Caveat venditor* involves the acceptance by government of a responsibility to regulate business operations for the protection of consumers.
• *Significance:* The freewheeling business practices of the nineteenth century period of laissez faire and *caveat emptor* have given way, in the twentieth century, to numerous national, state, and local laws and enforcement agencies which operate in the interest of consumer protection. Businesses that sell impure foods or drugs, engage in false advertising, give short measure to buyers, sell dangerous items, or misrepresent their products, may be subject to criminal prosecution. National agencies which are particularly concerned with safeguarding consumer interests include the Food and Drug Administration of the Department of Health, Education, and Welfare, and the Federal Trade Commission. Regulation is intended to force business to present certain facts about their products for the information of the public, but sound investments and purchases still require careful buying methods by individual consumers.

Commerce.   The buying and selling of commodities, transportation and commercial intercourse, and the transmission of radio, television, and telephonic and telegraphic messages. The Constitution grants the Congress the power to regulate interstate and foreign commerce, and commerce with the Indian tribes. The states retain the power to regulate intrastate commerce.
• *Significance:* The power of the Congress to regulate interstate and foreign commerce has, over the years of American history, proved to be one of the most significant powers of the national government. Through successively broader interpretations by the Congress and the Supreme Court, the term "commerce" has come to include almost all forms of business activity, including manufacturing since 1937. Although many legal battles have been fought out over the years concerning the extent of the commerce power, the issue since 1937 has become largely a political question rather than a legal one,

to be settled by the Congress and the people and not, ordinarily, by the Supreme Court. Commerce which is intrastate may come under the regulatory power of the Congress if it directly or indirectly affects interstate commerce. Conversely, states may also regulate interstate commerce along with the national government so long as their regulation does not impede the free flow of that commerce and has a reasonable relation to the protection of the public safety, health, morals, or welfare.

Common Carrier.   Any company which offers its services to the public for the transportation of goods or persons. Common carriers include airlines, railroads, bus companies, taxicabs, ships, pipe lines, and trucking lines.
• *Significance:* Common carriers have been legally recognized throughout American history as businesses affected with a public interest because of public dependence upon their services. They may, therefore, be regulated for the public safety and convenience by the national, state, and local governments, each acting within its sphere of authority. National agencies involved in regulating interstate common carriers include the Civil Aeronautics Board, the Interstate Commerce Commission, and the Federal Power Commission. Regulation of common carriers by governments include various aspects of their services and the rates they may charge.

Copyright.   The exclusive right granted by the Copyright Office in the Library of Congress to the creative products of authors, composers, dramatists, photographers, and others. A copyright grant is made to anyone who wants one, following publication of his material and its submission to the Copyright Office. A copyright confers an exclusive privilege for a period of 28 years, with the option of renewal for another 28-year period. Typical copyrighted items include books, newspapers, magazines, musical compositions, translations, cartoons, sermons, motion pictures, photographs, paintings, maps, and charts. The copyright power is based on the constitutional grant to the Congress to promote science and the arts by granting authors "the exclusive right to their respective writings. . . ."
• *Significance:* Copyrights are intended to foster creative efforts and to reward talent, and, like patents, they constitute an exception to the laws against monopolies. The Copyright Office makes no effort to enforce the exclusive grant, however, and the individual grantee must take civil suit or injunctive action through the federal courts when he believes his copyright has been infringed.

Corporation.   A business unit created by law and owned by stockholders which is legally regarded as an artificial person. Private and public corporations are chartered under state or federal law, the former being owned by private individuals and the latter partially or wholly owned by government—national, state, or local. Corporations may enter into contracts and sue and be sued.
• *Significance:* The corporation has become the major form of business enterprise in the United States. Individually owned and partnership businesses, although more numerous than corporations, are dwarfed by the corporations in terms of volume of business, numbers of employees, assets, and in the wielding

of economic and political power. The corporate form has tended to promote urbanization, industrialization, and increasing impersonality in business life. National defense requirements, corporation mergers, and a high mortality rate for small, noncorporative business have all tended to accelerate the growth of huge corporations in recent years. National and state legislation extensively regulate the chartering of corporations, their financial and general business operations, and their impact upon competition in the market place.

Depression.   A business cycle period characterized by a serious economic slump, inadequate purchasing power, deflation, and high unemployment. Typically, major depressions have followed peak periods of prosperity when production facilities and credit have been overextended.

• *Significance:* The American economy has experienced numerous depressions of serious proportions, but all previous ones were dwarfed by the great depression of the 1930's. Classical economic theory held that depressions are inevitable in a free enterprise economy and that self-correcting economic forces set in motion by the depression would in time provide the corrective adjustments without governmental interference. Today, economic theory and analysis is aimed at preventing a depression, and most economists believe that governmental monetary and fiscal policies can prevent or quickly remedy a serious depression if they are wisely used and properly timed. Four post-World War II economic recessions have been attacked with monetary and fiscal measures, and the serious downturns in the economy have been arrested and reversed before they could assume depression proportions.

Economic Planning.   The establishment of economic goals and the means for reaching them, usually under governmental direction. Economic planning may be concerned with providing some protection against violent swings of the business cycle in a capitalistic economy. At the other extreme, it may involve total government control and direction of investment, production, consumption, and other economic forces.

• *Significance:* The national government, since the depression of the 1930's, has increasingly used economic planning to fight recessions and to promote full employment. Long-range resources planning was first begun by the National Resources Planning Board, established in 1934, which was charged with studying economic trends and recommending national policies to avoid runaway booms or major slumps in the economy. In the Employment Act of 1946, the Congress created a new planning group, the Council of Economic Advisers. The Council is charged with responsibility for short-term planning to recommend government policies which will give stability to the nation's economy, promote full employment, and avoid major booms and busts. In Communist and Socialist countries, economic planning is based on setting up national goals for a specific period, such as in a five-year plan, and the marshalling of the nation's work force and resources, often through authoritarian control, to achieve these goals.

Franchise.   A privilege conferred by government upon an individual or a corporation to operate a public utility and to use public property for the welfare or convenience of the public. Franchises are granted by the national, state, and local governments to bus companies, railroads, telephone and electric power companies, pipe lines, and other types of public services performed by private companies.

• *Significance:* In granting a franchise, a government recognizes that a condition of limited competition or natural monopoly exists and that free and unrestricted competition would not be practicable. In restricting competition, the government accepts a subsequent responsibility to regulate the service and the rates of the franchised company to ensure that it operates in the public interest. Most franchises are granted by city governments, and franchise fees constitute a sizable source of municipal funds.

Holding Company.   A corporation whose assets consist of stocks in operating companies, usually a controlling share in each of several allegedly competing companies (subsidiaries). Holding companies, although illegal under the common law, have been legalized by statute in many states. The policies and pricing of subsidiary companies are controlled through stock ownership and the membership of holding company officers on the boards of directors of subsidiaries.

• *Significance:* In the late nineteenth and early twentieth centuries, holding companies were used to establish monopoly or near-monopoly pricing conditions in certain industries, especially in electric and gas utilities. By the 1930's, holding companies were recognized as a threat to free enterprise competition and to the welfare of consumers in the gas and electric industries, and the Congress enacted the Holding Company Act of 1935 to control the operations of such companies engaged in interstate and foreign commerce. One section of this law, the so-called death sentence provision, halted the pyramiding of holding companies by limiting them to the second degree only, i.e., only two holding companies are permitted beyond the operating level. The effect of the law in dissolving many of the complicated holding company structures that had been built up over the years has generally been salutary in revitalizing competition and keeping consumer prices at reasonable levels.

Interlocking Directorates.   A means by which competing companies reduce or eliminate competition among themselves by having the same individuals as members of the boards of directors of their companies.

• *Significance:* Through interlocking directorates, companies supposedly in competition with each other could establish uniform pricing policies and take other actions of a monopolistic nature. The device came into use in the world of big business as a means of evading the provisions of the Sherman Antitrust Act prohibiting combinations in restraint of trade. This loophole was largely closed by the Clayton Act of 1914 which prohibits interlocking directorates in companies with a capitalization of $1 million if they are engaged in interstate or foreign commerce and are natural competitors.

License.   A certificate of permission granted under law by administrative officials permitting private individuals to engage in certain business or professional activities. Licensing power is exercised primarily by the state and

local governments, but the national government also uses it to regulate such fields as atomic materials, securities, market exchanges, and radio and television.
• *Significance:* Persons seeking a license must meet the requirements established by law. Discretion is exercised by administrative officials in choosing from among many qualified applicants for a limited number of licenses. The power to grant licenses includes the power to suspend, revoke, or refuse to renew licenses for cause. Licensing by government is often demanded by professional or skilled groups, such as physicians and beauty operators, to ensure proper standards and, in some cases, to restrict competition in the field.

Merger.   The pooling of assets of two companies to form a single company. Various kinds of mergers are possible, including those between competing companies (horizontal), those aimed at gaining control of raw material suppliers (vertical-backward), those involving retail outlets (vertical-forward), and those of unrelated businesses (conglomerate).
• *Significance:* For many years, mergers were regarded as reasonable business combinations not in violation of the antitrust laws. As a result of a rapidly increasing number of business mergers and growing pressure for government action, the Congress enacted the Celler Antimerger Act in 1950 as an amendment to the Clayton Act. Mergers that reduce competition or foster the growth of monopoly conditions are prohibited by the law. Many controversies have arisen concerning the application of the Celler amendment because of its vague and general language which leaves considerable discretion in the hands of enforcement officials. Most such controversies involve the question of whether the mergers will increase or decrease competition. Companies often seek approval from enforcement officials prior to undertaking a merger.

Monopoly.   A market condition characterized by the absence of competition and the artificial fixing of prices for services or commodities.
• *Significance:* Monopolies result from the tendency of business firms to establish conditions in which prices are rigidly controlled through mergers, holding companies, interlocking directorates, conspiracies to restrain trade, collusive bidding, and by driving competing firms out of the market through unrestrained price wars. In the Sherman Act of 1890, the Clayton Act of 1914, and the Federal Trade Commission Act of 1914, the national government has sought to break up monopolies and restrain their price-fixing techniques so as to foster real competition in the free enterprise system. In some cases, however, the national government has permitted and even encouraged monopolies, as, for example, in granting exclusive franchises to public utilities, in conferring patent and copyright privileges, and in fostering the export trade (Webb-Pomerene Act).

Nationalization.   The transference of ownership and operation of private enterprises to a national government. Nationalization may result from purchase or confiscation with or without compensation, and may apply to properties owned by citizens or foreign nationals.
• *Significance:* Although American nationalization has been limited to the

seizure of enemy assets during time of war, other democratic nations, such as Britain, have nationalized some of their basic industries and communications, transportation, banking, and health facilities. Nationalization of private business and industry is a goal of the Socialists and Communists, and in many countries private assets have been confiscated without compensation to the owners. Fear of nationalization has been a significant factor in limiting American private investments abroad, especially in the newly emerging nations of Asia and Africa. American constitutional guarantees limit the nationalization powers of the national government, although private property may be appropriated by law for a public purpose and with the payment of just compensation to the private owners.

Navigable Waters.   All waters within the boundaries of the United States which are or may be used as highways for interstate or foreign commerce, such as rivers, streams, lakes, and inlets.
• *Significance:* The Supreme Court in its decision in *The Daniel Ball* case, (10 Wall. 557 [1871]), declared that the jurisdiction of the Congress extended to all natural waterways which can be used for the transmission of commerce among the states and with foreign nations. Although the beds of such waterways are under state jurisdiction, no state may constitutionally impede or obstruct the flow of commerce on the waters. Approval for construction of bridges over navigable waters by state or local governments must be obtained from the national government through the United States Corps of Engineers.

Oligopoly.   A market condition wherein the supply of a commodity is controlled by a few companies, consequently limiting competition. Oligopoly is sometimes referred to as a situation of partial monopoly because the market price can be fixed through collusion or passive competition.
• *Significance:* Oligopoly conditions have tended to increase in many areas of the nation's economy in recent years, especially as a result of business mergers. They constitute an especially difficult enforcement problem in the national government's efforts to maintain effective competition in business because competition appears to exist when it may not exist in fact.

Original Cost Theory.   An approach used in fixing rates to determine a fair return in profits for public utilities regulated by government. The original cost theory is based on ascertaining the total investment made by the stockholders when the corporation was organized, plus subsequent capital expansions, less depreciation.
• *Significance:* The original cost theory is usually favored by utility companies if their major investments have been made during periods of high cost. If made during periods of deflation, "reproduction cost" would be regarded more favorably. Federal regulatory agencies generally follow the original cost less depreciation theory modified by the "prudent investment theory." Supporters of the original cost thesis argue that it is the only way of accurately computing a company's actual investment and that all other theories are hypothetical and subjective. Those who oppose original cost regard it as inaccurate and unfair because of its failure to take inflationary and deflationary factors into account.

Original Package Doctrine.   A limitation on the state taxing powers which exempts commodities from state jurisdiction so long as they remain in their original shipping containers. The Supreme Court applied the original package doctrine to products imported from foreign countries (*Brown v. Maryland,* 12 Wheaton 419 [1827]) and to those commodities produced in the United States and shipped in interstate commerce (*Leisy v. Hardin,* 135 U.S. 100 [1890]).
• *Significance:* The Supreme Court's original package doctrine was intended to restrain the states from imposing a burden upon the flow of interstate and foreign commerce. Otherwise, commodities could be subjected to a series of crippling taxes levied by each state that the commodities passed through on their way to their final destination.

Patent.   An exclusive grant to an inventor by which the national government extends to an individual or corporation "the right to exclude others from making, using, or selling the invention throughout the United States" for a period of 17 years. Patent grants are made only for bona fide "discoveries," and not for improvements upon existing inventions. They apply to any new machine, design, process, composition, substance, or plant variety. The Constitution grants the Congress exclusive power to grant patents. Patents are granted by the United States Patent Office in the Department of Commerce.
• *Significance:* In 1961, the United States Patent Office issued its three millionth patent since the Act of Congress of 1836 establishing it. In recent years, patent applications have been made at the rate of 1500 each week, and there is a backlog of almost 200,000 applications in various stages of processing. As the Founding Fathers intended, the monopoly granted to inventors has served as a major incentive in developing the thousands of useful products which typify the American economy. The United States has entered into patent agreements with most foreign states, although a few, including the Communist countries, have jeopardized inventor's international patent rights by refusing to conclude reciprocal protection agreements.

Proprietary Function.   A government activity involving business-type operations ordinarily carried on by private companies. Proprietary functions include such activities as supplying electricity and gas, operating recreational facilities, garbage collection, transportation, and the liquor business.
• *Significance:* Governments engage in proprietary functions to secure revenue, to provide proper regulation of certain activities, or to offer services that private companies cannot or will not provide. Neither level of government can tax the other level's purely governmental functions, but the problem of distinguishing between proprietary and ordinary governmental activities has been a troublesome one for the courts. For example, the supplying of water to a city was held by the courts to be a regular function of government, whereas the bottling and selling of mineral waters by a state was held to be a proprietary function.

Prudent Investment Theory.   An approach used in fixing rates to determine a fair return in profits for public utilities regulated by government. In its application the rate base is determined by ascertaining the original cost of investments in the utility and subtracting from this figure those which have been imprudent or wasteful.

• *Significance:* The prudent investment theory is based on the assumption that it would be unrealistic to include imprudent or dishonest investments in calculating the rate base of a utility for determining a fair return on investment. The Supreme Court in recent years has favored the use of the prudent investment theory by federal regulatory agencies, although it has not tried to establish a single formula (*FPC v. Hope Natural Gas Co.,* 320 U.S. 591 [1943]). The prudent investment theory has also been favored by many state courts for use by state regulatory agencies.

Public Service Commission. A regulatory agency found in each of the states which regulates the rates and services of public utilities operating within the state. Public service commissions vary in size from one to seven members, with most states fixing the number at three. Private utility companies regulated by the commissions include gas and electric suppliers, buses, interurban railway transit systems, taxicabs, oil and gas pipe lines, telephone and telegraph services, and in some states, municipal utilities. Some of the larger cities have also established public service commissions, and in many other cities the city council functions in this role.

• *Significance:* Public service commissions are expected to regulate utilities in the public interest to provide good service and fair rates for consumers. In most states, their efforts are hampered by complicated, court-imposed valuation formulas for determining rates, by inadequate operating funds, and by politically appointed staffs. In some states, the regulated companies are accused of having an inordinate influence over the commissions, which undermines the latter's regulator role and results in higher rates. In many cases, utility companies operating in interstate channels are more effectively regulated by federal commissions than are their counterparts in the states. Organized consumer groups in some states have successfully exerted political pressure to strengthen the regulatory function of commissions.

Public Utility. A privately owned business which performs an essential service for the community and is extensively regulated by government. Congress and the state legislatures determine the need for public utilities within the nation and the states respectively. They establish general criteria for regulation and create government commissions to perform the regulatory function subject to review by the courts. Typical examples of public utilities include transportation facilities, electric and gas suppliers, communication services, and water suppliers.

• *Significance:* A public utility is given a license or franchise by government when noncompetitive conditions are desirable (natural monopoly). When government grants franchises to private businesses to carry on operations in the public interest free from competition, it has a resulting responsibility to regulate their services and rates. Many Supreme Court decisions have concerned the types of businesses which can be regulated as public utilities, the respective regulatory spheres of the nation and the states, and the methods of calculating a fair return for the company in fixing rates.

Public Works.   Improvements in public facilities financed or built by government for the public welfare and convenience. Public works include such projects as parks, bridges, public buildings, roads, sewers, dams, harbors, housing, hospitals, canals, reclamation, irrigation, and navigation.

• *Significance:* Public works projects are important not only in providing additional facilities for public benefit, but they are also useful in carrying out countercyclical fiscal policies to combat economic recessions. Economists generally agree that public improvements should be carefully planned in advance and, during an economic downturn, be quickly put into effect. Governments on all three levels generally cooperate in carrying out public works programs, with major financing usually provided by the national government. In addition to stimulating the economy by increasing purchasing power and reducing unemployment, public works can greatly strengthen the nation by meeting present and future needs.

Rate Making.   The determination by government regulatory agencies of the charges which public utilities will be permitted to levy for their services to the public. Rate-making agencies usually fix only maximum rates, although minimum rates may be fixed in the public interest to avoid rate wars.

• *Significance:* Rate making is one of the most difficult problems of utility regulation, involving the problem of protecting consumer interests while permitting rates high enough for the utility to earn a fair return. Rates are usually fixed to give a return of from 5 to 8 percent, but the difficulty remains of determining the base on which this profit is to be calculated. Utilities often appeal to the courts when they regard their return as too small. Theories of valuation on which rate making has been based include original cost, reproduction cost, market value, and prudent investment; federal regulatory agencies generally follow the original cost approach, modified by prudent investment.

Reproduction Cost Theory.   An approach used in fixing rates to determine a fair return in profits for public utilities regulated by government. The reproduction cost theory is based on ascertaining the cost of reproducing the assets of a utility at current prices less depreciation over the period of their use.

• *Significance:* The reproduction cost theory is favored by utilities during periods of inflation because higher prices tend to increase the size of the rate base on which rates and a fair return are computed. The case for the reproduction cost theory is based on its realistic acceptance of current market conditions as the basis for rate making, whereas the case against it is based on the view that a fair return can be accurately determined only if based on an actual investment figure (original cost theory) and not one established by government rate makers.

Restraint of Trade.   The use in the business world of trusts, monopolies, price fixing, collusion, conspiracy, or other devices and practices which hamper or eliminate a market economy based on free competition in buying and selling goods and services. The phrase is used in the Sherman Act of 1890 wherein it forbids any "conspiracy in the restraint of trade. . . ."

• *Significance:* Although the laissez-faire theory of free enterprise calls for economic freedom from governmental controls, some measure of regulation of business and commerce has proved necessary to maintain free competition. Major federal statutes which have sought to prevent private actions in restraint of trade and free competition include the Sherman Act of 1890, the Clayton Act of 1914, and the Federal Trade Commission Act of 1914.

Rule of Reason.   A Supreme Court position which modified the enforcement of the Sherman Act of 1890 by forbidding only those business combinations which were "unreasonably restrictive" of competition. The Court held that size alone is not a factor in restraint of trade; the government has to show that monopoly was the intent of accused violators to gain a conviction. The Supreme Court's rule of reason was laid down in two cases, *Standard Oil of New Jersey v. United States,* 221 U.S. 1 (1910), and *United States v. American Tobacco Co.,* 221 U.S. 106 (1911).
* *Significance:* Although the Congress in the Sherman Act had banned every contract or combination in restraint of trade, the Supreme Court modified it by following the common law rule of reason. This is a pointed example of how laws enacted by the Congress may be substantially modified or altered through judicial interpretation. Although public indignation was aroused by the new rule, the decision has been sustained. The result has been a haphazard enforcement of the Sherman Act in which government prosecutors and large business concerns have sought to anticipate what the courts might regard as "reasonable" or "unreasonable" business activity.

Subsidy.   Financial aid bestowed by government upon private individuals to improve their economic position. Subsidies may be direct, as in the payment of sums of money to shipbuilders and farmers, or indirect, as in the tariff which protects American business, labor, and agriculture from foreign competition.
* *Significance:* Although subsidies are granted to private individuals by all three levels of American government, the national government has been the most active. Since Alexander Hamilton first proposed subsidies in his Financial Program, they have been a continuing and significant function of the national government, amounting to billions of dollars annually in recent years. Major beneficiaries of government subsidies are or have been railroads, airlines, farmers, businessmen, home builders, defense contractors, the unemployed, and veterans. In some cases, subsidies to one group may imperil the economic position of another group, as, for example, the effect on railroads of extensive subsidies to airlines.

Trademark.   A name, mark, or symbol used by a manufacturer or dealer to identify his product or service to the consuming public. Trademarks are granted by the Patent Office through a procedure similar to that for obtaining patents. Registered trademarks are valid for 20 years provided registrants file affidavits with the Patent Office every five years attesting to their use, and are renewable for subsequent 20-year periods. Trademark protection is left up to registrants who can take civil suit action in the courts when infringements occur.
* *Significance:* Much of the confusion surrounding trademarks was eliminated

when the Congress enacted the Lanham Trademark Act of 1946, which revised and codified numerous federal statutes relating to trademarks. Like patents and copyrights, a trademark bestows a monopoly right upon an individual or company. Trademarks are significant not only to registrants whose sales of products may be increased through such identification, but to consumers as well who are protected from a welter of confusion of similar marks and symbols when making purchases.

Trust.   Two or more corporations linked together in a common business policy as a result of the assigning of voting rights of a majority of stockholders in each corporation to a single group of trustees. The term is also commonly used to describe any huge corporation or group of corporations which pursue monopolistic policies in the production or supplying of goods or services.
• *Significance:* The trust as a business combination was used extensively to reduce or eliminate competition among previously competing companies, until outlawed by the Sherman Act of 1890. The Supreme Court, however, subsequently modified the antitrust provisions with its "rule of reason" which applied the Sherman Act only to those combinations which are unreasonably restrictive of competition and in which a clear intention of monopoly can be shown. Many trusts continued to flourish until the late 1930's when the Department of Justice engaged in a vigorous trust-busting campaign. In recent years, the Department has turned its attention to preventing mergers and collusive practices which, like the trusts of an earlier period, tend to reduce competition.

Unfair Trade Practice.   Any business activity which deceives or misleads the consumer and results in his being sold shoddy, dangerous, or overpriced goods or services. Examples of unfair trade practices include false and misleading advertising, misbranding, improper labeling, conspiracies to fix prices, collusive bidding, discrimination against buyers, price cutting to eliminate competition, and other practices in restraint of trade.
• *Significance:* Unfair trade practices were outlawed by the Congress in two laws enacted in 1914, the Clayton Act and the Federal Trade Commission Act. The former forbids price discrimination, price cutting to restrain trade, and purchases of stock among competitors. The latter seeks to promote fair competition and, through the Wheeler-Lea Act amendments of 1938, outlaws unfair and deceptive practices and false advertising of foods, drugs, cosmetics, and other commodities. Both acts are administered by the Federal Trade Commission. Consumer interests are also protected by the Food and Drug Administration of the Health, Education, and Welfare Department, which safeguards against misbranding, adulteration, and false labeling.

Usury.   The charging of interest in excess of the maximum rate permitted by law. State usury laws provide for civil and criminal actions against persons or lending institutions charging illegal interest rates.
• *Significance:* All states have enacted usury laws, although the legal maximum rates permissible vary considerably. Provisions of usury laws are particularly effective in holding down interest rates charged by small loan companies and

pawnbrokers. Usury laws have gained in importance as the American economy has become increasingly dependent upon consumer credit.

IMPORTANT AGENCIES

Antitrust Division.   One of the major divisions of the Department of Justice which has responsibility for enforcement of the antitrust laws.
• *Significance:* The forcefulness with which the national government has carried on its antimonopoly programs has depended often on the person chosen by the President and the Attorney General to be placed in charge of the Antitrust Division. For example, when Thurman W. Arnold, a law professor dedicated to breaking up trusts, headed the Antitrust Division, almost as many legal proceedings were initiated in the five years of his tenure, from 1938 to 1943, as had been started in the preceding half century since the enactment of the Sherman Act. Stanley N. Barnes as chief "trust buster" under the Eisenhower Administration, and Lee Loevinger of the Kennedy Administration have compiled good records in vigorously enforcing antitrust laws in recent years.

Civil Aeronautics Board (CAB).   A five-member independent regulatory agency which controls the business aspects of American airlines engaged in domestic and foreign transportation. Board members are appointed by the President with the Senate's approval. The CAB was established under the Civil Aeronautics Act of 1938 which gave it responsibility for the "encouragement and development" of civil aviation. Its functions include the regulation of the economic aspects of domestic air lines and of the operations of both domestic and foreign air lines in the United States. It grants permission to companies to fly specific routes, exercises jurisdiction over rates and fares, and regulates mergers and other business relations in the interest of maintaining competition.
• *Significance:* In a reshuffling of responsibilities under the Federal Aviation Act of 1958, the powers for making and enforcing safety and traffic regulations in the air were transferred to a new Federal Aviation Agency. The CAB still plays an important role in investigating air accidents.

Council of Economic Advisers (CEA).   A staff agency in the Executive Office of the President. It consists of three leading economists who advise the President on measures to maintain stability in the nation's economy. The Council was established by the Congress in the Employment Act of 1946 and was given responsibility by that Act to formulate proposals "to maintain employment, production, and purchasing power." The Council's recommendations are included in the President's annual economic report to the Congress in which he sets forth the economic problems facing the nation and recommends legislative solutions.
• *Significance:* The Council of Economic Advisers reflects the fact that the American people look to their President for leadership in keeping the nation's economy healthy. The Council has played a significant role in recommending specific fiscal and monetary policies to help overcome several post-World War II recessions.

Department of Commerce.   One of the ten major departments of the national administration headed by a Secretary with Cabinet standing. The Department of Commerce and Labor, founded in 1903, was split in 1913 by the Congress into the two separate departments of Commerce and Labor. Units found in the Department, and the major responsibility of each, include (1) the Bureau of the Census conducts decennial census; (2) the Coast and Geodetic Survey maps coastlines and waterways; (3) the Foreign Commerce Bureau promotes American business interests abroad; (4) the Federal Maritime Board regulates water carriers in foreign commerce; (5) the Maritime Administration administers grants to shipbuilders and operators; (6) the National Bureau of Standards maintains basic units for testing and measuring in business and industry; (7) the Bureau of Public Roads adminsters highway programs; (8) the Patent Office examines and grants patents and trademarks; and (9) the Weather Bureau forecasts weather and provides meteorological data.
• *Significance:* The Department of Commerce has major responsibility for providing services for the business community. It promotes and protects the interest of businessmen in the government and abroad. It is primarily a service, rather than a regulatory agency. The Secretary of Commerce is, typically, a businessman or a person who has been identified as friendly to the business community.

Export-Import Bank of Washington.   A government corporation which makes loans to foreign and domestic businessmen to promote the flow of trade. The Export-Import Bank was originally chartered under the laws of the District of Columbia in 1934. Since that time, the Bank has financed over $10 billion in loans and has earned a profit of about $1 billion.
• *Significance:* The Export-Import Bank was originally created to foster trade between the United States and the Soviet Union and with Latin America, but its operations have become almost world-wide in scope. Its loans must be repaid in American dollars, and equipment needed by the party receiving the loan must be purchased in the United States. The Bank has become an important contributor to the aid programs to underdeveloped countries, financing the building of steel mills, roads, dams, manufacturing plants, and other projects.

Federal Aviation Agency (FAA).   An independent agency, headed by an Administrator, which makes and enforces traffic and safety regulations for civil aviation. It was created by the Federal Aviation Act of 1958 which provided for the transfer of functions of the expired Civil Aeronautics Administration and the safety responsibilities of the Civil Aeronautics Board (CAB) to the new FAA. Its activities include control over airspace of the United States for both civil and military aircraft. It was also given a general responsibility by the Congress to promote, encourage, and develop civil aviation.
• *Significance:* The traffic and safety functions of the FAA have grown as increasing numbers of civil and military airplanes fill the skies. Its main concerns are licensing planes and pilots, providing regular and emergency landing fields, mapping, lighting, and marking air routes, and encouraging research.

Federal Communications Commission (FCC).   A seven-member independent regulatory commission which controls interstate and foreign communication via radio, television, telephone, telegraph, and cable. The FCC was created by and administers the Federal Communications Act of 1934. Under the Act, the FCC grants licenses to broadcasters, enforces regulations prohibiting indecent language and lotteries, and requires equal time for political candidates. The FCC has no power to regulate rates charged sponsors of radio and televison programs, but the Congress has designated telephone, telegraph, and cable services as "common carriers" and, therefore, subject to extensive regulation of rates and services.

• *Significance:* The major responsibility of the FCC in recent years has been that of granting licenses to broadcasters. A limited number of radio frequencies and television channels are available. A television license, for example, is granted free by the FCC but may be worth millions of dollars to the licensee. As a result, the FCC has often had to select from a number of applicants who may bring various kinds of political pressure to bear on the commissioners, as revealed in congressional probes late in the 1950's. Although its regulation of broadcasting is exercised exclusively, it shares regulation of telephone services with state utility commissions. The latter control rates and services of independent telephone companies and local calls, whereas the FCC controls most long-distance calls and all telegraph and cable services.

Federal Deposit Insurance Corporation (FDIC).   A government corporation created in 1933 to insure depositors' accounts in participating banks for up to $10,000 for each account. The FDIC insurance system is financed through annual assessments levied on the privately owned banks. Member banks of the Federal Reserve System must participate and nonmember banks may request to join the program. The FDIC is directed by the Comptroller of the Currency and two directors appointed by the President and the Senate.

• *Significance:* The FDIC program is aimed at promoting stability in the banking system by maintaining the confidence of depositors that their money is safe. Prior to the establishment of the government's guarantee, "runs" on individual banks and general bank "panics" were quite common. They were difficult to control because banks do not normally keep enough cash on hand to meet widespread demands from depositors for their money. Because such fear is restrained by absolute guarantees of the national government offered through the FDIC, the banking system and, as a consequence, the entire American economy have achieved greater stability. All but a small fraction of the commercial bank and trust companies in the United States are insured by the FDIC. The Federal Savings and Loan Insurance Corporation (FSLIC) similarly insures each depositor's account for up to $10,000 in all federally chartered and in most state chartered savings and loan associations.

Federal Maritime Board (FMB).   A three-member regulatory agency in the Department of Commerce which controls rates and services of water carriers engaged in foreign commerce and related dock and wharf facilities. Members are appointed by the President with the Senate's approval, and one of the three is designated chairman by the President. Decisions made by the FMB are carried out by the Maritime Administration, a related administrative agency also located in the Department of Commerce. The FMB's authority includes the approval of routes, the settling of disputes, and the prescribing of working conditions for seamen.

• *Significance:* The Congress, in replacing the Maritime Commission in 1950, established two agencies so that the regulatory and service functions could be exercised separately. Foreign shippers under Maritime Board regulation are freer from government controls than are coastal and inland waterway shippers under Interstate Commerce Commission jurisdiction. The Board's powers over rates are limited to prohibiting discriminatory practices among American shippers. The Maritime Administration aids shipbuilders and operators through the payment of "construction differentials" and "operating differentials" as subsidies to enable American shippers to compete with foreign companies.

Federal Power Commission (FPC).   A five-member independent regulatory commission which controls the production and the interstate transmission and sale of electrical energy and the interstate transportation and sale of natural gas. Commissioners are appointed by the President with the Senate's approval. The FPC was created as a Cabinet committee in 1920, and given its independent status by the Federal Power Act of 1930. Its functions include granting licenses to private companies to build hydroelectric plants on navigable waters, determining wholesale rates for electric power transmitted across state lines, regulating security issues of private power companies, planning for multipurpose river basin development, developing power resources at government-built dams, and controlling pipeline transmissions and sales of natural gas.

• *Significance:* National regulation through the FPC of electrical power and natural gas operations of private utility companies stemmed largely from the inability of state utility commissions to protect the public interest in these areas. The FPC has engaged in extensive studies and detailed investigations to determine fair prices and reasonable services, rather than relying on information supplied by utility companies at formal hearings, a practice which characterizes much state regulation. The major issues in this area in recent years have been whether the national government or private utility companies should develop some of the few remaining sites for major dams, and the scope of natural gas regulation.

Federal Trade Commission (FTC).   A five-member independent regulatory commission created by Congress in 1914 to promote fair competition in business and to restrict unfair business practices in interstate and foreign commerce. Commissioners are appointed by the President with the Senate's approval for seven-year terms. The FTC enforces the Clayton and the Federal Trade Commission Acts of 1914. It seeks to prevent illegal combinations in restraint of trade, deception, price discriminations, price fixing, interlocking directorates, fraudulent advertising of foods, drugs, and cosmetics, and other business activities which reduce competition or endanger or defraud the consumer. The operations of the FTC include making rules and regulations to establish a code of fair competition, holding hearings concerning alleged violations, and enforcing decisions through cease and desist orders and with injunctions granted by federal courts.

• *Significance:* Most of the work of the FTC is carried on through the persuasion of officials of various businesses to cease some activity of doubtful legality. The Commission has played a relatively minor role in enforcing antimonopoly legislation and has directed most of its efforts toward protecting consumer interests by preventing deceptive advertising, fraud, and the sale of dangerous products. Most observers credit the FTC with raising the ethical level of business operations in the United States.

Interstate Commerce Commission (ICC).   An 11-member independent regulatory commission, created in 1887, which regulates the business operations, services, and rates of interstate carriers. Commissioners are appointed by the President and confirmed by the Senate for seven-year terms. The jurisdiction of the ICC extends to railroads, express companies, bus and truck companies, oil pipe lines, intercoastal and inland waterway carriers, and terminal facilities used in transporting goods or persons. The ICC enforces the Interstate Commerce Act of 1887 and six other supplementary statutes, plus numerous amendments. It employs a staff of over 2,000 attorneys, investigators, economists, examiners, and technicians. Its responsibilities include fixing rates, both maximum and minimum, controlling poolings and consolidations of operating companies, regulating their sales of stocks and bonds, prescribing accounting systems, granting permits and licenses, and providing traffic management.
• *Significance:* The ICC was the first of the independent regulatory commissions, all of which have come to play a major role in the national government's regulation of substantial sectors of the nation's economy. The ICC, like the others, performs a threefold function of making rules and regulations (quasi-legislative), administering them, and holding hearings concerning violations and disputes (quasi-judicial). Commissioners are divided into three-member panels to carry out most of the routine work of the ICC. The role of the ICC has become increasingly difficult as competition among the various carriers has intensified in recent years. Decisions of the ICC can be appealed to the federal courts for review to ensure protection of property rights from arbitrary actions.

Post Office Department.   One of the ten major departments in the national administration. The Postmaster General who heads the Department is appointed by the President with the Senate's approval and is a Cabinet officer. The national chairman of the party which wins the presidency often receives the appointment in a new administration. The Post Office Department operates 35,000 post offices around the country. In addition to carrying the mail the Department operates a parcel-post service, a system of registering, certifying, and insuring mail, postal savings, money orders, C.O.D. and special delivery services, and sells government bonds.
• *Significance:* The Post Office is the biggest business operation in the world. Each year the Department incurs a substantial deficit in its operations, resulting mainly from the fact that many politically powerful groups are subsidized through postal operations. These subsidies include below-cost rates for certain types of mail, including business advertising, books, newspapers, and magazines. Free postage privileges are granted to various groups, and rail, air, and other carriers are paid high prices to carry the mails. Although the Congress has

raised rates in recent years, as recommended by the Hoover Commission and several Presidents, they have not been raised high enough to overcome deficits.

Securities and Exchange Commission (SEC).   A five-member independent regulatory commission created by the Securities Exchange Act of 1934 to regulate the buying and selling of securities (stocks, bonds, etc.). Commissioners are appointed by the President with the Senate's approval, for five-year terms. In addition to the Act of 1934, the SEC enforces the Securities Act of 1933 which compels full disclosure of information concerning new security issues, and the Public Utility Holding Company Act of 1935 under which the SEC tries to limit mergers and combinations of utility companies.

• *Significance:* The creation of the SEC and adoption by Congress of the Acts of 1933 and 1934 grew out of the shocking disclosures of deception, manipulation, fraud, and dishonesty revealed by a Senate investigation of causes of the stock market crash of 1929. The SEC does not guarantee the financial soundness or money-making possibilities of any security; it merely requires disclosure of all pertinent information to prospective buyers and forbids any attempts to manipulate prices.

Small Business Administration (SBA).   An independent agency in the national government, established to make loans to small businesses and to assist them in obtaining government contracts. The SBA was given temporary status by the Congress in 1953, and was expanded and made a permanent agency in 1958. Some of its operations since 1961 have been carried on through small business investment companies around the nation. Principal functions of SBA include financing plant expansion and modernization, aiding disaster victims, helping businessmen to cut through red tape to secure government procurement contracts, and giving managerial advice to small firms. Applicants for loans must show they have been turned down by private banks; the maximum amount per loan was raised, in 1961, to $400,000.

• *Significance:* The SBA was the first agency established for the specific purpose of aiding small business. There are approximately 4 million small businesses in the United States today with an annual turnover rate of about 10 percent. The SBA has a revolving fund of $650 million which gives it a measure of freedom from dependence upon annual budget grants from the Congress. Although the agency was criticized in its early operations for granting, mainly, large loans to sizable businesses, it has increased the number of its loans and reduced the average amount of each loan to about $40,000, in recent years.

IMPORTANT CASES

Brown v. Maryland, 12 Wheaton 419 (1827): Established the "original package" doctrine, which holds that the authority of the Congress over foreign commerce does not end until the merchandise arrives at its ultimate destination, the contents of the package are sold or removed for the purpose of selling, and they become commingled with the general property of a state. The case invalidated a law of Maryland which had required importers of foreign goods to obtain a license before being permitted to sell them.

• *Significance:* The original package doctrine established in the *Brown* case remains a significant factor in restricting state interference with foreign commerce. The regulatory power of the Congress continues to be more extensive over foreign than interstate commerce, resulting from the vast powers exercised by the national government in foreign affairs. However, in *Leisy v. Hardin,* 135 U.S. 100 (1890), the Court expanded the original package doctrine to include products shipped in interstate as well as foreign commerce.

Cooley v. Board of Wardens, 12 Howard 299 (1851): Upheld the right of the states to regulate interstate commerce so long as the Congress has not already covered the field with its regulations and so long as the subject regulated by the states is not of a nature to require exclusive national regulation. The case involved local regulations for port pilots, which were upheld as a reasonable regulation of interstate commerce since such regulation does not lend itself to a national uniform policy.
• *Significance:* The *Cooley* case established the precedent on which a vast amount of state regulation of interstate commerce is based today. By permitting states to enter the field, the Court recognized that the national government would be unable to provide all of the regulations needed to control the flow of commerce. Under the *Cooley* rule, the permissible extent of state regulation of interstate commerce in the absence of federal regulation is left to the courts to decide.

Gibbons v. Ogden, 9 Wheaton 1 (1824): Nullified a state grant giving exclusive rights to navigate certain state waters. It was the first case involving the commerce clause, in which the powers of the Congress to regulate interstate commerce were broadly interpreted by Chief Justice Marshall and the Court. They defined interstate commerce to include not only traffic but all commercial intercourse. The Court held that congressional control over interstate commerce includes navigation.
• *Significance:* The *Gibbons* case opened the door to a vast expansion of national control over commerce through liberal interpretations of the commerce power. Today, the powers of the Congress to regulate interstate commerce include the regulation of transportation, communications, buying and selling, and manufacturing. There are few areas of economic activity remaining outside the regulatory power of the Congress.

Munn v. Illinois, 94 U.S. 113 (1876): Held that a state could validly fix maximum rates for a "business affected with a public interest." Regulation of a privately owned grain warehouse by the state of Illinois was upheld on the ground that when a proprietor devotes his property to a public use, he "must submit to be controlled by the public for the common good. . . ."
• *Significance:* The *Munn* case was a landmark in establishing the power of government to regulate businesses other than public utilities. National and state legislatures have continued to use the flexible criterion of "business affected with a public interest" to regulate many business activities.

Smyth v. Ames, 169 U.S. 466 (1898): Declared, in an historic rate-making case, that government regulatory agencies must consider a number of factors in fixing rates, rather than a single one. The facts in the case involved a dispute over rate-setting for Nebraska railroads, in which the government agency based its formula chiefly on "reproduction cost," and the railroads demanded that the rate base be "original cost." The Court held that many factors should be considered in determining fair value, including original cost, cost of improvements, value of securities, reproduction cost, earning capacity, and operating expenses.

• *Significance:* Because due process requires that rates fixed by government for private businesses be fair and reasonable, the problem of determining the base upon which the fair return will be calculated is a basic one. In recent years, the Court has modified the *Smyth* decision, adopting the "prudent investment" theory as a guide and using a pragmatic approach to determine whether the rates permit companies to operate successfully (*FPC v. Hope Natural Gas Co.,* 320 U.S. 591 [1943]).

IMPORTANT STATUTES

Atomic Energy Acts of 1946, 1954.   The Act of 1946 created the Atomic Energy Commission (AEC) to control and develop the uses of atomic energy. Private mining of fissionable materials was permitted, but all other aspects of atomic energy were kept under strict government control. The Act of 1954 modified the public monopoly by permitting private development and operation of atomic power plants and the use of nuclear fuels and the sale of by-products by private firms under government licensing.

• *Significance:* The first Atomic Energy Act placed atomic energy, which had been developed by the military, under civilian control. Growing Soviet achievements in the atomic field awakened the Congress to the need to stimulate more rapid development of atomic energy for industrial purposes. As a result, the second Act, which sought to unleash private energies within limits of government control, was passed. Because of the extremely high cost of producing electricity in atomic power plants, the government must contribute a major portion of the cost in building private facilities. Considerable government effort is also going into research to try to develop cheaper power.

Clayton Act of 1914.   A major antitrust act which was aimed at increasing competition in business. Provisions of the Clayton Act include the forbidding of price cutting and other abuses which tend to weaken competition, restricting corporations from acquiring stock in competing firms or building interlocking directorates, making corporation officers individually liable for violations, and facilitating civil suit procedures by injured parties. Labor unions and agricultural organizations not carrying on business for profit were exempted from the provisions of the Act.

• *Significance:* The Clayton Act was intended to supplement and reinforce the Sherman Act of 1890, which had been weakened by the Supreme Court's interpretation limiting its application to "unreasonable" combinations in restraint of trade. The Act was aimed at reducing the confusion surrounding the Sherman Act by more clearly defining unfair business practices. Enforcement of the

Clayton Act, however, has been weakened through administrative unconcern and judicial tolerance, except for a few periods of vigorous enforcement by the Antitrust Division and the Federal Trade Commission.

Employment Act of 1946.   The Act establishes a responsibility for the national government to maintain stability in the nation's economy. A Council of Economic Advisers (CEA) was created by the Act and placed in the Executive Office to advise the President on economic matters. The Act requires the President to make an annual economic report to the Congress setting forth the major economic problems confronting the nation and recommending appropriate legislation.

• *Significance:* The Employment Act of 1946 was the first legislation to recognize a continuing responsibility of government to use its fiscal powers to promote the nation's economic well-being. Specific goals of the Act include the maintenance of high levels of production, employment, and purchasing power. Since 1946, many demands have been made to include price stability as an additional responsibility of government. Congress has created a Joint Committee on the Economic Report, with seven members from each chamber, to study the President's recommendations and to recommend legislative consideration of specific programs. Although some recommendations and decisions undertaken under the Act have been controversial, the acceptance by government of a responsibility to combat economic downturns has been generally accepted by the American public.

Natural Gas Act of 1938.   An act which placed the regulation of the interstate shipment (largely by pipelines) and sale of natural gas under the Federal Power Commission (FPC).

• *Significance:* Much controversy has surrounded the regulation of natural gas by the FPC, especially since manufactured gas is not subject to federal regulation. On two occasions, the Congress has passed bills freeing the natural gas industry from federal regulation. The first was vetoed by President Harry Truman; the second was supported by President Dwight Eisenhower but vetoed because of the distasteful tactics of natural gas lobbyists.

Robinson-Patman Act of 1936.   An antitrust measure, called the Anti-Chain Store Act, which seeks to curb transactions in which large purchasers receive special discounts and rebates which tend to injure competitors and reduce competition.

• *Significance:* The Robinson-Patman Act was pushed through the Congress by pressures from small independent retail merchants who claimed that the big chain stores were being given favored treatment by manufacturers and wholesalers. Difficulties in enforcing the measure have resulted in the continuing growth of chain stores and discount houses and a reduction in the number of independent merchants.

Sherman Antitrust Act of 1890.   The basic federal antimonopoly law which forbids "every contract, combination . . . or conspiracy in the restraint of trade or commerce." Enforcement of the Act is provided through criminal penalties, civil suit action with triple damages to injured parties, injunction, and seizure of property. Responsibility for enforcement is vested in the Antitrust Division of the Department of Justice.

• *Significance:* The Sherman Act was a recognition by the Congress that, paradoxical as it might appear to be, governmental intervention in the free economy was essential to preserve competition and free enterprise. Soon after its enactment, the Act was seriously crippled in two major Supreme Court tests. In the first, the Court held that manufacturing trusts were not engaged in commerce and, therefore, could be regulated only by the states (*United States v. E. C. Knight Co.,* 156 U.S. 1 [1895]). In the second, the Court laid down the "rule of reason" by which not *every* combination in restraint of trade (as the Congress had explicitly stated in the Act) was illegal, but only those *unreasonably* so (*Standard Oil Co. v. United States,* 221 U.S. 1 [1910]). To supplement and reinforce the Sherman Act, the Congress has since adopted the Clayton Act of 1914, the Federal Trade Commission Act of 1914, the Robinson-Patman Act of 1936, and the Celler Antimerger Act of 1950. The history of the Sherman Act demonstrates the great influence of the Supreme Court, the President, the Attorney General, and other high officials in interpreting the language of the Act narrowly or broadly and in vigorously or reluctantly enforcing it.

Webb-Pomerene Act of 1918.   An act which exempts business associations engaged in export trade to foreign lands from the provisions of the antitrust laws. Such organizations must register with the Federal Trade Commission (FTC).

• *Significance:* The Webb-Pomerene Act was enacted to promote American foreign trade and to put American exporters on a competitive basis with countries which have little or no effective antitrust or anticartel legislation.

13

Government and Labor

AFL-CIO.   The American Federation of Labor and Congress of Industrial Organizations, a federation of national and international unions which merged in 1955. Approximately 74 percent of the unions, comprising 80 percent of the membership of organized labor, are members of the federation. The remainder of organized labor is in independent unions, such as the Teamsters, the Mine Workers, the Railroad Brotherhoods, the Longshoreman, and a number of smaller unions. Over 130 unions are members of the AFL-CIO, with a total membership of 15 million.
• *Significance:* The merger of the formerly separate AFL and CIO has greatly enhanced the power of organized labor within the labor movement as well as it has in national politics. Within the labor movement, the merger has reduced interunion competition, and a code of ethics has been established to eliminate corruption and Communist influence. In national politics, the merger has given labor a stronger, more unified voice and much effort is put into political education, electioneering, and lobbying through the Federation's Committee on Political Education (COPE).

Agency Shop.   A recent innovation in labor-management contracts which provides that a worker need not join a union but must pay the union a sum equal to union dues in order to hold his job. This payment represents a fee for the services of the union since it acts as the worker's agent in collective bargaining.
• *Significance:* The agency shop has been approved by the National Labor Relations Board. With the closed shop outlawed, the agency shop satisfies the labor union demand that nonunion workers contribute to the efforts of the union in collective bargaining.

Arbitration.   The submission of a labor-management dispute to an impartial board or individual whose decision is binding upon the parties to the dispute. A few states have passed statutes requiring compulsory arbitration of disputes in public utility enterprises, such as electric, gas, and water.
• *Significance:* A large number of labor disputes are submitted to private,

professional arbitrators. Many strikes are thereby avoided. Compulsory arbitration has been used in wartime, but both management and labor fear compulsory arbitration since both prefer to keep the government out of labor disputes and to pursue their ends through collective bargaining. Compulsory arbitration procedures are provided under the Railway Labor Act to supplement, rather than substitute for, collective bargaining. However, these procedures have not proved successful and have often been bypassed during a railroad labor dispute.

Boycott.   Action taken by a union to refuse to deal with an employer or to prevent others from dealing with an employer. Two types of boycotts may be distinguished, primary and secondary. A primary boycott involves withdrawal of patronage, and the urging of others to withdraw their patronage, from an employer with whom a union is having a labor dispute. A secondary boycott involves a refusal to deal with or patronize anyone who deals with the employer with whom there is a dispute. Secondary boycotts are outlawed by the Taft-Hartley Act of 1947 and, with certain exceptions, by the Landrum-Griffin Act of 1959.
• *Significance:* The primary boycott is lawful but often ineffective for a union. People may continue to cross a picket line to patronize a strikebound store and, in the case of large industrial plants, suppliers may continue to sell to the plant and dealers continue to sell its products. Labor prefers the secondary boycott which enables it to bring pressure to bear upon others whose continued dealing with the strikebound plant hinders the successful conclusion of the strike. However, secondary boycotts are illegal since they interfere with the rights of persons not involved in the dispute, and public policy seeks to confine the dispute to the particular parties involved. Most states also outlaw the secondary boycott.

Checkoff.   The withholding of union dues from a worker's wages by the employer who turns the funds over to the union. The employee must agree to this procedure in writing, under provisions of the Taft-Hartley Act.
• *Significance:* The checkoff is considered by unions as an essential element of union security: no one working under a collective bargaining agreement can avoid or delay payment of dues. It assures the union of a continuous flow of funds, while freeing it from extensive record keeping and other mechanics of dues collection. It also tends to ease the dues burden of the individual employee. The checkoff is used in the overwhelming majority of business establishments with union agreements.

Child Labor.   The employment of children below the legal age limit. The national government and most states prohibit the employment of children below the age of 16 and, in certain hazardous occupations, below the age of 18. Children are permitted to work outside of school in nonhazardous jobs.
• *Significance:* Until about 1910, large numbers of children 10 to 15 years of age were regularly employed. State governments then began to impose restrictions, but states which did not do so were at an advantage over those which did. Agitation for national regulation led to the passage of legislation.

However, the Supreme Court struck down a law aimed at banning products of child labor from interstate commerce (*Hammer v. Dagenhart,* 247 U.S. 251 [1918]), and another law which taxed such products (*Bailey v. Drexel Furniture Co.,* 259 U.S. 20 [1922]). In 1924, the Congress submitted a constitutional amendment to the states which would authorize federal regulation of child labor. Strong opposition prevented its ratification, though, by 1937, 28 states had ratified it, eight short of the required three fourths. However, a more liberal view of national power resulted in the passage and Supreme Court approval of the Fair Labor Standards Act of 1938 (*United States v. Darby*), 312 U.S. 100 [1941]), which, among other things, prohibits child labor. Today, child labor poses no major problem, particularly in view of compulsory education laws.

Closed Shop. An industrial plant which agrees to hire only those persons who are members of a labor union. The closed shop is outlawed by the Taft-Hartley Act of 1947, although later legislation has modified this restriction with regard to the building trades.

• *Significance:* The closed shop is opposed by management because it allegedly places the hiring power in the union rather than in the hands of management. Approximately 30 percent of organized labor, largely in craft industries, were under closed shop agreements prior to 1947. Though forbidden by the Taft-Hartley Act, many establishments continue to operate as closed shops through the mutual agreement of the union and management who are reluctant to upset customary patterns.

Collective Bargaining. Negotiation between an employer and a union representing the employees. It is to be distinguished from negotiation between an employer and an individual employee. The right of workers to organize and to bargain collectively through their representatives has been the official policy of the United States since 1935. Collective bargaining imposes upon the employer and labor union an obligation to confer in good faith with respect to working conditions and to execute a written contract embodying the agreements reached. Refusal to bargain, on the part of an employer or a duly recognized union, is an unfair labor practice.

• *Significance:* Official recognition of the principle of collective bargaining was the culmination of years of industrial strife in which unions sought recognition from employers as legitimate bargaining agents for employees. Both national and state labor-management relations laws were enacted to guarantee the right of collective bargaining in the interest of avoiding continued industrial unrest. The principle of collective bargaining is recognition of the inequality of bargaining power between an employer and an individual employee. National and state laws now extensively regulate the procedures by which agreements are to be reached, the administration of agreements, and the problems attending the breakdown of collective bargaining procedures.

Cooling-off Period. A period of time, stipulated by the Taft-Hartley Act of 1947, during which parties to a labor-management controversy may not engage in a strike or lockout. Under the Act, an existing collective bargaining contract can be terminated or changed only after 60 days notice to the other party. If no agreement is reached within 30 days, the Federal Mediation and Conciliation Service must be notified. During the 60-day period no strike or lockout is permitted. In the case of disputes threatening the national welfare, the Taft-Hartley Act authorizes the President to seek an injunction from the courts which maintains the status quo for 80 days, during which time fact-finding and conciliation efforts are to be made and the workers given a chance to vote on the employer's last offer. If, at the end of the 80-day period, no solution is reached, a strike or lockout may take place. Similar procedures are provided for the rail and air transport industries in the Railway Labor Act. • *Significance:* The 60-day and 80-day cooling-off periods are designed to give the parties to the dispute a chance to reach an amicable settlement without resort to disruptive practices. Oftimes, in practice, the parties "warm up" rather than "cool off" during this period. Both labor and management tend to judge any government intrusion into collective bargaining arrangements according to its effect on their respective positions.

Featherbedding.   A labor practice which requires an employer to pay for services which are not performed. Featherbedding is considered to be an unfair labor practice and is outlawed by the Taft-Hartley Act. An example of feather-bedding is a requirement that a radio station pay musicians who do not play, since phonograph records, rather than "live" musicians, are used. Feather-bedding may also take the form of deliberate slowdowns in production or insistence that a job be performed by a particular individual though others can do it as well. • *Significance:* The increasing automation of industry has caused concern in labor circles. Featherbedding practices are designed to maintain the employment of persons whose jobs are rendered useless by new techniques. Labor leaders defend the practice by comparing it to the businessman who restricts output to keep prices high, to professions which restrict the licensing of persons seeking to join the profession, and to farmers who are paid not to grow crops. Featherbedding practices are likely to be part of the labor scene except in times of full employment.

General Counsel.   An official charged with the responsibility for the investigation and prosecution of unfair labor-management practices under the Taft-Hartley Act. His functions include supervision of all regional offices of the National Labor Relations Board and final authority to issue complaints in unfair labor practice cases. These functions were formerly vested in the National Labor Relations Board. The General Counsel is appointed by the President for a four-year term with the Senate's approval. • *Significance:* The office of General Counsel was created by the Taft-Hartley Act to meet the criticism that the National Labor Relations Board was both prosecutor and judge in unfair labor practice cases. The net effect of this move was to make the Board primarily a quasi-judicial agency to hear appeals from decisions rendered by trial examiners in cases brought by the General Counsel. In the early stages of this new development, some friction arose between the

Board and the General Counsel, but basic policy matters remain in the hands of the Board.

Injunction. A court order to compel or restrain the performance of an act. In the field of labor, the injunction became a weapon in the hands of management to restrain the activities of labor unions during their formative period. For many years, the injunction was used to enforce the Sherman Antitrust Act against unions. The Norris-LaGuardia Act of 1932 outlawed the use of the labor injunction when labor pursues lawful ends by legitimate means. The Taft-Hartley Act of 1947, however, empowers the President to seek an injunction when a labor dispute threatens the national welfare.

• *Significance:* The labor injunction used prior to 1932 was based on the theory that organized labor was a conspiracy in restraint of trade and that, when a union conducted a strike, it threatened the property rights of the employer. The injunctive power exercised by an unfriendly judiciary made it virtually impossible for labor to pursue its goals. From 1890 to 1932, the major political aim of labor was to eliminate the injunction from labor-management disputes, and success was achieved in the Norris-LaGuardia Act. The return to the injunction device in the Taft-Hartley Act caused resentment among labor leaders, and presidents have been reluctant to use this power. However, under the Taft-Hartley Act, the injunction can last only 80 days, after which labor is free to strike.

Jurisdictional Strike. A strike brought about by a dispute between unions rather than between a union and an employer. Jurisdictional strikes may occur over the question of which union has the right to represent the workers or over the question of which workers are to do a specific job. For example, both carpenters and metalworkers may claim the right to install metal framed windows, or one union may try to "raid" another union's territory. The Taft-Hartley Act and many state laws make the jurisdictional strike unlawful.

• *Significance:* Jurisdictional strikes generally are viewed with little sympathy by the public. The consumer and the employer suffer the consequences of a fight in which they are innocent bystanders. Unions, too, recognize that such strikes harm them in the public eye and have tried to reach voluntary agreements on problems likely to lead to jurisdictional disputes. Nevertheless, workers may be vitally affected by problems arising over which group is to do a specific job. The jurisdictional strike still erupts from time to time but, in recent years, the number has diminished.

Lockout. Action taken by an employer to close down his plant to keep workers from their jobs in order to force them to accept his position in a labor controversy. Lockouts are lawful unless practiced in violation of a collective bargaining agreement or to accomplish a goal which the law declares to be an unfair practice.

• *Significance:* The lockout is to the employer what the strike is to the union —a major weapon to force agreement. Lockouts are not commonly used, but some labor authorities point out that what the public usually considers to be a strike may also be a lockout since the employer closes his plant by refusing to meet union demands.

Maintenance of Membership.   A modification of the union shop whereby workers are free to join or not join a union. Those who join, however, must remain in the union for the duration of the contract in order to hold their jobs.

• *Significance:* Maintenance of membership provisions in labor-management agreements resulted from the problem posed during World War II when employment expanded greatly and unions sought to compel membership of all workers in a particular plant. Under the Taft-Hartley Act, maintenance of membership agreements are authorized if the union represents a majority of the workers. Frequently, the contract stipulates a particular period during which a worker may leave the union without losing his job.

Mediation and Conciliation.   These terms are used interchangeably to refer to the attempt of a third party to settle a labor dispute by bringing the parties together and persuading them to reach a compromise. Unlike arbitration, the mediator has no power to make his suggested solutions binding upon the parties.

• *Significance:* Elaborate mediation and conciliation machinery has been established by both the national government and most state governments. The Federal Mediation and Conciliation Service, an agency established in 1913 in the Department of Labor but given independent status by the Taft-Hartley Act, may be called into a dispute by either party, or it may offer its services. State mediation services operate only on a part-time basis in most states, but the larger industrial states have established full-time agencies. In the railway and air transport industries a federal agency, the National Mediation Board, has been established to mediate disputes in those critical areas of industrial relations.

Picketing.   Patrolling the site of a business establishment by workers who are on strike. Peaceful picketing is considered to be a form of free speech protected by the First Amendment (*Thornhill v. Alabama,* 310 U.S. 88 [1940]). However, under national and state laws picketing may not be used to promote any purpose which is contrary to law or public policy. The Taft-Hartley Act and the Landrum-Griffin Act forbid picketing for such purposes as encouraging secondary boycotts or trying to force employers to recognize a union other than one already lawfully recognized.

• *Significance:* Picketing by a labor group serves both the purposes of informing the public of the controversy and persuading customers and other workers to refrain from dealing with a business establishment. It is a potent labor weapon since many people will not cross a picket line, either out of sympathy for the strike or fear of retaliation. Labor leaders hailed the 1940 Supreme Court decision which made picketing a free speech right, but subsequent legislation and court decisions have placed numerous restrictions upon the practice.

Right to Work Law.   A law which prohibits making union membership a qualification for employment. About 19 states now have constitutional or statutory provisions which provide that one may not be compelled to join a union or to remain a member of a union to hold his job. Right to work laws establish the principle of the "open shop."

• *Significance:* Right to work laws are designed to curtail the closed shop and union shop. Though a union shop is permitted by the Taft-Hartley Act, that Act also permits states to pass right to work legislation. These laws are prompted in part by exposures of union corruption and by concern for workers who are penalized by not holding union membership. Some states seek to attract industry by enacting right to work laws which greatly weaken labor unions. Labor leaders strongly oppose right to work laws. They argue that nonunion members benefit from the union's efforts and that the laws will destroy unions and the principle of collective bargaining. With the exception of the state of Indiana, no major industrial state has enacted a right to work law.

Strike.   A stoppage of work by employees for the purpose of winning concessions from their employer on matters of wages, hours, or working conditions. The right to strike, except for purposes prohibited by law, is considered to be a fundamental right of free workingmen. Government employees, however, are not permitted to strike. National and state laws contain a variety of limitations on the right to strike. For example, strikes may not be used to promote a secondary boycott or other unfair labor practice. Procedures are also provided by law for cooling-off periods, injunctions, fact-finding boards, and mediation services in order to avoid strikes.

• *Significance:* The strike is labor's most effective weapon but is often damaging to both sides and to the public. A strike in one industry has an effect on other industries dependent upon the struck plants for supplies. The Taft-Hartley Act of 1947 permits the President to obtain an 80-day injunction if a strike might cause a national emergency. Workers on strike are not considered to have given up their jobs and a lawful dispute may not be interfered with by "strikebreakers" or "scabs" who replace the striking workers. Many unions provide strikers with subsistence allowances during a strike.

Unfair Labor Practice.   Activity by a labor union or an employer which is defined by law as constituting a threat to industrial peace. Unfair labor practices are defined in the Taft-Hartley Act of 1947. Employers are forbidden to interfere with the rights of unions to organize, to discriminate against union members, or to refuse to bargain collectively. Unions may not discriminate against or coerce employees who are not union members, or engage in such practices as secondary boycotts, featherbedding, jurisdictional strikes, charging excessive dues or fees, or refusing to bargain collectively.

• *Significance:* By listing unfair labor practices, the Congress sought to cope with the more common causes of labor-management unrest. The Taft-Hartley Act represented a departure from previous legislation by listing unfair union tactics as well as unfair employer behavior. The National Labor Relations Board (NLRB) and its General Counsel are charged with the duty of policing unfair activities. Exactly what constitutes an unfair practice is often open to dispute since the law cannot cover every eventuality. Many NLRB decisions on unfair practices are appealed to the federal courts.

Union Shop.   An establishment in which all newly hired workers must join the union after a specified period of time, usually 30 days. Unlike the closed shop, now outlawed, the employee need not be a member of the union in order to be hired.
• *Significance:* The union shop is the major form of union security permitted by law. About 75 percent of organized labor works in union shops. The union shop eliminates "free riders" who would benefit from collective bargaining agreements without supporting the union. Many employees object to being forced to join a union, but they must remain members in order to hold their jobs. The Taft-Hartley Act authorizes union shop agreements, but permits states to eliminate them through right to work laws.

Workmen's Compensation.   An insurance program, in effect in all states, which provides compensation for workers injured on their jobs and for dependents of workers who are killed in the course of employment. In most states, the program is financed entirely by the employer who must take out private or public insurance for this purpose. Occupational diseases are also covered in many states. An administrative agency is generally established to settle claims arising under the law with appeal to the courts possible. State laws vary with regard to types of employers and occupations covered.
• *Significance:* Workmen's compensation has replaced the system which required an injured worker to bring a lawsuit against his employer to recover damages. In such lawsuits, the employer could be freed from liability if he could show that the injury was the fault of the worker or of another employee. Workmen's compensation is based on the theory that whatever the cause, workers cannot bear the financial burden of a lawsuit and that insurance is to be carried as a regular cost of production. Workmen's compensation laws have reduced hardship and have sustained families who might otherwise have to seek welfare aid.

IMPORTANT AGENCIES

Department of Labor.   A major department of Cabinet status which administers and enforces statutes which seek to promote the welfare of wage earners through improved working conditions and employment opportunities. The Department, established in 1913, is headed by the Secretary of Labor. Its major divisions and bureaus include (1) Bureau of Employment Security which administers grants-in-aid to the states for unemployment compensation programs and the operation of the United States Employment Service; (2) Wage-and-Hour and Public Contracts Division which administers the Fair Labor Standards Act and the Walsh-Healey Act; (3) Bureau of Labor Statistics which performs a major fact-finding function in various aspects of working conditions; and (4) Bureau of International Labor Affairs, which considers the effect of American labor problems on foreign policy and is responsible for American participation in the International Labor Organization. The Department also includes the Women's Bureau, Bureau of Apprenticeship and Training, Bureau of Labor-Management Reports, Bureau of Veterans' Re-employment Rights, Bureau of Employees' Compensation (for federal employees), Employees' Compensation Appeals Board, and the Office of the President's Committee on Employment of the Physically Handicapped, all of which perform duties indicated by their titles.

• *Significance:* The Department of Labor was established to give labor a direct voice at the highest level of government operations. As a result of increased federal labor legislation and the vast involvement of the United States in foreign affairs, the Department has gained in stature and influence as a major force in meeting national and international problems related to labor and the economy in general.

Federal Mediation and Conciliation Service. An agency formerly within the Department of Labor but given independent status under the Taft-Hartley Act of 1947. The Service is headed by a director appointed by the President with the Senate's consent. The Service has no law-enforcement authority but relies upon persuasion to prevent strikes which will impede the free flow of interstate commerce. Professional mediators employed by the Service assist in the settlement of labor-management disputes and try to promote good relations between labor and management. The Taft-Hartley Act requires that employers and unions must file notice of any dispute not settled 30 days after either side has expressed an intention to terminate an existing contract. The Mediation and Conciliation Service then tries to conciliate the dispute, but neither side is compelled to accept the solution suggested by the Service. The Service may also offer to enter a dispute on its own motion or at the request of parties. The Service often helps in the selection of arbitrators when both sides accept arbitration.

•.*Significance:* The Federal Mediation and Conciliation Service reflects government policy to prevent the disruptive influence of strikes whenever possible. The Service has been highly successful in carrying on its functions because of the high prestige of its employees and its independent status in the government organization.

National Labor Relations Board (NLRB). An independent regulatory commission, created in 1935, which administers the National Labor Relations Act and the Taft-Hartley Act relative to unfair labor practices and the designation of appropriate bargaining units. The NLRB consists of five members appointed by the President with the Senate's consent for five-year terms, and a general Counsel similarly appointed for a four-year term. The Board is authorized to issue cease and desist orders, to hold bargaining representative elections, and to seek court injunctions and other enforcement orders. The General Counsel conducts investigations, issues complaints, and conducts prosecutions before the Board. Actual hearings are held by trial examiners with final orders issuing from the Board.

• *Significance:* The NLRB, like other independent regulatory commissions, reflects the policy of utilizing an independent agency to perform quasi-legislative and quasi-judicial functions in important sectors of the economy. Controversial charges alleging prolabor bias on the part of the NLRB led to an increase in the size of its membership, from three to five, to provide broader representation, and the establishment of the office of General Counsel by the Taft-Hartley Act of 1947. The NLRB has played a crucial role in the development of broad policies as well as specific rules to meet the complicated problems posed by the growth of labor unions and the increasing problems of labor-management relations in an industrial society.

National Mediation Board.   An independent agency established in 1934, under an amendment to the Railway Labor Act of 1926, to mediate differences between management and labor in the railroad and airline fields and to determine bargaining representatives. The Board consists of three members appointed by the President with the Senate's consent. For the settlement of disputes growing out of the application of collective bargaining contracts, the National Railroad Adjustment Board, consisting of representatives of the unions and the carriers, is called into action. In the event of deadlocks in the Adjustment Board, the National Mediation Board appoints a referee. Parties may appeal to the courts for enforcement of any settlements reached through this procedure. If the dispute does not involve a collective bargaining agreement, and the National Mediation Board cannot effect a solution, the law authorizes the President to appoint a special fact-finding board and, if this fails, the President may place the carrier under government operation.

• *Significance:* The National Mediation Board and the related procedures are designed to prevent strikes and lockouts in the crucial areas of rail and air transport. With occasional lapses, these procedures have proved effective and work stoppages in these fields are relatively rare. Every effort is made to avoid government-imposed solutions and to help the parties reach agreement.

IMPORTANT CASES

NLRB v. Jones and Laughlin Steel Corp., 301 U.S. 1 (1937): Upheld the National Labor Relations Act of 1935 which guarantees labor the right to organize and bargain collectively and establishes the National Labor Relations Board to regulate labor-management relations. The Act was upheld as a valid exercise of the Congress' power to regulate interstate commerce.

• *Significance:* This case reflected a major shift in attitude by the Supreme Court toward New Deal regulatory legislation. The Court asserted the right of the Congress to regulate activities having "a close and substantial relation to interstate commerce" and to prevent strikes and other industrial disputes which might burden or obstruct the free flow of commerce. In its decision, the Court took a broad view of the power of the Congress to meet the challenges of an industrial society. The *Jones and Laughlin* case was a turning point for the American labor movement, and has been followed by extensive involvement by the national government in labor-management relations.

United States v. Darby Lumber Co., 312 U.S. 100 (1941): Upheld, in a major decision, the Fair Labor Standards Act of 1938. The Act imposes wage-and-hour regulations upon businesses engaged in or producing goods for interstate commerce and places restrictions upon the use of child labor.

• *Significance:* The *Darby* decision climaxed many years of national efforts to regulate wages, hours, and other conditions of employment in the face of hostile judicial decisions. The *Darby* case specifically overruled *Hammer v. Dagenhart,* 247 U.S. 251 (1918), in which the Supreme Court held unconstitutional a statute which barred goods made by child labor from interstate commerce. In the *Darby* case the Court repudiated long-held notions that the Congress could not regulate production or control wages and hours. The decision virtually put an end to legal challenges to the power of the Congress to regulate aspects of business which directly or indirectly affect interstate commerce. The decision also made it unnecessary to secure ratification of the proposed child labor amendment to the Constitution.

West Coast Hotel Co. v. Parrish, 300 U.S. 379 (1937): Supported a minimum wage law of the state of Washington. The Court held that a minimum wage law did not violate freedom of contract under the due process clause of the 14th Amendment.

• *Significance:* The *Parrish* case put an end to the use of the due process clause of the 14th Amendment by the Court to restrict state regulation of working conditions. It specifically overruled *Adkins v. Children's Hospital,* 261 U.S. 525 (1923), in which the Court struck down a federal law establishing minimum wages for women in the District of Columbia. In the *Parrish* case, the Court rejected the notion that wages were beyond state legislative control. It also rejected the concept of freedom of contract which the Court had in earlier decisions injected into the due process clause. Such regulation was upheld as a valid exercise of the police power in the interest of protecting the health, safety, morals, and welfare of the people.

IMPORTANT STATUTES

Fair Labor Standards Act of 1938. An act establishing minimum wages and maximum hours for employees engaged in interstate commerce and outlawing the use of child labor. An eight-hour day at $1.25 per hour is now established as the basic requirement, with time and a half for work exceeding 40 hours a week. Persons not engaged in interstate commerce are not covered unless state laws make similar provisions. Certain types of work are exempted from coverage, such as agricultural workers, seamen, retail trade employees, and salesmen.

• *Significance:* The Fair Labor Standards Act was designed to eliminate substandard working conditions and to minimize competition among the states which might be inclined to have lower standards in order to attract industry. The Act has also been successful in eradicating the worst aspects of child labor. Responsibility for enforcement of the Act is lodged in the Wage-and-Hour and Public Contracts Division of the Department of Labor. Earlier, in 1936, the Congress passed the Walsh-Healey Act which establishes minimum wages, maximum hours, and outlaws child labor for persons working on federal contracts. The Fair Labor Standards Act was patterned on the Walsh-Healey Act, but has broader coverage.

Landrum-Griffin Act (Labor-Management Reporting and Disclosure Act of 1959). Informally known as the Labor Reform Act of 1959, this law strengthens the Taft-Hartley Act's restrictions upon internal procedures of labor unions and provides a "bill of rights" for members of labor unions. The Act requires detailed reports on union finances and the operations of union constitutions and by-laws, and it makes misuse of union funds a federal crime. Ex-convicts, Communists, and labor officials with conflicting business interests are barred from holding union office. The "bill of rights" provisions secure the secret ballot in union elections, freedom of speech in union meetings, hearings in disciplinary cases, the right of members to sue the union for unfair practices, and authorize member access to union records.
• *Significance:* The Landrum-Griffin Act was a direct result of investigations by the Senate Rackets Committee which revealed a variety of corrupt practices by some labor leaders. The Act is designed to protect the integrity of law-abiding labor unions as well as the rights of individual members. Many labor leaders feared that the Act would result in increased government interference with organized labor, but the full impact of the Act remains to be tested. Both the Taft-Hartley Act and the Landrum-Griffin Act reflect a change in government policy as expressed in the Wagner Act of 1935, from promotion of labor interests to regulation of unions.

Norris-LaGuardia Act of 1932. An act which outlawed "yellow-dog" contracts by which workers agreed not to join unions, and limited the use of the injunction in labor disputes.
• *Significance:* The Norris-LaGuardia Act was one of the first pieces of pro-labor legislation. Its main purpose was to free labor from two major weapons used against it and to enable labor unions to pursue lawful goals. The Act was instrumental in providing the climate in which labor could develop as an economic power. It led to the passage of the Wagner Act in 1935 which guaranteed the right of labor to organize and bargain collectively.

Taft-Hartley Act (Labor-Management Relations Act of 1947). A major revision of the Wagner Act of 1935 which seeks to equalize the power of employers and labor unions. The Act places limitations upon labor union practices, regulates certain internal arrangements of unions, and strengthens the position of the individual worker. Provisions of the Wagner Act relative to unfair practices by employers against unions are retained. Among the major limitations placed upon unions by the Taft-Hartley Act are those outlawing the closed shop (but permitting the union shop), jurisdictional strikes, secondary boycotts, political expenditures, and excessive dues. The Act also permits unions and employers to sue each other for contract violations and provides for the use of the injunction and other "cooling-off" procedures in strikes which threaten the national welfare. Internal affairs of unions are regulated to the extent of requiring unions to file reports on the use of union funds and organizational procedures. The National Labor Relations Board (NLRB) was increased from three to five members and a General Counsel was created to investigate and prosecute unfair labor charges.

• *Significance:* The Taft-Hartley Act was a reaction to growing union strength, to allegations that the Wagner Act and the NLRB favored unions over employers, and to revelations of communism and corruption in some unions. The Act was passed over the veto of President Harry Truman and has been a major political issue since its enactment. Many observers are fearful of the extent to which the Act involves the government in labor-management relations and restricts the range of free collective bargaining for both labor and management. Many states have passed "little Taft-Hartley" acts. Several states, under a permissive provision of the national law, have passed "right to work" laws which have further limited the power of unions by curtailing the union shop. Both the national and state laws gave great impetus to the merger of the AFL-CIO in 1955, and have intensified the political activity of organized labor.

Wagner Act (National Labor Relations Act of 1935). A major enactment of the New Deal period which guarantees the right of labor to organize and bargain collectively through representatives of its own choosing. The Act established the National Labor Relations Board (NLRB) to administer the Act. The Board was authorized to issue cease and desist orders to employers who commit unfair labor practices as defined by the law and to certify bargaining representatives for unions.

• *Significance:* The Wagner Act was a boon to the American labor movement. Until the year 1947, when the Act was amended by the Taft-Hartley Act, union membership grew from 4 to 15 million and the overwhelming majority of manufacturing plants were covered by union contracts. This growth was accompanied by increased economic and political power for unions. Criticism of the Act as being too one-sided in favor of organized labor, and discriminatory against employers and individual workers, led to the passage of the Taft-Hartley Act in 1947. Nevertheless, the Wagner Act has significantly altered labor-management relations in the United States. "Little Wagner" acts were also passed in many states to cover workers not engaged in interstate commerce. The underlying purposes of the law—to foster and protect the right of collective bargaining—remains basic to public policy in the labor field.

14

Agriculture and Natural Resources

American Farm Bureau Federation.   A major national farm organization comprising a federation of state units which, in turn, are based on federations of county farm bureaus. The Farm Bureau, now a private organization, grew out of the promotional activities of county agents under the agricultural extension services sponsored jointly by the land-grant colleges and United States Department of Agriculture. Created in 1915, the farm bureaus achieved national stature in the 1920's through the Federation.

• *Significance:* The American Farm Bureau Federation has become the most powerful and energetic spokesman for farmers' interests. Although its membership of about 1.5 million farm families covers all states and represents all kinds of farmers, its main strength lies with the fairly prosperous cattle, corn, and cotton farmers of the Midwest and South. The Farm Bureau has been politically effective in working through the farm bloc in the Congress, and has generally succeeded in achieving its demands for government subsidy programs, extensive research, expanded extension services, and high tariffs on agricultural products. In recent years, the Farm Bureau has opposed government production controls.

Colorado River Compact...   An interstate agreement concluded among seven states concerning their respective rights to the waters of the Colorado River and its tributaries. The Colorado River Compact was concluded in 1922 after years of negotiation and was approved by Congress in 1927. Parties to the compact are Arizona, California, Colorado, Nevada, New Mexico, Utah, and Wyoming.

• *Significance:* The Colorado River Compact helped to alleviate a long-standing disagreement over the use of the Colorado River waters, permitted Los Angeles to draw an essential water supply from 300 miles to the east, and laid the groundwork for the building of the first huge reclamation dam, the Hoover Dam, by the national government. In addition to these direct benefits, the Colorado River Compact stands as a model to other states of how regional conflicts can be settled through cooperative "horizontal" federalism.

280

Columbia River Compact.　　An interstate agreement concluded in 1925 among four states, Idaho, Montana, Oregon, and Washington, concerning their respective rights to the waters of the Columbia River and its tributaries.

• *Significance:* The Columbia River Compact helped lead to the construction of the huge, multipurpose Grand Coulee and Bonneville Dams by the national government. Programs of great benefit to the four compact states have been cooperatively developed, including flood control, reclamation, power production, improved navigation, and the conservation of the famed Columbia River salmon.

Conservation.　　The careful management and wise use of natural resources to prevent depletion and to maximize the production of wealth from their use. Conservation involves the protection, preservation, and replenishment as well as the planned use of land, forests, wildlife, minerals, and water by private individuals and national, state, and local governments.

• *Significance:* Conservation suddenly was recognized as a new problem area around the turn of the century as a result of growing apprehension over the squandering of the nation's natural wealth and the crusading zeal of President Theodore Roosevelt. The first conservation programs were begun by the national government in the vast areas of the public domain, followed by state efforts, cooperative nation-state programs, and educational and publicly financed efforts in privately owned areas. The major impetus behind the conservation program remains with the national government, although some states have developed extensive programs covering water resources, mineral production, reclamation and irrigation, forest protection and reforestation, and protection of wildlife. Conservation has increasingly come to mean not only the preservation of existing natural wealth, but the planned use of resources to increase wealth and to turn unproductive areas into productive natural assets. Major conservation programs of the national government are carried on by the Departments of Agriculture and the Interior, and conservation and agriculture departments in state governments have primary responsibility for implementing state programs.

County Agent.　　The local official charged with promoting agriculture under the federal, state, and county cooperative extension program. The Federal Extension Service supervises the program through which agricultural, home demonstration, and Four-H Club agents are located in most American counties to aid farmers. The Smith-Lever Act of 1914 created the modern extension service under which the county agent program was developed.

• *Significance:* County agents seek to improve agriculture by encouraging farmers to adopt new methods developed in laboratories and in agricultural research centers. They try to reach the ordinary farmer through advice, demonstrations, and exhibits, and the great increase in farm productivity testifies to their success over the years. The county agent has also been an important factor in many states in the development of the American Farm Bureau Federation, a leading farmers' organization. Although the early integration of the county agent system with the Farm Bureau has been ended, the county agent continues to work closely with the organization in some states.

Ever-normal Granary.   The concept behind the national government's farm programs since 1938 which aims at securing a stable supply of, and stable prices for farm products through government action. The ever-normal granary system provides for accumulation of reserves of basic farm products by the government during periods of oversupply as a means of maintaining price levels. During droughts or other times of short supply, when prices rise above support levels, the government reverses the process by selling from its granaries to meet market demand and to stabilize price levels.

• *Significance:* The ever-normal granary system seeks to maintain some semblance of equilibrium between supply and demand for basic farm products, while maintaining most of the traditional freedom of the farm economy. In the years since 1938, however, generally good weather, parity price support incentives and, especially, the scientific revolution in farm technology, have all contributed to surplus production and the growing mountains of government-owned farm products. Over the years, the government has been able to dispose of little of its granary holdings in the American market, although below-cost sales abroad and foreign aid programs have helped to keep the government's granary supplies from getting completely out of hand.

National Farmer's Union.   A major farm organization active in about one half of the states. The National Farmer's Union was created in 1902 and currently has about 400,000 members.

• *Significance:* The National Farmer's Union is considerably more liberal and reform-minded in its policies than either of the two other major farm organizations, the National Grange and the American Farm Bureau Federation. Its membership comes mainly from the less prosperous, marginal farmers of the Great Plains states. It favors government price support programs, farm cooperatives, low property taxes, the family farm, and, unlike the Grange and Farm Bureau, is not opposed to production controls.

National Grange.   A major farm group active in all states and through a national organization. The Grange was founded in the 1860's as a fraternal organization dedicated to glorifying rural life.

• *Significance:* The National Grange is the most conservative of the three major farm organizations in the United States. Its membership today is located largely in the New England and Middle Atlantic states. Although a radical and politically effective organization in the two decades following the Civil War, it has been replaced by the American Farm Bureau Federation as the major spokesman for farm interests.

Parity.   A government price policy designed to maintain a level of purchasing power for farmers equal to that of a previous base period which was favorable to agriculture. This means, for example, that if a farmer was able to sell 10 bushels of wheat in 1910 and buy a bicycle with the receipts, at full parity today he should be able to work out the same exchange. Parity support price levels are determined by the Congress, and actual parity prices for specific crops are determined each year by the Department of Agriculture.

• *Significance:* The concept of parity has become a significant part of the national government's farm program. It recognizes that the agricultural sector of the economy is basic to the well-being of the rest of the nation's economy, and any serious imbalance might result in a serious slump for the entire economy. Parity does not provide a maximum price, only a minimum, which has often been exceeded on the free market in recent years. Government price support programs have generally ranged from 60 to 90 percent of parity, depending upon the supply of each basic crop.

Price Support.   A national government program to help stabilize agricultural prices near parity by buying up market surpluses. Price supports, which have been used since 1933, are usually accompanied by some production controls. The Commodity Credit Corporation (CCC) administers much of the price support program through outright purchases and, more commonly, by granting loans to farmers, their stored crops being the collateral. The individual farmer can, in effect, turn the loan into a government purchase of his crop by simply not paying it off. If, however, the market price of the commodity goes above support level, he may pay off his loan, redeem his stored crop, and sell it on the free market.

• *Significance:* Important commodities which have come under the price support program include corn, cotton, rice, tobacco, wheat, wool, and milk. The price support program recognizes the significance of agriculture as the basic industry supplying Americans with foods and raw materials, and it demonstrates the extent of agriculture's power in national politics and of the farm bloc in the Congress. The price support program accepts the proposition that the basic problem of agriculture is to bring the supply of farm products into line with the demand for them. As a result of a technological revolution in farming methods in the 1950's and 1960's, productivity has increased to the point where the national government has a huge and ever-growing amount of farm surpluses on its hands amounting to billions of dollars, with annual storage costs running into hundreds of millions of dollars. Although price supports have been backed by both major parties, the Democratic party has advocated high, rigid supports at or near 90 percent of parity, whereas the Republicans have supported flexible price supports. Each party criticizes the other's position as likely to stimulate greater overproduction and unlikely to provide the farmer with a fair return.

Public Domain.   Public lands owned by the United States government. The public domain consists of national parks and forests, grazing districts, Indian reservations, and miscellaneous holdings. The Bureau of Land Management in the Department of the Interior has custody over a large portion of the public domain.

• *Significance:* Most of the land area of the United States today, with the exception of the 13 original states and Texas, was once under the proprietorship of the national government. Through many programs, including homesteads, state grants, sales, grants to railroads, aids to education, and grants to soldiers and sailors, the national government has divested itself of most of its public lands. Today, the public domain comprises approximately 1.9 billion acres, about 21.5 percent of the nation's total land area. Most of these public lands are found in 11 Western states, where in many cases one half or more of the state's lands are held by the national government. In the new state of Alaska, 99 percent of the land remains part of the public domain. Considerable political controversy in recent years has concerned the leasing of vast areas of the public domain for exploitation by private parties.

Public Power.　　The production of electrical energy by government built and operated dams and power plants. Millions of kilowatts are produced and sold by the national government, especially from generating plants on the Colorado, Columbia, and Tennessee rivers. Public power production has become one of the major functions of the huge government dams, along with reclamation, irrigation, navigation, and flood control. Many cities and towns also produce and sell public power.
• *Significance:* Public power development by the national and local governments was negligible until the depression years of the 1930's. The case for public power is based on the multipurpose nature of government dams, and on the claims that water power is a public resource and should not be used for private gain, and that public power is necessary to build up underdeveloped regions. The case against public power holds that it is dangerous to free enterprise, that government facilities do not pay taxes or dividends, that the taxpayers of the entire nation subsidize the people of the regions with public power, and that where multipurpose government dams are necessary, a partnership should be worked out with private business for buying wholesale power and selling it to the consumers. Over four fifths of the electricity used in the United States is produced by private companies.

Rural Electrification.　　The government program to bring electric service and telephone lines to rural people not serviced by private enterprise. The Roosevelt Administration initiated the program in 1935 with the creation of the Rural Electrification Administration (REA) by executive order.
• *Significance:* The REA has encouraged rural electrification by making low interest loans to farmer cooperatives and local governments to build transmission lines, and to private electrical companies engaged in wiring individual farms. When the program started, only 10 percent of the nation's farms were electrified, whereas, today, about 95 percent of the almost 5 million farms have light and power, and well over one half have telephone service. The second Hoover Commission charged that the rural electrification program involved a considerable subsidy by the nation's taxpayers because of the low interest loans, the high administrative costs, and tax exemptions to cooperatives. Supporters of the REA program defend it on the ground that private enterprise has refused to bring electrical services to the farmers because of the lack of profit possibilities, and they note that the improvement of farm conditions benefits the entire nation.

Soil Conservation.　　A cooperative program of the national government, states, local units, and individual farmers to preserve valuable top soil from being washed or blown away through erosion and dust storms. Primary responsibility for carrying out soil conservation programs is vested in the Soil Conservation Service of the Department of Agriculture.

• *Significance:* Although government can spark soil conservation programs and provide some financing, their effectiveness depends almost wholly upon the efforts of individual farmers. Soil-conserving methods include proper drainage, crop rotation, terracing, contour plowing, and strip cropping. The national government has provided an incentive for individual farmers to cooperate by requiring all farmers participating in price support subsidy programs to use soil conservation methods. Both the Eisenhower and Kennedy Administrations have sought to improve soil conservation and reduce agricultural surpluses by paying farmers to retire overworked cropland by planting soil-conserving grasses and trees.

Tidelands Oil.   The vast oil and other natural resources lying under the waters adjacent to the states of Texas, Louisiana, Florida, and California. President Harry Truman claimed national jurisdiction over the tidelands, and his claim was upheld by the Supreme Court. After much dispute, the Congress enacted the Submerged Lands Act in 1953 which constituted a "quitclaim" giving the states jurisdiction up to three miles in the Atlantic and the Pacific Oceans and up to 10½ miles in the Gulf of Mexico, depending upon each state's seaward boundaries when admitted to the Union. The Act also sought to establish national jurisdiction over resources within the "continental shelf," the shallow waters beyond the three-mile limit which stretch over 100 miles into the Atlantic and the Gulf.

• *Significance:* The tidelands oil issue involved the question of whether the national government should divest itself of legal jurisdiction over oil resources worth an estimated $46 billion and constituting almost one half as much as total proved oil reserves in the United States. The four states concerned sought jurisdiction because of the extensive royalties which would accrue to them. Oil companies backed the states, preferring state control to the stricter, federal oil conservation laws. The case for state jurisdiction was based on claims going back to the era before the above four states had joined the Union, and was passed by the Congress despite a filibuster. Opponents of the Submerged Lands Act of 1953 argued that the divesting of federal jurisdiction over territorial waters constituted a serious and dangerous precedent, that the oil resources were the property of the entire American people and should remain so, and that royalties should be used to support public education. The national government's claim to the continental shelf may involve international legal complications because of the three-mile limit to sovereignty generally recognized by international law.

Water Conservation.   The planned use and protection of water resources. Water conservation programs include promoting the navigibility of streams, flood control, irrigation, river basin development, pollution control, recreation, reclamation, hydroelectric power, and the use of water for home and industrial consumption.

• *Significance:* The Bureau of Reclamation of the Department of the Interior, and the United States Army Corps of Engineers play a significant and sometimes competing role in developing the nation's water resources. Pollution control is carried on mainly by the states, through interstate agreements and joint action on waterways which flow through several states. The most pressing problem for the future is that of providing adequate supplies of fresh water for human consumption and industrial use. President John F. Kennedy has initiated a program to develop practical means for converting salt water from the oceans into fresh water.

IMPORTANT AGENCIES

Corps of Engineers. A branch of the United States Army which is charged with planning and constructing public works on navigable waterways. The Engineers have constructed dams and power-generating facilities on many major rivers and have engaged in extensive flood-control projects.

• *Significance:* The construction of government dams and other public projects involving multipurpose river development have often produced jurisdictional battles among the Corps of Engineers, the Department of Agriculture, the Department of the Interior, and advocates of valley authorities like the TVA. The Corps of Engineers with strong congressional support has been able to maintain its position as a major agency in the development of river programs.

Department of Agriculture. A major department of the national government which provides numerous services for farmers and regulates various aspects of agriculture and related fields in the interest of farmers and the general public. The Secretary who heads the Department is appointed by the President with the Senate's approval and serves as a member of the Cabinet. A variety of activities are carried on by the Department's major operational units: (1) The Agricultural Research Service conducts research in crop and livestock production and marketing. (2) The Extension Service works cooperatively with land-grant colleges and county agents to provide research information to farmers. (3) The Forest Service protects the national forests from fire and disease. (4) The Soil Conservation Service conserves soil resources through programs of research, erosion control, reforestation, and flood control. (5) The Commodity Exchange Authority supervises trading on commodity exchanges where agricultural products are bought and sold. (6) The Commodity Credit Corporation makes loans to farmers and purchases from farmers to stabilize agricultural prices. (7) The Federal Crop Insurance Corporation insures farmers against loss or damage to their crops. (8) The Farmers Home Administration makes low-interest loans to low-income farmers to improve their crops or facilities. (9) The Rural Electrification Administration makes loans to finance the extension of electric power to rural areas.

• *Significance:* The Department of Agriculture, regarded by many as a model agency with good organizational and operating procedures, was involved in charges of political favoritism in 1962. Because of the nature of its task, however, its expenditures have increased considerably in recent years. The farm economy is undergoing a scientific revolution in production resulting in huge surpluses, low prices for farm products, and an increasing need for governmental assistance. Some critics point out that the Department is largely responsible for the great increases in productivity through its laboratory, experimental farm, and county agent programs. Others have noted that with the population explosion in the United States and in the entire world, new agricultural technologies are essential. In recent years, the Department's budget has averaged more than $5 billion annually, the major portion of this amount going for price support programs, although storage of surplus products already purchased by the Department costs about $1 million each day.

Department of the Interior. A major department of the national government which has responsibility over a variety of affairs concerning the territories and properties of the United States. The Secretary who heads the Department is appointed by the President with the Senate's approval and serves as a member of the Cabinet. Some of the major operating units found in the Interior Department are (1) Fish and Wildlife Service which improves commercial fishing, and hunting and fishing for sport through research and conservation programs; (2) Bureau of Mines which promotes health and safety in privately owned mines and compiles statistics on mine operations; (3) Geological Survey which surveys and classifies public lands and conducts geologic research; (4) Bureau of Indian Affairs which provides health, welfare, and educational facilities on Indian Reservations; (5) Bureau of Land Management which supervises the exploitation of natural resources of the public domain by private companies; (6) National Park Service which develops and administers natural beauty spots and historic sites for the enjoyment of the American people; (7) Office of Territories which offers services to the peoples of overseas territories; (8) Bureau of Reclamation which constructs and operates public facilities to generate electric power, promote flood control, and provide irrigation; and (9) the Bonneville, Southeastern, and Southwestern Power Administrations which market electric power generated by national dams and power stations in different sections of the country.
• *Significance:* Most of the agencies in the Department of Interior are concerned with conservation. Conservation as practiced by the Department means not only the preservation of land, water, forests, natural resources, and wildlife, but their wise and systematic use as well. The importance of the Department's activities is emphasized by the fact that almost one half of the land of 11 Western states is owned by the national government, and in the state of Alaska 99 percent of the land is part of the public domain.

Tennessee Valley Authority (TVA). A major corporation of the national government created by the Congress in 1933 to provide for the development of the Tennessee River and its valley area. The TVA has responsibility for the generation, transmission, and sale of electric power, flood control, improvement of navigation, production of fertilizers, reforestation, reclamation, and soil conservation. The TVA operates under a board of three directors appointed by the President with the Senate's approval. Its operations cover an area of over 40,000 square miles in the states of Alabama, Georgia, Kentucky, Mississippi, North Carolina, Tennessee, and Virginia. Development projects are financed through the issuance of bonds by the Authority and through the sale of electric power to private companies.
• *Significance:* The TVA is an outstanding example of regional development fostered by a single, independent government corporation. Almost 30 major

dams have been constructed and others are planned. The flood-prone Tennessee River has been tamed. Navigation and farming have been improved and the cheap power supplied by the TVA has encouraged the industrial development of the entire region. All essential features of the program have been sustained by the Supreme Court. Yet, in spite of its success, much opposition remains. Many businessmen oppose it as unfair, subsidized government competition with private power companies. It is often charged with being another step toward national planning and socialism. Some critics in other parts of the country oppose the use of government tax money to subsidize the people of a single region with cheap power. Much opposition has resulted from the attraction of industry away from other sections of the country to the Tennessee Valley. Private power companies operating in the area oppose the use of TVA rates as a "yardstick" to measure the fairness of the rates which they charge consumers. Despite the political controversy over TVA, several additional valley authorities have been planned, including a Missouri Valley and a Columbia Valley authority, but none has received congressional approval.

IMPORTANT CASES

Ashwander v. TVA, 297 U.S. 288 (1936): Upheld the construction of major dams by an agency of the national government under the war and commerce powers, and upheld the authority of such an agency to build transmission lines and to sell electric energy generated at the dams. The Court held that the Congress could properly build huge dams if needed for national defense and to improve navigation, and that it could, under the Constitution, dispose of property belonging to the United States.

• *Significance:* The *Ashwander* decision provided the legal basis for the vast complex of the TVA and its multipurpose program. It also has served to encourage further river basin development on the Columbia, Missouri, and Colorado rivers by the national government.

Mulford v. Smith, 307 U.S. 38 (1939): Sustained the constitutionality of the Agriculture Act of 1938 on the grounds that the Congress may limit the amount of a crop sold in interstate commerce, and that the delegation of powers to the Secretary of Agriculture by the Congress was proper since definite standards were laid down in the Act. It also held that the Congress may validly exercise its power to regulate interstate commerce through a regulatory tax.

• *Significance:* The *Mulford* case sanctioned the attempts by the Congress and the Department of Agriculture to provide a more orderly marketing system for the basic crops of cotton, wheat, corn, tobacco, and rice. National government procedures involved under the Act included loans, marketing quotas, storage of crop reserves, and the parity concept aimed at securing fair prices for farmers. This case had the effect of overruling the Supreme Court's earlier decision in *United States v. Butler,* 297 U.S. 1 (1936), in which it was held that national regulation of farm prices invaded the reserved powers of the states. Since the *Mulford* decision, the national government's handling of the farm problem has involved primarily political and economic problems rather than legal ones.

IMPORTANT STATUTES

Agriculture Act of 1958.   A new approach to the farm problem which combined lower price supports on three basic commodities—cotton, rice, and corn—and a reduction of federal production controls over individual farmers growing these crops.
• *Significance:* The 1958 Act was enacted following President Dwight Eisenhower's veto of an agricultural bill which would have frozen farm price supports at high levels. The Act was indicative of the growing internal strife among farmers and farm organizations as to the best approach to meet the problems of huge surpluses and low farm prices, as reflected in the increasing conflict within the farm bloc in the Congress. The program has since been modified by the Kennedy Administration, which has sought to reduce surpluses through increased exports and by encouraging farmers to take some of their land out of production. Direct payments are made to individual farmers for crops not grown. Government surpluses would be reduced under the Kennedy program by selling them on the free market to meet the demand resulting from reduced farm production.

Agricultural Adjustment Acts of 1933, 1938.   Broad agricultural programs sponsored by the Roosevelt Administration and enacted by the Congress to maintain farm income through parity price supports and production controls for basic crops. After the first Agricultural Adjustment Act (AAA) had been declared unconstitutional by the Supreme Court in *United States v. Butler,* 297 U.S. 1 (1936), a second AAA was adopted in 1938, containing much of the first program but eliminating or modifying those sections which had failed the constitutionality test. The 1933 Act was held to be an invalid use of the taxing power, whereas the 1938 Act was upheld as a valid exercise of the commerce power (*Mulford v. Smith,* 307 U.S. 38 [1939]).
• *Significance:* Most of the procedures for aiding agriculture which were initiated in these two AAA programs remain as the basic approach used by the national government today. Features continued today include direct government payments to individual farmers for reducing acreage for soil conservation purposes, government loans on surplus crops when overproduction drives prices down, support of farm crop prices at a parity level, and establishment of acreage allotments and marketing quotas on basic crops when farmers choose them through a two-thirds majority vote in a national referendum.

Homestead Act of 1862.   Congress offered 160 acres of the public domain to any person who would pay a $10 registration fee and live on the land for five years.
• *Significance:* The Homestead Act was intended as a means of opening up the vast areas of the public domain in the Midwest and West to farming. Millions of acres were parceled out to pioneering "homesteaders," and by 1910 restrictions had to be imposed to keep some government lands under public ownership. The Homestead Act contributed greatly to the growing strength of the nation by opening the West and encouraging land and home ownership.

15

Health, Education, and Welfare

Aid to Dependent Children.   Financial aid provided under the categorical assistance program of the Social Security Act of 1935 for children who lack adequate support but are living with one parent or relative. Some provision also has been made for support of children in foster homes as well as for children of the unemployed. The program is administered by the states with the assistance of federal funds and under regulations established by the national government. The program is supervised by the Bureau of Public Assistance of the Department of Health, Education, and Welfare.
• *Significance:* The aid to dependent children program is designed to preserve a private home environment for children who otherwise would have to be put into orphanages, institutions, or foster homes. The program makes it possible for children to remain with a parent, grandparent, or other close relative and to receive the love and attention unavailable in even the best institutions.

Aid to the Blind.   Financial aid given to the needy blind under the categorical assistance program of the Social Security Act. Payments are made by the states with funds provided by the states and the national government to persons whose eyesight deficiencies make it impossible for them to engage in normal work. The program is supervised by the Bureau of Public Assistance.
• *Significance:* About one third of the blind people in the United States are aided through this categorical aid program. Though the payments are not high, the blind are able to live outside of public institutions. The specific degree of eyesight deficiency which makes a person eligible for aid is determined by each state.

Aid to the Totally and Permanently Disabled.   A program inaugurated in 1950 as part of the categorical aid program of the Social Security Act which provides for financial aid to persons over 18 whose physical condition makes it impossible to engage in gainful employment. The program is administered by the states with the assistance of federal funds under the supervision of the Bureau of Public Assistance.
• *Significance:* As is true of the categorical aid programs which preceded it,

290

the eligibility requirements for aid to the disabled are determined by each state. Most states have established broad categories of disability ranging from shut-ins to those with various diseases or mental conditions who are unable to hold employment.

Categorical Assistance.   Welfare programs provided under the Social Security Act. These programs include (1) old age assistance, (2) aid to the blind, (3) aid to dependent children, and (4) aid to the totally and permanently disabled. Persons who fall within these categories and are in need of financial assistance may receive aid from their state from funds supplemented by federal grants.

• *Significance:* The categorical assistance program is designed to establish a continuing program of aid for major categories of destitute people. The states may establish their own requirements which a person must meet to receive assistance, such as residence, conduct, and need. Categorical assistance has made it possible for many helpless people to continue living outside of public institutions. In former years, it was common for local governments to provide poorhouses or almshouses for the care of the needy. Congress requires that any state participating in the program must establish a state agency, staffed by the merit system, to conduct the program or to supervise local units which conduct the program. Persons denied aid must be given opportunity to appeal to the state supervisory agency.

Federal Aid to Education.   Various programs of federal grants-in-aid to the states for educational purposes. Such aid has taken the form of land grants for schools and colleges, grants for vocational education and vocational rehabilitation, school lunch programs, scholarship funds for science, mathematics and other programs in the interest of national defense, grants to veterans to attend school, and grants to areas with a heavy influx of students because of the establishment of a military base or other national facility. In recent years, numerous proposals have been made for a general program of federal aid to education for school construction and the improvement of teacher salaries.

• *Significance:* Much current controversy has been engendered by proposals for general federal aid to education. Opponents of such proposals point out that education has traditionally been a state and local concern, and that federal aid would be followed by federal supervision and control of the school system and curriculum. Proponents of federal aid point to the wide variety of federal aid programs already in existence. They claim that the states are in no position to finance the increasing need for better educational facilities. Deeply involved in the controversy are issues relating to aid for parochial and private schools and the segregation of the races. Many persons oppose aid to religious institutions and to schools which segregate pupils because of race. Others argue that all children should benefit from such aid, and, hence, no restriction should be placed on the type of school affected.

Indoor Relief.   Care of the needy in public institutions. Indoor relief is usually provided for the aged, the chronically ill, and the mentally incompetent. Prior to 1935 and the passage of the Social Security Act, many poor but healthy persons were cared for in public almshouses, poorhouses, poor farms, asylums, county homes, or institutions of like names. Indoor relief has largely been replaced by "outdoor relief" which provides money, food, and medical care to persons who continue to live in their own homes.

• *Significance:* Indoor relief is largely the responsibility of local governments. At one time, it was common practice to put all kinds of helpless people into one home—dependent children, the blind, the aged, the sick. National and state programs now make separate provisions for many of these people under the categorical assistance program. Many public institutions are maintained, however, largely for the aged who are unable to care for themselves, and for other persons who cannot be provided for in private homes. Modern institutions now take the form of nursing homes, many of which are supported by local and state governments.

Land-grant College.   An agricultural and mechanical college, or the agricultural and mechanical school of a state university, established under the provisions of the Morrill Act of 1862. The Morrill Act provided for the granting of land (amounting to nearly 11 million acres) by the national government to the states for the support of colleges to teach agriculture, engineering, and home economics. Since that time, the Congress has continued to make money grants to these institutions, supplementing funds given by state and private agencies. Experimental stations for agriculture, and an extension service which carries education directly to the farmer in the rural areas, have also been established at land-grant colleges.

• *Significance:* Most of the great state universities and agricultural colleges in the United States are a direct result of the land-grant policy. Congress did not exclude the teaching of other subjects from these schools and all of them provide education in the humanities and scientific fields. However, the agricultural and mechanical divisions continue to receive special attention from the Congress. The farmer has benefited most from the facilities made available through the land-grant college.

Maternal and Child Welfare Program.   A feature of the Social Security Act of 1935 which provides for grants to the states for maternal and child health services, crippled children services, and general child welfare programs. Grants are made to the states not for payments to particular persons, as is true under the categorical aid programs, but for support of state welfare programs. Maternal and child health services include care of mothers before and after childbirth, and immunization of children against communicable diseases. Another program seeks to provide therapy and rehabilitation for crippled children whose parents lack independent means to care for them. Child welfare activities include counseling and care of neglected, mentally retarded, and emotionally disturbed youngsters, and care of delinquent children.

• *Significance:* The maternal and child welfare program has had remarkable success in reducing infant and maternal mortality and has benefited thousands of crippled, neglected, and emotionally disturbed children. All states have established agencies to carry out these functions. Overall administration is in the hands of the Children's Bureau of the Department of Health, Education, and

Welfare. This has caused some friction among the Children's Bureau and the Bureau of Public Assistance, which administers the aid to dependent children program, and the Public Health Service. However, it has been considered desirable to vest control over most children's programs in a single agency.

National Health Insurance.   A system of government-sponsored insurance for health and medical care. In the United States, most official proposals for medical care have involved application of the principles of the Old-Age and Survivors' Insurance program whereby all persons would contribute to a general fund from which they could draw funds when needed. None of these proposals has met with congressional approval, but the Congress has responded to pressures for legislation in this field by increasing grants to the states for medical aid to the aged.

• *Significance:* Illness is the one major hazard for which no social insurance exists. A protracted illness can easily exhaust the resources of families who otherwise require no welfare aid. Proposals for compulsory health insurance seek to overcome this problem. Though many voluntary health insurance programs are in effect, many people find these plans too expensive. The American Medical Association and other groups have opposed any government-sponsored plan. They fear that it will lead to "socialized medicine" with bureaucratic control over doctors and the impairment of doctor-patient relationships.

Old-Age and Survivors' Insurance (OASI).   An insurance program, commonly called "social security," administered by the national government under the provisions of the Social Security Act of 1935. Its major purposes are to provide a retirement income for elderly persons, income for workers who are totally disabled, and income for the widows and minor children of deceased wage earners. Specifically exempted from coverage are federal employees under the civil service retirement system, self-employed doctors, ministers who choose not to participate, state and local employees not authorized coverage by state law, and some persons whose incomes are not sufficient to qualify. All other persons are required to contribute a certain percent of their income which is matched by the employer. These contributions are credited to each worker's account and, upon death, retirement, or disablement, funds are provided in accordance with the formulas provided by law for each eventuality. Retirement usually takes place at the age of 65, but one may retire at 62 with reduced benefits. Retired persons may continue to work but may have their benefits reduced if they earn more than $1200 a year. After the age of 72, no limitations are placed on earnings. The program is administered directly by the Bureau of Old-Age and Survivors' Insurance in the Department of Health, Education, and Welfare.

• *Significance:* OASI is a compulsory savings plan designed to meet the problems of an increasingly aging population. Modern health programs have contributed to a rapid increase in the number of persons over 65. In addition, OASI seeks to provide for the disabled and the families of deceased workers who would otherwise become public charges. Insurance has taken the place of public and private charity, and maintains the dignity of those who receive funds from the program. The program is a direct result of the depression of the 1930's during which many people became destitute. Some persons object to the compulsory nature of the program and to the amounts spent on its administration. However, the program has received the endorsement of both major parties and benefits and coverage have been regularly increased.

Old-Age Assistance.   Financial aid provided under the categorical assistance program of the Social Security Act for the needy aged who are not covered by the Old-Age and Survivors' Insurance program. Old-age assistance is furnished through the states under grants-in-aid from the national government under supervision of the Bureau of Public Assistance. The program is in effect in all states, the amount granted to an individual varying with his need, the responsibility of relatives, and other requirements established under state laws. • *Significance:* Old-age assistance is designed to provide aid to those needy people who retired prior to the enactment of the Old-Age and Survivors' Insurance program or whose occupations are not covered by the insurance program. Congress has extended the coverage of social security insurance to many more occupations in recent years. In future years, the need for the old-age assistance program should diminish considerably.

Outdoor Relief.   Financial aid or food and medical care provided needy persons outside of public institutions. Outdoor relief programs are administered by state and local governments under a general relief program or with the aid of the national government under the categorical assistance program. • *Significance:* Outdoor relief is generally preferred to indoor relief unless the health or mental incompetence of an individual compels that he be placed under constant institutional care. Outdoor relief permits greater flexibility in administration and preserves the dignity of those in need of aid. One drawback of outdoor relief is that it may encourage persons to seek aid who, under the threat of having to go to a poorhouse, would make greater efforts to rehabilitate themselves. Yet, careful administration of the program can assure that only those in need are provided with aid. In this way, the needy can continue to maintain their homes and play a useful part in society.

Public Housing.   Government construction and maintenance of dwellings for low-income families. Since 1937, and with increasing emphasis since 1949, the national government has given assistance to local governments through the Public Housing Administration to clear slum areas and to construct housing. Local governments need state authorization to participate in the program and the local community can reject public housing by referendum. A local housing authority must be established. It administers the funds provided by the federal government and floats bonds. Rentals are used to repay the federal loan and private bondholders. Rentals are kept very low and the federal government subsidizes the difference between costs and rental receipts. Only persons with limited incomes are eligible to occupy the housing. Some cities and states have undertaken their own public housing programs without federal aid. • *Significance:* The depression and World War II contributed to a housing shortage and continuing deterioration of slum areas. Rising costs have made it impossible for many low-income families to secure decent housing. Poor housing and slums, it is contended, increase delinquency, impair family ties, and are costly to the community in such things as welfare services and police and fire protection. Opponents of public housing object to the government competing with private industry. It is argued, too, that the availability of public housing discourages tenants to earn higher incomes since they may be forced to move if their income rises.

Unemployment Insurance.   A program of insurance under the Social Security Act of 1935 which provides for payment of funds for a limited period of time to workers who are laid off or discharged for reasons beyond their control. The program is administered by the states under national supervision. Under the plan, the Congress imposes a tax of 3 percent on the payroll of employers of four or more workers, but each state which chooses to come under the act (all do) may receive 2.7 percent of the tax with only 0.3 percent going to the national government for administrative purposes. All proceeds of the tax are held by the national Department of the Treasury in separate state accounts to be paid out as needed by each state. Each state determines the amount to be paid to each unemployed person, for how long, and under what conditions. Generally, benefits amount to about $26 per week for 20 weeks and are provided to unemployed persons who register with the proper state agency and are willing to accept suitable employment. Most states reward employers with good employment records by reducing their payroll tax. Over-all supervision of state plans is in the hands of the Bureau of Employment Security in the Department of Labor.
• *Significance:* Unemployment insurance, along with Old-Age and Survivors' Insurance, compose the major programs of social insurance in effect today. Unemployment insurance makes public relief unnecessary and preserves some purchasing power in the hands of the unemployed. Critics of the plan charge that it encourages laziness, and many oppose the compulsory nature of the plan. Supporters point out that unemployment tends to have a chain effect and that the loss of purchasing power endangers other jobs.

Urban Renewal.   A program conducted by cities with the aid of the federal government to prevent the spread of urban blight, to rehabilitate areas that can be restored, and to clear and redevelop slum areas that are beyond repair. The Housing Act of 1949 and subsequent legislation provide for procedures by which cities can submit programs to the Urban Renewal Administration to get federal aid. Aid is provided for planning and clearance programs and for public housing. Federal mortgage insurance is made available to private investors in reconstruction and rehabilitation projects.
• *Significance:* Urban renewal is designed to restore rapidly deteriorating cities and to make the city an attractive place to live and to work. The growth of suburbia has cost cities a good deal in tax resources. Slum areas are a blight on a community and a drain on its financial resources. Suitable housing is needed in most large cities to attract residents and to rehabilitate slum dwellers. Downtown areas need restoring to attract business concerns and customers. Industrial areas need to be developed to provide jobs. All of these problems, and the need to prevent future blight, are the underlying concerns of the

urban renewal program. It represents a major attempt on the part of the national government to gain the cooperation of both local governments and private capital to save the cities.

Vocational Rehabilitation.   The training of the physically and mentally handicapped for useful work. The national government provides grants-in-aid to the states for such programs under supervision of the Office of Vocational Rehabilitation in the Department of Health, Education, and Welfare. Another major program is in the hands of the Veterans Administration which cooperates with various state educational agencies for the training of handicapped veterans.
• *Significance:* Vocational rehabilitation is made available to any handicapped person who can become self-sufficient. If the person can pay for the service, he is required to do so, but those unable to pay are provided free training. The program has been expanded in recent years on the theory that it is better for the individual and for society to rehabilitate the handicapped rather than to provide them with a dole. The restored worker is not only able to sustain himself but contributes taxes to the community as well.

IMPORTANT AGENCIES

Department of Health, Education, and Welfare (HEW).   The newest federal department established in 1953 to unify administration of federal activities in the fields of health, education, and social security. The Department is headed by a Secretary who is a member of the Cabinet. Its major operating units include (1) the Social Security Administration which includes the Children's Bureau, the Bureau of Old-Age and Survivors' Insurance, and the Bureau of Public Assistance; (2) the Office of Education which administers grants-in-aid for educational purposes; (3) the Public Health Service which carries on far-flung programs in health and hospital care; (4) the Food and Drug Administration which prevents misbranding and adulteration of food and drugs; and (5) the Office of Vocational Rehabilitation which works with states to aid the physically and mentally handicapped.
• *Significance:* The Department reflects the commitment of the national government to protect the public health and welfare through vast programs of social security, education, and disease prevention. Most of these programs, once highly controversial, are now accepted by both major political parties and by the American people.

Housing and Home Finance Agency (HHFA).   An independent agency established in 1947 which administers the housing and urban renewal functions of the national government. It is headed by a director appointed by the President with the Senate's consent. Its major units include (1) the Federal Housing Administration (FHA) which encourages improved housing standards and stabilizes the mortgage market through insurance programs; (2) the Public Housing Administration (PHA) which administers federally aided public housing; (3) the Urban Renewal Administration which administers grants for slum clearance and urban renewal by state and local governments; (4) the Federal National Mortgage Association (FNMA, sometimes called "Fanny

May") which supplements private mortgage lending and ensures availability of funds for housing for veterans and farmers; and (5) the Community Facilities Administration which provides technical and financial assistance to state and local governments and to nonprofit organizations for construction of multiunit housing and public works.

• *Significance:* The Housing and Home Finance Agency now includes under one roof the major housing functions of the national government. Considerable agitation exists to raise the functions of the agency to a Cabinet level department of urban affairs and housing. The great depression and World War II created an emergency in housing which the national government has tried to meet through HHFA.

Veterans Administration (VA). An independent agency established in 1930 to coordinate the administration of various laws providing benefits for veterans and their dependents. Included are such programs as compensation for service or nonservice connected disabilities or death, vocational rehabilitation, education, home insurance, life insurance, hospitalization, care of disabled veterans, and burial of veterans. The agency is headed by an administrator appointed by the President with the Senate's consent.

• *Significance:* The Veterans Administration spends more money than any other civilian agency; it is exceeded only by the Post Office and the Department of Defense in numbers of employees. More than 20 million Americans are veterans and, if their families who are actual or potential beneficiaries are included, almost one half of the American people are concerned with the operations of this agency. Various suggestions to make the VA a part of a major department, such as Health, Education, and Welfare, have met resistance from veterans' organizations which prefer the independent status of the VA.

IMPORTANT CASES

Social Security Cases: Two cases in which the Supreme Court upheld the Social Security Act of 1935. In *Steward Machine Co. v. Davis,* 301 U.S. 548 (1937), the Court upheld the unemployment insurance feature of the Act. The Court reasoned that the tax for relief of the unemployed was within the power of the Congress to provide for the national welfare and that the states were not coerced to join the plan. In *Helvering v. Davis,* 301 U.S. 619 (1937), decided the same day, the Court upheld the Old-Age and Survivors' Insurance provisions. The Court recognized the broad power of the Congress to promote the general welfare and maintained that the scope of the general welfare was for the Congress to determine. The Court denied that the tax on payrolls for Old-Age and Survivors' Insurance benefited only a particular class of persons or invaded the powers of the states.

• *Significance:* The Social Security Cases were major interpretations of the general welfare clause of the Constitution. The decisions gave the Congress an almost unlimited power to tax and spend for whatever purposes it deems necessary to promote this goal. A far-flung system of social welfare measures is now sponsored by the national government with the cooperation of state and local governments.

IMPORTANT STATUTES

Housing Act of 1949.   An act providing for federal assistance to local governments for low-rent public housing, slum clearance, and urban renewal. The Housing Act of 1949 continued a program begun under the Housing Act of 1937, which had been interrupted by World War II. The 1949 Act called for the construction of 810,000 housing units over a period of six years but the Congress reduced this figure in subsequent legislation. Since 1949, the urban renewal aspects of the law have been expanded and various specialized housing programs have been instituted, such as those for college dormitories and housing for the aged. Funds have also been made available for municipal public works, such as sewers and transportation. All but a few states have authorized their local governments to participate in various aspects of the program. The Housing and Home Finance Agency supervises administration of the Act.
• *Significance:* In the Housing Act of 1949, the Congress declared as its goal "a decent home and a suitable living environment for every American family." The national government is now committed to a "total" housing program which takes account of all aspects of community development. These programs result from an acute housing shortage for low-income families and increasing urbanization which tends to breed slums and blight. Many persons object to the intrusion of the national government into these areas, but the Congress has continued to expand existing programs, encouraging the use of private capital when possible.

National Defense Education Act of 1958.   An act to encourage education in science, mathematics, engineering, languages, and teacher education. The Act provides for loans to needy college students, with preference given to those pursuing these courses of study; one half the loan is forgiven if the student teaches for five years after graduation. In addition, the Act provides funds for graduate fellowships, and for public schools to purchase science and language equipment and to improve guidance and testing services.
• *Significance:* Congress enacted the National Defense Education Act in response to Soviet achievements in the field of science. Many observers see in this Act the start of a trend toward greater national government involvement in education. The Act is designed to serve national security needs by equalizing educational opportunities throughout the nation in critical subject matter fields. A requirement of a loyalty oath from recipients of loans and grants has resulted in the refusal of a number of schools to accept the funds. Some educators object to the emphasis put upon science to the neglect of the social sciences and humanities. In order to meet the major objections to federal aid to education, the Act specifically provides that no national official may exercise any control over curriculum or personnel in any school system.

National Mental Health Act of 1946.   A nationwide program for the care and treatment of the mentally ill. The Act provides for grants-in-aid to the states for psychiatric personnel, community psychiatric services, and research into prevention and care of mental illness. The Act is administered by the Public Health Service in the Department of Health, Education, and Welfare.

• *Significance:* Mental health is one of the most pressing health problems in the United States. Though more than half the hospital beds are occupied by the mentally ill, an acute shortage of trained personnel and facilities exists. Much progress has been made since the passage of the National Mental Health Act. The national government has also taken action to provide grants for hospital construction and for the control and treatment of other serious diseases such as tuberculosis, cancer, and heart diseases.

Smith-Hughes Act of 1917. An act providing for federal grants-in-aid to the states for vocational training in agriculture and home economics. The Act has since been expanded to cover vocational education in trade and industry and for training of teachers in vocational subjects. The Office of Education in the Department of Health, Education, and Welfare administers the grants.

• *Significance:* The Smith-Hughes Act is often pointed to as an example of federal aid to education without undue control by the national government. The vocational training programs have supplemented the regular academic programs of public schools and have provided trained personnel for the farm, home, and business.

Social Security Act of 1935. The basic social welfare legislation embodying social insurance, public assistance, and child health and welfare services. Social insurance programs include Old-Age and Survivors' Insurance and unemployment insurance. Public assistance is provided under the categorical assistance program to the needy aged, blind, permanently and totally disabled, and to dependent children. Child health and welfare services are provided under the Act for maternal care, crippled children, and general child welfare services. With the exception of the Old-Age and Survivors' Insurance program, which is financed and administered exclusively by the national government, all these programs are administered by the states under grants-in-aid from the national government. Responsibility for over-all supervision rests with the Social Security Administration in the Department of Health, Education, and Welfare. In addition, the Social Security Act provides for widespread public health services through grants to the states under supervision of the Public Health Service in the Department of Health, Education, and Welfare.

• *Significance:* The Social Security Act is the most comprehensive social welfare legislation passed in the United States. The program grew out of the experience of the great depression and reflected a basic change in public attitudes toward the needy and the role of the government in providing basic security for the aged and unemployed. The Act, at first highly controversial, is now generally accepted by the American people; both major political parties have expanded the scope of benefits available under the law. The partnership of the national and state governments in the administration of the Act provides a leading example of cooperative federalism in action to meet common national problems.

16

Foreign Policy and International Affairs

Aggression.   An unwarranted attack by one state against another. Much of the literature of international law is concerned with the problem of identifying aggression and differentiating it from self-defense. Recent cold war history has been characterized by nations arming themselves and concluding alliances to protect themselves from aggression. The United Nations collective security system was established primarily for the purpose of protecting states from aggression.

• *Significance:* The community of nations has never been able to agree on a definition of what constitutes aggression. The United Nations Charter does not define aggression; aggression has occurred when an authorized organ of the world organization makes such a determination through its voting procedure. Such was the case in 1950, when the Security Council branded North Korea an aggressor. The International Law Commission of the United Nations has tried for several years to establish objective criteria to be used in deciding whether acts of aggression have been committed. Extensive studies have been carried on but no agreement has been reached.

Alliance.   An attempt by a state to improve its power position by joining with other states in defense of their common interest. Most alliances are now characterized by an agreement to regard "an attack upon any member of the alliance as an attack upon all." When a nation is attacked, it goes to war in self-defense. Hence, an alliance is a way of informing friend and foe that an attack against any individual nation will precipitate a general war. Balance of power systems tend to create the need for alliances.

• *Significance:* Throughout most of American history, President George Washington's advice to "steer clear of permanent alliances" was carefully observed. Since the advent of the Cold War, the United States has been catapulted into a position of leadership of the free world, unable to continue its time-honored policy of isolation. The United States has become the world's leading advocate of security through defensive alliances. Alliances have been concluded with over 40 nations in recent years in an attempt to forestall a Soviet attack, or to deal with it if it should occur. Mutual security alliances include

300

the North Atlantic Treaty (NATO), the South East Asia Treaty (SEATO), a trilateral treaty with Australia and New Zealand (ANZUS), and bilateral pacts with Japan, the Philippines, Nationalist China, and South Korea.

Alliance for Progress.   A program of foreign aid developed by the Kennedy Administration for Latin America. Congress authorized $500 million in 1961 to initiate the program. Nineteen Latin American countries—all except Cuba —are participating. Continued aid to these nations will be offered if internal economic reforms are instituted and social progress moves forward with economic development. The Inter-American Development Bank was created in 1961 to play a major role in implementing the program through development loans. Its efforts are supplemented by the Development Loan Fund, the Export-Import Bank, and the Agency for International Development.
• *Significance:* The emphasis in the Alliance for Progress program is on securing progress in Latin America through close hemispheric cooperation. American help is intended to aid these countries in getting started on the road to self-sustaining growth. Closer economic ties leading to some measure of economic integration are encouraged by the program. Additional objectives include the strengthening of political relations through the Organization of American States (OAS) and the collective security system under the Rio Treaty.

Ambassador.   The top-ranking diplomat sent by a sovereign state as its official representative to another state. An ambassador is the head of an embassy in the capital city of the foreign state. Official relations between governments are carried on mainly through an exchange of ambassadors. American ambassadors are sent to important countries that send ambassadors to the United States.
• *Significance:* In the United States, ambassadors are appointed by the President and confirmed by the Senate. Personal and political considerations, such as campaign contributions and party service, may be important in making such appointments. The trend, however, is in the direction of appointing foreign service career diplomats. An ambassador is the personal representative of the President, and, as such, is charged with implementing the foreign policy of the administration in power in the United States. A new president will usually select an entirely new staff of ambassadors. In addition to his official duties, much of an ambassador's time is spent in promoting better relations between the peoples of the two countries.

ANZUS Pact.   A tripartite security treaty among Australia, New Zealand, and the United States, signed at San Francisco on September 1, 1951. The treaty, which has no terminal date, declares that an attack upon any of the members would constitute a common danger and each would act to meet it according to its constitutional processes.
• *Significance:* ANZUS is an attempt to provide security against Communist encroachment in a large area of the Pacific. The Pact reflects a growing dependence upon the United States for leadership in providing security in the Pacific. In 1954, the security system of the ANZUS Pact was expanded into

the South-East Asia Treaty Organization (SEATO) defense arrangement, but the ANZUS Pact remains in force.

Appeasement.   A term used to describe concessions made to a warlike, potential enemy in the hope that these will satiate his appetite for expansion, and peace will be secured. Prime Minister Neville Chamberlain's agreement at Munich to accept Adolf Hitler's demand for the partition of Czechoslovakia is regarded as a classic example of appeasement.
• *Significance:* The fear of appeasement makes diplomatic negotiations extremely difficult. Successful diplomacy requires concessions from both sides. Frequently the cry of "appeasement" can sabotage a diplomat's position. Concessions are played up while counterconcessions are overlooked. The problem of appeasement is particularly acute when diplomats are engaged in "open" or "public" negotiations.

Arbitration.   A method of settling a dispute between states by judges selected by the parties to the dispute. The judges, who have standing as international jurists, must render a decision or award based on international law, and the parties agree in advance to accept the decision as binding. Arbitration dates back many centuries, but its modern use began with the famous *Alabama Claims* settlement between the United States and Great Britain growing out of Civil War controversies.
• *Significance:* Many conflicts between states involving their secondary interests have been solved through arbitration. Generally, states are reluctant to submit disputes involving their *primary* national interests to an arbitration tribunal. Contrary to popular myth, states which have accepted arbitration have almost always abided by the decision of the tribunal. The main weakness of arbitration is the difficulty of getting states to accept it as a means of settling their dispute.

Attaché.   A military, commercial, or other official with diplomatic rank who is attached to an embassy or foreign mission.
• *Significance:* Attachés seek to establish good relations with similar officials in the country to which they are accredited. They also comprise the eyes and ears of the United States in gaining specialized information concerning the conditions which exist in that country.

Balance of Payments.   The net balance between total income and expenditures of a nation in its business and trade relations with the rest of the world. Included are all monetary transactions, such as imports and exports of goods, tourist expenditures, investments, and income from investments.
• *Significance:* Nations usually seek to maintain a "favorable" balance of payments. This means that they strive to increase income over expenditure to the extent that balances of foreign currencies and gold can be built up. Nations with "unfavorable" or deficit balances are like individuals who spend beyond their income. In the short run, this situation may not be serious. If it persists, corrective action must be taken. This may take the form of higher tariffs, exchange controls, export subsidies, austerity programs, currency de-

preciation, or other kinds of state action. The United States has suffered from a deficit balance of payments for several years, which has resulted in an outflow of gold into foreign hands.

Balance of Power.   A system of power alignments in which peace and security may be maintained through an equilibrium of power between the rival blocs. Participating states enter into alliances with friendly states in attempts to protect and enhance their power positions.
• *Significance:* If the balance works well, peace will be maintained for a period of years. So long as a near equilibrium is thought to exist, neither side will dare to launch an attack upon the other. However, with the military build-up characteristic of a balance of power system, there is always the danger that war will result from border incidents, miscalculations, or causes other than planned attack. Historically, balance of power systems have kept the peace for short and long periods, but have in time deteriorated into war. Today, a worldwide balance of power system exists between the Communist and the free world camps. This system is accompanied by the greatest armaments race in the history of the world.

Bilateralism.   Action undertaken in the international field involving two states.
• *Significance:* Bilateralism is a compromise between unilateralism (a lonewolf policy) and multilateralism (concluding agreements with several states). A state pursues a bilateral policy when it fears both isolation and entanglement. In international trade, bilateralism refers to agreements made between two states for exchanges of goods, usually on a barter basis.

Bipartisanship.   The close cooperation between the two major American political parties in dealing with foreign affairs problems. Bipartisanship usually takes the form of frequent consultations between the leaders of both parties in the Congress, and between these leaders and the President. During time of war or threat of war, when bipartisanship typically comes into vogue, the President may appoint members of the opposition party to key Cabinet posts.
• *Significance:* Bipartisanship is a means by which a democracy can overcome its divisions and present a solid front to the world. "Partisanship ends at the water's edge" is a frequently repeated description of bipartisanship. Disadvantages resulting from such cooperation include the loss of the function of the "loyal opposition" within the government and the lack of "issues" to place before the voters in subsequent elections.

Chargé d'Affaires.   The Foreign Service official temporarily placed in charge of an embassy or legation in the absence of the ambassador or minister.
• *Significance:* When the United States seeks to indicate displeasure with the actions of a foreign government, but does not wish to take the serious step of severing diplomatic relations, it has usually withdrawn its ambassador. Under such conditions, the chargé d'affaires assumes a position of grave importance. In this way, a "listening post" to the foreign country is kept open, as are the diplomatic channels.

Charter of the United Nations.   A multilateral treaty which serves as the constitution for the United Nations Organization. The Charter was drawn up and signed at San Francisco by 50 nations on June 26, 1945, and was ratified and put into effect on October 15, 1945. The document consists of a preamble and 111 articles which provide for the creation of six major organs and set out the powers to be exercised by each.

• *Significance:* The Charter represents an effort by the community of nations to establish norms of international conduct by outlawing war, providing for the peaceful settlement of international disputes, and by encouraging cooperation among nations in dealing with economic and social problems. Like the United States Constitution, the Charter has proved to be a flexible document, subject to many broad interpretations. Without this feature of adaptability, the United Nations would probably have collapsed under the impact of the Cold War.

Cold War.   A term used to describe the extreme state of tension existing between the western powers and the Soviet Union since 1947.

• *Significance:* The era of the Cold War has been characterized by diplomatic offensives, economic penetrations, psychological warfare, ideological conflict, political battles, an armaments race, and other clashes falling short of an all-out "hot" war. The Cold War has also had a considerable impact on American domestic politics and policies in such areas as budgets, civil rights, education, and the nation's economy.

Collective Security.   A world-wide security system by which all or most nations agree in advance to take collective action against any state or states which may break the peace by committing aggression. Collective security is based on the assumption that, normally, no nation or group of nations would dare to challenge the power of the world community, but, if an attack should occur, all nations would honor their commitments to take police action. The United Nations embodies the concept of collective security. Under Chapter VII of its Charter, the Organization can take such action, including military, as may be necessary to preserve world peace. Primary responsibility is vested in the five great powers (U.S., U.S.S.R., Britain, France, China), each having the veto power in the Security Council. Since 1950, the General Assembly also has been empowered under the Uniting For Peace Resolution to authorize collective security action if the Security Council is stymied with a veto. Sometimes, collective security is also used to describe alliances established under a balance of power system.

• *Significance:* The first universal collective security arrangement, the League of Nations, broke down in the 1930's under the impact of aggressions by the Axis powers, Germany, Italy, and Japan. Collective security military sanctions were invoked by the UN in 1950 against North Korea in its attack upon South Korea. Although this police action left much to be resolved, the UN was successful in halting the aggression. In 1956, the world organization was faced simultaneously with an attack by the Soviet Union upon Hungary and an attack by Britain, France, and Israel against Egypt. Although the UN was able to cope with the latter successfully, in the Hungarian case only moral sanctions were employed because of a fear of general war.

Comity.   Courtesies extended between nations in their formal relations with each other. Examples include extradition of fugitives in absence of a treaty, and immunity of diplomats.
• *Significance:* Most acts of comity between nations are based on customary international practice. It is important that nations abide by certain principles of conduct so that their relations can be harmonious and fruitful. Comity is not regarded as binding in character or enforceable in court.

Consul.   An official appointed by a government to reside in a foreign country in order to assist citizens of the appointing state and to advance their commercial interest. American consuls are members of the Foreign Service.
• *Significance:* The United States maintains consulates in most of the important commercial cities of the world. Responsibilities of an American consul include jurisdiction over American vessels (the settling of shipboard disputes, sanitary inspections, sending mutinous and shipwrecked sailors home, etc.), granting visas to foreigners seeking entry into the United States, and opening up new business and trade opportunities.

Containment.   A general policy adopted in 1947 by the Truman Administration to establish "situations of strength" around the globe in order to contain Communist power within its existing boundaries. Underlying the policy was a belief that, if Soviet expansion could be stopped, communism would collapse of its own internal weaknesses.
• *Significance:* Under general guidelines of containment policy, the Truman Administration embarked on vast new programs which included (1) rearmament; (2) establishment of military bases around the world; (3) mutual security alliances with friendly powers; (4) an economic aid program to rebuild war-shattered economies in western Europe (Marshall Plan); (5) a program of technical and economic aid to underdeveloped countries (Point Four Program). Through these and other programs, Communist expansion was slowed down but not completely halted.

De Facto Recognition.   The preliminary recognition of a new state or government by another state. It is usually followed by *de jure* or full, legal recognition with exchange of ambassadors. The term also refers to a theory advanced by some international jurists that new states and governments should be recognized if, in fact, they do exist.
• *Significance:* Premature granting of recognition to a revolutionary regime, or continued withholding of it from a government on ideological grounds, has produced much turmoil in the world. Today, Communist China and East Germany are subjects of recognition controversies. Great Britain has maintained a *de facto* recognition of Communist China for more than ten years without an exchange of ambassadors.

De Jure Recognition.   Full, legal recognition of a new state or government by another state, usually accompanied by an exchange of ambassadors or ministers. Also, a theory which holds that only those states and governments that have come into existence through peaceful, constitutional means are deserving of recognition.

• *Significance:* The *de jure* theory is used mainly by those nations which seek to preserve the status quo in the world. In an ideological struggle, like the present day Cold War, rigid theories frequently give way to mere expediency as each side uses its power to recognize or to withhold recognition as a diplomatic weapon.

Diplomacy.   The process in its totality by which states carry on political relations with each other. The machinery of diplomacy includes a policy-making Foreign Office (Department of State in the United States) and diplomatic missions abroad (Foreign Service).

• *Significance:* Diplomacy is an art which can only be mastered by skilled negotiators. A good diplomat knows how, when, and what to compromise and how to achieve maximum benefit from compromise. War may result if diplomacy fails.

Diplomatic Immunity.   Under international law, diplomatic officials are immune from the jurisdiction of the state to which they have been accredited. The embassy grounds may not be trespassed upon by local officials unless permission is granted by the diplomat. He, his family, and his official staff are immune from arrest and from civil jurisdiction unless his own government waives this immunity.

• *Significance:* The purpose of diplomatic immunity is to ensure that the diplomat will have the freedom to carry on effectively the relations between the two states. Though not subject to the laws of the state to which he is accredited, he nevertheless is expected to abide by them under normal conditions. A diplomat who misuses his immunity may be reported to his superiors for discipline or, in severe cases, his recall may be demanded by the government of the state to which he is accredited.

Dollar Diplomacy.   A term used by Latin Americans to show their disapproval of the role the American government has played in using diplomatic and military power to open up foreign markets and safeguard financial interests. Under the Roosevelt Corollary of the Monroe Doctrine, American Marines were frequently sent into countries of Central America. Protectorates were established over Cuba, Haiti, Nicaragua, and Santo Domingo in the early part of the twentieth century. The term might also be used to describe any use of a state's political or military power to further the economic interests of its citizens abroad.

• *Significance:* American relations with Latin America have considerably improved since the inauguration of the "Good Neighbor Policy" in the 1930's and the "Alliance for Progress" aid program of 1961. Treatment as equals and mutual solving of problems through the Organization of American States has greatly improved the position of the United States with the Latin American republics. Yet reservoirs of ill-feeling remain and are occasionally exploited by political leaders unfriendly to the United States.

Dumping. The selling of a commodity in foreign markets at a price below existing world market prices. The purpose of dumping is usually to reduce heavy surpluses or to drive competitive groups out of the market by sustaining temporary losses.
• *Significance:* Dumping is regarded in international trade circles as unfair competition, regardless of the motives behind it. It tends to distort world market situations and create bitter feeling which frequently crystallize into retaliatory trade action. A nation confronted with a threat of the loss of home markets because of foreign dumping practices would usually take refuge behind a high protective tariff.

Economic and Social Council (ECOSOC). A major organ of the United Nations concerned with promoting higher standards of living and social justice throughout the world. The Council includes 18 members elected by the General Assembly, six chosen each year for three-year terms. Responsibilities include (1) coordinating the activities of the Specialized Agencies, such as the World Health Organization (WHO) and the Food and Agriculture Organization (FAO); (2) administering United Nations functions in economic, social, educational, cultural, and related areas; (3) promoting world-wide observance of human rights and fundamental freedoms.
• *Significance:* The Economic and Social Council has successfully coordinated the operations of diverse agencies in seeking to meet the pressing social and economic problems of today. It has established regional Economic Commissions for Asia and the Far East, for Europe, for Africa, and for Latin America to make comprehensive studies and recommendations on how economic conditions can be improved. It has established various commissions to study international problems, including: Fiscal, Human Rights, Narcotic Drugs, Population, Social, Statistical, Status of Women, and Transport and Communications.

Economic Nationalism. An economic policy by which a nation seeks to attain economic prosperity by protecting the home market and/or opening up foreign markets through unilateral or bilateral government action. It is the opposite of a multilateral trading system with free flow of trade and free convertibility of currencies. It is characterized by extensive governmental control of trade and the subjection of economic matters to overriding considerations of political and military policy. Techniques employed by states pursuing policies of economic nationalism include (1) austerity programs; (2) barter arrangements; (3) currency depreciation; (4) exchange controls; (5) export subsidies; (6) licensing; (7) quota restrictions; and (8) tariffs.
• *Significance:* A state cannot normally pursue a policy of economic nationalism without inciting retaliatory action from other states which have suffered harm from such policies. The great danger is that, once started, the process becomes cumulative, with action and counteraction building up to the point of stifling most trade. This is what happened in the 1930's, when the Smoot-

Hawley Tariff Act raised tariff rates to the highest point in American history in an effort to protect the home market from foreign competition. The action touched off extensive retaliation which precipitated a world trade crisis. Today, bloc trading systems, such as the European Economic Community (Common Market) and the Soviet bloc, tend to reduce restrictive trade practices among member nations but to encourage increasing economic warfare between blocs.

Executive Agreement.   An international agreement between the President and foreign heads of state which need not be ratified as a treaty. Most notably, trade agreements are concluded under powers granted to the President by the Congress. Others are concluded by the President alone, acting under his constitutional powers over foreign relations. The Constitution makes no explicit provision for executive agreements. *See* EXECUTIVE AGREEMENT, page 160.
• *Significance:* Legally, an executive agreement is the same as a treaty. In recent years, the trend has been toward more agreements, fewer treaties. For example, in 1930, 11 agreements and 25 treaties were concluded; in 1958, there were 182 agreements and 3 treaties. Advantages of the executive agreement include avoidance of the power of the Senate to cripple or kill a treaty, and the maintenance of secrecy when desirable, as in a wartime agreement. Disadvantages include the frequent need for further implementation of the agreement by *both* houses of Congress through statutes and appropriations. When secrecy is involved, congressional and public suspicions may be aroused, as in the case of the Yalta Agreement with the Soviet Union which became a major issue in several national elections. When substantial public support is needed, presidents usually fall back on the treaty procedure.

Extradition.   Delivery by a nation to another nation of a person accused of having committed a crime in the latter. The process resembles that of interstate rendition which occurs within the United States. In the international field, extradition usually depends upon treaty arrangements between the two nations concerned. Some international jurists regard it as a matter of reciprocal interest covered by customary international law in the absence of any treaty.
• *Significance:* Because there is no international criminal law, without extradition a criminal could escape punishment by simply crossing a border. The whole process of law enforcement would become infinitely more difficult under such circumstances. States usually extradite persons sought by other states; however, political offenses are not generally recognized as ground for extradition. In the United States, the President is not legally empowered to extradite in the absence of treaty provisions.

Free Trade.   The elimination of all governmental regulations and controls so as to allow the free flow of commodities into and out of a country. The theory was first postulated by Adam Smith who believed that a free trade system would foster an international specialization which would result in higher productivity and standards of living for all nations.
• *Significance:* Desirable as free trade appears in theory, all nations practice varying degrees of protectionism. Many economists still support the idea of free trade, but political considerations have tended to override economic

theories. Many nations seek to obtain a measure of self-sufficiency, particularly in critical sectors of their economy, rather than becoming overly specialized. World peace and security are indispensable conditions to a system of free trade.

General Assembly.   The major organ of the United Nations in which all members (104, in 1962) are equally represented. The Assembly has evolved into the focus of the multifold activities of the UN. In one sense, it is a continuing international conference; in another, it is an international forum in which each member nation can discuss its international problems with all others. It is a "Town Meeting of the World" through which world public opinion can be aroused and brought to bear on a problem. Its functions directly or indirectly relate to almost all of the activities carried on by the world organization. Specific responsibilities include (1) election of some or all members of the other five major organs; (2) an annual review of the activities of all segments of the Organization; (3) control over the budget; and (4) decision making and recommendations to members on all subjects within UN jurisdiction. Measures are adopted ordinarily by a simple majority vote, but "important questions," as defined by the Charter, require a two-thirds vote of members present and voting. The most important power of the Assembly —to deal with acts of aggression and breaches of the peace when the Security Council is stalemated by a veto—was not vested in the Assembly by the Charter but was assumed by it in 1950.
• *Significance:* Through an evolutionary process, the Assembly has become the sun of the UN solar system. Until, and unless, the great powers begin to cooperate more fully, the Assembly seems destined to overshadow completely the Security Council. With the admittance of many new members, mostly African states, the prestige and responsibilities of the Assembly have grown accordingly.

Good Neighbor Policy.   American policy toward Latin America initiated in the early 1930's. President Franklin Roosevelt described the change in policy in his inaugural address in March 1933 as follows: "In the field of world policy, I would dedicate this nation to the policy of the good neighbor—the neighbor who resolutely respects himself and, because he does so, respects the rights of others. . . ." Although the policy was directed toward the world at large, it soon came into general usage as descriptive of the United States new policy of treating Latin-American nations as friends and equals.
• *Significance:* From the turn of the century until the adoption of the Good Neighbor policy, the United States played the role of "Big Brother" toward Latin America. Unilateral actions, dollar diplomacy, and frequent military intervention characterized that policy. Terms such as "Yankee imperialists" and "Colossus of the North" came into common usage south of the border to indicate displeasure with American policies. The Good Neighbor policy was an about-face, a repudiation of earlier actions. Since its inception, the policy has resulted in two military pacts of mutual assistance (the Act of Chapultepec of 1945 and the Rio Treaty of 1947), the creation of the Organization of American States (OAS), and a general improvement in relations between the

United States and the Latin-American countries. The policy occasionally has been strained over United States relations with dictatorial regimes like Perón's Argentina and Castro's Cuba.

Good Offices.   A method of peaceful settlement by which a third nation seeks to bring two disputing nations into agreement. The state offering its good offices merely seeks to create favorable conditions under which the states in conflict can talk over their differences. Good offices does not include participation in the negotiations nor the offering of a suggested solution, although the disputing states may request such. When this occurs, good offices is converted into mediation.

• *Significance:* Good offices can be a useful device in "breaking the ice" between disputing states by getting them to talk things over. Neither disputant may be willing to initiate proposals for such talks for fear of demonstrating weakness in its position. The third state that offers its good offices is playing the role of peacemaker on behalf of the world community. In recent years, the United Nations has generally taken over the role of offering good offices to disputing states, usually through the Security Council, the General Assembly, or the Secretary General.

Ideological Warfare.   One of the tactics used by the Communist and free world blocs on the cold war battleground. Each side has sought to achieve ideological conformity among its own people, while trying to convert the large masses of mankind outside its borders to its "way of life." Ideology comprises the ideas and ideals of a political and economic system. The struggle involves competition between Soviet-style communism and dictatorship, and western-style capitalism and democracy.

• *Significance:* The ideological war has developed an inclination toward "black and white" classification as each side tries to convince millions of peoples of the soundness and rightness of its position and the imperialistic, warlike, aggressive nature of the other side. Various psychological techniques are used in disseminating propaganda. Never before in history has the battle for men's minds reached such proportions.

Inherent Powers.   Powers exercised by the national government in foreign affairs which are neither expressed nor implied in the Constitution. They are derived from the concept that the United States exists in a world of many nations and, therefore, must possess powers to meet its international responsibilities. *See* INHERENT POWERS, page 33.

• *Significance:* The inherent powers doctrine enables the national government to act in foreign affairs to protect the security and well-being of the American people. The extent to which such action would be permissible has not been specified, although the Supreme Court has stated (*United States v. Curtiss-Wright Export Corp.,* 299 U.S. 304 [1936]): "As a member of the family of nations, the right and power of the United States in that field are equal to the right and power of the other nations of the international family."

International Bank for Reconstruction and Development.   A Specialized Agency of the United Nations known informally as the World Bank, which makes loans to member nations for economic rehabilitation or development purposes. The Bank was created by the Bretton Woods Agreement of 1944 to promote the growth of world trade and higher standards of living by making loans when private capital is not available. The Bank's chief sources of funds are capital subscriptions from member nations and sales of its own bonds to private investors. By 1962, the subscribed capital of the Bank was approximately $20 billion of which almost one third was supplied by the United States. The Bank operates by insuring private loans or, if necessary, by providing the funds itself. As of 1962, 72 countries were members.

• *Significance:* The Bank has made several hundred loans to over 50 countries and territories, mostly in the underdeveloped category. Loans are made only after careful and detailed studies convince the directors of the soundness and usefulness of the ventures. To meet criticism of the Bank's conservative lending policies, the International Finance Corporation (IFC) was created in 1956 to invest in private enterprises and, in 1960, the International Development Association (IDA) was created to offer long term, low interest loans.

International Court of Justice (ICJ).   An international tribunal created as one of the six major organs of the United Nations to adjudicate justiciable disputes among nations and to render advisory opinions to organs of the United Nations. The World Court was established in 1945 under an agreement which was annexed to the United Nations Charter, and to which all UN member states are parties. Nonmembers of the UN may adhere to the agreement under conditions set by the General Assembly and the Security Council. Other states may use the Court if they accept its jurisdiction. The Court, with its headquarters at the Hague, has 15 judges elected by the General Assembly and the Security Council, no two of whom may be nationals of the same state. Decisions rendered by the Court are final and, if any party to a case refuses to heed the judgment of the Court, the other party has recourse to the Security Council, which may decide on a course of action.

• *Significance:* The usefulness of the Court has been impaired because its jurisdiction extends only to cases in which the parties concerned have given their consent prior to or after the dispute has occurred. No national court system could function under such limitations, and the International Court of Justice has suffered a lack of effectiveness as a result. Attempts to correct this weakness through compulsory jurisdiction under the "optional clause" which nations may accept have largely been unsuccessful because of reservations attached to the acceptance of compulsory jurisdiction by many nations, including the United States (Connally Amendment). Over a dozen cases have been decided by the Court, and no party in a case before the Court has refused to abide by the judgment rendered. But, unless leading members of the United Nations resolve their political differences, the Court will continue to play a limited role, having little impact on world affairs. Many people believe that world peace and security cannot be achieved without world law and a court system to enforce it.

International Labor Organization (ILO).   A Specialized Agency of the United

Nations which seeks through research and recommendation to improve working conditions throughout the world. Established in 1919, the ILO was the only agency associated with the League of Nations in which the United States participated. The ILO is concerned with problems of full employment, labor standards, migration of workers, collective bargaining, social security, and workers' health. Its headquarters are in Geneva, and it functions through a General Conference comprised of delegates representing labor, employers, and government. Between annual conferences, an executive Governing Body supervises the operations of ILO committees and commissions and prepares the agenda for future conferences.

• *Significance:* Although the ILO cannot make binding decisions, its recommendations have been adopted by many member countries, resulting in the raising of working and living conditions of millions of workers. Improvements in labor standards can best be accomplished when instituted simultaneously by many nations, otherwise those nations acting unilaterally would be placing themselves at a competitive disadvantage costwise. In recent years, much of the ILO's activity has been directed toward improving working standards and raising productivity in the underdeveloped areas of the world. Hundreds of ILO experts have provided technical assistance to countries in Asia, Africa, Latin America, and the Middle East.

International Law.   A body of rules and principles which guides the relations among nations and between governments and foreign nationals. Sources of international law include treaties, authority (e.g., decisions of international courts), reason, and custom. Treaties are the most important source today, as custom was earlier in the development of international law. The law has been classified into three categories: peace, war, and neutrality, based on the nature of the law, and into public, private, and administrative, based on the different sources of the law.

• *Significance:* Although international law evolved out of the European nation-state system, it has gained nearly universal acceptance by the world community of states. Some theorists reject the entire concept of international law, holding that law must be handed down by a sovereign authority, enforcement agencies must exist, and courts must provide sanctions against violators. Because none of these conditions exist in the state system, the existence of *law* is denied. Others refute this position by noting the universal acceptance of some elements of international law by the world community (e.g., diplomacy and commerce), and the general obedience of states to its rules. Today, with the world caught up in revolutionary ferment, international law has depreciated in importance, despite efforts of the United Nations to foster its growth and adherence to its principles.

Isolationism.   A policy pursued by the United States, during the nineteenth and part of the twentieth century, of political noninvolvement in the affairs of Europe. Isolationism as a political ideology was nurtured by geographical, ideological, and cultural separateness.

• *Significance:* American isolationism never expanded to the point of nonintercourse with Europe. It was particularly operative, however, in American intentions to remain aloof from the power struggles of Europe by remaining independent of Europe's system of entangling alliances. The doctrine was instrumental in conditioning the American public's belief that the United States should maintain neutrality during the early stages of World War I and World War II and not join the League of Nations. Most vestiges of isolationist thinking have disappeared since 1941.

League of Nations. The first general international organization created to preserve peace and security and to promote cooperation among nations in economic and social fields. The League was created by the victorious powers of World War I in 1919 under the leadership of President Woodrow Wilson, but the United States did not join. The Organization operated under a constitutional system established through its Covenant, which was a treaty that all members signed and ratified. A Council and Assembly were the major organs (similar to the Security Council and General Assembly of the United Nations) and subsidiary committees and commissions were established to deal with special problems in areas such as mandates, military affairs, and disarmament. A Secretariat headed by a Secretary-General and staffed with international civil servants provided continuity and expertness in record keeping and research. A World Court (the Permanent Court of International Justice, forerunner of the present International Court of Justice) and the International Labor Organization were independent of the League but worked closely with it. Sixty-one nations joined the League and its headquarters were at Geneva, Switzerland. • *Significance:* In its first decade, the League resolved many postwar problems and settled numerous disputes which threatened the peace. The great depression which swept across the world in 1929–1930 rekindled aggressive nationalism and reduced the League's effectiveness. Failure of the League to deal resolutely with the Japanese conquest of Manchuria in 1931, the Italian conquest of Ethiopia in 1935, and the Nazi aggressions in the late 1930's brought about its collapse. Most observers believe that the League's breakdown resulted not from internal constitutional weaknesses, but from the failure of key member states to support its principles and the refusal of the United States to join. Despite its failure to maintain peace, the League did succeed in promoting extensive international cooperation in economic and social affairs and in developing new ideas and procedures for international organizations which have proved useful to its successor, the United Nations. The League voted itself out of existence in 1946.

Marshall Plan. A proposal made by Secretary of State George C. Marshall in 1947 for a vast program of American economic aid to reconstruct the war-devastated economies of western Europe. The United States Congress accepted the Plan and, in 1948, established the European Recovery Program under which 16 nations of western Europe (later joined by West Germany) received $21 billion in loans and gifts from 1948 to 1952. Under the Marshall program, the participating European nations on American request joined together in the Organization for European Economic Cooperation (OEEC) for the purpose of drawing up a collective inventory of resources and requirements. The

U.S.S.R. and other Communist countries were invited to participate but rejected the offer.

• *Significance:* The Marshall Plan was successful in thwarting Communist aims of exploiting the economic collapse and political turmoil of the post-World War II era in western Europe. By 1951, all participating members had raised their production capacities beyond prewar levels. American attempts to promote the integration of European economies through the program were partially successful, especially on the continent. Since 1952, the rebuilt and modernized economies of European countries have increased their competition with the United States for world markets.

Monroe Doctrine. A unilateral declaration of American foreign policy made by President Monroe in his annual message to the Congress in December 1823, opposing any European intervention in the affairs of the American continents. He also reaffirmed the American intention to refrain from interfering in European affairs. The Doctrine was intended to stop the Holy Alliance from aiding Spain in a reconquest of the newly created Latin-American republics.

• *Significance:* The Monroe Doctrine at the time of its enunciation was largely meaningless because only the British fleet stood between the Holy Alliance and the reconquest of Latin America. Over the years, however, it developed into one of the basic tenets of American policy through restatements, corollaries, and through the growing ability of a powerful United States to intervene actively whenever the Doctrine was challenged. Since the Declaration of Lima in 1942, and particularly in the Rio Treaty of 1947, the Doctrine has become a common principle by which all American republics have declared their determination to defend themselves against foreign intervention. In recent years, the problem of implementing the Doctrine has centered around the creation of procommunist governments in certain Latin-American states, especially the Castro government in Cuba. This poses a problem because of the conflict between those portions of the Doctrine which rule out foreign intervention and those which guarantee that each Latin-American state may choose its own economic and political system.

Neutralism. A "third force" in the cold war power struggle comprised of states which pursue policies of nonalignment with either the free world or Communist bloc. Most of the nations of Asia, Africa, and the Middle East and a few states in Europe have refused to join military alliance systems propagated by either the United States or Soviet Russia. Although some of these states profess ideological sympathy toward one side or the other, none has committed itself to any kind of military involvement.

• *Significance:* Neutralist leaders have consistently emphasized that neutralism is a positive force which endeavors to prevent another catastrophic global war by encouraging a rapprochement between the east and west. Both rival power blocs have been seeking to win the favor of the neutralists. Some of these neutralist states, such as Sweden and Ireland, are ideologically identified with the West whereas others, such as Yugoslavia and Ghana, are more sympathetic with the goals of the Communist bloc. Others, such as India and Burma, have tried to steer a middle course. None, however, has committed itself to any military alliance.

Neutrality.   The legal status of a nation which does not participate in a war between other states. It is free to defend its territory or neutral waters against attack by belligerents. Although public opinion and even the government of a neutral state may sympathize with one side or the other, to retain its neutral position a state may not engage in action which might favor one side in the war. Some states have espoused a doctrine of perpetual neutrality, such as Switzerland, Sweden, and Ireland.

• *Significance:* The concept of neutrality has lost some of its meaning in modern times because of the increasingly ruthless nature of war, its expansion into global struggles, and the tendency of neutrals to show some favoritism based on ideological sympathies. In a future global war, neutrals may be placed in as great a position of danger as belligerents because of the possibilities of radioactive fall-out, the spread of poisonous gases, and the employment of biological warfare by belligerents.

North Atlantic Treaty Organization (NATO).   A permanent organization established under the North Atlantic Treaty of 1949 to create a single unified defense force to safeguard the security of the North Atlantic area. Members agree under Article V of the Treaty to regard an attack upon any of them as an attack upon all, and, if an armed attack occurs, each will render such assistance as it deems necessary. NATO now includes 15 members, the original 12 (Belgium, Britain, Canada, Denmark, France, Iceland, Italy, Luxembourg, Netherlands, Norway, Portugal, and the United States) and three states which joined NATO in the 1950's (Greece, Turkey, and West Germany). NATO's members seek, in addition to attainment of mutual security, "the further development of peaceful and friendly international relations . . . and to eliminate conflict in their international economic policies."

• *Significance:* For over a decade, NATO has represented the basic framework of the political-military structure of the west. Important questions, such as the rearmament of West Germany, the establishment of missile bases in western Europe, the employment of nuclear weapons, and over-all strategic and tactical strategy have been worked out through the political and military channels of cooperation established within the NATO framework. NATO's solidarity has tended to wax and wane over the years as the Cold War grew more intense or cooled off through Soviet peace offensives. In recent years, pressures have been brought by European statesmen to implement more fully the treaty provisions calling for expanded political and economic cooperation. The future importance of NATO as a military "sword and shield" will likely depend upon the nature of the new weapons developed by the United States and the Soviet Union.

Organization for Economic Cooperation and Development (OECD).   An international organization created in 1961 to achieve expanded cooperation and joint action between the United States and western Europe and Canada. The OECD is an outgrowth of the Organization for European Economic Cooperation (OEEC) established in 1948 to decide how American aid granted under the Marshall Plan would be distributed. When the OEEC went out of existence in 1960, its membership included 18 European nations which, with the addition of the United States and Canada, comprise the present membership of OECD. Fifteen of the 20 members of OECD are NATO allies—the United States, Canada, Belgium, Britain, Denmark, France, Greece, Iceland, Italy, Luxembourg, Netherlands, Norway, Portugal, Turkey, and West Germany. The other five are Austria, Ireland, Spain, Sweden, and Switzerland.

• *Significance:* The objectives of the OECD are (1) to encourage economic growth and financial stability for member nations; (2) to expand and improve western aid to underdeveloped countries; (3) to expand trade among members and with the world through more liberal policies; and (4) to provide a forum where members can consult on mutual economic problems. The United States was the main force behind the creation of the OECD. American policy makers were particularly concerned with overcoming the balance of payments deficit, with penetrating the Common Market and Free Trade Association trading blocs in Europe, and with ensuring that all western nations would carry their fair share of the program for aiding the underdeveloped countries.

Organization of American States (OAS). A regional political organization comprised of the United States and 20 Latin-American republics which was created at the Bogotá Conference in 1948. The OAS consists of (1) the Inter-American Conference, which meets every five years to decide general policies; (2) the Council, with each member state represented by an ambassador, which oversees the implementation of general policies of OAS; (3) the Consultative Meetings of Ministers of Foreign Affairs, which occur whenever urgent problems confront the OAS; (4) the Pan-American Union, which operates through its headquarters, in Washington, D.C., as a general secretariat of the OAS; (5) the Specialized Conferences, which are called periodically to enable the members to cooperate in dealing with technical problems; and (6) the Specialized Agencies, which are responsible for eliciting cooperation in economic, social, education, technical, and humanitarian problem areas. The OAS is a regional organization of the type encouraged by the United Nations Charter. Important provisions of the OAS Charter are concerned with the peaceful settlement of disputes among members, and with procedures for mediation, arbitration, and adjudication.

• *Significance:* The OAS regional system has institutionalized the principles embodied in the Monroe Doctrine. All major hemispheric problems have been taken up since 1948 through the machinery of the OAS. In recent years, Communist infiltration into Latin America has been a major problem for OAS organs. In 1960, the foreign ministers approved the Declaration of San José condemning the intervention by any outside power in the affairs of the American republics. The OAS has also condemned and taken action against right-wing dictatorships; for example, in 1960 the foreign ministers levied an arms embargo and economic boycott against Rafael Trujillo's Dominican Republic and called for the breaking off of diplomatic relations with the Dominican government. The major challenge facing OAS in the future will be that of meeting increasing Sino-Soviet efforts to penetrate economically and politically into the western hemisphere.

Pacific Settlement of Disputes.   The peaceful adjustment of international disputes through the use of one or more of the following techniques: negotiation, inquiry, good offices, mediation, conciliation, arbitration, or adjudication. Pacific settlement may be employed through the traditional diplomatic channels, by regional organizations or arrangements, or through the organs or agencies of the United Nations. Chapter VI of the United Nations Charter sets out in detail the political procedures available to the Security Council and the General Assembly; Chapter XV delegates peaceful settlement responsibilities to the Secretary-General; and Chapter XIV prescribes the legal processes by which the International Court of Justice may attempt to settle justiciable disputes.

• *Significance:* War occurs not only as a result of planned aggression but also from failure to keep international disputes within peaceful bounds. The United Nations system has bolstered traditional and regional settlement channels by establishing the principle of member responsibility to settle all disputes peacefully and by providing permanent machinery readily available to take up disputes. The UN has a good record of settling or limiting the effects of many important disputes, including the Soviet-Iranian case, the Indonesian-Netherlands dispute, the India-Pakistan case, the Arab-Israel dispute, and various controversies which have arisen in the Cold War.

Pan-American Union.   The permanent organ and general secretariat of the Organization of American States (OAS). Its headquarters is in Washington, D.C., and it operates under a governing board of 20 Latin-American Ambassadors and the United States Secretary of State.

• *Significance:* The Union's four administrative departments—economic and social, cultural, international law, and administrative services—operate as advisers to the OAS agencies and as a clearinghouse to supply information to member governments. The Pan-American Union is a good example of the implementation of the Good Neighbor policy of the United States in treating Latin-American states as equals and in tackling common problems through mutual cooperation.

Persona non Grata.   An unacceptable person. *Persona non grata* relates particularly to when a nation declares that an ambassador or minister is no longer acceptable and requests his recall by his government, or dismisses him by handing him his passport.

• *Significance:* Each nation is free to accept or reject any person accredited to it as a diplomatic agent. When a diplomat is declared *persona non grata,* his government may consider it an affront, but the procedure is generally recognized and accepted. Numerous incidents in recent years involving the declaring of diplomatic agents *persona non grata* have resulted from the Cold War. In most such cases, retaliation has followed, with a diplomat of equal status declared *persona non grata* following the first dismissal.

Quid pro Quo.   A diplomatic bargaining concept meaning, literally, something for something. Negotiations conducted on a basis of *quid pro quo* depend on mutual compromises for success.

• *Significance:* Any nation unable to demand a *quid pro quo* in exchange for

its own concessions is in an inferior bargaining (and power) position. Reciprocal concessions are particularly useful in reducing tariffs and other trade barriers through *quid pro quo* bargaining.

Ratification.   The formal action of the President in giving effect to a treaty
which has been approved by the Senate. The President or his representative
meets with representatives of the other signatory parties and exchanges ratifications with them. The treaty then is officially proclaimed and becomes legally
enforceable. *See* RATIFICATION, page 165.

• *Significance:* Contrary to popular belief, the Senate does not officially ratify
a treaty when it gives its advice and consent. In giving its consent, the Senate
may attach amendments or reservations which may influence the decision of
the President on ratification. The Senate's amendments or reservations, under
which portions of a treaty will not be considered binding on the United States,
leave the President with three choices: (1) renegotiation of the treaty; (2)
ratification with reservations, if acceptable to other signatories; or (3) refusal
to ratify. In American history, over 900 treaties have been approved by the
Senate and ratified by the President. In approximately 100 other cases, the
Senate has either failed to act or has approved the treaties with reservations
or amendments of such a nature that either the President or one of the signatories refused to ratify them. In addition, over 60 treaties have been rejected
outright by the Senate, thus eliminating the question of ratification.

Recognition.   The discretionary function exercised by the President of
deciding whether or not the United States shall officially carry on relations with
a new state or a new political regime in an existing state. *See* RECOGNITION,
page 165.

• *Significance:* Each state in the world must determine for itself if and when
new states and governments are to be recognized. Premature recognition of a
revolutionary regime may lead to a threat of war by the government fighting
the insurgent group. Conversely, continued refusal to recognize an existing
state or an established government may engender hostility toward the state
which withholds it. American recognition policy has varied with different
presidents but, since World War I, it has generally been one of withholding
it from regimes distasteful to American citizens and of granting it to friendly
governments. The world-wide ideological struggle has influenced presidential
recognition policies in recent years. A major recognition controversy, linked
also with the question of representation in the United Nations, has involved the
refusal of the United States to accept Communist China into the family of nations.

Regionalism.   The development of limited systems of international organization which enable groupings of states to deal cooperatively with political,
economic, social, and military problems. Geographical proximity of states typi-
fies most regional organizations, although a community of common interests
appears to be the integrating force behind such movements. Regional organizations include the military alliance systems of both the western and Soviet blocs,
political systems like the Organization of American States and the Council

of Europe, and economic groupings such as the Common Market and the Free Trade Association.

• *Significance:* Although the United Nations Charter encourages regionalism (Article 52), the prolific growth of regional organizations has had a limiting effect on the fostering of world-wide cooperation through the world organization. Supporters of regionalism point out that it represents a gradual approach toward world unity and is more realistic than either unilateralism or universalism because of the disharmony and conflict which exists in the world. Opponents argue that international problems are world-wide in scope and that increasing economic and security interdependence can best be met by a universal system.

Rio Treaty.   The Inter-American Treaty of Reciprocal Assistance of 1947 by which 21 American republics agreed "that an armed attack by any State against an American State shall be considered as an attack against all the American States. . . ." The Rio Treaty was the first mutual security pact entered into by the United States and it became a model for all subsequent ones. The treaty establishes a hemispheric security zone stretching from the North Pole to the South Pole. If an attack occurs within the zone, members agree to consult upon collective measures to be undertaken while retaining freedom to act individually "in accordance with the principle of continental solidarity." The treaty also includes principles and means by which conflicts between American states can be settled peacefully. Decisions concerning implementation of the treaty are reached through the Organization of American States (OAS) machinery.

• *Significance:* The Rio Treaty has gained new importance as a result of increasing economic and political penetration into Latin America by the Soviet Union and Communist China. The major difficulty has been that posed by the establishment of a Communist regime in Cuba without a direct military attack by a nonhemispheric power. The Organization of American States sought to close this loophole in August 1960, when it adopted the Declaration of San José calling for action against Communist infiltration and subversion in the hemisphere.

Sanctions.   A collective, punitive action involving diplomatic, economic, or military measures against a state committing an aggression. Under the United Nations Charter (Chapter VII), when the Security Council determines that a "threat to the peace, breach of the peace, or act of aggression" exists, members may be called upon to invoke military or nonmilitary sanctions against the lawbreaking state. Since the adoption of the Uniting For Peace Resolution in 1950, the General Assembly is also empowered to levy sanctions against an aggressor by a two-thirds vote. Sanctions may include such actions as breaking diplomatic relations, embargo or blockade, and the use of force.

• *Significance:* An international law-enforcement system, like a nation's, must provide enforcement action to be effective. The threat of collective sanctions may frequently be more effective in preventing aggression than the enforcement system is in dealing with actual aggressions. The League of Nations attempted only once to employ sanctions (an economic boycott was levied against Italy after its attack upon Ethiopia in 1935) but failed to deter the aggressor. The United Nations levied military and economic sanctions against North Korea in 1950 and applied economic measures against Communist China.

San Francisco Conference. The United Nations Conference on International Organization at which 50 states wrote and signed the United Nations Charter in the period from April 25 to June 26, 1945. The deliberations at San Francisco were based on the *Proposals* which had been formulated by representatives of Britain, China, the Soviet Union, and the United States at the Dumbarton Oaks Conference in 1944.
• *Significance:* Contrary to later developments, the major conflicts which occurred at San Francisco in drafting the Charter were not among the great powers but between them and the small states. The great powers were in substantial agreement concerning their pre-eminent position in the new world organization and successfully fought off all attempts to challenge it. The United Nations Charter went into effect October 24, 1945 (since declared United Nations Day) after it had been ratified by 51 states, including Poland which sent no delegation to the Conference.

Secretariat. An organized body of officials and civil servants who have the responsibility of fulfilling administrative, secretarial, and housekeeping functions for an international organization. The United Nations Secretariat is one of the six major organs of the world organization. Its formal structure includes a Secretary-General and eight Assistant Secretaries-General, each of the latter heading a major Department (Security, Economic, Social, Trusteeship, Legal, Information, General Services, and Administrative and Financial).
• *Significance:* The success or failure of an international organization often depends on the efficiency of its secretariat and the capabilities and dedication of its staff. The United Nations has fostered the concept of an international civil service whose members serve the United Nations without regard for the views of their own countries. The concept of an independent secretariat, however, has been endangered in recent years by the Soviet Union's refusal to accept the UN Secretariat's administrative actions, as in the Congo crisis.

Secretary-General. The chief administrative officer of the United Nations who heads the Secretariat. The Secretary-General is chosen by the General Assembly upon recommendation by the Security Council for five-year terms. He is responsible for translating, recording, printing and distributing debates and documents, and he sits in at meetings of the Assembly and the three UN Councils to offer assistance when requested. The UN Charter, in an attempt to strengthen the office of Secretary-General over its League predecessor, gave him authority to place security questions before the Security Council.
• *Significance:* The role of the Secretary-General has greatly expanded with the assignment of various political responsibilities in addition to his administrative duties. In theory, the position of Secretary-General is somewhat analogous to that of a city manager; in practice, however, it has evolved into a position of real leadership. Although he must operate within the framework of Assembly or Security Council resolutions, much decision-making power is left to him

in the implementing of these resolutions. Trygve Lie of Norway, first Secretary-General of the United Nations, provided effective leadership until a western-Soviet split over the Korean War reduced his ability to function in that role. Dag Hammarskjold of Sweden, who replaced Lie in 1953, further expanded the executive role of the office and maintained the support of all UN Members until the Congo crisis of 1960. At that time, the Soviet Union charged Hammarskjold with partisanship in his handling of the Congo situation and demanded that he be replaced by a three-man presidium ("troika"), representing western, communist, and neutralist blocs. The death of Hammarskjold in 1961 left the problem unresolved. U Thant of Burma was appointed to complete the unexpired two years of Hammarskjold's term.

Secretary of State.   The leading Cabinet officer who heads the Department of State and is charged with the responsibility of formulating policies and conducting relations with foreign states. The Secretary of State has been recognized by statute as first of the Cabinet officials in the line of succession to the presidency following the Vice President, Speaker, and President pro tempore. His responsibilities include the direction and supervision of policy-making and administrative functions vested in the State Department in Washington, D.C., the diplomatic and consular services, and special missions and agencies abroad.
• *Significance:* The role of the Secretary of State as a decision maker may be as great or as insignificant as the President may decide. Some presidents, like Woodrow Wilson and Franklin Roosevelt, largely ignored their secretaries of state and handled foreign policy matters directly and personally. Other presidents have delegated full responsibility to their secretaries of state in all foreign affairs. Often in American history, the Secretary of State has become a political target of the opposition party.

Security Council.   One of the six major organs of the United Nations which was given primary responsibility for maintaining peace and security in the world. There are five permanent members—Britain, China, France, Soviet Union, and the United States—and six nonpermanent members elected by the General Assembly for two-year periods, three chosen each year. Procedural and substantive decisions are made by an affirmative vote of seven members but, in the latter case, a negative vote cast by any permanent member constitutes a veto and stops all action. When considering peaceful settlement measures, a Council member which is a party to the dispute must abstain from voting. Nations which are not members of the Council may be invited to participate without a vote in Council deliberations if they are involved in a dispute being considered. The Charter in Chapter VII gives the Security Council the responsibility to "determine the existence of any threat to the peace, breach of the peace, or act of aggression. . . ." The Council can make recommendations or take enforcement action to restore peace and security.
• *Significance:* The Security Council was given the most important responsibilities by the Charter on the assumption that the great powers would continue to cooperate in the postwar period to maintain peace and security. Instead, the major threats to world peace have involved great power rivalry, and over 100 vetoes have reduced the effectiveness of the Council. Many disputes and prob-

lems have been dealt with successfully by the Council, but few involving cold war questions have been resolved. As the Council's ability to act during crises faded, a new role was thrust upon the General Assembly, which today has replaced the Council as the dominant organ of the United Nations. The importance of the Council today lies mainly in its role of providing the machinery for a continuous forum for great power negotiation.

South-East Asia Treaty Organization (SEATO). A military-economic arrangement based on the South-East Asia Collective Defense Treaty signed at Manila on September 8, 1954. Members who agree to take collective action whenever any of their number are threatened by external aggression or internal subversion in southeast Asia are Australia, Britain, France, New Zealand, Pakistan, Philippines, Thailand, and the United States. SEATO headquarters are in Bangkok and include a council and secretariat.
• *Significance:* SEATO was created through the efforts of Secretary of State John Foster Dulles to safeguard vital interests against Communist penetration in the southeast Asia area. The economic cooperation sections of the agreement have been overshadowed by the military and anti-Communist provisions. Successive internal Communist threats, supplied with military equipment by Sino-Soviet forces, have challenged the effectiveness of SEATO to maintain the security of the southeast Asia area.

Sovereignty. A legal concept which, in international affairs, means statehood, political independence, and freedom from external control.
• *Significance:* The importance of sovereignty in the modern state system has come largely from the psychological effect it has had on the decision-making processes of states. It has been a difficult force to overcome in creating political, military, and economic international organizations with decision-making powers. Sovereignty remains one of the major legal and psychological obstacles to the effective operation of the United Nations system.

Status Quo. A descriptive term used by international political analysts to describe the foreign policy of a state which aims at preserving the existing distribution of power in the world. The concept is derived from the diplomatic term, *status quo ante bellum,* which is a clause typically inserted into peace treaties providing for the restoration of prewar conditions.
• *Significance:* The term "status quo" is used as an analytical tool in seeking to understand and describe the motivations and actions of states in the struggle for power which characterizes the state system. States pursuing policies of revision provide the challenge which forces the status quo grouping to develop defensive policies and alliances. Since World War II, the United States has pursued a policy of the status quo, vis-à-vis the expansionist policies of the Soviet bloc.

Tariff. A tax levied on imports to help protect a nation's industry, business, labor, and agriculture from foreign competition, or to raise revenue. Tariffs are discriminatory if they apply unequally on similar products from different countries, and are retaliatory if motivated by the creation of trade barriers by other countries.

• *Significance:* Tariffs have been used by the United States since 1789 as the principal means of protecting domestic producers from foreign competition. For many years prior to the adoption of an income tax, the tariff was also a primary source of revenue for the federal government. Since 1934, the United States has sought to encourage mutual reductions in tariffs through the Reciprocal Trade Agreements Program.

Treaty.   A formal agreement entered into between two or more sovereign states for the purpose of creating or restricting mutual rights and mutual responsibilities. The treaty process includes negotiation, signing, ratification, exchange of ratifications, publishing and proclamation, and treaty execution. Treaties having only two signatory states are called bilateral, whereas those with more than two parties are multilateral. Treaties may expire at the end of a specified time limit, when certain conditions have been met, or by mutual agreement. Renunciation of a treaty by one of its parties may occur when a state of war exists or when conditions have been substantially altered (*rebus sic stantibus*). In the United States, all treaties are negotiated under the direction of the President, with some members of the Senate occasionally participating under the constitutional provision that treaties be made "by and with the advice and consent of the Senate. . . ." Treaties must be approved by a two-thirds vote in the Senate, followed by presidential ratification if the Senate's version is acceptable. *See* EXECUTIVE AGREEMENT, page 308; RATIFICATION, page 318.
• *Significance:* Multilateral treaties have become the major source of international law today. In the United States, treaties are part of the supreme law of the land and take precedence over state constitutions and laws. The courts have never declared a treaty to be unconstitutional. The Supreme Court has held that a treaty may increase the powers of the Congress beyond the powers prescribed in the Constitution (*Missouri v. Holland,* 252 U.S. 416 [1920]). Increasingly, American presidents have come to depend on executive agreements rather than treaties; the latter are generally used only when strong congressional and public opinion support are essential to the success of the arrangements.

Truman Doctrine.   The policy adopted by President Harry Truman on March 12, 1947, which called for American support for all free peoples resisting armed subjugation by internal or outside forces. The policy was aimed expressly at halting Communist expansion in southeastern Europe and was expounded in a speech to the Congress in which President Truman asked for an appropriation of $400 million for military and economic aid to Greece and Turkey.
• *Significance:* The Truman Doctrine marked the first official acceptance of the "containment" philosophy of building up free world strength to halt Communist expansionism. The Truman Administration followed it up with the development of the Marshall Plan (1947), a technical assistance program (1949), the North Atlantic Treaty (1949), and a mutual security program (1951). The Truman Doctrine as applied to Greece and Turkey was successful in helping the Greek loyalists to win the civil war, and in building up Turkey as a bastion of free world strength with a modern army.

Trusteeship Council.   One of the six major organs of the United Nations which helps the General Assembly to supervise the administration of the international trusteeship system. Members of the Council include those nations which administer trust territories, permanent members of the Security Council, and elected members equal in number to the total of trust-administering states on the Council. Trust territories include (1) the former mandates of the League of Nations; (2) Axis colonies; and (3) colonies voluntarily placed under trusteeship. No colonial power has yet volunteered to place a colony under the system. Council powers include considering reports, accepting petitions, and making periodic visits to trust territories. Administration of "strategic" trust territories is supervised by the Security Council, rather than the Trusteeship Council, because of their military importance.

• *Significance:* Through its supervisory role the Trusteeship Council has helped move most trust territories toward self-government. Libya, Italian Somaliland, and Tanganyika, for example, have become independent states, and remaining trust territories are moving rapidly toward that goal. Little progress has been made toward the self-government of the three island groups under American strategic trust—the Marshalls, the Carolines, and the Marianas.

Yalta Conference.   A summit conference of President Franklin Roosevelt, Prime Minister Winston Churchill, and Premier Josef Stalin, held at Yalta in the Russian Crimea in February 1945, to make plans for the defeat and occupation of Germany, the future of eastern Europe, and the defeat of Japan. War decisions agreed upon were: (1) German surrender must be unconditional; (2) German war criminals would be swiftly brought to justice; (3) reparations would be exacted; (4) liberated eastern Europe would set up new governments based on free democratic elections; (5) Polish borders would be shifted westward at the expense of Germany; and (6) the Soviet Union would join in the war against Japan within three months following the end of the European war. Additionally, important decisions were made concerning the proposed United Nations Organization, including a formula for Security Council voting and the use of the veto, and the granting to the U.S.S.R. of three seats in the United Nations instead of the 16 seats demanded by Stalin.

• *Significance:* The Yalta Agreement largely determined the policies of the victorious Big Three powers toward the defeated Axis countries in the absence of a general peace treaty. It also influenced the reshaping of power structures and spheres of influence in Asia and eastern Europe. The Soviet Union regained in Asia essentially the position she had had there before her defeat in the Russo-Japanese War in 1905, and created a group of satellite states in eastern Europe. The Yalta Agreement became a major election campaign issue in 1948 and 1952, the Republicans charging a "give-away" to Stalin of Poland and eastern Europe, the Democrats defending Roosevelt's action and charging the Soviet Union with violation of the Agreement.

IMPORTANT AGENCIES

Agency for International Development (AID).   A semi-independent agency within the Department of State which directs economic and technical assistance aid programs to foreign nations. AID was created by the Congress in the Act for International Development of 1961, and it replaced the former International Cooperation Administration (ICA). AID works through United States Operations Missions in each country receiving aid. Each mission is responsible for developing programs jointly with government officials of the recipient state and for overseeing the work of the specialists attached to it. AID is headed by a director who has a dual role as chief of the operating agency and political adviser to the Secretary of State. In 1962, of the 38,000 personnel in the Department of State, 17,000 were in AID.

• *Significance:* AID has become an increasingly important agency as the Soviets have stepped up their world-wide economic offensive. Although military aid has outweighed economic aid since 1951, the Kennedy Administration has stressed the expansion of economic programs. Total foreign economic aid administered by the ICA and the AID since 1955 has averaged almost $2 billion each year. AID was created particularly to implement President Kennedy's Alliance for Progress program.

Department of State. The agency primarily responsible for making and executing American foreign policy. The Secretary of State who heads the Department is the President's official adviser on foreign policy matters. The first responsibility of the Department is to formulate programs and policies for the United States in its relations with other nations. Next in importance are its duties of administering laws relating to foreign affairs and conducting the day-to-day relations with foreign countries. The latter responsibility is carried out primarily by the Foreign Service which is administratively tied to the Department of State and has been undergoing a gradual process of integrating its personnel with that of the Department. Specific duties of the Department include (1) negotiating treaties and agreements with foreign states; (2) carrying on extensive communications with foreign governments and American units abroad; (3) issuing passports and, through consular officials abroad, granting visas; (4) promoting cultural relations between foreign peoples and the American people; (5) carrying on propaganda and information programs overseas; (6) planning and formulating short- and long-range programs. The Department and its Secretary are responsible to the President in carrying out these duties. Important policy making and primary contact with field operations and foreign missions are carried on through six regional bureaus. These include the African, Inter-American, European, Far Eastern, and Near Eastern and South Asian Affairs Bureaus, and a Bureau of International Organization Affairs, each headed by an Assistant Secretary.

• *Significance:* The Department is the major agency for foreign policy decision making. The importance of its role may depend on the individuals who are President and Secretary of State. For example, President Woodrow Wilson chose to depend largely on his own abilities and those of close friends in making foreign policy decisions. John Foster Dulles, as Secretary of State under President Dwight Eisenhower, preferred to deal with important matters personally, and the Department's staff declined in influence under his leadership. The main conflict over the role of the Department has involved the question of whether it should confine itself to policy making or be charged additionally with administering foreign programs. This problem has never been fully resolved, although today its primary responsibility is that of developing policy.

United States Information Agency (USIA).   Created in 1953, by a presidential reorganization directive, to take over responsibility and administration for all information programs of the United States in foreign affairs. The new agency absorbed the Voice of America and the International Information Administration. It operates a global network of radio stations which beam propaganda programs at Communist and neutral nations. Hundreds of information centers throughout the world provide outlets for reading materials designed to give a favorable impression of the United States.

• *Significance:* The USIA directs American governmental efforts in the psychological phase of the Cold War. Activities include round-the-clock radio broadcasts in almost 50 languages, numerous television programs over more than 150 free world stations, distribution and showings of documentary, feature, and newsreel films, and distribution of millions of leaflets, pamphlets, news bulletins, and related propaganda materials. The USIA has operated on the proposition that "truth is our weapon." Evaluations of the USIA generally have criticized its overemphasis on defensive responses to an aggressive Soviet propaganda while it places too little stress on developing a better understanding of American policies.

United States Tariff Commission.   An independent agency which gives information to the Congress and the President on American and foreign tariff and trade matters. The six members of the Tariff Commission, three from each of the major parties, are appointed by the President with the Senate's approval.

• *Significance:* The Congress has used the Tariff Commission as a means of keeping the President's tariff reductions, under the Reciprocal Trade Agreements Act, within some degree of congressional supervision and control. In the "peril point" provisions, the Tariff Commission indicates a rate for each imported product at which it might enter the American market in a quantity sufficient to threaten or injure domestic producers. Under "escape clause" provisions, the Commission can recommend to the President that a trade agreement be adjusted when its investigations disclose that low tariff rates are threatening to injure or are injuring American producers. If the President rejects the advice of the Tariff Commission, the Congress can override him and restore the higher tariff rate by a two-thirds vote in both houses. The escape clause has been invoked by the United States to modify agreements with foreign nations on only a few occasions.

IMPORTANT CASES

Missouri v. Holland, 252 U.S. 416 (1920): Upheld the validity of a federal statute based on a treaty with Great Britain for the protection of birds and waterfowl migrating between Canada and the United States. The question was whether the national government could acquire, through a treaty, power to legislate on domestic matters otherwise reserved to the states. A similar federal law, antedating the treaty and the law in question in this case, had earlier been declared unconstitutional by the lower federal courts. This decision means that the national government can actually add to its powers by concluding treaties with foreign states.

• *Significance:* Opponents of increasing federal responsibility have argued since 1920 that this case must be overturned because it almost obliterates the distinction between delegated and reserved powers. This viewpoint crystallized in the 1950's in the Bricker Amendment proposal which would have allowed treaties to become effective within the United States only through legislation which would be valid in the absence of a treaty. Supporters of the decision point out that the alleged danger has not materialized and that to limit the treaty-making powers would constitute a greater danger to the country.

United States v. Curtiss-Wright Export Corp., 299 U.S. 304 (1936): Upheld the validity of a statute of the Congress which delegated broad powers to the President to prohibit arms shipments to foreign belligerents. In question was a presidential proclamation levying an embargo on shipment of war materiel to either side in the Gran Chaco war between Bolivia and Paraguay. In the *Curtiss-Wright* case, the Court distinguished between broad delegations of congressional lawmaking power in domestic areas and in foreign affairs. The Court noted: "As a member of the family of nations, the right and power of the United States . . . are equal to the right and power of the other nations of the international family. Otherwise the United States is not completely sovereign."

• *Significance:* The Court recognized in this case the full responsibility of the national government in foreign affairs and the importance of the President's role in this field. By authorizing congressional and presidential actions in foreign affairs which might not be valid in domestic matters, the Court was recognizing that, in addition to the enumerated and implied powers, a third category of powers, inherent in nature, may be exercised by the President in foreign affairs. The Court reaffirmed the primacy of the national government in foreign affairs in *United States v. Pink,* 315 U.S. 203 (1942), asserting that power over foreign relations "is not shared by the states; it is vested in the national government exclusively." Federalism, the Court noted, stops at the water's edge.

IMPORTANT STATUTES

Battle Act.   An act passed by Congress in 1951 designed to prohibit trade with Communist countries in strategic goods and to deny American aid to any nation that carried on such trade.

• *Significance:* The Battle Act has resulted in a major reduction of American trade with the Soviet Union and other Communist countries. Much effort has been expended by American negotiators since 1951 to persuade allies and neutralist countries to cut off their trade with the Communists. The policy was moderately successful for a few years but, since the launching of the massive Soviet trade offensives in the latter part of the 1950's, most of the non-Communist nations of the world have progressively increased their trade with the Soviet bloc.

Reciprocal Trade Agreements Act of 1934.   A broad tariff program under which the President negotiates trade agreements with foreign countries that provide for mutual reductions in tariff rates. Enacted for a three-year period, it has since been renewed for periods from one to four years in duration. It incorporates the "most favored nation" principle, under which concessions contained in agreements apply to all other nations with which we have most favored nation arrangements. The original enactment in 1934 provided that tariff rates of the United States could be lowered or raised up to 50 percent of the existing rates, but more recent renewals have given the President authority to seek additional cuts. Amendments to the Act include "peril point" and "escape clause" provisions. The peril point amendment provides that the Tariff Commission inform the President and the Congress at what level a tariff rate might allow imports to threaten or injure a domestic producer. Escape clause procedures require that tariff rates be raised if they injure domestic producers.

• *Significance:* The Reciprocal Trade Agreements Act sought to increase the two-way flow of trade by transferring rate-setting powers from the Congress, where political considerations and logrolling tactics flourished, to the President, who was empowered to lower rates only on a *quid pro quo* basis. Agreements with 43 countries are currently in force. Reciprocal bargaining has been facilitated through multilateral negotiations carried on through the General Agreement on Tariffs and Trade (GATT) system with a membership of 35 nations. Protectionist sentiment, however, has increased in the Congress in recent years as a result of growing competition from imports.

Rogers (Foreign Service) Act of 1924.   The basic law which established the organization and functions of the Foreign Service as it exists today. The Rogers Act unified the diplomatic and consular services into an integrated Foreign Service, created a career service based on merit, and established the Foreign Service Institute. Subsequent amendments added in the Foreign Service Acts of 1946 and 1949 have sought to professionalize the Service. Additional changes based on the report of the Wriston Committee in 1954 have sought to "democratize" the Service and integrate its personnel with that of the State Department.

• *Significance:* The Rogers Act initiated a series of reforms which have reshaped the Foreign Service over the years and developed it into a first-rate organization. Appointment to the Foreign Service today is open to most Americans, yet involves the most careful selection process developed by any government agency. The Foreign Service organization and the quality of its personnel have a direct bearing on the wisdom and success of making foreign policy and conducting foreign affairs.

17

National Defense

Civilian Control. The American constitutional principle providing for civilian supremacy over the military to safeguard republican institutions.

• *Significance:* Civilian control is maintained through constitutional provisions which make the President commander in chief of the armed forces and grant the Congress power to raise and support armies, make military law, declare war, and appropriate money for only two-year periods for military expenditures. The Second and Third Amendments buttress the principle by forbidding the quartering of troops without consent and by granting the right of the people to keep and bear arms. Statutory enactments also encourage civilian control, such as the legal requirement that the Secretary of Defense and the Secretaries of the Army, Navy, and Air Force Departments must all be civilians. Civilian control is especially significant in a democratic nation which is beset by potential enemies and has built up a great military power. Several countries of the world today appear to be democratic but are controlled by military cliques. Some people in the United States have become fearful of the rising power and influence of the military during the period of the Cold War, yet national defense considerations have increased the nation's dependence upon them.

Commander in Chief. The role of the President, as provided in Article II, section 2, as supreme commander of the military forces of the United States and of the state militias when they are called into federal service. As commander in chief, the President exercises a vast array of "war powers." During periods of war or threat of war, he exercises both military and civilian powers related to defense.

• *Significance:* Under his war powers, the President can deploy American forces anywhere in the world and, as has happened many times in American history, order them into action against a foreign foe without a declaration of war by the Congress. President Harry Truman's ordering of American troops into combat in Korea without congressional action illustrates the extent to which a President can commit the nation to a course of military action under his powers as commander in chief.

329

Court-Martial.   A military tribunal which conducts trials of military personnel accused of violating military law. A *summary* court-martial consists of a single officer who tries enlisted men for minor offenses. A *special* court-martial, which can only be convened by a commanding general, consists of three officers who may impose moderately severe penalties, such as six months at hard labor, bad conduct discharges, and reductions in rank. A *general* court-martial may be convened by the President or Secretary of Defense. It consists of five or more members, one third of whom must be enlisted men if requested by the accused. Severe penalties, such as the death penalty, life imprisonment, or dishonorable discharge, may be imposed.

• *Significance:* The court-martial has become an important part of the American system of justice because of the large numbers of Americans in the armed forces. During World War II, almost one third of the nation's criminal cases were decided by courts-martial. Charges of unfair procedures and a lack of justice led the Congress to establish a new Uniform Code of Military Justice in 1950, to provide for enlisted men to serve on *general* courts-martial, and to create a three-man civilian Court of Military Appeals to which convicted military personnel can appeal.

Declaration of War.   A formal announcement by a nation that a state of hostilities exists with another nation. Constitutionally, only the Congress may declare war. Under the usual procedure, the President requests a declaration of war, the Congress adopts it by joint resolution, and the President signs it.

• *Significance:* In the conditions of modern war, the Congress has lost most of its discretionary power to determine when and if war should be declared. The Congress may merely recognize that a state of hostilities already exists, as in its declaration of war against the Axis powers following the attack upon Pearl Harbor. Moreover, the President as commander in chief may commit American forces to action without a congressional declaration of war, as when President Franklin Roosevelt ordered a naval convoy for merchant ships prior to America's actual entry into World War II. In the Korean War, American troops, ordered into action by President Harry Truman, fought from 1950 to 1953 under the United Nations banner without a formal declaration of war by the Congress. Today, with missiles and hydrogen bombs poised for attack, the decision to launch or repel an attack may be made by the President or, conceivably, by a military commander in the field, with the Congress having little to do with the decision.

Limited War.   Any war which is fought without the employment of all major weapons and for objectives other than the complete defeat of the enemy. Limited war today would involve the use of conventional military forces rather than the use of atomic superweapons.

• *Significance:* In the Korean War of 1950–1953, the United States and other nations fought a limited war with conventional military forces, under the United Nations flag. Efforts to contain the war from spreading into a general world-wide conflagration were successful, but the result was that a decisive victory became impossible to achieve. Many critics opposed American defense policies in the 1950's on the ground that too much emphasis was placed upon weapons of massive destruction at the expense of mobile tactical forces of the type needed to fight limited wars. This opposition was based on the belief that since neither the Soviet Union nor the United States would employ atomic weapons, the United States found itself in an inferior position to combat localized aggressions because of its overemphasis on atomic forces. The Kennedy Administration has sought to achieve a "balanced force" of conventional and nuclear weapons.

Martial Law. Military government established over a civilian population during an emergency in which military decrees supersede civilian laws and military tribunals replace civil courts. Martial law may be accompanied by the suspension of the writ of habeas corpus; vast discretion is vested in military officers. Although the Constitution does not delegate specific power to declare martial law, it is implied from military and defense powers and can be invoked by the President when necessary for the security of the nation.
• *Significance:* Martial law is sometimes erroneously used to describe the use of troops to aid civil authorities and civil courts in maintaining order, which is far more common than the suspension of civil authority. Rare occasions when federal martial law has been invoked by the President include Abraham Lincoln's placing the southern and border states under martial law, and Franklin Roosevelt's placing Hawaii under it following the attack upon Pearl Harbor. In the states, the governor as commander in chief of the state militia may declare martial law during an emergency occasioned by internal disorders or a natural disaster.

Military Government. Temporary government established by the conquering military forces over occupied enemy territory. Areas occupied by American forces are governed under statutes enacted by the Congress, supplemented by orders issued by the President as commander in chief. The military governor of a territory under military government exercises supreme legislative, executive, and judicial authority. Civil government operates to the extent permitted by the military governor.
• *Significance:* Military government was used extensively by the United States and its allies during and following World War II in the occupation of enemy territory. Special army military government units were trained to perform occupation duties. Efforts were made to teach the enemy populace the principles and practices of democracy, in most cases successfully. Today, sovereignty has been restored and military government units have been completely withdrawn from most of these formerly occupied territories.

Military Law. Law, enacted by the Congress, which governs the conduct of enlisted men and officers of the armed forces of the United States. Military law also establishes the procedures for trial by courts-martial for alleged infractions.
• *Significance:* Prior to 1950, separate Articles of War applied to the Army, Navy, and Coast Guard. To secure uniformity, and in response to criticism concerning the lack of military justice, the Congress, in 1950, enacted a single uniform code for all of the armed forces. This Uniform Code of Military Jus-

tice seeks to resolve the problem of balancing the needs for discipline with justice. It also permits the trial of servicemen by civil courts for off-duty offenses committed in the United States. Military law, however, does not ordinarily apply to civilians who are abroad with the armed forces (*Reid v. Covert*, 354 U.S. 1 [1957]) or to discharged servicemen for offenses committed while in the armed forces (*Toth v. Quarles*, 350 U.S. 11 [1955]).

Mobilization.   Preparing a nation to meet an attack or to fight a war. Mobilization involves placing the armed forces in readiness, calling up reserves to active duty, putting the nation's economy on a war footing, establishing government controls over manpower, production, resources, and prices, and generally regimenting the nation. Mobilization for modern war involves readying the totality of a nation's manpower and physical resources for military action.
• *Significance:* Mobilization is directed by the President whose constitutional authority as commander in chief is buttressed by vast delegations of emergency powers by the Congress for the duration of the war or crisis. Under the stress of war or threat of war, the courts have not generally interfered with the President's exercise of mobilization powers. Mobilization by a nation during peacetime may decrease the possibility of war by calling a potential aggressor's bluff; conversely, it may increase the likelihood of war if other nations consider it a threat to their security.

National Guard.   The volunteer armed forces of the states formerly called the militia. The Constitution provides for a cooperative system under which each state is responsible for appointing officers and the Congress provides for organizing, arming, and disciplining the Guard.
• *Significance:* During much of American history, the state militias constituted a relatively powerful and autonomous group of armed forces. Since 1916, the militias have been organized as the National Guard, an auxiliary of the regular army subject to substantial national control. Congress may call the Guard into federal service at any time, and has done so during World Wars I and II and in other emergencies, such as in the 1961 Berlin crisis. The President as commander in chief decides when units will be called, and all state jurisdiction ceases when the Guard becomes part of the regular army. Under state authority, each governor is commander in chief of his state militia and may call it out for serious emergencies, such as floods, fires, or civil disorders.

Reserves.   The Army, Navy, Air Force, Coast Guard, and National Guard units not on active duty but available to supplement the regular military services during emergencies. Reservists are divided into "ready reserves," "standby reserves," and "retired reserves." The ready reserve, with up to 2.9 million men authorized, may be called to active duty by the President or the Congress. The standby reserve is a pool of trained military personnel who can be called up only in case of war or an emergency declared by the Congress. A third category, the retired reserve, can be recalled to active duty by the Congress during a major emergency.
• *Significance:* The reserves consist largely of men who have completed their

active military duty and take weekly training and attend summer training camps. The role of reserves in modern warfare depends on the nature of the military situation. In a major atomic war, for example, decisive blows might be struck before reserves could be mustered. In a limited war, conversely, a reservoir of trained manpower would probably be essential. During the Berlin crisis in 1961, President John F. Kennedy called up selected National Guard and other units of the ready reserves for one year of active duty to bolster the American military posture.

Selective Service.   The conscription system under which the national government drafts men for service in the armed forces. Selective service is based on the constitutional provisions which give the Congress the powers necessary "to raise" armies and "to provide" a navy.
• *Significance:* The national government has drafted manpower for military service during and since the Civil War for wartime or emergency service. During World Wars I and II, millions of Americans were conscripted for military service. Peacetime selective service systems were also instituted by the Congress in 1940 and again in 1948, the latter being currently in effect. The Supreme Court established a basic precedent in 1918 when it rejected the assertion that selective service violates the constitutional provision against "involuntary servitude" by holding that compulsory military service is, rather, an "involuntary duty" (*Selective Draft Law Cases,* 245 U.S. 366 [1918]).

Unification.   The integration of the military services of the United States. Under the National Security Act of 1947, the Army, Navy, and Air Force were unified under a single Department of Defense.
• *Significance:* Critics of separate military departments charged that the system promoted interservice rivalries, prevented integrated planning, increased military costs, encouraged recruiting competition, promoted budget battles, and resulted in duplication and inefficiency. Supporters of independent departments claimed that a single military chief would be too powerful, that it would encourage a Prussian-type general staff system, that it would lead to charges of favoritism against the single head, and that the separate service approach had proved itself in World Wars I and II. Unification has not, in fact, eliminated interservice rivalries, and serious cleavages among the three branches concerning such questions as basic strategy, budget allocation, and missile development responsibility have continued.

War Powers.   The authority expressly granted by the Constitution, implied from it, or inherent in the duty of protecting the nation from its enemies. War powers include those granted to the Congress to tax and spend for the common defense, to declare war and make rules concerning captures, to raise and support armies and provide a navy, to enact military law, and to oversee the state militias. Moreover, the elastic clause permits the Congress to do whatever is necessary and proper in executing these powers. The President as commander in chief has the inherent power to do whatever is necessary to protect the nation, subject to judicial scrutiny. In times of crisis, the Congress delegates legislative powers to the President as "emergency powers."

• *Significance:* Although defense and war powers are subject to constitutional limitations in the same way as other powers, they have been stretched to their limits during times of serious crises. Presidents Abraham Lincoln, Franklin Roosevelt, and Harry Truman regarded the war powers as a special and undefined category of powers which can be exercised whenever the security of the nation is threatened. The Congress, the public, and the courts have generally accepted the primacy of the President's role and his exercise of vast powers during time of war. Under conditions of modern warfare, the war powers include control over the domestic economy as well as the military phases of the conflict.

IMPORTANT AGENCIES

Atomic Energy Commission (AEC). An independent agency of the United States government which has responsibility to foster research and development of atomic energy and to regulate all private efforts in the field. The AEC consists of five commissioners appointed by the President with the Senate's approval for five-year terms. Responsibility for enforcement of the Atomic Energy Acts of 1946 and 1954 is vested in the Commission. *See* ATOMIC ENERGY ACTS OF 1946, 1954, page 264.
• *Significance:* The AEC has been primarily concerned with developing and stockpiling a vast array of nuclear weapons. Its major research activities are carried on at Argonne National Laboratory at Chicago and at Brookhaven National Laboratory at Upton, New York. Its major production facilities are at Oak Ridge, Tennessee, and Richland, Washington. The AEC has become one of the major spending agencies of the national government with an annual budget of about $2 billion. Its activities are supervised by the Congress through a Joint Committee on Atomic Energy.

Central Intelligence Agency (CIA). An agency which functions under the National Security Council to coordinate intelligence activities in the interest of national security. The CIA evaluates raw intelligence data supplied by the Army, Navy, Air Force, the State Department, and other intelligence-gathering, civilian and military agencies. This information is disseminated among various units of the national government to aid in decision making.
• *Significance:* The CIA operations are supersecret in nature, and even most congressmen cannot inquire into its activities. Experts estimate that the major portion of intelligence information is secured through foreign publications and other materials of an open nature, with only a small amount of information secured through clandestine "cloak-and-dagger" methods.

Department of Defense. A major department of the national government which has responsibility to formulate military policies and to maintain the armed forces of the United States. Since 1961, it has assumed responsibility for civil defense functions. The Secretary who heads the Department of Defense is a civilian appointed by the President with the Senate's approval, and he serves as a member of the Cabinet. The three major military departments of the Army, Navy, and Air Force are each headed by a civilian secretary who is responsible to the Secretary of Defense. The Chiefs of Staff of the Army and the Air Force and the Chief of Naval Operations are the top military officers in each service who advise the civilian secretaries. These three military leaders join with the Chief of Staff to the Secretary of Defense to form the Joint Chiefs of Staff, the nation's highest military advisory body. Other advisers to the Secretary of Defense include the Armed Forces Policy Council composed of both the civilian secretaries and their chiefs of staff, a Director of Guided Missiles who advises the Secretary on military developments in that field, and a host of civilian and military individuals, boards, and committees to offer advice on a variety of defense subjects. In matters affecting the Marine Corps, its Commandant sits on the Joint Chiefs and the Policy Council as an equal with other chiefs of staff.

• *Significance:* The Defense Department has become the most important department in the national government in numbers of employees and the amounts of money spent. Defense has over one million civilian employees, almost one half of all national civil servants. In recent years, its annual budget has averaged more than 60 percent of all expenditures of the government. The Secretary of Defense ranks after the Secretaries of State and Treasury as Cabinet adviser to the President and in the line of succession to that office. The Department of Defense has primary responsibility for building an adequate military organization to protect the people of the United States. Major expenditures of the Department fall into four categories: procurement of military items, salaries and benefits to personnel, operations, and research and development. Military bases are maintained around the world, and coordinated programs are worked out with over 40 nations with which the United States is militarily allied. Increasing emphasis is being placed on research and development as the technological race with the Soviet Union accelerates. Unity of command has been achieved through the National Security Acts of 1947 and 1949 and the Defense Reorganization Act of 1958, but interservice rivalries have not completely given way to unity of purpose, especially during budget making. Critics express concern over the growing decision-making power of the military in American life.

National Aeronautics and Space Council (NASC).   A staff agency in the Executive Office of the President which advises the President on policies, plans, and programs concerning the American space program. Members include the Vice President of the United States, who serves as chairman, the Secretaries of State and Defense, the Administrator of the National Aeronautics and Space Administration (NASA) which carries out space program decisions, and the Chairman of the Atomic Energy Commission. The NASC was established under the National Aeronautics and Space Act of 1958.

• *Significance:* The Council was created to meet the challenge posed when Soviet scientists placed the first "sputnik" into space in an orbit around the earth in 1957. The American failure to secure a "first" was blamed on many factors, among them the lack of a unified program to eliminate duplication and to achieve a common effort. Rival military space teams were brought into an integrated program directed by the civilian NASC and NASA agencies.

National Security Council (NSC).   A staff agency in the Executive Office of the President, created by the National Security Act of 1947, which advises the President on domestic and foreign matters involving national security. The Council is composed of the President, the Vice President, the Secretaries of State and Defense, and other civil and military officials appointed by the President with the Senate's approval. The Central Intelligence Agency (CIA), headed by a director, functions under the direction of the Council. The Council's main functions are to assess and appraise the objectives, commitments, and risks of the United States in the interests of national security and to make recommendations to the President on specific policies and decisions.

• *Significance:* The National Security Council is the highest policy-recommending body in defense and related fields. Whenever a serious crisis erupts anywhere in the world, the President usually summons the Council into an immediate session. The President is free to reject the advice of the Council, but this is unlikely because it is composed of the highest leaders of his administration in defense and foreign policy fields.

IMPORTANT CASES

Ex parte Milligan, 4 Wallace 2 (1866): Held that the suspension of the right of writ of habeas corpus and the trial of a civilian by a military tribunal while the civilian courts are operating violates the Constitution. The Court held that neither the President nor the Congress could legally deny the accused a civil trial by jury in an area outside an actual theater of war.

• *Significance:* The *Milligan* case reaffirmed the principles of civilian control over the military and the maintenance of due process of law free from military interference. There have been no further attempts to suspend the writ of habeas corpus in the continental United States. In 1941, following the attack upon Pearl Harbor, President Franklin Roosevelt placed the Hawaiian Islands under martial law and all civil courts were replaced by military tribunals. In a case after the war (*Duncan v. Kahanamoku,* 327 U.S. 304 [1946]), the Court held this action invalid.

Selective Draft Law Cases, 245 U.S. 366 (1918): Upheld the constitutional authority of the Congress to draft men into the military forces. The Supreme Court rejected the argument that conscription is "involuntary servitude" in violation of the 13th Amendment, holding that such service by the citizen was "his supreme and noble duty."

• *Significance:* Although the *Selective Draft Law Cases* dealt with a wartime conscription measure, the constitutionality of the peacetime draft is also based on this precedent. During war and in peacetime, the Army has depended heavily upon the draft to supply needed manpower, whereas the Navy and Air Force have mainly used volunteers.

IMPORTANT STATUTES

Defense Reorganization Act of 1958.   An act which sought to overcome administrative weaknesses in the Defense Department created by the National

Security Acts of 1947 and 1949. The Act of 1958 made it clear that the Secretaries of the Army, Navy, and Air Force were under the direct authority of the Secretary of Defense. A direct line of command from the Secretary to operational units in the field replaced the earlier system whereby the Secretary communicated decisions through the Army, Navy, and Air Force Secretaries.

• *Significance:* In the wake of spectacular Soviet space and missile successes, President Dwight Eisenhower proposed a sweeping reorganization of the defense organization. Congress accepted part of the President's proposals in the Act of 1958, but retained a legislative veto over the Defense Secretary's organizational changes, permitted the civilian and military heads of the three services to communicate directly with the Congress, and specifically exempted the National Guard and Marine Corps from alteration, except by the Congress. Although the Act of 1958 was designed to eliminate interservice rivalries over budgets and weapon development programs, some conflict and controversy among the services has continued. The Act of 1958 expressly denied any power to the President to merge any of the military services or to create a military chief of staff system.

National Security Acts of 1947 and 1949.   The Act of 1947 provided the nation's most comprehensive reorganization of its defense structure. It established a new National Security Organization and placed the three major military forces—Army, Navy, and Air Force—in a National Military Establishment under a single civilian Secretary of Defense. A National Security Council was created as a top-level advisory body. In the National Security Act of 1949 the National Military Establishment was replaced with a single executive department—the Department of Defense—and the National Security Council was transferred to the Executive Office as a staff agency to the President.

• *Significance:* The National Security Acts of 1947 and 1949 were aimed at unifying and coordinating the efforts of the nation's armed services. Although the Act stated that the services were not to be merged, it called for "their integration into an efficient team of land, naval, and air forces." The authority given to the Secretary of Defense in the Act of 1947 proved insufficient to unify in fact three separate military services, each largely autonomous in its operations and protective of its traditional role. The Act of 1949 sought to reduce these interservice rivalries further by strengthening the hand of the Secretary of Defense over the military departments.

18

State and Local Government

Alderman.   A member of a city council. The term originated in England and was used in the American colonies to designate officials chosen by the common council of the city to exercise judicial power and to share in the governing of the city. In the nineteenth century, when bicameral legislatures were common in cities, one house was designated as the Board of Aldermen, the other, the Common Council. In some cities, members of the city council or commission are popularly referred to as aldermen.
• *Significance:* The commission and council-manager plans of city government have been accompanied by the use of the terms commissioner or councilman to designate members of the city legislative body. Where used, the term alderman is generally associated with cities in which ward systems of representation for the city council function under a mayor-council plan of government.

American Municipal Association (AMA).   A national federation of state leagues of municipalities which seeks to develop a national municipal policy. Lobbyists are maintained in Washington. The AMA also provides information and consultative services to cities to solve municipal problems.
• *Significance:* The AMA is particularly interested in increasing municipal sources of revenue and municipal powers. It is typical of numerous organizations of state and local officials which seek to promote the interests of their particular activity.

Annexation.   The addition of territory to a unit of government. Annexation usually denotes the addition by a city of land adjacent to it, to meet the problems of metropolitan expansion. Procedures for annexation are established by state law and generally require an affirmative vote of both the central city and of the area concerned. In a few instances, as in Virginia and Texas, areas may be annexed by action of the city alone or through judicial procedures.
• *Significance:* Annexation is viewed as one solution to the problems caused by the urbanization of fringe areas of a city. Through annexation, a community seeks to eliminate conflicts of authority and duplication of services, and to protect orderly city growth which is hampered by the existence of numerous

338

units of government. Fringe-area dwellers often fear high city taxes and prefer to retain their identity as a community.

Assessor. A public official who determines the value of real and personal property for purposes of taxation. Assessors are commonly elected in towns, townships, or counties. In some midwestern townships, the supervisor serves as the assessor. About 15 percent of city assessors are still elected.
• *Significance:* Many students of government challenge the value of electing the assessor. The elective method is unlikely to secure competent assessors, and elected officials may under-assess so as not to antagonize the voters. Critics also charge that the town or township is too small a unit for assessment purposes. Many areas have moved in the direction of appointing assessors on a merit basis and making the county the assessment unit.

Attorney General. The chief legal officer of the state. The attorney general is elected in 42 states. He serves as legal adviser to the governor and to state agencies, represents the state in legal proceedings, and may have general supervisory powers over local prosecuting attorneys.
• *Significance:* The state attorney general holds an office which is frequently a pathway to the governor's chair or to a judicial appointment. Opinions of the attorney general have the force of law unless overturned by a court. Many students of state government argue that the office should be appointive since the governor should have full confidence in his chief legal adviser, similar to that placed by a client in his attorney.

Blue Laws. Laws which prohibit certain business operations on Sunday. Blue laws are on the books of many states. They often make exceptions for persons who observe a sabbath day other than Sunday. Exceptions are also made for amusements or essential activities.
• *Significance:* Blue laws are religious in origin and have been challenged as violations of religious liberty. Today, they are supported largely as welfare measures to encourage rest and relaxation. In 1961, the Supreme Court upheld a number of such laws on these grounds. Blue laws have not been rigorously enforced and permit many exceptions which render them ineffective in practice.

Board of Review. Public officials charged with the duty of reviewing individual assessments on property, made for tax purposes. The review function is to be distinguished from "equalization" which is the comparison and adjustment of assessments between entire tax-imposing units. The board of review may be elected or composed of local government officials serving ex officio.
• *Significance:* Citizens may appeal their assessments to a board of review in order to reduce their property taxes. The board's objective is to tax all citizens equitably, according to the value of their property. Most citizens fail to take advantage of their right of review, not wanting to take the time or trouble, or fearful that their assessment may be raised.

Borough. A municipal corporation, generally smaller than a city. Boroughs are found mainly in Pennsylvania, Connecticut, and New Jersey, and resemble villages or towns of other states. Borough is also the name assigned to major local government divisions in Alaska, comparable to counties. The city of New York is divided into five boroughs: Manhattan, Brooklyn, Queens, Bronx, and Richmond.

• *Significance:* The term borough is a holdover from England and colonial America. In New York City, the boroughs represent an attempt to decentralize the operations of that huge metropolis. The use of the term in the constitution of Alaska represents a noteworthy departure from tradition. In order to avoid some of the pitfalls of county government and to adapt local government to their peculiar needs, the people of Alaska provided for the creation of boroughs which would embrace an area and population with common interests and would have a high degree of home rule.

Charter.   The basic law of a local governmental unit which defines its powers, responsibilities, and organization. Charters are granted, under state constitutional or statutory provisions, to municipal corporations and, in some states, to counties or townships. Charters may be provided by (1) special act of the legislature applicable to one city, (2) general laws applicable to all cities within a certain classification, (3) optional charter laws whereby a city may choose a charter from a group provided by law, or (4) home rule whereby the people of a city draw up their own charter.

• *Significance:* In one sense, every unit of local government has a "charter" composed of the local government provisions of state constitutions, statutes, and the common law. Many cities, or other municipal corporations such as villages, do not have *a* charter in the form of a *document,* particularly when they operate under special acts or general laws. A charter document is generally found in cities operating under home rule and, sometimes, under optional charters. All local governments are subject to the state constitution and laws, and all actions taken under a charter must conform to these higher laws and to the charter as well.

City.   A municipal corporation, chartered by the state, which is usually larger than a village, town, borough, or other incorporated area. The term is a legal concept and exactly what constitutes a city is defined by state law. This is usually based on population but may be based on assessed valuation.

• *Significance:* Cities are generally accorded more authority over fiscal matters and services than are other incorporated units. Cities, too, are organized differently, with the mayor-council plan, commission plan, and council-manager plan generally made available by state law. Most Americans live in cities today, and city culture is replacing the traditions of a rural society. Cities have long fought for greater freedom from state control and the trend is toward giving cities home rule.

City Council.   The policy-making and, in some instances, the administrative board of a city. The structure and powers of city councils vary with the plan of city government. In the weak-mayor and commission plans, the council plays a large role in lawmaking and in the direction and control of administrative departments. In the strong-mayor and council-manager plans, the council's job is largely in the realm of lawmaking, with only general oversight of administration. In all cases, the most important job of the council is to pass ordinances which determine public policy, including control over the purse strings. Other functions, which vary from city to city, may include serving as a board of review for tax assessments, issuing licenses, and making appointments. Members of city councils are elected, on a partisan or nonpartisan basis, from wards or districts, at large, or by a combination of both.

• *Significance:* City councils are typically unicameral bodies most commonly of five or seven members, but range up to fifty. The commission and council-manager forms of city government, with which reform movements replaced the cumbersome and often corrupt bicameral city councils, have raised the prestige and quality of councilmen. Each state determines by law the structure and powers of city councils. Whatever its form, the council continues in its historic role as the legislative representative of the people, responsible for the conduct of city government.

City-County Consolidation.   The merger of county government with all other units within the county to form one unit of government. The plan is suggested as one solution to the problems of a metropolitan area, particularly when it coincides with the county boundary.

• *Significance:* City-county consolidation simplifies the government of a metropolitan county by eliminating duplication of services and allowing for area-wide planning and administration of services. In many areas, such as Philadelphia, Boston, and New Orleans, city and county boundaries are actually or substantially the same. Where several units are involved, residents of smaller municipalities and rural parts of the county tend to resist consolidation. They fear increased costs and want to maintain their individual identity. The consolidation of Baton Rouge, Louisiana, with its county is the leading example of successful consolidation. As a solution to metropolitan problems, however, the city-county consolidation plan does not meet the problems of areas which overlap counties or extend through many counties or even states.

City-County Separation.   The separation of the city from the county. Cities are generally part of the county in which they lie and the city residents pay county taxes and receive certain county services. More than 30 cities in Virginia, and the cities of St. Louis, Denver, Baltimore, and San Francisco, are separated from their counties and provide their residents with county services.

• *Significance:* City-county separation is designed to increase the efficiency of the urban area and to eliminate overlapping government. However, the urban area tends to continue to spread beyond the city limits. Moreover, the rural areas of the county and smaller municipalities are left without the financial help of the city, and the county must continue to provide services. At one time, city-county separation was considered a solution to metropolitan problems, but, except for the state of Virginia, it is rarely used.

Classification of Cities.   The grouping of cities according to population by the state legislature for purposes of enacting laws or city charters. The practice of classification results from the requirement found in most state constitutions that the legislature must deal with local governments by general law rather than by special act applicable to one unit. Since general laws may result in putting all cities, large and small, into a uniform mold, legislatures have classified cities and passed general laws applicable to each class.

• *Significance:* A classification must be reasonable, and attainable by others not yet within the group. For example, state legislatures have tried to evade the purposes of general law requirements by creating classes based on location which, in effect, was a special act applicable only to one community. However, laws applicable to cities with populations exceeding one million, for example, may actually apply to one city, but, theoretically, other cities may reach that population figure. Classification schemes are used to determine forms of government as well as specific powers which a city may exercise. The courts determine whether a scheme of classification is reasonable.

Commission Plan.　　One of the forms of city government in the United States wherein legislative and executive powers are exercised by a commission of three to nine members. Variations in structure are found around the country but the essential ingredients of the commission plan include (1) the concentration of legislative and executive powers in a small group elected at large on a nonpartisan ballot; (2) the collective responsibility of the commission to pass ordinances and control the purse strings; (3) the individual responsibility of each commissioner to head a city department, such as public works, finance, and public safety; and (4) the selection of the mayor from among the commissioners but reducing the office to that of ceremonial leadership.

• *Significance:* The commission plan enjoyed great popularity from its inception in Galveston, Texas, in 1901 until about 1920. Its simplicity and its resemblance to business corporation organization appealed to reformers who sought an end to the long ballot and the extremes of partisan politics in municipal government. However, as its defects became apparent its popularity declined. A major defect is the failure to separate legislative and executive authority, with the result that there is little check on spending and administration is in the hands of amateurs. The absence of an over-all executive makes it difficult for the voter to fix responsibility. Furthermore, trying to fit the number of city agencies to the number of commissioners leads to rigidity in organization. To meet these defects, many cities followed the lead of Des Moines, Iowa, and added the initiative, referendum, and recall to the plan, as well as a merit system for selection of government employees.

Congressional Township.　　A six-mile-square area of land established under laws of the Congress for the purpose of surveying the land. The system was started by the Confederation Congress in 1785, and was applied to the land in most states. Excluded are the original 13 states and Maine, Kentucky, Tennessee, Vermont, West Virginia, and Texas. Under the law, land is divided into townships six miles square and each township is divided into 36 mile-square sections. Each section is further subdivided into quarter sections and less. By the assignment of numbered base lines, similar to the longitude and latitude patterns on maps, any parcel of land may be easily identified.

• *Significance:* The congressional township system of land survey was instituted to replace the haphazard "metes and bounds" method of identifying tracts of land wherein landmarks were used rather than precise, numerical points of reference. Accurate records, particularly for real estate transfers, are made possible by the congressional township plan. A congressional township is not a unit of government and, frequently, the township will overlap county and state boundaries. However, many township units of government do follow the congressional township line, accounting for the six-mile-square civil township. The Congress reserved one section of the township (section 16) for the support of public schools and many states provide that the proceeds from this section constitute a permanent fund for school purposes.

Consolidation.   The union of two or more units of government to form a single unit. Consolidation is often recommended as a solution to metropolitan area problems, but it is also recommended in rural areas as a means of reducing the large number of local governments in existence. State constitutions or statutes designate consolidation procedures, generally requiring the separate consent of all units.
• *Significance:* In the metropolitan areas, consolidation has the same benefits and meets the same opposition as do annexation proposals. It eliminates conflicting authority and duplication of services but meets opposition from suburban communities desiring to retain their identity. In rural areas, consolidation is viewed as a means of strengthening counties and townships which were established many years ago and no longer contain sizable populations or the means to carry on governmental functions efficiently. By joining together, it is expected that services may be improved and much confusion eliminated. However, legal intricacies, tradition, and the opposition of vested interests militate against consolidation. Many school districts, however, established prior to modern means of transportation, have found it desirable to consolidate in order to realize the benefits of larger enrollments and school plants, although this, too, meets with strong opposition.

Constitutional Amendments, State.   Changes in or additions to a state constitution. The procedures are detailed in the specific constitution and vary from state to state. Generally, two proposal methods are available—legislative, by an extraordinary majority, and initiative of the people. Ratification by the people is usually accomplished by simple majority vote, but a few states require an extraordinary majority. Under the initiative method, permitted in 13 states, the voters draw up a petition with a specified number of signatures (8 or 10 percent of the voters) requesting the desired change. If the petition is in order, the proposal goes on the ballot for ratification by the people.
• *Significance:* Most state constitutions have been amended numerous times to meet changing conditions or the desires of strong interest groups. The legislative proposal method has been used most often to effect constitutional change. It is simple and inexpensive compared to a constitutional convention. The requirement of extraordinary majorities, however, often make it difficult to propose controversial measures. Unlike the national Constitution, however, state constitutions have required frequent amendment due to their inflexibility. The initiative method serves as an important weapon for the people when the

legislature fails to respond to their demands. However, it tends to be abused by pressure groups, and many such proposals are rejected. Many states with extremely difficult amending procedures suffer from outmoded organization and procedures in the daily workings of government. Oftimes, the average citizen fails to realize that his state constitution is a stumbling block to effective government.

Constitutional Commission.   A group of citizens selected by the legislature and/or the governor of a state to study the state constitution and to make recommendations for change.
• *Significance:* Constitutional commissions have been used in a number of states when revision of the constitution has been under consideration. The most notable instance took place in Georgia, in 1945, where a commission, established by the legislature, had its proposed revision of the entire constitution ratified by the people as a single amendment to replace the old constitution. In other cases, a commission has served as an educational medium, prior to the calling of a constitutional convention. In still others, the legislature submitted to the people specific proposals of a commission as amendments. Through the commission device, a group of leading citizens, making use of expert advice, can contribute to better understanding of constitutional problems.

Constitutional Convention.   A body selected by the people to rewrite the constitution. Most state constitutions make provisions for the calling of a constitutional convention but, even if no provisions are made, the power to call a convention is considered to be inherent in the people in their sovereign capacity. Ten states provide for a mandatory, periodic submission to the people of the question of whether they wish to call a convention. The procedures for a constitutional convention generally involve (1) the placing of the question on the ballot by the legislature, usually by an extraordinary majority unless it be mandatory for that year; (2) the election of delegates, should the people approve the call; (3) the meeting of the convention which has deliberations similar in method and procedure to legislative bodies; and (4) the submission of the new constitution to the people for ratification.
• *Significance:* A constitutional convention is an historic event; over 200 have been held in the United States. About 16 states have held just one convention, but some states have held ten or more. The most recent conventions have been held in Missouri (1945), New Jersey (1947), Tennessee (1953), and Michigan (1961). The new states of Alaska and Hawaii framed their constitutions in conventions held in 1955 and 1950 respectively. Constitutional conventions are expensive and many people fear that vested interests or long-standing practices will be disturbed. Yet, conventions represent the highest voice of the people and have tended to attract able citizen talent. The voter is brought into the picture at several stages and the entire process has an excellent educational effect. The provision for the mandatory call of a convention is based on the assumption that each generation should have the opportunity to revise its basic law. Agitation for conventions is underway in most states today.

Constitutional Officer.   A public official, usually in the executive branch, whose office is created by the constitution. State constitutions generally name numerous state and local government officials and designate their terms of office and duties. For example, most state constitutions provide for the election of such state-wide officers as secretary of state, attorney general, state treasurer, and state auditor. On the local level, the constitution may name such offices as sheriff, county clerk, township supervisor, and highway commissioner.

• *Significance:* Constitutional officers present one of the troublesome aspects of state government today because they enjoy much immunity from legislative and executive power and, oftimes, may resist direction from the executive. Reform of state and local government is difficult since these offices cannot be abolished without constitutional change. Students of government prefer that the constitution be free of such provisions, and that these officers be appointed if needed.

Constitutions, State.   The organic law of a state which defines and limits governmental power and guarantees the rights of the people. Each state has a constitution and its provisions may not conflict with the United States Constitution. Since state governments have all powers not delegated to the national government, state constitutions, typically, are filled with restrictions on legislative and executive power rather than grants of authority.

• *Significance:* State constitutions tend to be unduly lengthy and filled with details better left to statutes. The authority of the legislature and executive is, typically, restricted in taxation, expenditures, and administration. Local governments and major state services, such as education and highways, tend to be frozen into a specific mold. These defects, among others, have led to considerable agitation for state constitutional reform since the people's representatives often have their hands tied by the constitution in attempting to meet day-to-day problems. This has resulted in the frequent amendment of many state constitutions and the thorough revision of others. Proponents of constitutional reform seek a document more closely related to the national Constitution, with emphasis on fundamentals rather than details. Strong opposition to change, however, comes from those whose interests are protected by specific provisions as well as from many who tend to view a constitution as a sacred document.

Council-Manager Plan.   A form of city government in which the city council appoints a professional administrator, a manager, to act as the chief executive. With variations from city to city, the essentials of this plan are (1) a small council or commission of five or seven members elected at large on a nonpartisan ballot, with power to make policy and to hire and fire the manager; (2) a professionally trained manager, with authority to hire and fire his subordinates, who is responsible to the council for efficient administration of the city; and (3) a mayor chosen separately or from within the council, but with no executive functions. The council must refrain from bypassing the manager by interfering with his subordinates or in the details of administration, and the manager must follow the policies outlined by the council. A merit system of employment is generally consistent with this plan.

• *Significance:* The council-manager plan is a product of the twentieth century and, since its inception, more than 1600 cities have adopted it. About 65 cities have abandoned the plan after trying it, usually because of lack of citizen understanding of its operations. It is used by cities of all sizes except very large ones. Advantages of the plan include its simplicity, clarification of responsibility for both policy and administration, and its use of experts to adopt and utilize modern techniques of budgeting, planning, and over-all administration. The profession of city manager has gained in status and many universities train managers. The manager may also be of invaluable aid to the council and the public in suggesting policy alternatives. Opponents of the plan criticize the lack of a strong political leader, particularly essential in large cities where strong mayors play this role, and charge that the manager plan is undemocratic since the executive is appointed. However, the council is responsible to the people and has full control over the manager. The plan is now well established in the United States and is growing in popularity.

County.   The major unit of local government in the United States except in Connecticut, Rhode Island, and Alaska. Louisiana has county units but calls them parishes. Alaska has a new major division of local government called a borough. Connecticut abolished counties in 1959. In New England, counties are relatively unimportant for governmental purposes. Otherwise, county governments exist as principal agencies of the state for state-wide purposes, and as important units of local government. There are 3042 counties in the United States ranging from three in Delaware to 254 in Texas. Their powers and functions vary from state to state and within states as well. Generally, counties perform such functions as law enforcement, maintenance of courts, highways, schools, and welfare agencies. In urban areas, counties may perform a variety of services usually handled by cities. Counties are governed by a board which differs in composition from state to state. Counties have a large number of elected officials, such as sheriff, clerk, coroner, attorney, auditor, register of deeds, surveyor, and treasurer.

• *Significance:* Counties were originally established as administrative subdivisions of the state and for local government purposes. The number of counties and their organizational patterns have undergone almost no change through the years and tradition militates against change. Many are densely populated and part and parcel of metropolitan areas. Others have lost population and are thoroughly rural. The metropolitan counties are faced with the need to expand their services; the rural counties find it difficult to support their regular functions. Thus, in one case, the county has achieved new importance while, in the other, means are sought to relieve it of its burdens. Most counties suffer from outmoded administrative organization, the lack of a chief executive, the long ballot, and the spoils system.

County Board.   The governing body of the county. The official title of this body varies from state to state with as many as 27 different titles used. Most common are "board of commissioners," "board of supervisors," and "county court," but the term county board is the popular one. About two-thirds of the county boards are composed of three to five commissioners or supervisors who are elected by the voters of the county. In states with township government, the board is composed of township supervisors and representatives of cities within the county and usually numbers about 25. In several states the board is composed of county judges. The board administers state law in the county, levies taxes, appoints numerous officials, and supervises the general affairs of the county.

• *Significance:* County boards are important strongholds of political power. The growing importance of the county in urban areas has added to the powers and influence of these boards. In some areas, they have not been adequate to meet new responsibilities and many persons advocate the use of a county manager. Because many boards are composed of persons with other responsibilities, no individual has over-all responsibility for the county. Boards are also handicapped by the large number of elected county officials over whom they exercise little control.

County Clerk. A county official who is popularly elected in more than half the states. His principal duties include acting as secretary to the county board, supervision of elections, issuance of various business certificates and licenses, and handling of birth, marriage, and death records.

• *Significance:* The county clerk's office tends to become a central clearing house for county affairs, and the clerk tends to be an important political figure. The nature of the office has led some observers to consider it the logical place to vest principal administrative supervisory duties in the absence of a regular county executive.

County Manager Plan. The county manager plan is patterned after the council-manager plan which is widely used in cities. The county manager plan envisages a small county board for policy determination and an appointed, professional manager to serve as the executive officer of the county. Less than 20 of the more than 3000 counties in the United States have adopted the manager plan.

• *Significance:* The county manager plan is designed to overcome the defects common to most counties—the long ballot, the lack of an integrating executive officer, and the spoils system. General public apathy and a tradition-bound attitude toward county government have made for slow adoption of the plan. Constitutional provisions also make it difficult for counties to reorganize themselves. Such reforms as county home rule or optional charters will probably be necessary before the county manager plan can spread. Supporters of the plan hold that, in both urban and rural counties, it can make the operations of county government more efficient and can clearly fix responsibility. Critics argue that, since the county is principally an administrative arm of the state, the manager would obstruct state supervision of county activities.

Dillon's Rule. A rule enunciated by Judge John F. Dillon, an authority on municipal corporations, to the effect that a municipal corporation can exercise only those powers expressly granted to it, those necessarily implied from the granted powers, and those essential for the purposes of the organization. If any doubt exists, it is to be resolved against the local unit.

• *Significance:* Dillon's Rule underscores the subordinate relationship of local government to the state. The rule applies to all local units. Local government is a creature of the state and has only those powers permitted by state constitutions and laws.

Equalization.   The review and adjustment of tax assessments among taxing districts in the state. The equalization function may be exercised at the county level to adjust assessments among the townships, cities, and other units of the county and, at the state level, to equalize assessments among counties. If property in one area is assessed at 50 percent of value and in another at 80 percent, some adjustment is necessary to equalize the burdens borne by taxpayers. Equalization differs from the local review of assessments in which individual rather than area assessments are reviewed.
• *Significance:* One of the characteristics of local government in the United States is the multiplicity of taxing units. This, combined with under-assessment by popularly elected assessors, often results in unequal distribution of tax burdens.

Functional Consolidation.   The cooperation of two or more units of local government in providing services to their inhabitants. Several counties may join together for common administration of health services, or two cities may agree to have a common water supply or sewerage system.
• *Significance:* Recent years have witnessed an increasing use of functional consolidations. It can help metropolitan areas with their complex of overlapping governments as well as rural areas which lack financial resources. It provides a satisfactory alternative to complete consolidation of units which often meets strong opposition. Another form of consolidation of functions takes place when a state takes over a service, such as highways or education, and relieves local units of these burdens.

General Laws.   Laws applicable to all local government units of a similar type. Most state constitutions now provide that the legislature may pass only laws of general application rather than special acts applicable only to one unit. To allow for variations in the needs of small or large units of government, the legislatures often classify units according to population and then pass general laws applicable to that classification.
• *Significance:* General laws relieve the burden on the legislature by making it unnecessary to deal with each unit individually. More important, it restricts the favoritism and political in-fighting which characterized the special act system and permitted the legislatures to make decisions for individual cities. Often, however, the legislature's classifications are so specific as to apply, in fact, to a single unit of government.

Governor.   The chief executive officer of a state. In all states, the governor is elected by the people, serving for four years in most, and for two years in others. About one half the states limit the governor to one or two terms in office. A governor's executive powers include the power of appointment and removal (although this is severely restricted in most states), preparation and execution of the budget, the power to issue executive orders, and general law enforcement. In the legislative field, governors enjoy considerable power through exercise of the veto power (in all states but North Carolina), and in all but nine states the governor may veto items in appropriation bills. A governor may call the legislature into special session and, in several states, he may limit the special session to consideration of specified subjects. Like the President, the governor may exercise influence over the legislature through his party leadership, messages, and direct appeals to the people. Most governors have the power to pardon and grant reprieves to convicted persons. They also serve as commanders in chief of the National Guard of the state except when it is called into national service. Governors may be removed from office by impeachment and, in a few states, by the recall.

• *Significance:* The office of governor is one of considerable prestige and political power and has been steadily growing in influence. One of the major difficulties of the office is the requirement in many states that the governor share his executive authority with several other elected officials. In this respect, the governor is a weaker executive than the President since the governor may not have control over many high executive officials. Reorganization movements have sought to strengthen the appointive and removal powers of the governor by reducing the number of elected officers and eliminating many boards and commissions which characterize state government. Recent trends also include increasing the governor's term of office, reorganizing the executive branch, and expanding his budgetary, management, and personnel powers.

Home Rule.   The power vested in a local unit of government, usually a city, to draft or change its own charter and to manage its affairs. Home rule limits legislative interference in local affairs. More than half the states permit some degree of freedom for cities, but only 12 have granted it to counties. Home rule may be required or permitted by the state constitution or be granted by the legislature without specific constitutional authorization. Under home rule, the voters choose a commission to draft a charter which may be approved or rejected by the voters. This is in contrast to the granting of charters by the legislature under special acts, general laws, or optional plans. The city under home rule has control over its local problems provided it does not violate the state constitution or general laws of the state.

• *Significance:* Home rule introduces a measure of federalism into state-local relations to modify the usual unitary relation. The legislature is relieved of the burden of handling a variety of local problems which are best handled by those most intimately affected by them. Moreover, it strengthens democracy and local self-government, and increases citizen interest. The major problem of home rule is the determination of what constitutes a *local* problem. The attitude of the legislature and of the courts determines the effectiveness of home rule provisions.

Incorporated and Unincorporated Areas.   The legal status of a local unit of government. Incorporated units include cities, villages, and, in some states, towns and boroughs. Unincorporated units include counties, townships, New England towns, and school districts. Incorporated areas are also called munici-

pal corporations and unincorporated places are known as quasi-corporations.
• *Significance:* Though variations are found in the laws of the states, incorporated units or municipal corporations have a distinct legal entity and are
usually created at the request, and for the benefit, of the inhabitants of the
area. Incorporated units have a charter granted under special, general, or
optional laws, or under home rule. As municipal corporations they usually
have a large measure of self-government and provide services needed by the
residents. Unincorporated units or quasi-corporations are created by the state
constitution or laws without regard to the wishes of the inhabitants of the area
and are primarily designed to carry on state services. The distinction between
incorporated and unincorporated areas is rapidly disappearing in many states,
as unincorporated units are increasingly given powers usually reserved for incorporated areas.

Lieutenant Governor.   The elective official in 38 American states who succeeds to the governorship when that office is declared vacant. Typically, the
lieutenant governor presides over the state senate and casts the deciding vote
in case of a tie. He is elected in these states at the same time and for the same
term as the governor. In some states he serves as an ex officio member of the
governor's administrative council and several boards and commissions.
• *Significance:* The lieutenant governor, like his counterpart, the Vice President
in the national government, performs his most important function by being
available to take over as chief executive. When the governor is temporarily
absent from the state, the lieutenant governor usually takes over until the
governor's return. In states without a lieutenant governor, the president pro
tempore of the senate or the secretary of state succeeds to the office of governor.

Local Option.   Authority vested in local units to approve, reject, or select
specific or alternative forms of action. Local option often refers to the power
of local units to determine by popular vote whether or not liquor will be served
in the community. It may also be used to describe the action taken by communities to select a charter from those made available by state law.
• *Significance:* Local option provides a means whereby state governments are
prevented from imposing the same controls over all units of local government.
This has proved to be popular in the case of liquor consumption since each
community may decide for itself whether it will be "wet" or "dry." Local option
is in accord with traditional American theories of local self-government.

Mayor.   The chief executive and/or the ceremonial leader of a city. The
role of the mayor varies with the form of city government. Under the strong-
mayor–council plan, the mayor has extensive executive power including control over appointments and removals of city officials and the veto power. Under
a weak-mayor–council plan, the mayor has limited executive powers. The
mayor in the commission and manager plans is largely a ceremonial figure.
• *Significance:* The power and prestige of the mayor varies with the structure
of city government and with the personal qualities and political influence of
the individual. In small cities, the mayor generally is a part-time official, but in
cities like New York and Chicago his responsibilities are greater than those

of many governors. In all cities, people look to the mayor for leadership in municipal affairs.

Mayor-Administrator Plan.   A plan of city government wherein an administrative officer is appointed to assist the mayor in managing the affairs of the city. The plan has been adopted in a number of large cities to free the mayor for broader policy-making duties while using expert aid to supervise the routine administration of city government. The administrator, called the chief administrative officer (CAO), is appointed by the mayor with or without council approval and may have extensive appointment and removal power over administrative officials. His duties include budget supervision, coordination of city agencies, personnel direction, and the giving of technical advice to the mayor.
• *Significance:* The mayor-administrator plan is a recent development used in large cities under a strong-mayor plan of government. The plan makes use of some of the features of the city manager form of government while retaining the political leadership of a strong mayor. It differs from the council-manager plan in retaining the position of strong mayor and in making the administrator responsible to the mayor rather than to the council.

Mayor-Council Plan.   A plan of city government in which the mayor is elected to serve as the executive officer of the city and an elective council serves as the legislative body. Wide variations exist from city to city but the plan usually takes the form of a weak- or strong-mayor–council plan depending upon the position of the mayor in the system.
• *Significance:* The mayor-council plan reflects the traditional separation of powers between the legislative and executive branches. While the role of the mayor is the key to the nature of any specific application of the plan in a city, the council, in all cases, plays a major role as the legislative body of the city. In recent years, the mayor-council plan has lost ground to the council-manager plan, particularly in small and middle-sized cities. In large cities, however, the plan continues to be in use with the strong-mayor plan gaining favor over the weak-mayor plan. More than one half of American cities still use some form of the mayor-council plan.

Metropolitan Area.   A large city and its surrounding suburbs which are socially and economically integrated although composed of separate units of government. The term metropolitan is derived from the Greek terms "mētēr" (mother) and "polis" (city). In 1960, the Bureau of the Census identified 212 metropolitan areas. These include each city of 50,000 population or more and the county and other outlying areas which are socially and economically a part of it. The Census Bureau calls these "standard metropolitan statistical areas." New York and Chicago have been identified as "standard consolidated areas" because of the highly complex nature of these regions which combine several contiguous standard metropolitan statistical areas.
• *Significance:* Approximately 70 percent of the American people live in metropolitan areas although these occupy only about 10 percent of the land area of the United States. This phenomenon of the twentieth century has

brought with it a host of political, social, and economic challenges. Metropolitan areas are characterized by numerous governmental units sharing such major problems as transportation, housing, sewage disposal, and water supply. In recent years, the central city has been losing population to the suburbs, creating severe governmental and fiscal problems for both areas. Proposed solutions to the metropolitan problem include annexation, consolidation, federation, and functional consolidation. None of these proposals has, as yet, proved satisfactory, due largely to the reluctance on the part of the people to change established patterns. On the national scene, the metropolitan areas have had a strong political impact, but representation patterns in legislative bodies still favor rural constituencies which are large in area but small in population. About 85 percent of the total population increase between 1950 and 1960 took place in the metropolitan areas, and nearly 70 percent of this growth was in suburban regions.

Metropolitan Federation. A proposed solution to the problems of metropolitan areas which would create a central metropolitan government to handle problems of the entire metropolitan region, reserving to the local units control over local matters. The plan is based on the principle of federalism which is in effect at the national-state level. The plan has been put into effect in Toronto, Canada. No American area has adopted the plan, although the metropolitan government of Dade County (Miami), Florida, resembles a federation. Under a federated plan, the metropolitan or central unit might handle such common problems as highways, air terminals, water supply, sewerage, and air pollution. The local units could continue to act in the areas of police, schools, and other matters which the people desire to retain as strictly local functions.

• *Significance:* Federation is viewed as one of the more practical means of solving metropolitan problems because it does not destroy the identity of local units. At the same time, area-wide services can be provided to units unable to finance them alone. The plan is flexible, since functions can be arranged as need demonstrates and new units can be added as they become part of the metropolitan area. However, it is difficult to determine what constitutes an area-wide or local problem. Further, the plan simply adds another unit of government to an already large number. Disagreement is apt to arise over proper representation of local units in the metropolitan government.

Model State Constitution. A proposed state constitution prepared by the National Municipal League. Highlights of the Model include a unicameral legislature, a strong executive, and a unified court system with judges appointed by the governor. It also provides for modern techniques of budgeting, financing, auditing, and personnel management; for home rule for cities and counties, the initiative and referendum, simplified amendment and revision procedures, and a brief bill of rights. The Model is brief compared to most state constitutions and is restricted to fundamentals.

• *Significance:* The Model State Constitution is now in its sixth revised edition (1962). Its periodic revision demonstrates the need for adapting state constitutions to meet changing conditions. The Model is not likely to be adopted by any one state and it contains numerous highly controversial items. Yet, it is designed to stimulate discussion by presenting some guidelines proposed by experts. The major aim of the Model, however, meets with general approval from students of government, namely, a state constitution limited to fundamentals and with clear assignment of responsibility coupled with flexibility of action.

Optional Charter. A plan in effect in about one third of the states which permits a city to choose a charter from among several provided by state law. Typically, cities may choose various forms of the mayor-council plan, the commission plan, or the council-manager plan.

• *Significance:* The optional charter plan represents a compromise between complete legislative domination of cities through special acts and home rule. It permits cities to choose their own forms of government by public referendum. However, the plan is unlike home rule in that the legislature may change the options at any time. Under home rule, the city itself frames and changes its charter.

Ordinance. A legislative enactment of a local governing body. Ordinances have the force of law but the term is technically to be distinguished from the statute-making power of national and state legislatures. Ordinances are issued under authority granted by the sovereign power and, in the case of local governments, must comply with state constitutions, charters, and general laws.

• *Significance:* The subordinate position of local government in its relations to the state is underscored by the fact that it has only ordinance-making rather than statutory power as that term is generally understood. An interesting sidelight of the use of the term ordinance is that the Congress under the Articles of Confederation had only ordinance-making power, demonstrating the sovereignty of the member states.

Planning. Preparation and execution of projects for the future economic, social, and physical development of a community. Planning may be nationwide or state-wide where it would encompass all types of governmental problems, but it is more often associated with the physical development of municipal governments. This includes planning street layouts, parks, public utility routes, and the zoning of areas for residential and commercial purposes. In recent years, emphasis has turned from purely physical aspects of city planning and beautification to social and economic concerns such as urban redevelopment and housing. In metropolitan areas, stress is now being put on the need for county-wide or regional planning to provide orderly development of vast areas. Sound planning must take into consideration population and economic trends as well as future fiscal needs. Many cities and states have official planning agencies.

• *Significance:* The American people have been slow to accept the concept of planning, conceiving of it, perhaps, as similar to the planned economies associated with socialism. However, lack of planning has resulted in waste of natural resources and the need for expensive corrective action. The failure of most communities to provide for suitable streets and parking facilities to meet the demands of the automotive age is a major example. Today, planning is generally accepted as a necessary aspect of governmental operations although many communities still resist it. A large number of cities now have master plans for future growth and require that new developments fit into the master plan. Planning is now considered to be a professional specialty, with many colleges and universities offering courses of training.

Register of Deeds.   A county officer, sometimes called recorder of deeds, who is elected in about half the states. His major duty is to record and preserve legal documents relating mainly to real estate ownership and transfers. This function is designed to protect landowners and prospective purchasers of land against flaws in titles to property.

• *Significance:* Few students of government support the idea of electing a register or recorder of deeds. The position is an important one but is not of a policy-making nature. Some counties have adopted modern techniques of recording legal papers through microfilm or other technical processes, but most continue to keep records in longhand in bound volumes.

School District.   A governmental unit for the maintenance of schools. In about half the states, school districts are administratively and financially independent and do not follow township, city, or county lines. The town or township plan is dominant in New England and the county plan in the South. In Delaware and Hawaii, the entire state comprises one school district. Typically, school districts are governed by elective boards which choose a superintendent to administer the system. In some areas, the school is part of city government, and the board is selected by the mayor or council. Approximately half of all local units of government are school districts and they account for about one third of all local government expenditures.

• *Significance:* In 1942, school districts comprised more than two thirds of all local governments. There has since been a dramatic decrease in the number of districts and this trend continues. All over the country, small school districts are being consolidated to make larger, more efficient schools. The strong tradition of independent school districts is based on the assumption that schools should not be part of the politics of regular governments nor tied financially to other units. Some authorities claim, however, that the independent school district develops a "politics" of its own and tends to detract from the financial needs of other units.

Secretary of State.   A state official elected by popular vote in 39 states and appointed by the governor or legislature in others. His major duties include the preservation of official documents, administration of elections, issuance of business licenses and certificates of incorporation, and registration and issuance of motor vehicle licenses. He is also keeper of the state seal.

• *Significance:* The office of secretary of state is not considered by political scientists to be one that justifies popular election. The office has few, if any, policy-making responsibilities, but its elective position reduces the governor's control over state administration. Appointment by the governor is generally recommended. In most states, the secretary of state enjoys great political prominence because his name is affixed to numerous documents, such as driving licenses; many secretaries go on to higher office.

Special Act.   Legislation applicable to one unit of local government. The special act system prevailed from colonial times to the middle of the nineteenth century and is still in use in about a dozen states. Through special acts, state legislatures grant charters to municipalities, amend the charters, and pass legislation on a wide variety of purely local problems.

• *Significance:* Special acts have the virtue of flexibility but are often abused. The net effect of much special legislation is to vest complete authority over a local unit in the legislative representative from that area since other representatives rarely interfere with his desires. Oftimes, "ripper" acts are passed which abolish particular local offices, such as that of city manager, although it may be contrary to local wishes. Special acts put a great burden on the legislature and, in some states, more than half the legislation is special in nature. Most states now forbid special legislation by requiring general laws or by permitting home rule. In a few states, the people of an affected area may reject special acts by popular vote.

Special District.   A unit of local government established to provide a single service. About one half of the special districts in the United States are for fire protection, soil conservation, and drainage. Other common types of special districts provide cemetery, sewer, water, housing, and mosquito abatement services. A school district may be classified as a special district but the Census Bureau and political scientists classify it separately. Special districts are usually created to meet problems which transcend local government boundaries or to bypass taxation and debt restrictions imposed upon local units by state law. There has been a 75 percent increase in special districts since 1942, and they now comprise about 15 percent of all local units. The special district is created under state law, usually requiring the consent of the people in the district, and is governed by a small board which has taxing and bonding authority.

• *Significance:* The dramatic increase in the use of the special district device illustrates the inability of existing units of government to meet modern needs. Tax and debt restrictions can be evaded and high costs shared by several units without upsetting traditional governmental boundary lines. Paradoxically, while attempts are underway to decrease the number of local units of government, the special district is adding to the complexity of local government. However, the device has strong appeal to interest groups that want to keep a function separate, and to many people who believe that a special district keeps a function "out of politics."

State Aid.   Funds provided to local governments by the state in the form of grants-in-aid or shared taxes. State grants go primarily to school districts for educational purposes and to counties for welfare and highway functions. Shared taxes are administered by the state which gives a portion of sales or income taxes to local units, including cities.

• *Significance:* Local units must rely heavily upon the general property tax for income. Since this source has proved insufficient, state aid has increased substantially in recent years and accounts for about 30 percent of local revenues. Grants-in-aid are usually accompanied by state supervision of the expenditure and a requirement that the local unit put up a matching amount or some percentage of the grant. Such grants have improved local government standards while retaining some measure of local control. Shared taxes are usually free of state controls but, since tax collections vary from year to year, local units cannot depend upon specific amounts.

State Auditor. A state official elected in 31 states and appointed by the governor or legislature in others. In some states, the title "comptroller" is used. His major duty is to act as a watchdog over expenditures of state agencies by postauditing accounts. In some states, however, he has preauditing and accounting duties as well.

• *Significance:* The position of auditor is essential for ensuring accountability of public expenditures. However, political scientists doubt the wisdom of electing this official or having him appointed by the governor. Selection by and responsibility to the legislature is considered the most desirable situation, because the auditor's job is to ensure that expenditures have been made in accordance with the legislature's wishes.

State Treasurer. A state official popularly elected in 41 states and chosen by the governor or legislature in others. His major duties are the safekeeping of state funds and the payment of bills on proper warrant. In some states, he has tax collection responsibilities as well.

• *Significance:* The popular election of a treasurer is viewed as unnecessary by students of government. Financial matters, except for auditing, should be centralized in a finance office headed by an appointee of the governor. This would make the governor clearly responsible for the handling of state funds.

Strong-Mayor Plan. A plan of city government in which the mayor is given complete executive authority. Its major features include (1) election of a mayor as the only executive officer; (2) concentration of administrative power in the hands of the mayor, including powers of appointment and removal; (3) a veto power over the city council; and (4) strong budgetary controls in the hands of the mayor.

• *Significance:* The strong-mayor plan is used in most large cities and is favored by political scientists over the weak-mayor plan. The main advantages of the plan are the centralization of authority and the clear fixing of executive responsibility. The plan permits the mayor to exercise strong political or policy-making leadership, a particularly desirable condition in large cities with their variety of competing interests. In contrast to the weak-mayor plan, the strong-mayor plan encourages the use of modern administrative techniques and the appointment of able subordinates. Few people, however, combine top administrative and political talent. In several large cities, the mayor-administrator plan is in use to free the mayor from attention to administrative detail.

Superintendent of Public Instruction. An official elected in more than half the states to supervise the public school system of the state. In some states he is known as superintendent of schools or commissioner of education. In several states, he is chosen by the state board of education, and in a few, by the governor. In most cases, the superintendent serves on the state board of education and acts as its chief administrative officer. His duties generally include the establishment of standards for schools, curriculum development, setting up teacher qualifications, and control of state administered school funds. In some states, his authority extends to state teacher colleges or other educational institutions.

• *Significance:* The superintendent of public instruction holds a position of major responsibility because of the high value placed upon education in the United States. Because of the high professional standards desirable for this office, many educators and political scientists favor the superintendent's appointment by an elected or appointed board of education, or by the governor.

Supervisor. The chief elective officer of the township in some states and a member of the county board of supervisors. The chief township officer is also known in some states as the trustee. The supervisor has over-all responsibility for township government and presides over the township board. He represents his township on the county board and may serve as assessor and overseer of the poor.

• *Significance:* In states with township government, the supervisor is an important political figure. He may exercise considerable influence at the county and state levels. Often, however, the supervisor is inadequate to meet the challenges posed by the growing urbanization of many townships and counties.

Town. The major unit of local government in New England. The term is used in some states to designate a township or a small urban area but is generally used by political scientists to designate the New England town. With the exception of some incorporated cities, all six states of New England are divided into towns, which includes both the rural and urban portions of the particular area. The town is responsible for most of those governmental services provided in other states by counties and cities. The town is governed by all the inhabitants through the town meeting and, between meetings, by a board of selectmen and other town officers. In many towns, however, representatives are chosen for town meetings, and some utilize a town manager.

• *Significance:* The New England town developed in the colonial period and is deeply rooted in tradition. Growing populations and urbanization of many towns has put a strain upon governmental arrangements suitable for a frontier, rural society. Representative town meetings, special finance and budget committees, and town managers now characterize many towns.

Town Meeting. The governing authority of a town or township. All qualified voters may participate in the election of officers and in the passage of taxes or other legislation. Town meetings are used in New England towns and in many midwestern townships.

• *Significance:* The town meeting represents direct democracy in action. It is a product of rural society, however, and has lost much of its vitality in recent years. Areas with large populations cannot hold meetings of all qualified voters; no building can accommodate them and the meetings are unwieldy. Many people are apathetic and power falls into the hands of the few who do attend or to those who "pack" the meeting. Many midwestern townships have abolished the town meeting. In New England, representative town meetings are held which are composed of delegates elected by the voters, as is customary for most legislative bodies.

Township.   A unit of government, usually a subdivision of a county, found in 16 states principally in the midwest and in the northeast. The term "midwestern township" is often used to distinguish it from the New England town. Townships vary in shape and size but tend to cover an area of 36 square miles as a result of the congressional township system of identifying land. Some townships have an annual town meeting and all are governed by a township board, usually consisting of three members. Municipal areas are usually excluded from the township territory but in some states, villages or towns remain part of the township. Township functions tend to be rural in nature, such as maintaining roads, cemeteries, and drains, minor law enforcement, and assessment of property. However, in urban areas, townships have taken on numerous urban services, such as police and fire protection, and public works. In some states, the township is the unit for school administration.

• *Significance:* With some exceptions, township government has declined in importance. A product of frontier society and the New England town, it is too small for efficient administration. Modern communication makes it unnecessary as a subdivision of easily accessible county offices. Duplication of services in small areas results. Some states, such as Oklahoma and Iowa, have transferred most township functions to the county. A general lack of interest in township government seems to characterize many areas. In some states, the township has gained strength by taking on municipal functions. Most political scientists favor abolition of the township as a unit of government.

Uniform State Laws.   Laws proposed by the National Conference of Commissioners on Uniform State Laws, a few of which have been adopted by all or many states. Among those proposals which have had wide adoption are the Negotiable Instruments Act, the Warehouse Receipts Act, the Stock Transfer Act, and several others relating to sales, partnerships, bills of lading, and some traffic, criminal, and family matters. The National Conference has proposed over 100 uniform laws since its inception in 1892, but it has met with only minor success. The Conference consists of three Commissioners from each state, usually lawyers, appointed by the governor. The Council of State Governments acts as secretariat for the Conference.

• *Significance:* The wide diversity of state laws under the federal system has proved vexing to many people. Concerns doing business in several states are often inconvenienced and confused. Confusion exists, too, in such matters as marriage and divorce and traffic laws. The increasing mobility of business and private persons has increased the need for more uniformity. The effort has been retarded by apathetic state legislatures and by the desires of many states to gain an advantage over others by having less stringent rules concerning business transactions or divorce, for example, in order to attract more business to the state.

Urban County.   A proposed solution to metropolitan area problems which involves the transfer to county governments of functions exercised by several units of government within the county. Several counties in California have taken over the functions of law enforcement, health services, tax assessments and collections, and prisons. Dade County, Florida, has been established as a metropolitan or urban county. Twenty-six municipalities within that county, including Miami, have transferred to the county power over traffic problems, planning, sewerage, water supply, and other county-wide problems. The urban county plan is to be distinguished from city-county consolidation which contemplates the complete merger of county government with all other units within the county.

• *Significance:* Most metropolitan areas lie within a single county. This facilitates the transfer of functions, since the county is an established unit of government. No new government need be created nor need any unit be abolished. However, metropolitan areas are rapidly spreading beyond county lines. Most county governments are poorly organized and have made little progress in the use of modern administrative techniques or of the merit system of personnel management. Most are ill-equipped to handle urban services without considerable reform.

Village.   A small urban area, called a town or borough in some states, which is a municipal corporation but with less authority and simpler organization than a city. The term "village" is a legal concept, varying in meaning from state to state in which the designation is used. Village status may be based upon population but many villages are larger than regular cities. Villages usually are governed by a small council and a village president or mayor. Limitations are placed by the state upon the taxing and borrowing powers of villages as well as upon the types of functions which they may perform.

• *Significance:* Village government developed to accommodate the needs of trading centers in rural areas. Since the county or township could not provide needed services, such areas were permitted to incorporate as villages for limited purposes, such as street maintenance or water supply. Villages may attain city status by a vote of the people or by special act but many people prefer the lesser designation and the informality of village organization. However, increased population may compel change to city status in order to get greater taxing and service authority.

Ward.   The division of a city for purposes of electing members to the city council. The ward system is used mainly in cities with populations in excess of 500,000. Most cities now use an at large system of electing councilmen, particularly those using the commission or council-manager forms of government. A number of cities now use a combination of both methods, selecting some councilmen from wards and others at large.

• *Significance:* The ward system has declined in recent years but still has many adherents. It provides a more representative council since the voter can know his representative more intimately and, in turn, the councilman will know more about his ward. It is particularly favored by minority groups and labor interests who seldom gain representation under the at large system. The main disadvantage of the ward system is the emphasis which it tends to place upon special interests of neighborhoods rather than the interest of the community as a whole.

Further, it makes it more difficult to get qualified candidates and leads inevitably to gerrymandering and logrolling tactics. These factors have led to the growth of the at large system or a combination of both ward and at large elections.

Weak-Mayor Plan.   A plan of city government in which the mayor must share his executive authority with other elected officials and with the city council. Most cities under the mayor-council plan use the weak-mayor form rather than the strong-mayor plan. The major features of the weak-mayor plan include (1) a long ballot in which the people choose numerous department heads and boards and commissions for administrative purposes, as well as the mayor; (2) a limited power of appointment and removal in the hands of the mayor, requiring council approval; (3) the appointment of numerous officials by the council alone; (4) a weak, or complete absence of a veto power for the mayor; and (5) direct participation by the council in administrative matters, including preparation of the budget.
• *Significance:* In spite of its wide use, political scientists frown upon the weak-mayor plan. The long ballot, the difficulty of fixing responsibility because of the lack of a responsible executive, the lack of coordination, and the use of outmoded administrative and personnel techniques which characterize the plan, lead to a poor quality of municipal government. Yet, the plan, which is rooted in the traditions of Jacksonian democracy, prevents the concentration of power and establishes an elaborate system of checks and balances.

Zoning.   The division of a city or other unit of government into districts and the regulation, by law, of the uses of the land. Zoning is concerned with the nature of buildings (residential, industrial, or commercial), their height and density, and the uses which can be made of particular tracts of land. Zoning laws are enacted under the police power of communities to protect the health, safety, and welfare of the people. A zoning board of appeals is usually created to grant exceptions and variances to persons who might suffer undue hardships under a zoning regulation.
• *Significance:* Comprehensive zoning has been in effect only since the 1920's and still meets resistance in many areas where the people object to legislative and administrative control of their property. However, zoning protects property values in residential areas by forbidding industrial or commercial uses of property, and it contributes to the beauty of a community. Zoning makes possible better planning and administration of public services, such as fire protection and traffic supervision, and contributes to the health and well-being of a community by segregating industrial plants from residential areas. Zoning must be carried out with careful regard for constitutionally protected property rights.

IMPORTANT AGENCIES

Council of State Governments.   An agency maintained by the state governments to serve as a secretariat, research agency, and clearing house for the improvement of state legislative, executive, and judicial administration. It has encouraged interstate cooperation and the general improvement of federal-state relations and state-local relations. The Council is composed of Commissions on Interstate Cooperation found in each of the states which include legislative and executive officials. The Council serves as the secretariat for the American Legislators Association, the Governors' Conference, and similar organizations of chief justices, attorneys general, court, budget, purchasing, parole, and juvenile officials. It publishes a monthly magazine, *State Government*, and the biennial *Book of the States*. Its headquarters are in Chicago.

• *Significance:* The Council of State Governments has sponsored conferences and research in problems of common state concern from crime control to fisheries. It has promoted better interstate relations and has influence in Washington and in the state capitals. Its journal, *State Government*, carries informative and up-to-date information on state government developments and problems and the *Book of the States* is a major reference work on state and local government.

Index

Index